ORGANIZATIONS AT WAR IN AFGHANISTAN AND BEYOND

ORGANIZATIONS AT WAR IN AFGHANISTAN AND BEYOND

ABDULKADER H. SINNO

CORNELL UNIVERSITY PRESS
Ithaca and London

Published in South Asia by:

Cambridge University Press India Pvt. Ltd.
under the imprint of Foundation Books
Cambridge House
4381/4 Ansari Road
Daryaganj,
New Delhi – 110 002

First published 2008

ISBN-13: 978-81-7596-620-8

This edition of *Abdulkader H. Sinno / Organizations at War in Afghanistan and Beyond,* is published by arrangement with Cornell University Press.

Special edition for sale in South Asia only, not for export elsewhere.

Published by Manas Saikia for Cambridge University Press India Pvt. Ltd. and printed in India at Sanat Printers, Kundli.

In memory of Rafika and Hassan Sinno

Contents

Maps and Figures

Maps

Figures

Tables

Preface

This is a detached academic book that hardly mentions the suffering and dignity of those who inspired it. Their suffering and dignity are no less real because of my tone and arguments.

It took a bit longer than a decade to bring this work from concept to book. Along the way, I collected debts of gratitude to many people. Their help was crucial but all mistakes are mine.

Among fellow academics, I thank Fiona Adamson, Mahabat Baimyrzaeva, Scott Desposato, Lynn Eden, Jim Fearon, Jonathan Friedlander, Barbara Geddes, James Gelvin, David Karol, Deborah Larson, Brian Lawson, Mike McGinnis, Lin Ostrom, Nazif Shahrani, Ben Valentino, and John Zaller for their comments and suggestions during the different phases of this project.

I thank participants at Stanford's "Decade of the Taliban" conference for their comments on the paper that evolved into the eighth chapter of this book. I similarly thank participants, particularly Jim Fearon who was the discussant, in a Center for International Security and Cooperation (CISAC) workshop at Stanford University for helpful comments on a paper that was the basis of the statistical study.

I also thank Daniel Shroeter, Mike Herb, Michael Gunter, and Gregory Gause for providing me with some hard-to-find data on Palestine, Oman, Turkey, and Yemen, respectively. I thank Dan Van Fleet and Michael Radcliffe for assisting with collecting data on conflicts from the Americas.

The Office of the Vice Provost for Research at Indiana University graciously provided the funds for producing the index and procuring a jacket image.

I acknowledge the support provided by Stanford University's Center for International Security and Cooperation while working on this book and related projects. The CISAC fellowship provided income, facilities, a supportive environment, and research assistance. Most important, it allowed me to discuss my research with impressive scholars and practitioners with related interests. In particular, I acknowledge the support of Lynn Eden, Scott Sagan, and Steve Stedman.

I am heavily indebted to the Workshop in Political Theory and Policy Analysis and the Department of Political Science at Indiana University for organizing a one-day symposium on the manuscript. In particular, I am grateful to Mike McGinnis, Jeff Isaac, Lin Ostrom, and Amos Sawyer for organizing and participating in this event. I thank other wonderful colleagues at Indiana University who participated in the symposium and who graciously provided me with incisive comments: Gardner Bovingdon, Michael Ensley, Sumit Ganguly, Henry Hale, Iliya Harik, Lauren Morris McLean, Vincent Ostrom, Karen Rasler, and Armando Razo. I particularly thank our guest at the symposium, David Laitin, for his thorough, extremely helpful, and penetrating comments on the manuscript. David Laitin's boundless passion for the social sciences and his unmatched scholarship will always be a great model and source of inspiration for me.

I very much appreciate the helpful comments of two anonymous reviewers.

I recognize the marvelous help, dedication, and patience of my editor at Cornell University Press, Roger Haydon, and the outstanding staff at the Press. They helped make this a much better book.

Many thanks go to Shaykh Lenny Binder, a superb adviser, mentor, master of the craft we both practice, and exemplar of integrity and intellectual grace.

I thank all those who were kind enough to meet me and provide detailed interviews, whether Afghans, Pakistanis, Arabs, or Westerners who experienced Afghan conflicts as observers, analysts, or participants. I decided to withhold all of their names, some on their request and others because of the unfortunate twists in Afghan-Western relations since 2001. I made sure that all information in this book would not harm or benefit any participant or interviewee. The information they provided was essential. I kept no records beyond the information provided in the text.

My appreciation goes to relatives and friends who supported me while I was working on this project. I am particularly indebted to my uncles Afif Sinno, Ahmad Jabr, and Rafik Jabr (bless his soul and wonderful memory). They gave me sound advice, encouragement, and financial help when, once, I was in dire need.

I owe everything to my mother and father. I dedicate this book to their memory.

Note on Transliteration

I generally employ the transliteration system suggested by the *International Journal of Middle Eastern Studies*. For names and terms that have come into regular English usage, I do not transliterate (e.g., Shia instead of Shiʿa). I also drop initial hamzas and ʿayns for well-known names, like Ismail or Massoud, for convenience. I do not add long vowel lines or the dots for velarized letters, confident that those familiar with Middle Eastern languages will be able to recognize the correct word from the transliteration and that others will be unaffected because of lack of interest in such minutiae.

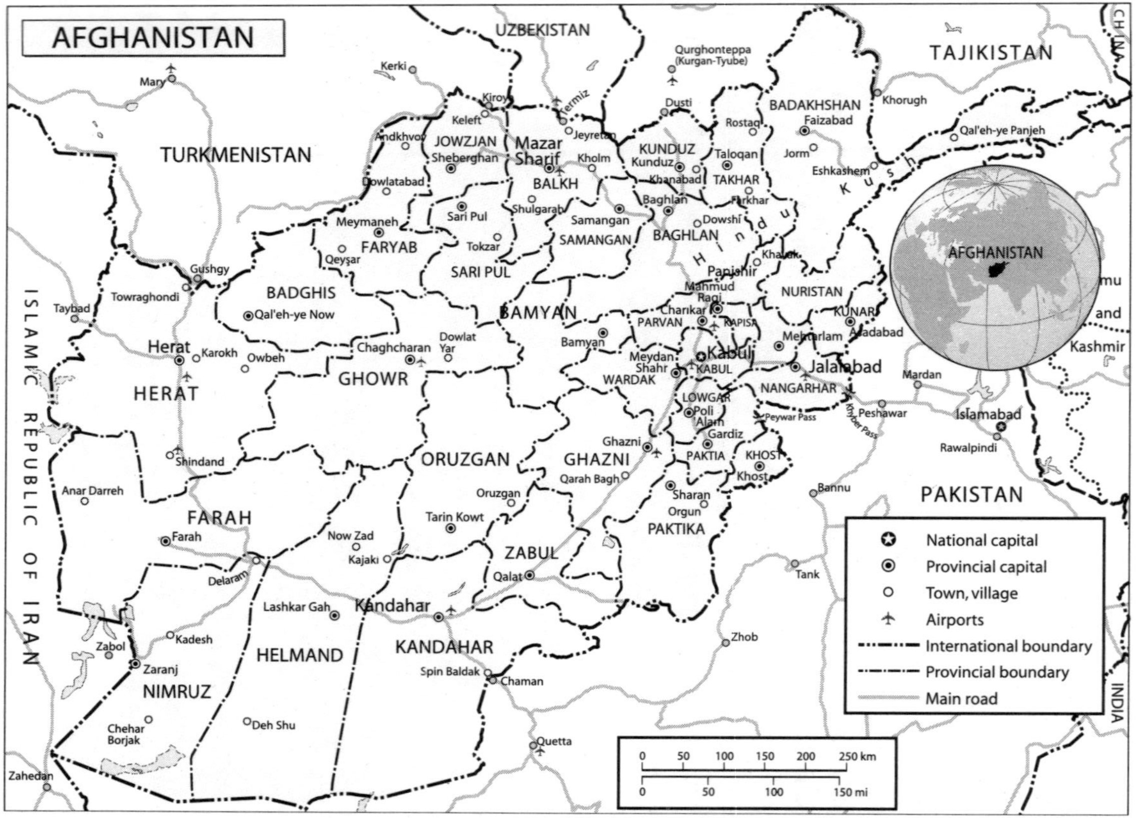
AFGHANISTAN
UZBEKISTAN
TAJIKISTAN
TURKMENISTAN
PAKISTAN
ISLAMIC REPUBLIC OF IRAN
CHINA
INDIA
Kashmir
Mary
Kerki
Kiroy
Termiz
Qurghonteppa (Kurgan-Tyube)
Khorugh
Qal'eh-ye Panjeh
Dusti
BADAKHSHAN
Faizabad
Rostaq
Jorm
Eshkashem
Hindu Kush
Keleft
Andkhvoy
JOWZJAN
Sheberghan
Mazar Sharif
Jeyretan
Kholm
BALKH
KUNDUZ
Kunduz
Khanabad
Taloqan
TAKHAR
Farkhar
Dowlatabad
Shulgarah
Samangan
SAMANGAN
Baghlan
BAGHLAN
Dowshi
Meymaneh
FARYAB
Sari Pul
Tokzar
SARI PUL
Qeysar
Gushgy
Towraghondi
Taybad
BADGHIS
Qal'eh-ye Now
BAMYAN
Panjshir
Mahmud Raqi
Charikar
PARVAN
KAPISA
NURISTAN
KUNAR
Asadabad
Mehtarlam
Herat
Karokh
Owbeh
Chaghcharan
Dowlat Yar
Bamyan
Meydan Shahr
Kabul
KABUL
WARDAK
Jalalabad
NANGARHAR
Mardan
Islamabad
Rawalpindi
Peshawar
Khyber Pass
Peywar Pass
HERAT
GHOWR
LOWGAR
Poli Alam
Gardiz
PAKTIA
KHOST
Khost
Ghazni
GHAZNI
Qarah Bagh
Bannu
Shindand
ORUZGAN
Oruzgan
Sharan
Orgun
PAKTIKA
Anar Darreh
FARAH
Farah
Tarin Kowt
Now Zad
Kajaki
ZABUL
Qalat
Tank
Delaram
Lashkar Gah
Kandahar
KANDAHAR
Zhob
Kadesh
Zabol
Zaranj
NIMRUZ
HELMAND
Spin Baldak
Chaman
Chehar Borjak
Deh Shu
Quetta
Zahedan
National capital
Provincial capital
Town, village
Airports
International boundary
Provincial boundary
Main road
0 50 100 150 200 250 km
0 50 100 150 mi

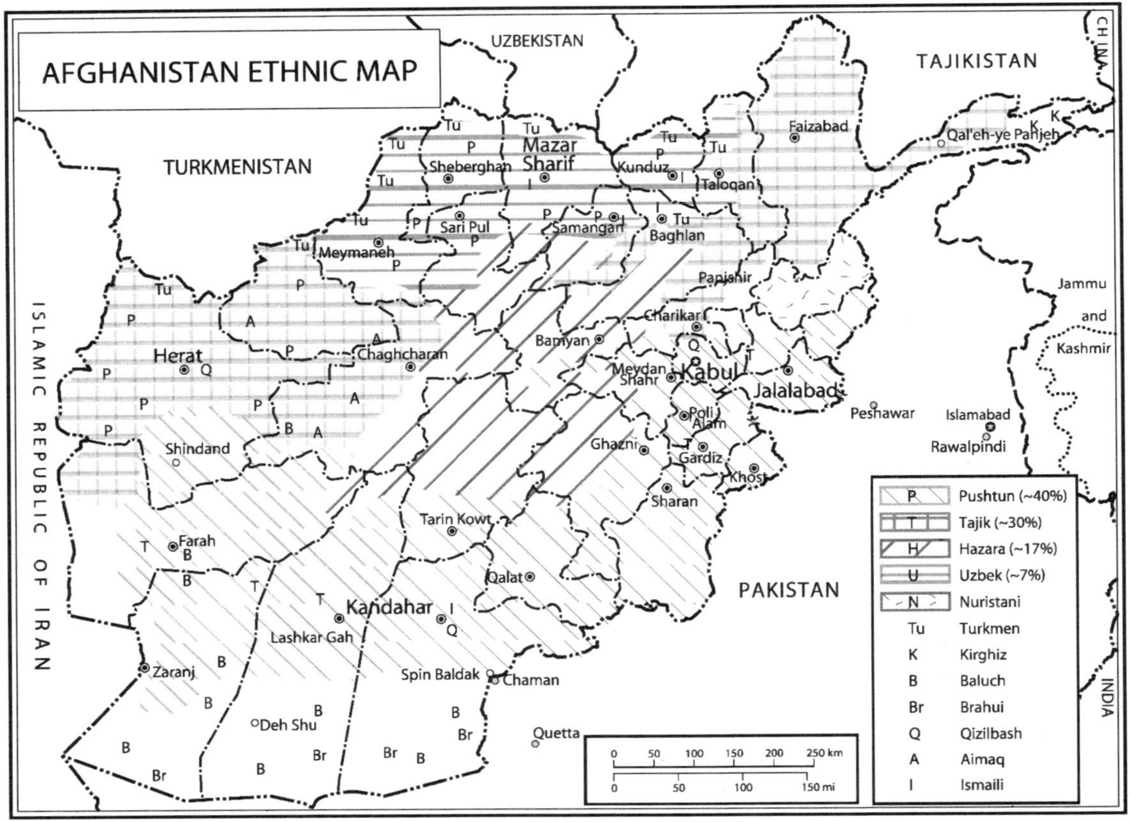
AFGHANISTAN ETHNIC MAP
UZBEKISTAN
TAJIKISTAN
CHINA
TURKMENISTAN
ISLAMIC REPUBLIC OF IRAN
PAKISTAN
INDIA
Jammu and Kashmir
Faizabad
Qal'eh-ye Panjeh
Mazar Sharif
Shebergham
Kunduz
Taloqan
Sari Pul
Samangan
Baghlan
Meymaneh
Panjshir
Charikar
Bamyan
Herat
Chaghcharan
Meydan Shahr
Kabul
Jalalabad
Peshawar
Islamabad
Rawalpindi
Poli Alam
Ghazni
Gardiz
Khost
Shindand
Sharan
Tarin Kowt
Farah
Qalat
Kandahar
Lashkar Gah
Zaranj
Spin Baldak
Chaman
Deh Shu
Quetta
0 50 100 150 200 250 km
0 50 100 150 mi
P Pushtun (~40%)
T Tajik (~30%)
H Hazara (~17%)
U Uzbek (~7%)
N Nuristani
Tu Turkmen
K Kirghiz
B Baluch
Br Brahui
Q Qizilbash
A Aimaq
I Ismaili

Chapter 1

Organizing to Win

> It was on the strength of their extensive organization that the peasants went into action and within four months [in 1926] brought about a great revolution in the countryside, a revolution without parallel in history.
>
> —Mao Tse-tung, 1927

After we had exchanged the requisite formalities over tea in his camp on the southern edge of Kabul's outer defense perimeter, the Afghan field commander told me that two of his bravest mujahideen were martyred because he did not have a pickup truck to take them to a Peshawar hospital. They had succumbed to their battle wounds. He asked me to tell his party's bureaucrats across the border that he needed such a vehicle desperately. I double-checked with my interpreter that he was indeed making this request. I wasn't puzzled because the request appeared unreasonable but because he was asking me, a twenty-year-old employee of a humanitarian organization, to intercede on his behalf with his own organization's bureaucracy.

I understood on this dry 1991 summer day in Khurd Kabul that not all militant and political organizations are alike. While officers in Gulbuddin Hekmatyar's Hizb-i Islami (Islamic Party) promptly honored written requests from their organization to allow me to set up basic clinics, field commanders (*comandan*) from other parties used the opportunity—and any other available leverage—to negotiate concessions from their party's bureaucracy. The Hizb was a centralized organization with semiprofessionally trained officers, whereas the six other major mujahideen parties were based on highly decentralized and continuously renegotiated arrangements: field commanders gave their loyalty, support, and assistance to a party in return for the resources necessary to maintain their resistance activities.

The internal structure of the resistance explains not only how its field commanders dealt with me but also how different parties have performed during all Afghan conflicts since the 1979 Soviet invasion. During this summer of 1991, the mujahideen were bogged down around the defensive perimeters of the Afghan regime's main garrison cities such as Kabul and Jalalabad. Jubilant experts expected that the regime of Dr. Mohammad Najibullah would collapse soon after the withdrawal of its Soviet patrons, but it lasted for longer than three years because the mujahideen were too loosely organized to mount the sustained assaults that would have led to victory. Ironically, their very decentralization had allowed them to be resilient in the face of overwhelming Soviet power for an entire decade earlier. I explain in this book how different modes of organization, such as these, affect the evolution and outcome of conflicts among organized groups in societies at war. But why should we try to understand the way group conflicts evolve and conclude?

Civil wars, revolutions, wars of liberation, guerilla wars, and other intrastate wars kill and maim millions every decade. Alas, they rarely end in negotiated settlements.[1] Yet social scientists have little understanding of the processes driving outcomes of civil wars other than those settled by negotiation. We generally focus on the rare negotiated settlement instead of decisive endings because the peaceful outcomes reflect our sensitivities and concerns.[2] Most of us, understandably, want to predict where conflicts will emerge and how to end them before they cause widespread human suffering or require costly intervention. Understanding the processes and correlates of decisive outcomes remains the concern of those directly involved in conflict—those in power, their advisers, and those dedicated to replacing them. Some participants survive long enough to analyze and share their experiences; but they may have good political reasons to ascribe their successes to the righteousness of their cause or the power of their ideology instead of the more mundane but critical factors that probably enabled them to defeat their rivals. Social scientists too should focus on decisive outcomes because winners of intrastate conflict shape the political system of the country, affect its economic performance, sometimes overhaul its culture and social structure, and rearrange the country's alliances with other states.

---

1. Only two out of forty-one conflicts in my dataset(chapter 10) concluded in negotiated settlements. Others find higher, but still modest, rates of negotiated settlement. For example, Barbara Walter (1997, 346) finds that only eight out of forty-one conflicts in her sample concluded in negotiated settlement.

2. Notable exceptions include Stam (1996) on the outcomes of interstate conflicts and Mason et al. (1999) on the outcomes of intrastate conflicts.

Our understanding of the dynamics of group conflicts is still very basic. Surprising developments such as the Islamic Revolution in Iran and the fall of the Berlin wall were the result of complex processes that few observers, no matter how thorough and seasoned, were able to foresee. Few Western scholars thought that the United States would face an insurgency in Iraq after 2003. The succession of conflicts that afflicted Afghanistan after the 1979 Soviet invasion included similarly baffling developments and unpredictable outcomes at every juncture. Very few observers expected the Afghan mujahideen to resist the mighty Red Army so stubbornly, or the Soviets to withdraw without achieving any of their original goals. Once they did withdraw, almost everyone predicted the prompt defeat of their puppet regime by the seemingly invincible mujahideen. But the Najibullah regime survived until aid from Moscow ceased completely. Once the victorious mujahideen entered Kabul, they shocked the world and their staunchest supporters by engaging in fratricidal warfare, with many organizations reserving their most aggressive behavior for their ideological kin. When the bloody balance of power between the five surviving organizations appeared to stabilize, a new entrant suddenly emerged to sweep aside parties, warlords, commanders, khans, bandits, and smugglers alike—the Taliban. The Taliban seemed poised to overtake the remaining 5 percent of Afghanistan when an attack by one of its key allies, al-Qaida, motivated a determined United States to actively support the nearly defeated Northern Alliance forces and become a direct participant in the conflict. U.S. intervention dismantled the Taliban as an organized force in a few weeks. But if the past is any indication, resistance to the U.S. and NATO military occupation will develop into a full-fledged insurgency.

Observers generally provide simple explanations for surprising developments in Afghan conflicts. Some would tell you that the Afghan resistance to the Soviet occupation was so resilient because of U.S. support, the provision of Stinger missiles, the deep religious motivation of the mujahideen, or cultural factors. Some would tell you that the meteoric rise of the Taliban resulted from Pakistani support and Saudi money, ideological purity, or a public that was receptive to their strict law-and-order agenda. But such explanations often fail to define how those factors led to the unexpected outcomes, and many do not withstand the weight of contrary evidence. I propose an alternative way of analyzing conflict, one that is grounded in the analysis of organizations in conflict.

Ethnic groups, social classes, civilizations, religions, and nations do not engage in conflict or strategic interaction—organizations do. When Samuel Huntington tells us that civilizations clash, he is merely informing us that there are organizations (states and nonstates alike) that are engaged in conflict across what he believes to be borders of civilizations. When Marxists talk of class revolt, they envision it as instigated by a dedicated organization that mobilizes the toiling masses. As any close observer of civil war will tell you, ethnic groups rarely fight each other en masse—organizations, which are either ad hoc or extensions of existing social structures, use an ethnic agenda to attract some members and wage conflict in their name. Engaging in conflict consists of performing a number of essential processes, such as coordination, mobilization, and the manipulation of information, to undermine rivals within a contested territory. Amorphous entities such as civilizations, ethnic groups, or the masses cannot perform such operations—only organizations can do so. To say that a certain conflict pits a politicized group against another is to use shorthand to indicate that organizations that recruit from among those groups are engaged in conflict. It is perfectly reasonable to use shorthand, but its use distracts the social scientist from focusing on the mechanisms that best explain how conflicts begin, evolve, and conclude.

An organizational approach to the study of conflict is both old and new. The fourteenth-century Muslim chronicler and analyst Ibn Khaldun (*Muqaddimah*, 130) tells us that "a dynasty rarely establishes itself firmly in lands with many tribes and groups." In the sixteenth century, Machiavelli theorized that an occupier's success in holding a newly conquered territory has much to do with the organization of its inhabitants:

> Whoever attacks the Turk must reckon on finding a united people, and must trust rather to his own strength than to divisions on the other side. But were his adversary once overcome and defeated in the field, so that he could not repair his armies, no cause for anxiety would remain. . . . But the contrary is the case in kingdoms governed like that of France, into which, because men who are discontented and desirous of change are always to be found, you may readily procure entrance by gaining over some Baron of the Realm. . . . But afterwards the effort to hold your ground involves you in endless difficulties, as well in respect to those who have helped you, as of those whom you have overthrown. . . . All those other Lords remain to put themselves at the head of new movements; whom being unable either to content or to destroy, you lose the State whenever occasion serves them.[3]

3. Machiavelli, Chapter IV. Callwell (1976, 34–36) also compares the centralized Ashantis and Dahomeyans to the decentralized and tribal Afghans. He argues that the former could be defeated after vanquishing their leader and army while the latter are much more difficult to subdue, even if their capital is occupied and their emir is defeated. Joel Migdal (1988, 28–9) also makes a similar argument.

His insight remains astonishingly relevant for today's conflicts.

Some three centuries later, Alexis de Tocqueville argued that patterns of societal organization governed the outcome of competition among colonial powers in the Americas. Decentralized states such as Britain, he said, endow their citizens with the characteristics (independence, initiative, autonomy) necessary to make successful colonists, unlike centralized ones such as France. This, he argued, explains why the Americas were ultimately dominated by people of British background and not by settlers of French descent. He also mentions that a society needs strong social groups and institutions capable of independent action in their own right to check the power of the established government, or any domestic or foreign usurper.[4] Tocqueville also focused on the importance of organization within classes as well as the centralization of power in his elegant explanation of the French Revolution.[5]

The lives and writings of perceptive participants in resistance and revolutionary conflicts suggest the importance of organizational matters. The unsuccessful experiences of European anarchists who disdained political organization show how detrimental fragmentation can be for revolutionaries. A premature shift from a decentralized structure (with its regional autonomy and specialization, cohesive small groups, and efficient local mobilization) to centralization has been widely recognized to be disastrous for revolutionary organizations by participants in the Greek Communist experience and the Tet offensive in Vietnam.[6] And Major (later General) Charles Callwell (1976, 157–58) notes in his late nineteenth-century manual on guerrilla war that it is in the best interest of the centralized state to assist in the transformation of its rivals into a centralized and specialized organization that mimics a modern army. The Chinese Communists accomplished the classic successful transformation from decentralized guerrilla forces into

4. De la Démocratie en Amérique, part 1, chap. 18, part 1, 9, 92–93, and 333–34; part 2, 93, 258, 271–72, and 296.

5. *L'ancien Régime et la Révolution*, part 2, chaps. 9 and 10.

6. See Chaliand 1982, 267–69. Rice (1988, 81–82) argues that the Tet offensive in South Vietnam was also such a mistake. It definitely was a disaster for the South Vietnamese Communist (Viet Cong) organization that lost most of its cadres and was reduced by as much as 80 percent of its fighting force. The war did go on, however, mostly because of *North* Vietnamese efforts. The Viet Cong was irrelevant when Saigon fell and the United States withdrew. Tran Van Tra, the Communist commander for the lower half of South Vietnam, later wrote that the Communists' mistake was to have failed to correctly assess the balance of forces between the two sides (Karnow 1983, 544). See also Leites and Wolf (1970, 57–60) for more on this issue.

a centralized conventional army after World War II.[7] This successful restructuring occurred after several failed and premature attempts (in Jiangxi between 1927 and 1934 and in northern China during World War II) that led to defeats but provided lessons that assisted the ultimate successful transformation.[8] Mao summarized his experience with the following recipe:

> There must be a gradual change from guerrilla formations to orthodox regimental organization. The necessary bureaus and staffs, both political and military, must be provided. At the same time, attention must be paid to the creation of suitable supply, medical, and hygiene units. The standards of equipment must be raised and types of weapons increased. Communication equipment must not be forgotten. Orthodox standards of discipline must be established.[9]

Vo Nguyen Giap applied Mao's formula to resist the three latest occupiers of Vietnam.[10] He successfully transitioned his forces from decentralized guerrilla bands into the three-tiered force—a mobile centralized force with specialized units, regional forces, and local militias, all flanked by a parallel system of political commissars—which defeated the French at Dien Bien Phu and caused the United States to abandon Vietnam. Giap's description of the process shows the care given to organization building by those who successfully practice the craft of resistance and revolution:

> In the early stage of the Resistance War, our army was in extremely difficult conditions, short of arms and munitions, its formation varied

---

7. An anecdote mentioned in Rice (1972, 62) illustrates how decentralized the Chinese Communist guerrillas were before their transformation into a centralized army. U.S. visitors to Yunan during World War II "found that Zhu De, the communist commander in chief, had no map room, possessed only a general idea as to the disposition of his forces, and—like other top leaders in Yenan—seemed to have plenty of time to talk to foreign visitors. One can also believe the truth of the assertion of one of his commanders in the field that he did not send telegraphic requests to Yenan because they were never answered. The decentralization of command over communist forces implied a similar decentralization of control over their support organization, and the field commanders had to look to it for support rather than to headquarters in Yenan." One would think that when Mao says in *The Strategy of Partisan Warfare* that "without centralized strategic command the partisans can inflict little damage on their adversaries, as without this, they can break down into roaming, armed bands, and then find no more support by the population" he is referring to the centralized phase.

8. See Rice 1988, 82.

9. Mao 1962, 113.

10. See Le Quang (1973, chapter 5) for a description of Giap's elaborate organizational efforts and the structure of his troops. Giap himself expounded on organizational matters in the *Military Art of People's War* and *People's War, People's Army*. For a description of how Giap developed the organization of his forces to suit changing circumstances, see *People's War* (1961, 132–50).

> from one locality to another. Parallel with the gradual development from guerrilla warfare to mobile warfare and with better supply and equipment, we had from scattered units, gradually organized concentrated ones, then regiments and divisions of a regular army. In the units of the regular army, the organization was unified step by step. The regiments and divisions were made up at first of infantrymen only. Later there were units of support and later sappers units and light artillery units, etc.[11]

We have research on Communist organizational thought because of the West's longstanding obsession with the Communist revolutionary threat, but Communists have no monopoly on concern with matters of organization. Members of the Egyptian Muslim Brotherhood engaged in tense debates about organizational matters that they believe to be extremely important. Such debates recur wherever Islamist movements develop, and different groups have adopted the organizational structure they felt best suited their situation. Nor is concern with organization restricted to territorially bound groups—it extends to transnational activities, as the words of Sheikh Fathi Yakan, a Sunni Islamist leader from Lebanon's northern city of Tripoli, reveal:

> Another principal feature that a unitary global Islamic movement should have is decentralization [*la-markaziyyah*]. . . . Emigration [*hijrah*] in the time of the Prophet (peace be upon him) was a profound indication that decentralization should be part of Islamic work and that the establishment of Islam could be easy and possible in one place and difficult, if not impossible, in another. It then becomes necessary to expand efforts where results are easier to achieve, to preserve time and energy.[12]

Advocates of decentralization, which would otherwise be abhorrent to Islamists because it might indicate an acceptance of the division of the Ummah (Muslim community), justify its adoption based on the writings of the fourteenth-century theologian Ibn Taymiyyah. Ibn Taymiyyah maintained that the Ummah does not necessarily need a single leader (imam) and that, when historical conditions require it, there could be several leaders so

---

11. People's War, 133. The influence of Mao and Giap was so powerful that even Che Guevara (more of an inspirational figure than a sophisticated strategist) mimicked Mao's theory that guerrilla troops should be centralized before ultimate victory in a motivational paragraph of his *Guerrilla War* (1985, 53).

12. Yakan (1993, 43–44), translated from Arabic.

long as they are worthy individuals. Sayyid Qutb, the foremost ideologue of the Egyptian Muslim Brotherhood, advocated extreme local centralization by recommending the formation of a tightly knit countersociety of believers in the midst of infidel society. The society of believers should be self-enclosed to avoid fragmentation and penetration by alien influences, but it should be able to engage the remainder of society to acquire what it needs but cannot produce itself.[13] The countersociety's goal is to become the majority and to later replace the old society. From an organizational perspective, this vanguard-based approach could appear to be similar to the Bolshevik approach to seizing power, but Qutb conceived of the possibility of many such countersocieties existing in the midst of society independent of one another.[14] Any three believers can form an independent society, and this multiplicity would be acceptable at the early stage of the process of transforming society from the state of *jahiliyya* (pre-Islamic ignorance of the divine message or current disregard for it) to that of *iman* (belief).

Alternatively, Yakan advises Islamist organizations that compete with the powers that be on a one-to-one basis to adopt a strictly centralized structural pattern to preserve discipline and internal cohesion.[15] He wants to avoid a repeat of the debilitating structural problems that plagued the Muslim Brotherhood, the original modern Islamist organization in the Middle East, among emerging ones.[16]

Revolutionary thinkers have given matters of organization their deserved importance, but their recommendations are not consistent. Some paid for their mistaken analyses with their lives. The findings in the balance of this study should show who was right.

Two factors hindered the modern emergence of theories of conflict and revolution based on the vertical stratification of society, such as Machiavelli's, or a mixture of vertical and class stratifications, such as Tocqueville's. The first is the adoption by many scholars and intellectuals of Marxist perspectives emphasizing class politics. The second is that many modern coups and revolutions that attracted Western attention until the 1990s were led by Communists who tried to develop class consciousness in even the least

13. Qutb n.d., 9 and 51.

14. Ibid., 10.

15. Yakan 1993, 15. See also pp. 23–27 where he argues that decentralization leads to loss of control over the actions of militants who, when lacking a thorough Islamic education, can discredit the Islamic movement with their irresponsible actions.

16. Ibid., 83–84. See Sivan (1985, 40–41) for an account of the Brotherhood's failure to withstand Nasserite crackdowns.

likely environments. Yet, political scientists have slowly regained awareness of the importance of social structure and other types of organizational patterns for a deeper understanding of conflict processes.

Charles Tilly (1978) tells us that political violence is likely to occur only when aggrieved groups have the means to mobilize resources through organization, which will allow them to develop the capability to control territory or topple the government. Some scholars of social movements (e.g., McCarthy and Zald 1973, 1977; several works by Tilly, Tarrow, and McAdam) have emphasized aspects of organization in mobilizing such movements in the West. Samuel Popkin (1979) argues that revolutionary movements succeed in attracting and holding mass support when, through the provision of good leadership, they succeed in solving local-level collective-action problems that could not be addressed by traditional leaders. Local organizers are able to generate a "revolutionary surplus" that they contribute to the nationwide revolution. Both Michael Taylor (1988) and David Laitin (1993, when applied to the development of nationalist movements) provide more general theories of collective action that argue that revolutions develop and are more likely to succeed where there is an abundance of well-knit small communities. More recently, Roger Petersen (2001), Stathis Kalyvas (2004, 2006), and Jeremy Weinstein have scrutinized the microsocietal dynamics that govern participation in civil wars. In this book I move beyond their insights by proposing that not all modes of organization are equal and by exploring how different organizational structures affect the outcome of conflict.

This book also benefits from breakthroughs in the field of organizational theory. The study of organizations has advanced dramatically in the last half century thanks to scholars of business management, sociology, and anthropology. I draw in particular on the development of contingency theory in management studies.[17] Contingency theorists try to predict the performance or effectiveness of an organization based on the extent to which the organization's structure matches contextual contingencies such as organizational size, technology, and the environment. I consider different organizational components and contingencies than classical contingency theorists, but the general principles of this approach apply equally well to business and militant organizations.

---

17. Contingency theory has its roots in the 1960s works of Peter Blau, John Woodward, Paul Lawrence, and Jay Lorsch, among others. One of the more innovative and compelling works on contingency theory is still Henry Mintzberg's *The Structuring of Organizations* (1979), which synthesizes and builds on the more basic preceding studies.

The similarities between a corporation and a warring organization are considerable: both compete with other organizations (the state and other revolutionary organizations in the case of the latter) to get a larger share of a market (popular support) and perhaps dominate it (take control of the state apparatus or an ethnic homeland). So why is the organizational study of corporations so advanced while scant attention is given to that of revolutionary and similar organizations? Perhaps because most corporations, unlike revolutionary organizations, encourage the study of their structures in their unrelenting pursuit of improved productivity. A second reason is that corporations pour huge sums into funding research that yields tangible results while scholars of conflict are not under pressure to provide practical advice. Yet another reason is that, in addition to scholars who study firms, there are legions of professional managerial consultants who are evaluated on the quality of their advice to the corporations to which they charge exorbitant fees. Specialized consultants and academics also frequently move in and out of firms, while few, if any, academics attain positions of leadership in militant organizations and return to academia to analyze their experiences in comparative context.

Modern armies are never more than a step behind corporations in adopting structural innovations.[18] Generals and military planners are often preoccupied with "chains of command," command and control (with a focus on redundancy), and the advantages and disadvantages of centralization.[19] Many sociologists have promoted the idea that organizations in different settings, such as corporations, states, and tribal societies, have much in common.[20] Although this may not always be true, there is no reason to believe that organizations at war are unlike any other kind of organization and cannot be more or less effective because of structural factors.

---

18. Bracken (1990) argues in a RAND Corporation note that the U.S. military has consciously borrowed structural innovations from corporate America in the past and that it should keep doing so in the future. Management scholars interested in corporate intelligence also draw for inspiration on the experiences of the military in organizing its security services (Roukis, Conway, and Charmov 1990).

19. Ries (1964), Barrett (1983), and Siccama and van den Doel (1994) provide insight into the enduring preoccupation of military circles with organizational structure. Military leaders of great empires have spent considerable energy on organizing and reorganizing their armies. Some historic examples include the organization of the Roman Legions, the evolution of the organization of Muslim armies from the days of the Prophet Muhammad through the successive Muslim empires (see Siddiqui, 1987), the military reforms of Frederick the Great of Prussia (Morgan 1997, 15–16), and the great Ottoman military reorganization that transformed the Turkic tribes into the most professional and best organized army of the sixteenth century, with the nontribal Janissaries as its elite force. See Hui (2005) and Cooley (2005) for studies of the organization of Chinese and Soviet empires.

20. Inter alia, Max Weber's writings, Lammers and Hickson 1979, Leites and Wolf 1970, and Kuhn and Beam 1982.

The Core of the Argument

The distribution of power within organizations (what we call structure) in conflicts such as civil war or resistance to occupation creates incentives that motivate the individual behavior of organizational members in ways that affect the organization's ability to outlast its rivals. Figure 1.1 provides the framework for an organizational theory of group conflict. The framework lists relevant organizational structures, the key processes they influence, and the possible outcomes for an organization engaged in conflict. It also represents the one contingency that affects whether a structure is advantageous: the organization's ability to keep its rivals from infringing on a territorial safe haven within the boundaries of the overall contested area. The adoption of specific structures by rivals in a territorial conflict affects their odds of survival and, consequently, the outcome of the conflict.

Types of Organizational Structure

I consider five basic organizational structures (ways that power can be distributed within and among organizations): centralized, decentralized, patron-client, multiple, and fragmented. *Centralization* is the measure of distribution of power over decision making among the top-tier leadership and second-level or subsequent cadres within the organization. Decision making deals with the formulation of strategy, making appointments, the distribution of resources, the control of communication, and enforcing discipline. Second-level cadres (e.g., field commanders, village leaders, imams of mosques, heads of associations) can only make such decisions for local matters, while the top leadership can be decisive on both the local and organizational levels. The more control second-level or subsequent cadres wield over the formulation of local strategy and other decisions, the more *decentralized* the organization.

A *patron-client* relationship is one of exchange in which a party (the patron) allocates a resource or is capable of providing a service to another party (the client) who needs it and is ready to exchange temporary loyalty, general support, and assistance for it. It is considerably easier for a client to exit a relationship with a patron than for a regular agent to do the same with his principal. To illustrate with familiar terms from the corporate world, a client is analogous to a contractor and an agent to an employee. Although some consider patron-client relations to be attributes of some cultures, I consider them to be structural links that can exist within any organization.

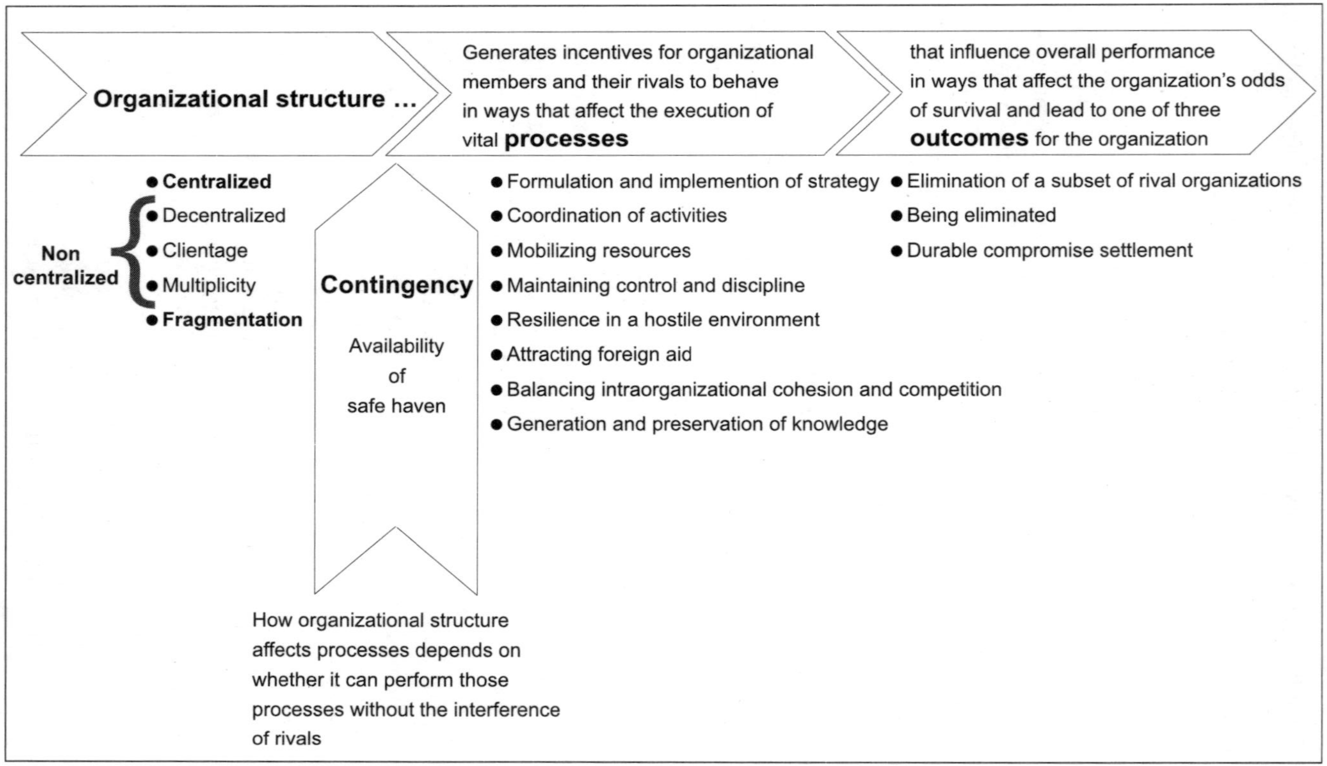

FIGURE 1.1. Framework of the organizational theory of group conflict

The two other dimensions of organization are movement-specific and only applicable to challengers. Some conflicts feature one independent challenger, some *multiple* independent challengers (two to four organizations), and others a *fragmented* opposition (five or more organizations). I decided on the cutoff between multiplicity and fragmentation after noticing a different dynamic in qualitative case studies once the number of organizations exceeds four—this is the empirical point of transition from competition with specific rivals to positioning the organization within an industry of conflict. What makes an organization independent is that its rank and file is bound to its leadership, and no other leadership, as agents or clients. I consider an organization to be significant if it musters reasonable popular support and its activities affect the strategies and operations of other significant organizations. If the incumbent (the government or occupier) has no organized challengers, then society is *atomized* for our purposes. Atomized societies do not produce sustained militant opposition.

The Safe Haven Contingency

The contingency that decisively influences how structure affects performance is the organization's control of a territorial safe haven—a portion of the contested territory where an organization's rivals cannot intervene with enough force to disturb its operations. A safe haven is important because each organization in conflict must perform eight critical processes well, and perform most of them better than the competition, to have a good chance of winning. The way power is distributed within the organization (i.e., structure) creates incentives that affect how organizational members perform such operations, and the availability of a safe haven (the contingency) affects whether they can achieve the levels of performance their organizational structure permits. The safe haven should be within the contested territory. Havens across the border are rarely safe for long because finicky sponsors may interrupt operations at will or distract the organization from its original goals by making it a tool to project influence in the neighboring country. Insurgents have a safe haven when the incumbent lacks the ability to effectively fight them in some regions of the country for any number of reasons—for example, loss of foreign aid, divisions within the military, or an underdeveloped state apparatus. Insurgents do not necessarily need a safe haven to win because regimes may collapse (e.g., Iranian Revolution) and occupiers may withdraw (e.g., Algerian War of Liberation) before they acquire one.

Organizations without a Safe Haven

The most important goal for organizations that are subject to the constant harassment of rivals is to survive long enough to take advantage of opportunities that may come up in the future that could advantage them. Centralized organizations are very vulnerable absent a safe haven because they rely on close coordination among their specialized branches and depend heavily on a few key leaders. Coordination can be frequently interrupted by stronger rivals, which makes the nonautonomous organizational components ineffective. The organization can also be incapacitated if decapitated, the way the Kurdistan Workers Party (PKK) was weakened by the capture of Abdullah Ocalan or the Shining Path (Sendero Luminoso, the Communist Party of Peru) by the capture of Abimael Guzmán. Centralized organizations without a territorial safe haven can also be routed through the use of sophisticated strategies that aim to isolate them from potential supporters. This is how the Omani Zhofaris, the Kenyan Mau Mau, and the Malayan Communists, among others, were defeated. Centralized organizations are also much less capable of mobilizing support than noncentralized ones absent a safe haven because they are less rooted in the social structure and their nonautonomous branches are not as responsive and adaptable to local needs.

Centralized organizations are also vulnerable to becoming tools for the projection of the power of their foreign sponsors instead of pursuing their independent goals because their leaders are able to bring the rank and file along with their shifts in strategy. Many Palestinian organizations shrank their way to near oblivion by becoming surrogates of Syria or Iraq in internecine Palestinian conflicts rather than pursuing a sensible agenda and popular policies so that they could grow at the expense of rivals. A foreign sponsor often requests exclusive sponsorship of a centralized organization and consequently manages to have strong leverage over its leader. Even more damaging can be the withdrawal of support by this one sponsor. Many organizations, such as the Sahrawi Polisario in the Western Sahara region of Morocco after the withdrawal of Algerian support, faltered this way. A centralized organization without a safe haven will also not be able to effectively use mechanisms otherwise available to it to enforce discipline, such as redundant structures and specialized branches, because they cannot be easily developed under duress and they require coordination and intensive communication. Centralized organizations also cannot manipulate and move information and knowledge effectively absent a safe haven: information needs to travel a long way from where it is produced to where it is needed in such organizations, and its flow can be easily interrupted or intercepted by rivals.

Noncentralized organizations are more resilient than centralized ones in hostile environments because their different components are more autonomous and less dependent on coordination. They are not as vulnerable as centralized organizations to shortcuts like decapitation or sophisticated strategies that aim to isolate the organization because the rank and file are both fairly independent and well ensconced within the social structure. The leader of a noncentralized organization will risk the noncompliance of its more autonomous rank and file if he tries to transform the organization into the surrogate of a foreign sponsor; the noncentralized organization is therefore less likely to squander its credibility and support. Some decentralized organizational setups (multiple patronage-based organizations) can even result in a strategic lockup when the insurgent organizational leaders cannot compromise with the powers that be regardless of their desire to do so or be pressured by sponsors because they would lose their rank and file (see chapter 6). Multiple organizations might even attract multiple sponsors, thus producing the kind of redundancy that would shield them in the aggregate from an abrupt cessation of support by any one sponsor. Noncentralized organizations are also advantaged in mobilizing support in a hostile environment because their more autonomous cadres are more responsive to local needs and are better able to mete out positive and negative sanctions than the officers of centralized ones. Control and discipline are easier to maintain within smaller and autonomous groups in hostile environments, which gives an advantage to noncentralized organizations enmeshed in intricate social structures. Information does not need to move far in noncentralized organizations: it is mostly produced and used locally with little input from the leadership and with little probability of interception by rivals.

Sophisticated incumbents can easily defeat a fragmented insurgent landscape because its different components are the equivalent of tiny vulnerable independent centralized organizations.

Organizations with a Safe Haven

An organization that can operate in a portion of the contested territory without much interference from rivals needs to take coordinated strategic action to decisively eliminate such rivals beyond its safe haven. If it doesn't, it will allow its rivals to repeatedly attack it and to perhaps ultimately defeat it. It might also lose supporters to organizations that make faster progress and be dropped from aid from sponsors that lose interest. Centralized organizations are much more capable than noncentralized ones of taking the strategic initiative and they have other advantages once they can operate without the intrusive intervention of rivals. Only centralized organizations can implement complex multistep strategies that require careful coordination, strict discipline, and concentrated decision making. Centralized organizations become less vulnerable to strategies that aim to isolate them from potential supporters if they acquire a safe haven because they have exclusive control over a portion of the territory where they can methodically mobilize the population through overlapping structures that police them and provide specialized services. Territorial control also allows taxation of the population and the extraction of resources, both of which reduce the centralized organization's reliance on sponsors who might distract it from its original goals. Redundant structures and specialized branches (e.g., political field officers) also enforce discipline within the ranks. Leaders of the organization can be well protected in a safe haven to reduce the probability of its decapitation. A centralized organization with a safe haven can also transmit information from where it is produced to where it is needed, accumulate knowledge, and centralize training with less fear of serious interruption.

Noncentralized organizations are incapable of taking the strategic initiative beyond locales abandoned by weakened rivals. They lack the ability to effectively coordinate large-scale actions, manipulate information, and enforce discipline among organizational components (in contrast to within those components, at which they excel) to do so. Their inability to take the strategic initiative to decisively defeat rivals can give their enemies time to reestablish themselves and further attempt to undermine them. It may also allow new organizations that are more capable of coordinated action to form in their areas and recruit their own followers (e.g., the Taliban's expansion). They may also lose the financial backing of impatient foreign sponsors with new priorities (e.g., the reduction of U.S. support for the mujahideen after they failed to take Kabul). Foreign backers might even cease to exist (e.g., the Soviet Union). Resilience, the major advantage of decentralization, is irrelevant for organizations that do not need to worry about constant harassment. The longer they take to centralize, the more likely they are to be defeated by rival organizations that can take the initiative or to fall apart on their own because of changing circumstances. Noncentralized organizations therefore must centralize once they gain control of a safe haven.

A highly fragmented insurgent landscape is even less capable than noncentralized organizations of engaging in decisive collective action. Fragmentation has no advantages.

Survival of the Fittest

The three possible conflict states for each organization are survival (which would be the equivalent of winning if it is the last organization standing); loss (becoming fragmented beyond the point where its surviving members and potential supporters can engage in effective collective action); or becoming part of an enduring settlement. Absent the rare negotiated settlement, the last organization to survive is the winner of the territorial conflict. If it happens to be a challenger to the powers that be, then one could also say that the revolution, war of liberation, or insurgency has succeeded.

Centralized organizations are generally more effective than noncentralized ones, but they are more vulnerable to the attempts of rivals to disturb their operations because of their dependence on coordination among their different specialized branches. An organization (such as the state, an occupier, or a strong insurgent group) that controls a safe haven that protects it from the easy disturbance of its operations by rivals must therefore adopt a highly centralized and specialized structure. Organizations that do not have such a space must adopt a noncentralized structure to increase their odds of outlasting their rivals. A safe haven is not essential to win a conflict, but it is essential that an organization organize properly depending on whether it has such a haven. An organization that suddenly gains control of a safe haven must transform itself into a more centralized structure or risk dissipating its resources (see figure 1.2 for a summary of predictions).

	Organizational Structure		
	Centralization	Patronage, Multiplicity, or Decentralization	Fragmentation
Safe haven	Good Fit	Bad Fit	Bad Fit
No safe haven	Bad Fit	Good Fit	Bad Fit

Good fit: organization more likely to survive by the end of the conflict

FIGURE 1.2. The organizational theory's predictions

An organizational approach explains otherwise puzzling behavior or developments that are regularly encountered in politicized group conflicts, such as the longevity of unpopular regimes, the surprising demise of some popular movements, why some seemingly advantageous strategies are never adopted, and why some who share a common cause are often more interested in undermining their ideological or ethnic kin than their ideological or ethnic enemies. Such events would be hard to understand if one conceived of conflict as being among ideologies, religions, civilizations, the masses, or ethnic groups.

I develop and provide a richer discussion of the theory in the three chapters of part 1. Chapter 2 defines the meaning of key terms and concepts. Chapter 3 explains how organizational structure affects the performance of the eight processes essential for organizational survival. I bring together the different threads of the organizational theory of group conflict and discuss its implications in chapter 4.

In part 2, I apply the organizational theory to explain the evolution and outcomes of consecutive Afghan conflicts since 1979. I explain in chapters 5 and 6 how the patronage ties that bound the party leaders in Peshawar to their client field commanders allowed the mujahideen parties to be quite resilient under the intrusive Soviet occupation, and how the failure of the Soviets and their client regime to centralize their institutions prevented them from benefiting from their overwhelming military power and abundant resources.

Chapter 7 explains how the Najib regime survived for three years beyond the withdrawal of its Soviet sponsors because the organizational structure of the mujahideen, beneficial as it was under duress, would not allow them to take the strategic initiative. What distinguished surviving organizations from losers after the Soviet withdrawal was not ideology or ethnic composition but the party structures they chose, or had to adopt, in a new environment that favored centralized organizations over patronage-based ones. Only centralized organizations endured beyond the collapse of the Najib regime to feud destructively until the rise of the Taliban.

I argue in chapter 8 that the Taliban, a centralized organization, eliminated its rivals by undermining the ability of local leaders (a fragmented opposition) to maintain the loyalty of their own followers and by skillfully manipulating pervasive regional rivalries among chieftains. I also explain how the Taliban defeated two of their larger rivals, General Abdul Rashid Dostum and Ismail Khan, by adeptly manipulating their ties with clients on the periphery of their domains.

Chapter 9 explains the failure of the United States to consolidate a loyal state in Afghanistan after it unseated the Taliban in November 2001.

I make the case in chapter 10 that the organizational theory explains organizational survival and the outcomes of territorially based politicized group conflicts well beyond Afghanistan. I test the theory on an original dataset of forty-one conflicts and the 133 organizations that participated in them—all ethnic, revolutionary, and secessionist conflicts that lasted longer than three years in post–World War II North Africa, the Middle East, and the Americas.

Part One

An Organizational Theory of Group Conflict

CHAPTER 2

Organization and the Outcome of Conflicts

> The principles of organization got more attention among us than they did then in universities. If what follows seems academic, I assure you that we did not think it so.
>
> —Alfred Sloan, the chief executive officer whose innovations made General Motors the largest car company in the world

Sustained action by either the state (or occupying power) and its challengers generally requires an organizational framework. Organization allows for coordination among participants, the maintenance of discipline, the minimization of free riding, the efficient mobilization and distribution of resources, the preservation and generation of necessary learning, and the purposeful use of sophisticated strategies to undermine rivals. The way such processes are executed by an organization and its rivals strongly affects their odds of success. In this chapter I discuss the meaning of organization and structure, describe how political organizations develop, how they can be structured, the possible outcomes of conflict, and the contingency that dramatically changes the way organizations need to be structured.

The Meaning of Organization

It is tempting, if only because of the fluidity of human interactions, to doubt that there is such a thing as an organizational structure, let alone a social structure. Marshall Sahlins (1985), for example, tells us that social structures are culturally and historically defined and that they do not really exist independently of exogenous influences that continuously cause them to reshape themselves.[1] If this were true, then I might not be able to use organizational and societal structure as an explanatory variable. Fortunately, Sahlins himself and many other keen students of traditional societies observe that change is often slow. Although tribal systems, for example, probably have not existed in the same form as long as tribal myths would have us believe, they normally are stable for the duration of many conflicts. Powerful shocks do cause structural changes, but the new structural forms often stabilize and allow us to use them as an independent variable, at least for the duration of a significant cycle of strategic interaction. And, perhaps both surprisingly and conveniently, organizations at war consistently follow a few widespread recognizable organizational patterns, despite the immensely large number of possible ways they could be structured.

Societal structures are not physical links, and organizations are not the charts used to represent them in managerial and sociological studies. So what are they? The terms "organization" and "social structure" are metaphors.[2] Further, because these metaphors illustrate something that needs to be explained with something that is not clear, they require yet another metaphor that is usually subsumed under the assumptions of the analyst.[3] Yet, as I show below, those twice-alienating metaphors represent some *thing*, and our understanding of this *thing* both benefits and suffers from the existence of the metaphors.

The words "organization" and "social structure" imply that the obligations, attachments, hatreds, competition, yearnings, needs, and desires of a group of people make up a coherent whole. They imply that such relations can make a purpose-oriented web of significant interactions that exclude others, who

1. The British social theorist Anthony Giddens (1979) also argues for the fragility and dynamic aspects of structure by recognizing that structure is created by interaction, which it also constrains. This idea that social structures are created by the activities they constrain is called the "duality of structure." Structure, the argument goes, is not a fixed and immutable object but a delicate cooperative moment of tentative and ever-shifting interactivity sustained by the desire of the individuals involved in a particular context to interact. For a critique of this approach, see Bunge (1996, chap. 10). Some writers (e.g., Kowalewski and Hoover 1995) emphasize that conflict outcomes can be best predicted by understanding that organizations and strategies, among many other relevant variables, are dynamic and fluctuate considerably during the period of confrontation. Hardin (1982, 125) goes even further by stating that "static analysis is fundamentally wrongheaded. . . . Most interesting group choices are made by groups that are ongoing; often those choices are even provoked by ongoing or repeated choice problems."

2. This argument is in tune with the social constructionist view that the categories of language used to understand and describe organizations are not real or natural in an objective sense. See Hatch (1997) for more on the social constructionist approach to organization theory.

3. For an excellent account of the use of metaphors to understand organization, see Morgan (1997). Also see Hatch (1997, chap. 2).

may, in turn, form rival webs of similar interaction.[4] The use of those two terms is metaphoric because it superimposes the illusion of a clearly defined chart or matrix on what might be no more than a set of relations, often merely dyadic, that happen to exist in a space, whether physical or conceptual. Journalists who used the term "army"—a large organized body of armed personnel trained for war, according to *Webster's Dictionary*—to describe the Kosovo Liberation Army (KLA) engaged in such a metaphoric use of a term depicting an organization. This seems to be the case as evidence surfaced that the KLA consisted of mostly isolated groups that adopted common symbols that gained wide acceptance among Kosovars. Often, however, a general consciousness of the existence of an organization or social structure only develops with the articulation of the structure in a belief system, such as an organizational chart or the Hindu scriptures, that is continuously enforced through material incentives. People need to be aware of the existence of an organization (or social structure) beyond their personal sphere of relationships and accept its existence for the concept of "organization" (or social structure) to become a reasonable first metaphor. Although the metaphor could be inaccurate and misleading, the idea that there is an "organization" can very well become a self-fulfilling prophecy. In addition, at least some of the sets of relationships that are necessary for the formation of the organization or social structure must exist for this awareness to develop and a truly self-contained, self-sustaining, coherent, and purpose-oriented web of relations to ultimately form.

In brief, the words "organization" and "social structure" are at worst empty metaphors and at best simplified parsimonious models of sets of relations that generally function far less coherently and convincingly than the metaphor would imply. Metaphors are of course problematic because they invite us to see similarities (both the KLA's small groups and regular armies fight) but deceive us into ignoring the differences (the KLA did not have a formal structure, the professional training, or the weaponry that characterize modern armies). Using terms such as "organization" as constructs and the basis for academic speculation brings us dangerously close to the realization of Plato's warning to Cratylus: "Well, but do you not see, Cratylus, that he who follows

4. This understanding is rooted in the pragmatist thought that is encapsulated in Charles Sanders Peirce's (1878) following two sentences: "Consider what effects, that conceivably have practical bearings, we conceive the object of our conception to have. Then, our conception of these effects is the whole of our conception of the object." In other words, a thing "is" what a thing "does," and if two hundred people coordinate their actions for the purpose of overthrowing a government then I see no reason why they should not be considered a revolutionary organization. Another elegant terminology can be found in Kuhn and Beam (1982, 17) who use "consciously coordinated actions toward a joint effect" in a way similar to my "purpose-oriented web of significant interaction."

names in the search after things, and analyzes their meanings, is in great danger of being deceived?"[5] It is indeed risky to invent and sustain the meaning of terms that we then use to understand the world, but a process of trial and error that involves the redefinition of deficient concepts is the only way for the social sciences to advance. One encouraging sign is that some organizations—particularly established corporations in lean times and bureaucracies in developed states—and a few social structures approach the models after which they have been created. This level of complexity in understanding the meaning of organizations and social structures is satisfactory for organizational builders and social reformers. Another group of people, however, finds the need to use yet one more level of metaphoric abstraction.

A scholar who observes individuals who behave as if there were such a thing as a coherent and purpose-oriented organization that affects their behavior ponders how to best explain its existence, its behavior, and its evolution; hence the need for a further metaphor. If the organization were like a machine, then it would not behave as if it were an organism, a brain, a culture, a political system, a psychic prison, or a tool for domination. Yet, as often is the case among scholars, there are people advocating each of the above metaphors to the exclusion of others. Scholars therefore deal with matters of organization by using twice-alienating metaphors, and lose much of their ability to both explain and predict in the process. There is a way out of this quagmire: the *thing* to describe and understand is not the organization but the interaction of the basic components of its structure. This solution does not push abstraction back one step because, while it is difficult to ascertain that an organization or a social structure is an elemental unit for the purposes of explaining its own performance, it is a more manageable task to argue that a principal-agent or patron-client relationship, for example, is. It is true that basic organizational components can be broken into even more basic interactive components (emotional impulses, complex economic decisions, feelings of loyalty, a chemical imbalance in either party's brain), but they are elemental enough and necessary (albeit not sufficient) to explain organizational performance. Although it is completely legitimate for those interested in studying the behavior of other types of entities to consider

5. Plato, *Diol.*, *Cratylus*. The same trap was also described by the cultural anthropologist Clifford Geertz (1973, 5), who wrote that "man is an animal trapped in webs of significance he himself has spun." In all fairness, the sin of the organizational theorist is no greater than that of the rational-choice analyst or any other parsimonious modeler when people in organizations fail to behave as if the lines on the organizational chart were real. We all dance precariously around the same dangerous pit.

finer or coarser elemental units than organizational components, I do not look beyond that level because I am interested in explaining the behavior of organizations. Focusing on the components of the organization also allows us to better explain change within an organization and otherwise unpredictable behavior by organizations. But what are the components of organizational structure?

Components of organizational structure are contained sets of relations among two or more individuals that create incentives to behave, communicate, and reward or punish in a specific way.[6] Individuals' behavior in the context of such relations is generally predictable because individuals are normally rational in long-term and iterated interactions that provide them with the opportunity to learn the consequences of their actions or to be socialized to do so.[7] Incentives take the form of positive and negative sanctions, such as giving resources commensurate with performance, physical punishment, deprivation of already acquired resources, and withdrawal of loyalty or support.[8] Although relations are conceptually contained within components of organizations, they can be affected by elements exogenous to the organizational component, or to the entire organization. Such exogenous factors could change

---

6. This is akin to the approach used by Etzioni (1975, xv–xvi and 5), who defined three types of power:

> Coercive power rests on the application, or the threat of application, of physical sanctions such as infliction of pain, deformity, or death; generation of frustration through restriction of movement; or controlling through force the satisfaction of needs such as those of sex, comfort, and the like. Remunerative power is based on control over material resources and rewards through allocation of salaries and wages, commissions and contributions, "fringe benefits," services and commodities. Normative power rests on the allocation and manipulation of symbolic rewards and deprivations through employment of leaders, manipulation of mass media, allocation of esteem and prestige symbols, administration of ritual, and influence over the distribution of "acceptance" and "positive response."

I simplify Etzioni's three categories under the two headings of positive and negative sanctions by breaking "normative power" into its positive and negative sanction components while acknowledging that they are of different importance and intensity when compared with other sanctions.

7. My understanding of structure is very close to that of Burton and Obel (1984, 4):

> In basic terms . . . the organization's structure influences its activities, which in turn influence the organization's performance. Simply put, Structure (→) Activities (→) Performance. The word "influences" is used purposefully. We did not say "determines," as there are clearly other concerns. The temperament of the CEO may also influence the organization's performance. But that is not an explicit part of our model. We focus on the structure and its consequences. For example, the way the firm is decomposed into smaller subunits is posited to influence what happens in the firm, and further how well the firm performs, say in terms of profit.

8. I define authority as the ability to apply positive and negative sanctions that are significant to others in a relationship.

the ability of parties to provide or inflict sanctions, reduce the value or impact of such sanctions, or lead to the renegotiation of the terms of the relationship.

As Herbert Simon has shown across the body of his work, there are many limitations on individual rationality, which is "bound," to use his term, by imperfect information, the complexity of problems and limited analytical ability, and time restrictions, among many possible factors. But it is virtually impossible to model aggregate human behavior without making simplifying assumptions. I therefore generally accept the simplifying assumptions of classical rationality for individual behavior. However, I do not accept them on the organizational level. The behavior of classically rational individuals within organizations could result in nonrational behavior by the organization as a whole. This occurs because individuals might value their influence within the organization over the interests of the organization, and those two goals might not always be aligned. The same could also occur because of disagreement among decision makers or because of the inability of the organization to channel the necessary information to those who need it. Some empirical research has shown that corporate decision making often degenerates from the rational to trial and error, or even to a process resembling the "garbage can" model of James March (March and Simon 1958). March argued that decisions sometimes form as a random stream of events intertwine, allowing some solutions to attach themselves to problems in the presence of a random set of individuals at a random point in time, much like the unsavory metaphor implies. War, however, has a way of focusing the mind and I will proceed by assuming that decisions by organizational members can be better understood once their interests within the context of structural incentives and constraints are unraveled.

Just like the no-nonsense pragmatists, I accept that I am observing a militant organization if a group of individuals coordinate their efforts to overwhelm and fragment other groups of similarly coordinated individuals or to preempt the formation of such rivals. The activity that defines the essence of the organization is not revolution, secession, or liberation; it is the effort to undermine rivals.[9] Revolution, secession, and liberation are simply the outcomes that might result from a successful challenge mounted

9. My definition of organizations based on their function and structure is in accord with many definitions found in the better works on organization theory. Scott (1981, 22) defines organizations as "collectivities oriented to the pursuit of relatively specific goals and exhibiting relatively highly formalized social structures." Although the "highly formalized" part of this definition goes against the fabric of my argument, other definitions he discusses (offshoots of the natural and open systems schools of organization theory) assume less structure.

by a rival of an incumbent organization. It is this perspective that allows me to subsume revolutionary, secessionist, separatist, guerrilla, and liberation conflicts under the same category to explain their evolutions and outcomes. To better understand the probability of success of such organizations, I look at how their internal structures allow them to perform vis-à-vis other political organizations in their particular environment. Adopting the pragmatist approach and focusing on organizational components relieves us of having to rely on alienating metaphors and the distracting analytical tools they suggest.

How Organizational Structures Develop

Although pervasive dissatisfaction with authorities, the shock of foreign invasion, or the atrocities that accompany occupation sometimes lead to impromptu street demonstrations or other widespread but uncoordinated acts of protest, such actions rarely have the resilience needed to achieve the aspirations of their participants.[10] As proof of the political weakness of atomized resistance, one need only consider the literature that has developed based on James Scott's (1976; 1986) work on atomized peasant resistance to centralized power. Among seven case studies in a volume edited by Forrest Colburn (1989) and based on Scott's work, none of the instances of atomized peasant resistance resulted in the overthrow of the government or colonial power. Furthermore, none resulted in the improvement of the peasants' political or economic conditions. The editor concludes that "for those in authority acts of atomized resistance are at best a nuisance and at worst a threat," and one contributor adds that "[such acts] were limited to provoking fear and unease among rulers. . . . At most, the Egyptian state's penetration of rural society may have been slightly slowed."[11] Atomization is so disadvantageous to those wanting to overthrow a regime that, as Guillermo O'Donnell and Philippe Schmitter (1986, 48) eloquently tell us, new autocratic governments make it their first order of business to fragment all nonregime organizational activities:

10. Some see the East German protests that led to the reunification of Germany as successful nonorganized ones. A number of mathematical models (Lohmann 1994; Kuran 1991) assume that these protests developed because of nonorganizational incentives for overcoming free riding, such as signaling (individuals with different tolerance for risk gauge the risk of participation based on the number of participants already protesting). I explain why atomized movements are generally weak in chapter 3.

11. Colburn 1989, xiii. Second quote is from Brown (1989, 118).

> [A revival of civil society] has to be set against the background of the success of most authoritarian regimes in depoliticizing as well as atomizing their respective societies. By physical repression, ideological manipulation, and selective encouragement, they manage to orient most of their subjects toward the pursuit of exclusively private goals. . . . Citizenship becomes a matter of holding a passport, obeying national laws, cheering for the country's team, and, occasionally, voting in choreographed elections or plebiscites.[12]

Although the complete lack of organizational structure (atomization) could arguably be advantageous in rare instances (when incumbent elites are already divided or when victimization could induce effective international intervention in support of the group after a spike in protests), politically oriented members of society soon realize the need to develop political organizations to achieve their own and their groups' political objectives.[13] Some organizations are shaped by preexisting societal ties while others are developed by political entrepreneurs to maximize their organization's probability of success or to achieve personal gains in areas where societal structures are weak.

The two patterns generally develop simultaneously in recently politicized societies. Political mobilization takes place along traditional sociostructural lines, where those exist, because they minimize the cost of convincing people to develop new loyalties and patterns of accountability and reduce resistance from those who would lose influence from their development.[14] The reduction of the cost of mobilization is so important in the initial stages of

---

12. O'Donnell and Schmitter 1986, 48.

13. Not everyone agrees with this statement. Jeffrey Simon (1989, 4–7) argues in a short RAND Corporation report that atomized mass protests can be more effective than organized militancy in toppling regimes. Others argue that spontaneous eruptions in atomized society take place because of the lack of more effective organized action (Greene 1974, 60–64).

14. Laitin (1993, 14) argues that a dense rural social structure is a necessary condition for nationalist mobilization and strife. Russell Hardin's (1982, 31–34) by-product theory shows how easy it is for nonpolitical organizations to perform political functions not originally intended for them because they have already overcome "latency." Historical analyses also support this view, as Zagorin (1982, 1:86) tells us while generalizing about peasant rebellion in early modern Europe:

> Agrarian rebellion almost invariably began in the mobilization of village communities, their members summoned to rise by the violent ringing of church bells in the parishes and then flowing together in growing crowds from all parts of the countryside. . . . The village community contained the main potentiality of joint action. It was the elementary cell from whose coalescence with other similar cells peasant struggles, whether against the state or landlords, developed.

See also Taylor (1988, 81–83) for additional historical accounts showing the ease and convenience of mobilizing and coordinating small communities.

conflict that it can temporarily relegate ideology to a secondary status, as Chalmers Johnson tells us happened early during the Chinese Communist experience:

> In their effort at defensive organization, the villagers welcomed whatever capable military and political leadership they could find—Communist, Nationalist, Sacrifice League (Shansi), secret society, KMT army remnants, or purely local leaders. . . . The Chinese Communist Party was the elite group that successfully placed itself at the head of the war-mobilized peasantry and became the political beneficiary of peasant mobilization.[15]

In the same vein, Ralph Thaxton attributes much of the success of the Chinese Communist Party in organizing peasants to the Communist offer of a renewed traditional system of rights and duties, and argues that Communist cadres had to adapt to the "alternate symbolic universe" of the peasantry.[16] Traditional patterns of authority often do not reach into urbanized areas and refugee camps, providing an opening for entrepreneurial talent to forge new ones.[17] If society is atomized, as in many industrialized and previously Communist countries, entrepreneurs become essential for the formation of any political organization.[18] Traditional and entrepreneurial political organizations have major structural differences that give them distinct advantages and disadvantages under different circumstances. Entrepreneurial political organizations are likely to be more centralized, aggressive, and integrated than traditional ones, which often rely on loose patron-client relations and are more reactive to local infringements on their authority but lack a coherent overall strategy. Traditional and ad hoc types of organizations often coexist, but organizations whose structural features best suit the conditions of the conflict ultimately prevail.

---

15. Johnson (1962, 3 and 71). The Communists restructured the peasant organizations as they strengthened their control of the villages. Although Skocpol (1979) discounts the village social structure in China, Taylor (1988, 73–76) argues that she is mistaken based on the much more meaningful accounts of scholars focusing on the Chinese village. The devil is indeed in the details.

16. Ralph Thaxton, "Mao Zedong, Red *Misérables*, and the Moral Economy of Peasant Rebellion in Modern China," reported in Weller and Guggenheim (1982, 4).

17. By "traditional," I do not mean to imply a "stiff cultural system imprisoned in the past," as David Apter (1967, 84–107, quote on page 84) warns us many wrongly understand the term. I simply call a social structure "traditional" to indicate that it was well established before the advent of a traumatic event such as colonial or despotic government. It might very well have metamorphosed many times in the centuries preceding the conflict.

18. On this specific point see McCarthy and Zald (1973, 1977), Freeman (1972), Evans (1979), and Jenkins (1983, 531).

The structure of traditional organizations is grounded in the existing social structure and often emulates it, with minor variations that might become amplified with the passage of time. One observer of a meeting of the men in charge of defending a Kosovar village (part of the loose structure of the Kosovo Liberation Army) found them seated in the traditional way: the village elder was surrounded by two distinguished figures, the most educated among the villagers (a tradition) and the commander of the armed villagers (the innovation in this case).[19] The longer the war, the more important the role of the fighters becomes (as opposed to the traditional elders), but the new allegiances are likely to mimic old ones—a phenomenon that is also illustrated by the Afghan shift from clans to clanlike fighting units centered around field commanders during the jihad.

Those who engineer ad hoc organizations have a greater ability to structure them to maximize their own power within them, while still giving the organization a chance to succeed. This universal trade-off between the power of the organizational entrepreneur and the potential of the organization to succeed explains why so many entrepreneurial revolutionary organizations are similarly structured, even if they differ in every other respect. It is indeed no coincidence that the Islamist Hekmatyar's party in Afghanistan was structured similarly to many Marxist organizations or that European parties in the first half of the last century engaged in what Duverger (1959, 25) calls "contagious organization."[20]

Sometimes organizations in a colonized society try to imitate the structure of their occupiers despite lacking the necessary skills, numbers, and resources. Societal leaders who believe that they can acquire the strength of their occupiers by mimicking their organizational structure generally discover the flaw in their reasoning at great cost, as Charles Callwell, the seasoned British colonial officer and small-war theorist, observes in his discussion of the Russian route of Central Asian resistance (see chapter 1).[21] More extreme examples are provided by armies established by weak non-European leaders in awe of European colonizers at the end of the nineteenth century. The British easily defeated the forces of Urabi Pasha in 1882 in Egypt, and the French did the same to Chinese troops they confronted in 1884–85. Both forces were ironically organized by their leaders following

19. *New York Times*, July 27, 1999, A8.

20. Pfeffer (1981, 267–71) argues that business organizations, before they had to become mean and lean or perish, acquired their structure as the result of "the political struggle to design organizations without any regard for their economic efficiency."

21. Callwell 1976 [1906], 157–58.

the European model in hopes of providing a deterrent for colonizers and other foes.[22] Their performance pales when compared with that of the traditionally organized Algerians and Afghans in reaction to the same colonizers. Once again, Callwell's extensive experience proves pithy: "It is an undoubted fact indeed the more nearly the enemy approximates in system to the European model, the less marked is the strategical advantage he enjoys."[23]

Shifting circumstances during conflict impose new trade-offs on members of rival organizations. Sometimes organizational changes take place because of the growing influence of new ideas, for example, the formation of the Wahhabi Ikhwan (brotherhood) under Ibn Saud or the many ill-fated imitations of the Che Guevara and Fidel Castro models by other South American revolutionaries.[24] More often, however, change happens because those at the helm of an organization and their rivals within and outside the organization attempt to affect the organization's structure to increase their power within or over it.[25] Kotchen and Deutsch suggest why this would happen:

> If a disfavored group or class is weak on the average across the aggregate domain of a service system, but strong in some smaller region, it should gain from decentralization; and a favored group, predominant on the average but weak in some localities, should gain from policies of centralization and amalgamation. As a group over time shifts from one of these conditions to the other, its attitudes toward decentralization are likely to reverse. Weak reformers, like weak conservatives,

---

22. Perhaps it is true, as Martin van Creveld (1991, 95) tells us, that

> war represents perhaps the most imitative activity known to man. . . . Strategy is interactive by definition. . . . Belligerents who were originally very dissimilar will come to resemble each other first in point of the methods that they use then, gradually, other respects. . . . One important way by which human societies of any kind develop their internal structure has always been through fighting other societies.

23. Callwell 1976, 157–58.

24. See Radu (1990, 14) for how even rightist and anticommunist revolutionaries study the strategies and tactics of glamorized Communist insurgents such as Mao, Fidel Castro, and Vo Nguyen Giap. Also see Duverger (1959, 25–26) for examples of how European parties imitated the organizational structures of more successful ones. The adoption of the structure du jour, even when it is not suitable for the company's situation, is also widespread in the corporate world (Mintzberg 1979, 292).

25. This opinion is shared by Kochen and Deutsch (1980, 185), who argue, "Often, the motive for centralizing is primarily someone's urge to maintain or increase power. Machiavelli suggested centralization as positive and decentralization as negative reinforcement for a ruling prince." Pfeffer (1981, 266–87) studies the effect of the power of actors in organizations on their structures.

often settle for local strongholds at least temporarily; whereas powerful reformers, like powerful conservatives, often prefer to centralize.[26]

Resources are important for individuals wishing to restructure organizations. Duverger (1959, 58–59) tells us that organizations financed by their rank and file are much more decentralized than those that feature a leadership with a monopoly on financial or other essential resources.[27] Although the case studies in part 2 show that this is not always true, those who control the flow of money gain some leverage in modifying organizational structure to increase their influence or to achieve other goals. Sometimes they can completely reshape the organization to maximize their power. And foreign sponsors encourage centralization of structure by giving their aid to the leaders they favor because they recognize that this facilitates their control over the organization.[28] This happened, for example, when Israel decided to channel all aid to southern Sudanese rebels through Joseph Lagu, the Anya Nya leader, who then eliminated all competition in the movement with the help of his newly mustered resources.[29] Another example is the failed British effort to unify Albanian resistance leaders who detested one another in World War II.[30] Shifts in power among relevant actors motivate the continuous deal making and compromises that cause the generally slow, but sometimes brutal, metamorphosis of organizational structures.

Components and Dimensions of Organizational Structure

Structure is difficult to describe and quantify, particularly in cases where the researcher is dealing with societies in flux that feature a myriad of overlapping human relations. I believe that the best way to manage the understand-

26. Kochen and Deutsch 1980, 199.

27. The other important factor that Duverger identifies, purpose, is not useful for this inquiry because all organizations considered here share the same purpose.

28. There is considerable and convincing evidence in the business management literature that shows that the greater the external control over the organization, the more centralized and formalized its structure. See Mintzberg (1979, chap. 16) for a summary of the literature and the argument that ensues: the most effective means to control an organization from the outside are to hold its most powerful decision makers responsible for its actions and to impose clearly defined standards on it. Mintzberg also argues that external control fosters bureaucratization and organizational inefficiencies.

29. Pirouet 1976, 208; Heraclides 1987.

30. Petersen 1993, 179.

ing, classifying, and coding of the organizational variable is to reduce it to its basic components. These components should suffice to represent significant and relevant webs of human interaction. I have identified six basic organizational components and dimensions, but I cannot say a priori that they are exhaustive because I need to actually find a specific case in which they do not suffice to accurately describe an organization's structure in order to be able to add new ones to the list.[31] I use these basic components to define the structures of rival organizations. It matters little if a politicized organization is ad hoc (e.g., centralized Communist parties, the Palestinian Izz ad-Din al-Qassam Brigades and Islamic Jihad, Polisario Front) or the extension of a preexisting societal organization (e.g., Kurdish or Afghan clans mobilizing, Sufi brotherhoods) so long as I can accurately and consistently code different patterns of organization by using the same structural building blocks. What once was an ad hoc organization can outlast the conflict to become a dominant societal organizational pattern (such as the change of village structure in postcolonial Vietnam), while some resilient societal arrangements have within them the ability to reshape themselves during crises and to revert back to their original patterns afterward (tribal societies, reserve armies).

The six basic organizational components I use to define organizational structures are the number of independent organizations, the existence of institutions linking the independent organizations, the existence of structural redundancy within independent organizations, the degree of centralization of each organization, the presence of patron-client arrangements, and the existence of specialized subgroups within organizations.

Number of Independent Organizations

What makes an organization independent is that its rank and file are bound to its leadership, and no other leadership, as agents or clients. As Sartori (1968) tells us, however, counting *relevant* organizations (political parties in his study) is not necessarily a straightforward matter. I consider an organization as relevant if it musters reasonable popular support and its activities affect the power or the strategies of other significant organizations. A contested territory can feature a single dominant politicized organization (e.g., Hafiz Assad's

31. I ignore some of the classic dimensions of organization used by business management scholars because of their irrelevance to my topic. Those dimensions, such as the average number of subordinates each manager supervises, are generally only relevant to very complex organizations with clearly delineated structures.

post-Hama Syria), two rival organizations (e.g., the challenge of the Algerian National Liberation Front [FLN] to French occupation at its advanced stages), or several (e.g., the Afghan resistance to the Soviets).

Supraorganizational Institutions

If a conflict features two or more independent organizations challenging a state or an occupier, some institutional structure that permits cooperation among them might develop. Such supraorganizational structures might not develop (e.g., among Iraqi Kurds before the 2003 U.S. invasion), be purely symbolic (e.g., among Afghan resistance parties during the 1980s), allow for effective communication and coordination (I have yet to hear of one), or be dominated by a strong organization and hence have a co-optive function (e.g., the pre-1982 Fatah-dominated Palestine Liberation Organization).

I list supraorganizational institutions in my typology of organizational components because they are the most visible organizational features when they do exist. Foreign sponsors always find it important to create "umbrella" structures that rival organizational leaders join with fanfare but later sabotage in so many ways. In fact, this organizational feature simply doesn't matter because it could either work too well and become the equivalent of a decentralized organization, or it could work poorly enough, which almost always happens, to deserve to be ignored for all purposes besides providing photo-ops to the satisfaction of foreign sponsors.

Redundancy

Redundancy is an organizational feature that sacrifices efficiency for improved reliability.[32] Critics of redundant structures dislike the added cost of their creation, the added cost of their competition (consider for example the added strain on the U.S. defense budget created by the acquisition of nuclear weapons by both the army and air force), and the difficulty of pinpointing responsibility before and after the occurrence of failure. The major argument in favor of redundancy is that it provides reliability under uncertainty: if one organizational unit fails to perform adequately then the other one is

32. Jonathan Bendor (1985) provides the detailed arguments for and against redundancy in organizational structures in the first chapter of a book dedicated to the topic. See also Landau (1969) and Niskanen (1971) for pioneering studies on the application of the concept of redundancy to organization theory.

fully equipped to perform its job.[33] The need for redundancy increases as the cost of failure and its probability increase. And since few settings are more conducive to operations going awry than territorial conflicts, redundant structures can be particularly valuable for organizations at war. It is no coincidence that states such as Hafiz Assad's Syria and Saddam Hussein's Iraq had more than a dozen overlapping security services each. Curiously enough, there is some evidence that, under some circumstances, redundancy increases productivity and effectiveness because of the competitive dynamics that develop among the redundant (sub)-organizations.[34] I therefore consider both competitive and noncompetitive redundancy. The way I use competitiveness as part of the independent variable here has everything to do with the incentive structure of the organization—Does the organizational component that is redundant get more resources (e.g., popular support, money, weapons) if it performs better than the others?—and nothing to do with outcome. The outcome is of course the cumulative performance of the organization. The redundant branches of the organization are by definition independent of each other, except for their hierarchical links to a common leadership.

Centralization

Degree of centralization is the measure of distribution of power over decision making among the top-tier leadership and second- or subsequent-level cadres within the organization.[35] Decision making relates to formulation of strategy, appointments, distribution of resources, control of communications, and administration of discipline. Second-level cadres (e.g., field commanders, village leaders, imams of mosques, heads of associations) can only make

---

33. Advocates of redundancy in numerically oriented fields would tell you that it is worthwhile to have a redundant system if increasing reliability by the square of its amount is worth doubling the costs of the system. The rationale here is that if you have two parallel and independent systems, each with a probability of failure of 1/10, then the probability of both systems failing is $(1/10)^2$, or 1/100. A third parallel system would increase the cost by 50 percent but reduce the possibility of failure to 1/1000. Of course, one might argue that the ratios should be discounted in human systems because each noncompetitive redundant unit might rely on others to perform adequately. In other words, noncompetitive redundancy could lead to "passing the buck."

34. See Niskanen (1971) for such an argument.

35. This is almost the same definition that Duverger (1959, 52) gives for centralization. Decentralization in this theory is equivalent to the first of Duverger's (1959, 53–56) four different types of decentralization: local, ideological, social, and federal. Decentralization may lead to ideological and social diversity, but it makes little sense to call an organization decentralized if it features such variety when only the top-tier leadership has a monopoly over decision making.

such decisions on a local level, while the leadership can be decisive on both local and organizational levels. The more substantial the control second- or subsequent-level cadres have over the local formulation of strategy and other decisions, the more decentralized the organization.

Patronage

A patron-client relationship is one of exchange in which a party (the patron) allocates a resource or is capable of providing a service to another party (the client) who needs it and is ready to exchange loyalty, general support, and assistance for it.[36] Although some consider patron-client relations to be attributes of some cultures, I consider them to be structural links that could exist within any organization.[37] Many students of clientage (anthropologists in particular) consider organizations and societies either to be based on ties of clientage or not to be. I adopt instead the more nuanced view that clientelism can exist alongside other structural links, such as more professionalized principal-agent relations (both centralized and decentralized).[38]

I keep the above definition of patron-client links skeletal to allow meaningful comparisons across different cultural and societal settings. This simplification makes it seem hard to distinguish between principal-agent and patron-client links, particularly because both forms of organization are asymmetrical, yield gains for both parties involved, and can fall apart if they become less advantageous to either one of the parties to the exchange. Clientage (itself a category with considerable internal variation) is a subset of principal-agent relations, albeit with enough distinctive characteristics to be considered a separate organizational feature for the purposes of this book. Patron-client bonds differ from principal-agent ones because they give the subordinate parties more autonomy in conducting their end of the bargain,

---

36. For slightly different definitions of patron-client relationships, see Clapham (1982, 4), Weingrod (1968), and Schmidt et al. (1977, pts. 1 and 8). Clapham's introductory chapter is particularly lucid and succinct in defining this class of relationships and evaluating its social scientific value. For a discussion of what patronage *is not* as well as what it might mean, see Ernest Gellner's introductory chapter (Gellner and Waterbury 1977). For a survey of the literature on clientelism, see Scott 1977.

37. The literature on clientelism was developed for explaining power distribution in traditional societies. The concept was later expanded to study power within certain bureaucracies, mostly from the same traditional societies.

38. Many students of bureaucratic organizations have adopted this understanding of the coexistence of formal and informal, professional and traditional, principal-agent and patron-client ties within organizations. See the bibliographical essay in Schmidt et al. (1977) for an illustration of how political scientists and anthropologists differ on this point.

allow them to defect to other patrons, and provide them with long-term opportunities to compete with their own patrons.[39]

Patron-client relations between the overall leadership and the second-level cadres (as well as between second- and third-level cadres, and so forth if applicable) allow the client to formulate local strategies. They may appear similar to ultimate decentralization, but they are in fact quite different from decentralized agency. An army commander may delegate much power to field commanders over local decision making with the underlying understanding that they will incur heavy penalties if they defect, while organizations featuring patron-client arrangements often experience defections by clients who are disgruntled with their patrons. The client's ability to defect from the patron-client arrangement gives the client considerable leverage within the organization, which justifies considering this organizational characteristic as distinct from regular agency.

Patron-client exchange is a dyadic phenomenon, but, as Eisenstadt and Roniger (1984, 167–202) show, the institutionalization of this mode of exchange often leads to the development of hierarchical networks of patrons and clients. The strategies of patrons and clients are concatenated in such networks. This can result in competition among clients at lower levels of the hierarchy to prove their ability to deliver a larger following to their own patron. Alternatively, midlevel patrons may wrest power from their own patron if he cannot continue to supply them with the resources they need, or if they develop a large clientele, or they sufficiently accumulate the resources that their patron once supplied. Reeves (1990, 160–62) provides an intuitive and simple model based on network analysis to explain how patron-client networks could collapse. He explains the ability of the patron at the top of the hierarchy to preserve his position by his ability to provide needed resources that he monopolizes, to mediate and arbitrate among his clients, and to protect them from each other. Reeves argues that such an arrangement works well in its early stages when the patron at the top of the hierarchy has a monopoly over essential resources, but it collapses as clients (who are also patrons in their own right) erode his monopolies over some resources and develop some of their own. When clients (or coalitions of clients) develop separate monopolies, they can negotiate with other clients without the added cost of involving the now monopoly-less or monopoly-poor previous patron, which would lead to the replacement of the single patronage

39. Some argue that for a relationship to qualify as one of patronage, it has to be regular, persistent, complex, dyadic, and multifunctional. These ideas are better developed in Clapham (1982, chap. 1).

network by several hierarchies. The previous patron becomes at best the first among equals in the new order.

Both governments and their challengers have used patronage to achieve their goals, with mixed results. The Afghan Najib regime met its demise because of its protracted reliance on patronage ties with the Uzbek, Ismaili, and other militias (see chapter 7). In 1934, however, the Austrian chancellor Engelbert Dollfuss developed such ties with a private fascist army, the Heimwehr, and successfully defeated the powerful socialist militia, the Schutzbund, which was effectively challenging his government. Although patron-client ties have the advantage of rapidly acquiring allegiance and increasing fighting ability, they are volatile and only last so long as both parties believe the other side will keep its end of the bargain and they cannot find a better bargain elsewhere.

Specialization

Suborganizational units can specialize in fighting in a certain terrain, training, the purchase or manufacturing of needed supplies, public relations and propaganda, logistics, or other tasks.[40] Centralization is generally a necessary prerequisite for effective specialization, because the lack of central control and coordination can lead to confusion and the collapse of the differentiated organization. Some kinds of specialization, however, do not require centralization. These types of specialization emerge when the population is socially or geographically heterogeneous. Politicized civil organizations are good examples of specialized units that can function as part of large decentralized organizations (e.g., the Egyptian professional syndicates and student associations are mostly dominated by the Muslim Brotherhood).[41] Such specialization helps the organization preempt the entry of competitors, because different branches can adapt to the requirements of different societal groups while benefiting from the prestige and resources of the wider organization.[42]

---

40. Scholars from the field of management often refer to the concept of specialization with the term "differentiation." Adam Smith was the first theorist of specialization.

41. This mode of organizing is comparable to the "network," the postindustrial organizational model that some believe is most suitable in rapidly evolving technological environments. What works in the regulated markets of industrialized countries, however, might very well fail under the yoke of a repressive regime. On the network organizational model, see Hatch (1997, chap. 6).

42. A similar point is made by Schwartz and Thompson (1986) in regard to oligopolistic firms. They argue that such firms can profitably forestall entry by creating new divisions, assuming that these divisions operate independently, and that incumbents can establish such new units more cheaply and more rapidly than potential entrants.

Regional variation could also allow indigenous groups to develop specialized resistance skills that are suitable for their environment while being part of a decentralized organizational structure.

One type of specialized organizational unit that has gained in importance in the recent past is the governance board (the *shura* council for Islamists). Governance boards of firms mostly deal with broad strategic issues, monitor management, and report to shareholders. Members of governance boards are generally not held liable for the actions of management but are given contractual incentives to keep senior management in check and report mismanagement to shareholders. A number of revolutionary and resistance organizations have developed structures similar to governance boards: a political leadership that provides the public face of the organization and sets the broad strategic direction for the other branches to follow but stays aloof from their specific actions. Such organizations can be quite resilient despite their structural looseness, as shown by Hamas and the Egyptian Muslim Brotherhood. The governance board–based structure is resilient because of the dependence of the organizational units on one another without the need for close coordination: the political leadership forming the governance board would be impotent without the other specialized branches (e.g., military, welfare, education) while the other branches would lose direction, the ability to coordinate, and risk having their actions be misinterpreted without the services of the board. The board can play other roles, such as fund-raising, and it can perhaps slowly centralize the structure of the organization. The board would then increase its control over the organization by assuming additional roles, but it might also make it more vulnerable to persecution.

Before the Israeli withdrawal from Gaza, Hamas was one of the most successful organizations featuring a governance board. Its political governance board was centered on the charismatic quadriplegic Sheikh Ahmad Yasin before his assassination by the Israelis and is mostly composed of highly educated and respectable Gazan figures who generally publicly address members of the Qassam Brigades (the military branch of Hamas) as if they are speaking *about* them, rather than speaking *for* or *to* them.[43] When asked about what the brigades will do in the wake of some event, such as the Israeli assassination of Islamist militants, governance board members normally have explained in their characteristically hands-off fashion how the military units were likely to respond as representatives of an oppressed people. Despite their harshness in dealing with Palestinians generally, the Israelis have rarely

43. See, for example, Sheikh Yasin's answer in the *New York Times*, October 20, 1998, A10.

jailed Hamas political leaders because they understood that such acts would not weaken the independent Qassam Brigades but perhaps make them more aggressive in the violent tit-for-tat that characterizes Hamas-Israeli relations. Even Sheikh Yasin was ultimately set free in the wake of a rare botched attempt to assassinate a Hamas activist in Jordan. The Israelis had no such reservations when dealing with the more centralized Islamic Jihad, whose leader—Fathi Shiqaqi—they assassinated in 1995. Hamas political leaders have the ability to restrain or unleash the Qassam Brigades through their moral authority. This, however, is not something the Israelis could rejoice about: no edict made in captivity by a Hamas political leader is accepted as legitimate by the rank and file. A governance board definitely yields some powerful advantages. The decision of Ariel Sharon to assassinate Hamas political leaders, including Sheikh Yasin, in a break with past practices was made after he decided to leave the Gaza Strip. The shift does not undermine the above logic; it merely shows that Sharon had other priorities. He needed to maintain the support of Israeli right-wingers while withdrawing.

The building blocks and dimensions of organizational structure can feature internal differentiation. Patronage ties, for example, can provide more leeway to the client in some organizations than in others. I do pay attention to such complexities in my analytical narratives of Afghan conflicts but ignore them in the statistical study and theory building to allow for useful generalizations.

Possible Outcomes to a Conflict

There are three possible outcomes to a conflict: (1) it is protracted and inconclusive; (2) there is a clear victory for a subset of rival organizations; or (3) a durable compromise settlement is achieved.

In a protracted inconclusive conflict rival organizations are still attempting to gain the upper hand.

A clear victory for a subset of rival organizations is represented by the withdrawal of the occupier (e.g., France's withdrawal from Algeria in 1962), the collapse of the government (e.g., Afghanistan in 1992), or a sharp decrease in the militant activities of one or more organizations challenging the state or occupier (e.g., the Iranian Kurdish organizations by 1986 and their ethnic kin in Turkey after the capture of Abdullah Ocalan, the head of the PKK).

A durable compromise settlement needs to have lasted for at least a decade. Ten years is enough time to show real durability without imposing an impossible hurdle. This cutoff point is arbitrary, but I cannot think of one that is less so. The Iraqi Kurds and the non-Muslim Sudanese almost managed to achieve such a conclusion at certain points in their respective conflicts.

One element seemingly complicates the measurement of this variable: How should we classify the outcome of conflicts that result in the defeat of the insurgents and the adoption of some of their demands by the incumbent government? This rare outcome has occurred mostly as a result of British counterinsurgency efforts (Malaya, Kenya, and the Dhofar region of Southern Oman), but also in other conflicts such as the Huk rebellion in the Philippines. Such outcomes are equivalent to the defeat of the insurgents because their organization did not replace the incumbent's institutions.[44] The fact that the British and the Philippine government managed to foster limited economic development in areas where they wanted to deprive the revolutionaries of support is by no means an achievement for the revolutionary organization. All it indicates is that the incumbent organization was more successful at motivating people to be on its side than the rival organization. Even British promises to give autonomy or independence to Malaya and Kenya at the end of the revolts did not constitute an achievement for the insurgents because their organizations were annihilated and power was given to those who were loyal to the colonial rulers throughout the conflict. In the Huk case, the rebel organization collapsed when it failed to provide incentives for peasants to remain loyal. Huk supporters deserted in droves when the government restrained its military's abuses, provided a modicum of services, and eliminated the absurd penalty for being *loyal*: the exorbitant share of the harvest peasants had to give to the landlords.[45] This clearly contrasts with the outcomes of, for example, the Algerian War of Independence that resulted in the Front de Liberation National(FLN) taking over all the institutions of the newly independent state.

Another potentially complicated outcome is the co-option of the insurgents into the state apparatus. Theoretically, one could argue that such an outcome lies somewhere between failure and a compromise solution. In reality, it is easy to tell which one it is, and it rarely lies in-between. If the rival organization disappears when its leaders are co-opted then the result is failure. If the entire organization is co-opted as part of a comprehensive agreement, then the outcome is a negotiated settlement. Slobodan Milosovic provided an illustration of the first outcome when he co-opted Vuk Draskovic, one of the most prominent leaders of the street demonstrations against his rule, into his

44. For more musings on this issue see Welch (1980 chap. 8).

45. Kerkvliet (1977, 207–10 and 236–69, inter alia) makes this point convincingly.

government in 1998. The unity arrangement between the two Yemens provides a good example of the second outcome, despite chronic problems in the relationship between the previous leaders of the North and South.

The Contingency

The considerable literature generated by contingency theory has generally shown that, all else being equal, the same organizational structure could perform differently contingent on the presence of some factors, such as technology, environmental characteristics, or organizational size. For example, the availability of technology that facilitates coordination among small independent groups would favor decentralized organizations in environments that value innovation and interorganizational competition. Matters are decidedly simpler for the analysis of organizations in conflict—only one contingency is relevant for organizational analysis.

Technologies available for rivals in revolutionary conflicts have been fairly stable in the second half of the twentieth century. Innovations that favor the centralized specialized organization (armor, for example) were soon countered by affordable technologies that canceled the advantage (rocket propelled grenades), and the cold war spread both advances and their antidotes wherever there was conflict. New media such as the radio became so ubiquitous that it is irrelevant to consider their availability to be a contingency. The recent development of the Internet, satellite television, and other late-coming technologies has only started to have an impact on collective action in the twenty-first century. I consider their impact to be generally insignificant for the discussion of twentieth-century conflicts.

Different aspects of the environment, such as the nature of the terrain, the distribution of the population, the size of the population, and the wealth and resources available could make relevant contingencies. Yet, the quantitative study in chapter 10 shows that it is reasonable to dismiss them as such. And I show in the following chapter that the ability to mobilize and attract resources is endogenous to the organizational theory.

The one contingency that is relevant here is the availability of a safe haven to the organization. A safe haven is a portion of the contested territory where an organization's rivals cannot intervene with enough force to disturb its operations. The safe haven must be part of the contested territory, not a shelter across the border. The reason is that cross-border shelters allow foreign sponsors to manipulate the organization and to restrict its activities at will.

Centralized organizations are generally more effective than noncentralized ones, but they are more vulnerable to the attempts of rivals to disturb their operations because of their dependence on coordination among their different specialized branches. An organization—such as the state, an occupier, or a strong insurgent group—that controls a safe haven that protects it from the easy disturbance of its operations by rivals must therefore adopt a highly centralized and specialized structure. Organizations that do not have such a space must adopt a more resilient noncentralized structure to increase their odds of outlasting their rivals. Decentralized structures are more resilient than centralized ones under duress because the autonomy and self-sufficiency of their components allow them to continue to do well even when other parts of the organization are eliminated or coordination among organizational components is disrupted.

A safe haven is not essential to win the conflict; what is essential for the organization is to organize properly based on whether it has such a space. The Lebanese Hizballah, a tiny force of no more than two thousand fighters, reached this point when Israel reduced the area of Lebanon it occupied to a nine-mile-deep strip of land north of its border. The vacuum and Syrian support provided a safe haven where Hizballah was able to restructure to take the initiative. The Algerian FLN, a much larger properly decentralized organization under constant pressure from the French and largely isolated from whatever cross-border bases were available to it, never reached this point until the French withdrawal. An organization that suddenly gains control of a safe haven must centralize its structure to be able to take the strategic initiative and defeat its rivals beyond its own haven. If the organization fails to take coordinated action to decisively defeat its rivals, it allows them to regain their footing and attempt to undermine it again, thus reducing its odds of outlasting them.

CHAPTER 3

Advantages and Limitations of Structures

> Without a guiding organization the energy of the masses would dissipate like steam not enclosed in a piston box.
>
> —Leon Trotsky, *History of the Russian Revolution*, 1932

How do the structures of the state (or occupier) and the organizations challenging its control affect their interaction? Organizational structure is intimately intertwined with the ability to formulate, implement, and counter strategies; to coordinate among participants; to mobilize resources; to enforce control and discipline; to allow for either resilience or flexibility; to assist in attracting outside aid; to develop intraorganizational cohesion and competition; and, finally, to generate and preserve knowledge. The way organizations perform those eight basic processes affects their odds of outlasting their rivals. Different structural components and dimensions restrict or affect all of them in ways that can be decisive. The absence of a safe haven renders otherwise superior modes of organization (centralization) ineffective.

Strategy

Organizational structure and strategy are closely intertwined. A certain structure can limit the strategic options available; make the adoption of a certain strategy more or less credible to the organization's opponents, sponsors, and supporters; limit the ability of the organization to resist its rivals' strategies; and provide additional incentives to adopt some strategies.

When I say that organizational structure can limit both strategic and tactical options I do not intend to be as stringent as the determinism of social structuralists. I do not mean that there is only one winning strategy and that this strategy is always adopted, the way Theda Skocpol sees things evolving during the Chinese Revolution.[1] All I mean is that the range of strategies that can be initiated and the range of those that can be countered can be limited by the structure of the organization. If the top-tier leadership decides to pursue a strategy outside the range that the structure of the organization allows, then one of four things could happen: the leadership is replaced or readjusts its strategy; the rank and file leave in droves; the organization is thoroughly defeated; or a difficult organizational restructuring process takes place. I draw on the metaphor that James DeNardo (1985, 29–32) uses to criticize Skocpol's strategic determinism to illustrate the different ways the three of us see strategic options. Consider a game of chess, DeNardo tells us, and you soon realize that the structure of the board and the configuration of pieces constrain the players' choices. Those restrictions do not determine the subsequent course of the game and its outcome, the way Skocpol believes social structure determines the outcome of revolutionary action. The metaphor of the chessboard, like all others, has its limitations, but it suffices to illustrate my understanding of restrictions on strategy. Although Skocpol might not consider a chessboard a good metaphor for revolutionary interaction and DeNardo finds it a fine one to illustrate the availability of many alternative strategies, I believe the chessboard could provide a good metaphor if the pieces were tied to one another with threads. The threads represent organizational restrictions that might limit the availability of complex strategies, and each structure can be represented by a different assortment of threads tying different pieces. If the rooks were attached to the queen with threads the length of two squares, then the player would be deprived of a number of strategies that depend on those pieces. The same player would also be limited in evading any of his or her opponents' strategies that aim to eliminate those pieces or that would be inconvenienced by a defense that requires their habitual movement. This is how I envision organizational structure reducing the range of strategies available to the state and its challengers.

Some modelers tell us that there are three broad strategies: sensitive (tit for tat); imperturbable (not responding to shifts in strategies by opponents); and opportunistic strategies (reacting to changes by others with changes designed to maximize gains, a reverse tit for tat).[2] Others tell us that there are only two

---

1. Skocpol 1979, 252. Most other structuralists argue that strategy doesn't even matter.

2. See Kowalewski and Hoover 1995, 2–7.

types of strategies: purist (conflictual) and pragmatist (accommodationist). The second classification is more intuitive than the first one in the case of territorial conflicts because an imperturbable strategy can only be a purist and conflictual one (there would be no conflict otherwise) and opportunistic strategies are also conflictual. There are, however, other more complex strategies that are harder to model in game-theoretical terms but that are critical to understanding the evolution and outcomes of conflicts. Three such strategies are divide and conquer (rule), "hearts and minds," and co-option.

Conflictual versus Accommodationist Strategies

Such strategies are available for both incumbent organizations and their challengers. The organizational structures of the parties in conflict can both encourage them to adopt an accommodationist or a conflictual strategy (through attrition or a direct attack to dismantle rival organizations) and lock them into those tactics.

One way societal leaders or the incumbent can force aggrieved groups to adopt an accommodationist nonviolent strategy is to keep them atomized as long as possible. Starting with an accommodationist strategy while clearly expressing collective demands provides an opportunity to end the conflict without much bloodshed, if the government cooperates. It also allows for international recognition for the cause and for the intervention of outside powers on behalf of the nonviolent protesters. One disadvantage of such a strategy is that atomization and peaceful protests are generally considered signs of weakness by the government or occupier whose clampdown could be brutally effective in reducing protests to bitter and isolated complaints in immigrant communities, the only locales where such complaints could then be voiced. Another disadvantage is that established leaders who fail to form organizations allow political entrepreneurs who disagree with their peaceful approach to form organizations that pursue armed resistance, as illustrated by the KLA challenge to Ibrahim Rugova in Kosovo.

Unlike fragmented groups, centralized organizations with strong hierarchical control are capable of rapidly adjusting their strategies in response to changes in the environment or the strategies of rivals. The ability to switch could be either to the advantage or detriment of the organization, because both resilience and flexibility have their distinct virtues. The ability of a centralized organization to adopt an accommodationist strategy toward the incumbent can, however, be impaired by the existence of rival organizations. A multiplicity of organizations encourages the consistent adoption of a confrontational strategy by the challengers because a dissatisfied population is likely to shift its support to the organization that shuns the conciliatory route.[3] The resistance organization that fails to understand this dynamic and appeases the occupier is likely to see its rivals grow at its expense.[4] Such was the destiny of Draza Mihailovic's Chetnik, as Chalmers Johnson and participants in the conflict tell us.[5]

This resulted, according to Tito companion and official Yugoslav Communist Party historian Vladimir Dedijer, in entire Chetnik units joining the partisans when they became disgusted with the policy of waiting or refused to accept their leadership's orders to stop attacking the Germans.[6] Another example is the radicalizing effect of ETA (Basque Homeland and Freedom) on other Basque organizations such as the PNV (Partido Nacionalista Vasco, or Basque National Party) and many Basque politicians (Laitin 1993, 26). Defeat was also the fate of the Chinese Kuomintang, which accommodated the Japanese while Mao's Communists engaged in active resistance.[7] And perhaps nothing can shed light on why the Chinese Communists were so aggressive in their resistance to the Japanese better than Mao's own words:

> Today, whoever can lead the people in driving out Japanese imperialism, and introducing democratic government, will be the savior of the people. *If the Chinese bourgeoisie is capable of carrying out this responsibility, no one will be able to refuse his admiration; but if it is not capable of doing so,* the major part of this responsibility will inevitably fall upon the shoulders of the proletariat.[8] (emphasis mine)

This quote is from Mao's 1940 essay "On New Democracy." The italicized words, which candidly express his understanding that the organization that resists harder will ultimately dominate China by wooing more supporters, were deleted from later versions of the text. They were probably deleted

---

3. This argument is akin to the one made by the philosopher René Girard (1977). Kramer (1991) applies these ideas to the resistance against the Israeli occupation of southern Lebanon.

4. Extremist groups (Hamas in Palestine, Protestant militants in Northern Ireland, supporters of Zulu chief Mangosuthu Buthelezi in South Africa) might try to derail deals concluded between the central power and more moderate groups through the use of violence. They don't always succeed, but their anticipated strategy reduces the incentive for the moderates to compromise and radicalizes all resistance groups. The success of such strategies is generally underestimated because it is hard to recognize cases in which moderate resistance leaders do not even enter negotiations because they realize that excluded groups will derail their efforts by increasing confrontation.

5. Johnson 1962, 164. This argument is also made by Vladimir Dedijer in Chaliand 1982.

6. From Dedijer's World War II diary, in Johnson 1962, 69.

7. Chaliand 1982, chap. 2.

8. Mentioned in Stuart Schram's introduction to Mao's *Basic Tactics* (1966a, 28–29).

because the Communists realized that resistance should be made to appear as the result of ideological motivation and powerful nationalism, not as a tool to overcome rival Chinese class-based organizations. Such thinking is not unique to Mao, and such dynamics are often replicated in the presence of more than one resistance or revolutionary party.[9]

Competitive redundancy also encourages the adoption of a conflictual strategy because of each branch's consistent drive to outbid and outperform others. The combination of redundancy and decentralization produces a dynamics very similar to the one resulting from competition among multiple organizations, because lack of central control generally prevents the regulation of competition.

Some structures go beyond influencing the adoption of a certain strategy; they lock the organization into this strategy. This occurs when structure creates a set of incentives that make it a dominant personal strategy for each organizational member to persist in the role he plays as part of the overall organizational conflictual strategy. Multiple organizations featuring ties of patronage are particularly prone to create such strategy lockups, as can be seen in chapter 6 in the Afghan mujahideen's tenacious resistance to the Soviets.

Decentralization puts more decision-making power in the hands of second-tier cadres, making them more flexible on the local level, unlike their peers in centralized organizations. This local flexibility—the ability to switch strategies—comes at the expense of overall organizational flexibility. Decentralized organizations are held hostage by their most extreme cadres, because the execution of a conflictual act by one segment of the organization is generally viewed by rivals as representing the intentions of the entire organization. The top-tier leadership of the organization will find itself in the awkward position of having to choose between denouncing part of the rank and file or pretending that it supported them all along while hoping that the confrontational strategy will succeed. Unfortunately for them, the same lack of control that dragged them into adopting an overall organizational conflictual strategy is likely to weaken their ability to motivate the nonaggressive segments. The Palestinian Authority under Yasir Arafat was no stranger to this situation. A governance board is less likely to be induced to adopt a conflictual strategy by aggressive organizational branches than a

9. The history of Palestinian conflict with Israel provides vivid examples of how the multiplicity of resistance organizations radicalizes the entire movement. Abu Ayad ("Al Fatah's Autocriticism" in Chaliand 1982), once Fatah's second in command, writes that radical organizations centered on George Habash and Nayef Hawatmeh "have consistently sought to raise the ideological stakes, launching provocative actions that have dragged us into adventures we would otherwise have avoided."

regular leadership of a decentralized organization because it does not claim to have control over them or to deserve credit for their actions. On the other hand, any organizational feature that isolates a decision maker from the consequences of the acts of the rank and file is likely to encourage the adoption of a confrontational strategy.

Divide and Conquer

Divide and conquer (rule) is a strategy for territorial control initiated by the colonial power (regime) that consists of dividing the population into interest groups (either horizontal or vertical) with a low probability of achieving their most preferred political outcome (to assume power) but that can achieve an outcome that is better than their worst one (having rival groups in power) by having the colonial state (regime) in power. For example, let us assume that a number of solidarity groups (e.g., ethnic groups) have the following preferences because of a history of enmity:

1. Control of the center and the resources it confers (be in power)
2. Colonial power (regime) controls center
3. Anarchy/secession (no central power)
4. Rival group(s) control(s) the center

If P(1)—the probability of outcome number one being achieved—is negligible or its cost is too high, then supporting the colonial power (regime) becomes the dominant strategy for the group. P(1) becomes smaller as the size of the group gets smaller and its distance from the center of power increases.[10]

Few writers describe the conditions under which a policy of divide and rule is likely to be successful as eloquently as Alexis de Tocqueville did when he explained why the rule of the Corsican Napoleon was easily accepted:

> All parties, indeed, reduced, cold, and weary, longed to rest for a time in a despotism of any kind, provided that it were exercised by a stranger, and weighed upon their rivals as heavily as on themselves. . . . When great political parties begin to cool in their attachments, without softening their antipathies, and at last reach the point of wishing

10. The Syrian Alawites are a glaring exception here, but they did become very close to the center of power by infiltrating the army before they controlled the institutions of the Syrian state.

less to succeed than to prevent the success of their adversaries, one must prepare for slavery—the master is near.[11]

If, however, the colonizer or regime is perceived as wanting to use the resources of the center to subvert the group, instead of keeping other groups from doing so at a cost, then the group has no incentive to support it. Anarchy and secession are often too costly and only become appealing alternatives if the rival group controls the center and uses its resources (e.g., legitimacy, institutions, rents, foreign aid) to subvert the group with the above preferences. Secession (de facto self-rule) can be a more appealing alternative to colonial (regime) control if it is easy to achieve because of competition among rival groups and the colonizer/regime.

If we relax the assumption of animosity or competition (either historical or stoked by the colonizer or regime) among societal groups, we can expect the different groups to coalesce in an effort to get rid of the colonizer or regime that is in control of resources that could otherwise be shared among them in their entirety.

In brief, divide and conquer is more likely to succeed (1) the greater the animosity and fear among societal groups, (2) the smaller the size and greater the distance of groups from the center, (3) the more costly secession is for the concerned groups, and (4) the greater the ability of the colonizer/regime to be (or to appear) neutral in the conflict among rival groups.

In one study of a skillful use of the divide-and-rule strategy, Laurie Brand (1999) shows how King Hussein of Jordan worked throughout his long reign to shape conditions in his country so that these four factors would allow him to keep his precarious throne. Hussein allowed resentment between Transjordanians and Jordanians of Palestinian descent to fester by giving Transjordanians a monopoly over state employment and allowing, some claim encouraging, the development of Transjordanian nationalist parties that excluded Palestinians from their conceptual construction of Jordan as a nation (factor 1). Both Transjordanians and Palestinian Jordanians coexist in the larger cities, and secession by any one group would be very difficult and costly, as demonstrated by the civil war of the early 1970s (factors 2 and 3). Finally, Hussein *was* an outsider (a descendant of the sharif of Mecca, with no family roots in Jordan). Although previously both Transjordanians and Palestinians could have envisioned a better Jordan without him, they ultimately preferred enduring his mild despotism to the

11. From the two completed chapters of the sequel to the *L'Ancien Régime*, in Tocqueville (1980, 246).

rule of extremists from the opposing side after he managed to fan ethnic distrust (factor 4).

Only a centralized organization can execute a divide-and-conquer strategy because of the dexterity and coordination required to fan intergroup hatreds (factor 1) and the necessity of projecting a consistent finely tuned image as a neutral party above those hatreds (factor 4). Divide and conquer is not meant to be applied to atomized societies or against a single centralized rival organization for obvious reasons—the latter situation generally invites a hearts-and-minds strategy. The ability of other structures to resist divide and conquer hinges on their ability to affect the four factors that govern its success. Factors 1, 3, and 4 are not clearly affected by structural matters, but factor 2 (the lesser the size and greater the distance of groups from the center) can be. Multiplicity and decentralization increase the role of this factor. Patronage, on the other hand, could either encourage or discourage it, depending on whether the strategy "lockup" is already in place. A governance board tempers factors 1 (animosity and fear among societal groups) and 4 (perceived neutrality of regime). It is unlikely, however, that divide and conquer will be applied against a single organization with a governance board.

Hearts and Minds

The British refined and successfully applied the "hearts and minds" strategy in a number of colonial conflicts, particularly in Malaya and in the Mau Mau and the Dhofar revolts.[12] This strategy is, in principle, available to government rivals, but it requires extreme centralization and considerable resources, more often attributes of the government or colonizer than of its rivals. The strategy consists of:

1. Differentiating among active fighters, passive supporters, genuine neutrals, and government loyalists. This, of course, requires a centralization of the flow of information.
2. Geographically, physically, or psychologically isolating those identified as the active challengers from others. This requires a highly coordinated and thus centralized military and intelligence operation.[13]

---

12. The term "hearts and minds" was coined by the British high commissioner in Malaya, General Gerald Templer. He was appointed in 1952 when things looked bleak for the British and successfully applied the general guidelines I describe in this section.

13. An obvious response to the famous Maoist aphorism that the successful insurgent is one who lives among the people as a fish in water.

3. Providing positive sanctions to potential supporters of rival organizations and protecting them from abuse by undisciplined troops to discourage them from supporting rivals.[14]

When those steps are well executed, it becomes much easier to subdue the isolated rebels who cannot replenish their ranks or rely on external material support.[15] To execute them well can be a considerable challenge, however, particularly if the revolutionaries avoid the fatal mistake of centralizing their structure in response to the regime's efforts. The best structures to counter a hearts-and-minds strategy are traditional ones, preferably based on patron-client ties and featuring an abundance of redundant structures. The density of ties in traditional structures makes it easier to conceal fighters within their own communities and prevent their isolation. Patron-client ties, if both patrons and clients are on the same side, maintain cohesion in the face of a hearts-and-minds strategy. Such ties also make it more costly for the regime to woo either patrons or clients to its side, because the more dependent a member is on a relationship (that is, the more costly it is to leave it in terms of opportunities forgone), the higher the cost will be to sever him from it. Such was the case during the Soviet occupation of Afghanistan, but not during the Huk rebellion, where previous patrons (landlords) and clients (farmers) were on opposite sides after a serious dislocation of their traditional ties. The Philippine government of Ramon Magsaysay followed the hearts-and-minds strategy to the letter under the guidance of Western advisers and was assisted by the clumsy attempt of the Communist Party of the Philippines (PKP) to control and centralize the peasant rebels. The Chinese Communist rebels in Malaya, as many observers have noted, suffered tremendously from their stubborn adoption of a centralized organizational structure inspired by their dogmatic beliefs when faced with the British hearts-and-minds strategy.[16] Redundancy, decentralization, and multiplicity

14. Some might argue that another necessary ingredient to "hearts and minds" is making plenty of concessions because, after all, the British did commit to withdraw from Malaya and gave it independence. This is not true: no such concessions were made in other cases where this strategy was successfully applied, including the Dhofar and the Huk rebellions. In both cases the government provided positive sanctions (step 3) but very little in terms of political concessions. While not necessary, however, affordable political concessions (especially developing a sense of political participation) would facilitate the government's task within the framework of a hearts-and-minds strategy.

15. Some erroneously say that the United States used "hearts and minds" in Vietnam. Such individuals fail to identify all the components of the strategy and believe it means only a massive propaganda effort.

16. Bell 1976, 184.

are useful because they hinder the collection of information on active militants by the regime: it is easier to fill the name slots in a single rigid organizational chart than in numerous ones in flux. Governance boards are helpful because they weaken the psychological isolation of the organization by being its shielded mouthpiece.

Co-option

Selznick (1948, 34) defines co-option (or co-optation) as "the process of absorbing new elements into the leadership or policy-determining structure of an organization as a means of averting threats to its stability or existence."[17] I generalize this definition as follows: Co-option is a strategy initiated by a dominant organization or coalition of organizations that consists of offering positive sanctions to other threatening organizations or key individuals within them in return for accepting the norms of interaction desired by the dominant organization or coalition.[18]

Co-option is a cooperative strategy that can result in a co-optive arrangement that is not self-enforcing: both parties, the co-opter and the co-optee, have to offer something in return for what the other offers for a co-optive arrangement to succeed. The co-opter hopes to reduce risk by co-opting some rival organizations or their leaders. The co-optees could obtain substantial gains from a co-optive arrangement but forfeit their ability to challenge the co-opter outside its institutions. The co-optee's acceptance of the co-optive arrangement might be valuable to the co-opter if it is one of many challengers and can therefore provide a precedent for more important attempts at co-option. A co-optee can also be valuable if it provides two-step leverage over other organizations or groups.[19] Co-opting for two-step leverage is a common strategy in colonial situations where the colonizer co-opts a small highly militarized minority to police the rest of the population. Frisch (1993) provides us with a vivid illustration of the use of this strategy by the Israeli

17. Selznick (1949) provides the classic case study of co-option as strategy. See Saward (1992) for a rare discussion of this important strategy and its general application to international relations and strategic interaction in general. Co-option is widely used and has received too little academic attention.

18. The terms "co-option" or "co-optation" are most often used to indicate an outcome. I am only interested in co-option as strategy here. When needed, I refer to the outcome as a co-optive arrangement.

19. See Gargiulo (1993) for a stimulating discussion of two-step leverage and indirect co-optive behavior in organizational politics.

government. The co-optees in this case are the highly martial Druze, whose units in the Israeli army are often assigned the task of suppressing Palestinian resistance in the Israeli-occupied territories in return for favorable treatment for their tiny community. Another form of two-step leverage consists of co-opting the leaders of an organization rather than the entire organization. This kind of co-option is highly cost effective because it is much cheaper to co-opt one or a few individuals than an entire organization, the way the CIA may have reasoned when it put Jordan's King Hussein on its payroll.[20] Tribal politics sometimes facilitates personal co-optation because of the loyalty tribal leaders generally, but not always, command among members of the tribe, whom they can restrain or unleash at will.

Two factors differentiate co-option from alliance (the short-term aggregation of capabilities against a common enemy). First, the co-opter generally offers positive sanctions in the hope of producing a co-optive agreement because the acceptance by a lesser organization of the norms of the hegemonic organization without concessions would be tantamount to defeat. Second, the co-opter must be more powerful than the co-optee, which must necessarily accept the hegemonic stature of the co-opter and the applicability of its norms to their future interaction (e.g., that all differences are solved in the parliamentary arena or the acceptance of the monarch's authority). Either party could defect (not continue to co-opt or be co-opted), sometimes even after a co-optive arrangement is reached or even institutionalized, if incentives change. Institutionalization, however, generally makes the cost of defection higher.

Co-option is costly to the co-opting organization and its leaders. It is costly because positive sanctions need to be offered to the co-opted individual or organization and because power and information need to be shared with them.[21] The powers that be therefore need to carefully assess candidates for co-optive arrangements. An organization makes a good candidate for co-option if it is powerful enough to substantially disturb the operations of the co-opting organization, or is likely to do so in the future, but not powerful enough to take over the organization from within, and the cost of co-opting it is less than the cost of fighting it.[22]

20. "Payments by CIA to Hussein Charged," *New York Times*, February 18, 1977, p. 5.

21. On the effect of co-option on power within the co-opting organization, see Pfeffer (1981, 166–77).

22. Some maintain that organizations other than adversaries can be "co-opted." This is a loose use of the term and seems to imply alliance more than co-option.

Whether it is advantageous or detrimental for an organization to be co-opted depends on the terms of the co-optive agreement (the positive sanctions and the norms adopted), as well as the opportunity cost of forfeiting confrontation. The only kind of co-option that could be safely assumed to have negative consequences for an organization is the co-option of its leaders, not the organization itself—if the leaders are awarded positive sanctions instead of the organization. In addition, early co-optees tend to benefit more than subsequent ones because the regime wants to co-opt the minimum number of rivals necessary to remain in power while lowering the cost of co-option, and it therefore may pay a premium to form a minimum organizational quorum.

Only centralized organizations are likely to adopt and implement co-optive strategies because of the necessity of bringing along the rank and file in support of the arrangement, which represents a strategy shift. Vulnerable societal leaders in fragmented societies are easy targets for co-option. It is easier to co-opt a centralized organization whose leadership has more control over organizational strategy than a decentralized one. Decentralized structures are also less likely to be able to enforce respect of the co-opter's norms on their rank and file, an essential condition for the success of the co-optive arrangement. It is even harder to co-opt organizations with governance boards, because it is even more difficult for them to impose change on organizational branches if co-opted.

A multiplicity of organizations eases the implementation of co-option by the powers that be because of the incentive for each organization to be the first co-optee with the most favorable co-optive arrangement, but it also makes defection more likely if the rank and file defect to non–co-opted challengers. Patronage-based organizations are likely to be immune to co-optive efforts once a lockup is triggered and to be vulnerable if the co-optive arrangement is concluded before the dynamics for a lockup are set in motion. Since this book is concerned with well-developed conflicts, I assume that patronage-based organizations are likely to resist co-optive offers. I believe specialization and redundancy are irrelevant for the analysis of organizational ability to resist co-option.

The results of this discussion of the effect of organizational structure on the ability to both pursue (top half) and resist (bottom half) different strategies are summarized in figure 3.1. A dark square indicates that a structure hinders executing or resisting a strategy while a lightly shaded one indicates that the structure facilitates execution or defense. Decentralized structures are generally incapable of taking the strategic initiative but can

	Fragmentation	Centralization	Multiplicity	Decentralization	Patronage	Governance board
Accommodation and Confrontation	Accommodate only	Both (flexible)	Encourages confrontation	Attrition and accommodat-ion only, low flexibility	Attrition and accommodat-ion only	Encourages confrontation, more flexibility than pure decenralization
Divide and conquer	No	Yes	No	No	No	No
Hearts and minds	No	Yes	No	No	No	No
Co-optation	No	Yes	NR	Unlikely	Unlikely	No

ABOVE: ABILITY TO EXECUTE STRATEGY

BELOW: ABILITY TO COUNTER STRATEGY

	Fragmentation	Centralization	Multiplicity	Decentralization	Patronage	Governance board
Confrontation	Nil, unless induces outside intervention	Yes if has safe haven, otherwise not	Depends on availability of safe haven helpful if doesn't have one otherwise, not			Helpful
Divide and conquer	NR	Yes, strategy useless versus one centralized organization	Probably weakens ability to counter		Yes in case of widespread lockup	Probably helps
Hearts and minds	NR	No	Both are better than a single centralized organization		The best	It helps
Co-optation	Vulnerable to individual co-option	Easier to co-opt than decentralized organization	Easy to co-opt	Harder to co-opt than centralized organization	Yes	Yes

Shading code: disadvantageous advantageous No shade = Not Relevant (NR) or not clear

FIGURE 3.1. How structure affects the ability to execute and counter different strategies

effectively resist complex strategies. Centralized structures generally can take the strategic initiative and execute complex strategies but are less able to counter them. Organizations without a safe haven would benefit from adopting a noncentralized structure, because centralized organizations are not capable of coordinating their operations well enough to effectively implement complex strategies absent a safe haven. The noncentralized organization without a safe haven will at least be more capable of fending off its rivals. Once an organization acquires a safe haven, it makes sense for it to centralize to be able to take the strategic initiative in a coordinated way beyond its safe haven.

Coordination

Russell Hardin is so convinced of the importance of coordination that he insists that "most revolutions require that both sides of the dual coordination theory be met: the current leadership must suffer falling coordination while the alternative leadership is backed by increased coordination."[23] Although I find Hardin's exclusive concern with coordination somewhat extreme, all else being equal the more coordinated a group the more capable it is of dominating its rivals. Coordination is important because often parts of an organization can only achieve their goals after other parts achieve theirs. It might be necessary, for example, for a certain military commander to secure strategic heights before another commander is able to effectively attack a rival's base. This type of coordination might seem an easy matter to achieve for modern militaries, but it can require intense negotiations and generate gross inefficiencies in other organizations. Let us say that our two commanders belong to a decentralized organization and that the one who should secure the strategic heights realizes that such an action would cost him X in resources, both human and material. If the other commander invades the base after the heights are secured, he will incur a cost Y, which is dramatically less than the cost Z he would incur if he attempts to invade with the heights still in enemy hands. The organization to which the two commanders belong, as well as the second commander, would gain a substantial benefit (B) that far exceeds X + Y but that would be dwarfed by Z, if the base is invaded ($X+Y<B<Z$). The equilibrium without coordination is that the first commander would not secure the heights (only the second commander enjoys B) and that the second would not allow his forces to be routed in a risky attack. This outcome, which describes quite well long stalemates such as the many stagnant fronts during the 1989–92 Afghan conflicts, is obviously not Pareto optimal for the organization. Absent coercion or guarantees from a strong central authority capable of imposing negative sanctions, the two commanders will have to bargain. The second commander will have to offer an amount greater than X to the first one to entice him to occupy the heights, if he knows the value of X. The first commander is likely to exaggerate the value of X, however, by keeping the information necessary to evaluate it (e.g., weaponry available to him, intelligence on how many enemy troops are occupying the heights) private. If $X^{\star}$ is the value of the exaggerated X and $X+Y<B<X^{\star}+Y$ then

23. Hardin 1995, 32–36.

the attack on the base is not likely to take place. If $X+Y<X^{\star}+Y<B$ then coordination might very well take place, but this leaves out the cost of uncertainty: there is a risk that either the first commander will be paid first and then shirk or that the second one will fail to pay after the heights are secured. Assuming this risk could be considered as a cost R_x (where R_x = the probability of defection of party other than x multiplied by the cost of defection, with X being the cost for the first commander and Z for the second one) we end up expecting coordination to take place only if $X^{\star}+Y+R_1+R_2<B$, a high threshold indeed. Such calculations make it clear both how essential and difficult coordination is to achieve in most organizations, particularly in noncentralized ones. The organization fails to achieve a gain of $B-X-Y$ when action is not taken every time $X+Y<B<X^{\star}+Y+R_1+R_2$. This forfeited gain is the cost of the inability to coordinate. The following quote by Mao illustrates the severity of the challenge raised by this readiness to shirk and his remedy for it:

> When there is punishment for those who, in order to preserve their own forces, fail to advance, or fail to carry out their tasks energetically, thus bringing about the defeat of another unit of our army, the case should also be the object of large-scale propaganda within the unit. In this way we give a lesson to the officers and soldiers of the whole unit, or of other units, and make them afraid to commit similar offenses.[24]

The highest levels of coordination, for which control is a prerequisite, can only be achieved in centralized organizations.[25] Being centralized, however, does not guarantee successful coordination, as an observer of the Malayan insurgency reports:

> The Communist high command convened only about twice a year to map out policy for the entire six-month period to come, and their communications were poor. As a result, the British gained . . . advantage over a considerable period if they could change the situation in such a way as to make the agreed policy inapplicable. [There was] at least one instance where the guerrillas recognized a certain method as

24. Mao 1966a, 144–45.

25. Both clinical and empirical studies support my argument that centralization is more conducive to coordination than any other structural form. See Gibson et al. (1973, 168–84) for a review of such studies. The related statement that the more centralized the organization the more it needs to allocate resources to coordination is also true. For an intelligent discussion of the costs of coordination in centralized versus decentralized settings, see Klibanoff and Morduch 1995.

> bad, but were unable to change it until the next semi-annual meeting of their high command.[26]

Most centralized organizations do take advantage of their structure to maximize coordination when possible, normally when they have a safe haven that protects coordination efforts from being disrupted. Noncompetitive redundancy within a centralized organizational structure enhances coordination among its members because it increases control by eliminating information asymmetry—this, of course, reveals the capabilities and limitations of all groups to the central coordinating body. Competitive redundancy, on the other hand, might have the opposite effect.[27] Lesser levels of coordination could be achieved through other modes of organization that are more realistically available to nonstate organizations. A lesser level of coordination might be perfectly acceptable in revolutionary or resistance situations because the interests of the challengers to the state might converge and lessen the need for it. In other words, participants might react similarly to cues, the way they would have done if ordered to do so by a centralized leadership. Such unintended cooperation without coordination happens when a decentralized or patron-client organization consists of many regionally segregated small groups that separately interact with the incumbent and can simultaneously benefit from its weakness or suffer from its strength. By way of illustration, see how the thoroughly decentralized Kosovo Liberation Army reacted in 1998 to Serb withdrawals prompted by NATO threats: each local group had an incentive to reoccupy the space left by the Serbs without having to be told to do so. It is wrong, however, to assume that coordination through convergence of interests happens often enough to allow for efficient resistance. An extremely decentralized organization might suffer from information overload while coordinating operations because of the large amount of information that needs to be exchanged to clarify preferences and reach acceptable compromises. Hence the need for an organizational structure that falls short of extreme centralization—a luxury resistance and revolutionary movements can ill-afford—but that provides adequate and consistent levels of coordination when the need arises.

One structural remedy to raise the level of coordination in decentralized organizations is the creation of a governance board. The different branches of the decentralized organization can follow the broad strategic path that the governance board draws for them while taking full responsibility for

---

26. Brigadier David Powell-Jones, in *Counterinsurgency: A Symposium* (RAND Corporation, R-412-ARPA, January, 1963, Santa Monica, Calif., 27–28), mentioned in Leites and Wolf (1970, 60–61).

27. For more on the use of redundant systems to improve control, see Drenick 1986, chap. 7.

implementation and tactical details. The governance board helps in matters of coordination by interpreting cues from the environment for the other members of the decentralized organization and signaling to them what actions would benefit them. The patron could also encourage cooperation among different clients in patron-client–based organizations by linking the distribution of resources to the amount of coordination among them, among other considerations.

In brief, coordination is maximized by an extremely centralized structure, enhanced by noncompetitive redundancy, weakened by competitive redundancy, and achieved to a sometimes satisfactory level by the creation of governance boards in extremely decentralized organizations or through the allocation of resources in patron-client–based ones. Coordination is practically nonexistent in atomized groups (unless signaling is used, as argued by Kuran and Lohmann) and largely autonomous small groups, but these groups and individuals can behave as if they are coordinating their actions if their interests converge.

Mobilization

The more popular approach used to explain mobilization in conflict emphasizes collective action in the pursuit of public goods. I propose another approach to understand mobilization in territorial conflicts: analyzing the positive and negative sanctions applied by competing organizations.

The widely accepted public-good approach assumes that the goal of mobilization is to produce such a good and that the challenge for political entrepreneurs is to solve the collective-action problem to produce this good. The challenge exists because it is supposedly not rational to participate in the generation of a public good produced through the efforts of large groups because one's participation is unlikely to decisively affect the outcome. A rational actor (one who considers all available options and chooses the one with the highest benefit/cost ratio) tries to free ride on the efforts of others working to produce the public good.[28] The consequence is that no one would pursue an activity that produces a public good unless his or her own efforts are decisive for the generation of the good. Efforts to understand why we encounter collective action in spite of expectations have centered on revising both the assumptions and the logic of the argument on free riding. Some reconsider the assumption

28. Those popular ideas were developed by Mancur Olson (1971).

that people are well described by the above definition of rationality: they overestimate the importance of their own role; they do not calculate costs and benefits in a detached way; or they are driven by impulses, emotions, and cultural indoctrination. People might even behave in an altruistic manner (not solely to irritate economists) or because they derive satisfaction from being part of a collective endeavor that generates a public good.[29] Timur Kuran (1991) reduces those factors to a variable in the decision-making equations of individuals. He simply assumes that every individual has a certain inclination to participate in the collective endeavor and that a person's threshold for participation is reached when a certain number of other individuals with lower thresholds go first and reduce the cost of participation by spreading out risk.[30] Although this approach might very well describe the decision-making process of potential participants during ephemeral conflicts, it does not have predictive power because it is impossible to know a priori the inclination of individuals to participate in very large groups and it is impossible to isolate this factor after the fact. Russell Hardin (1995, 47) adds to Kuran's consideration of personal cost the individual's assessment of whether self-interest and group identification are congruent. This line of thinking propels us toward greener intellectual pastures: developing a model of mobilization that discards the concept of the public good and solely relies on the consideration of threats and incentives.[31]

There is a public-good dimension to territorial conflicts, but participation is not always driven by the provision of such a good. What would villagers in remote areas who rarely see a colonial official gain from joining an uprising? They are not likely to expect to benefit or experience improvement in their living standards if the organization that is fighting for independence ousts the colonial power. Organizational members are likely to be the beneficiaries. Potential participants in insurgency also realize that they might experience a public "bad" in the guise of curfews, roadblocks, searches, and other punishments before they achieve the public good, if ever. Sometimes the desired public good seems so remote that it matters little in affecting individual calculations. A public-good approach also fails to explain how insurgent organizations that often fight each other instead of the incumbent still manage to mobilize support.

Long conflicts (the kind I address in this study) have a way of making individuals more rational and less interested in public goods than they would be during impulsive moments of revolutionary outburst. Individuals do not free

29. See Margolis (1982) on the first point and Scitovsky (1976) on the second.

30. A similar approach consists of ascribing a value to the psychological rewards earned from participation. This approach suffers from the same shortcomings of Kuran's method.

31. Such an argument was initially made by Tullock (1971).

ride. Instead, they try to maneuver their way out of sight or into the organization that would offer them the most, hurt them the least, and protect them from others who would hurt them. An individual who could potentially be mobilized does not make a binary decision to join a revolutionary activity or not to do so. Every individual who could be useful for a political organization is potentially a part of the state or occupier's governing apparatus, of any one of the organizations challenging the state and each other, or is completely neutral in his or her organizational adherence. Further, each one of the organizations, including the state, that seeks to win an individual's support or neutrality could subject her or him to positive and negative sanctions.[32] Those positive and negative sanctions tend to play a powerful role, overwhelming issues of psychological satisfaction and readiness to sacrifice. Those who doubt that rival organizations use negative sanctions need only consider Mao's words: "In order to prevent the enemy relying on a hostile population from . . . making a surprise attack on us . . . by methods of intimidation we warn the local population, we arrest and detain people."[33] ETA (the Basque nationalist organization) provides another example of the use of negative sanctions:

> [Radical Basque leaders] had a more daunting task than did the Catalans in altering subjective pay-offs. When it becomes irrational for any more Basques to adopt the Basque language, radicals can raise the costs of maintaining the status quo by intimidating those who refuse to shift. The sources of harassment and perhaps even terror can be found in a rational calculus of radicals that the movement would stagnate without adding the cost of fear to those who find comfort in the status quo.[34]

One of the most powerful positive sanctions an organization can offer is social acceptance, a factor so essential for personal fulfillment that it often dwarfs political preferences.[35] The regional focus of many supposedly ideological (even nonnationalist) organizations supports this view, and

32. Another way to put it is that every organization tries to convey the impression to its members and potential recruits that they are involved in an endless iterated interaction with it, whether they like it or not, and that they will be rewarded if they cooperate and punished if they defect. Of course, the first defection could define the last round of interaction. This type of strategic interaction is well described in Axelrod (1984) and, less extensively so, in Hardin (1982).

33. Mao 1966a, 119. See also chaps. 2 and 3 of Leites and Wolf (1970) for anecdotal examples. Another example of the use of negative sanctions (Callwell 1976, 128–29) is provided by Emir Abdulkader and the French general Thomas-Robert Bugeaud. Both opponents punished those who sided with the other side with cattle raids, crop burning, and other penalties. Callwell argues that the tide turned in favor of the French when they adopted those tactics.

34. Laitin 1993, 24.

35. For more on this issue, see Berman (1974), Hechter (1987), and Hoffer (1951).

David Laitin's adaptation of Thomas Shelling's (1978) tipping game gives it a theoretical framework. Laitin (1989, 1993) argues that an organization wishing to mobilize a population to support its views needs first to convert a critical mass of supporters whose participation makes further conversions much easier. Reaching this "tipping point" at which recruiting the next individual shifts from being costly to becoming easy and cheap therefore becomes crucial and encourages the use of all available positive and negative sanctions, including terrorism. Some like Barry (1970) and DeNardo (1985) deride any argument that delegates ideology to a secondary status in affecting mobilization, but it is widely observed that organizations often provide positive and negative sanctions to convert people to their ideological views, as evident from the work of Christian missionaries, Zionist agents among North African Jews in the 1950s, and the extensive welfare activities of many Islamist organizations.

It is easier to understand why free riding is less frequently possible than some collective action theorists would have us believe when we realize that each individual makes a decision to be part of the state or occupier's governing apparatus, to join any one of the organizations challenging the state and each other, or to be completely neutral instead of making a simple binary decision (whether to revolt or not to revolt). Free riding is rational when the only good to be gained is a public good, less compelling if positive sanctions are provided, and often not an option if powerful negative sanctions are imposed on the individual decision maker. Consider, for example, the massacres that have taken place during the Algerian conflict pitting the Groupe Islamique Armé (GIA) against the military junta. Most Algerians (theoretically even the Berbers) could have chosen to join either side. Villagers were often induced to join the government's side when it offered them weapons and the GIA levied harsh taxes. Unlike the FIS (Islamic Salvation Front) with its specialized branches, the GIA was loosely organized and lacked the ability to provide incentives through welfare programs, free clinics, or other such services. The GIA therefore could only attempt to shift the balance in its favor by applying *negative* sanctions such as massacring the inhabitants of any village whose male members joined the government militias.[36] Such massacres signaled to the population that they

36. When adopted alone and for a long time, however, negative sanctions tend to backfire. Such was the case for the GIA and for the Philippine peasants who flocked to the ranks of the Huk rebels because of governmental negative sanctions before the Magsaysay reforms (which combined both types of sanctions simultaneously). In Etzioni's (1975, 7) words: "Applying force usually creates such a high degree of alienation that it becomes impossible to apply normative power [such as loyalty based on nationalism or religion] successfully."

were still involved in an iterated interaction with the organization that involved a considerable probability of severe punishment if they defected to the government or even shifted from support of the GIA to neutrality. Even those who did not join one side or the other could find themselves subjected to threats and other negative sanctions. In brief, the public good is rarely what drives people to join the state or its rival organizations in protracted conflicts. Short- and long-term incentives and punishments play a greater role, and make the issue of free riding moot.

Although the consequences of short-term positive and negative sanctions are often clear, the probability of being subjected to long-term ones is often difficult to estimate. Those subjected to negative sanctions or courted with positive sanctions evaluate the probability of those sanctions lasting long enough to be worth accepting. Such calculations are important because the survival of the state and its rivals as well as their reach into different geographic areas is often in doubt during territorial conflicts. Consider, for example, the choices available to Iraqi Shiite and Kurdish rebels in the wake of the first U.S.-Iraq War (Gulf War) when the regime of Saddam Hussein was unstable and President George Bush Sr. encouraged them to rebel. Tribal and ad hoc organizations, villages, and neighborhoods from both groups had the opportunity to rebel against the generally disliked Hussein at the risk of being harshly punished if his regime regained its footing and control over their neighborhoods. The positive sanctions offered by a victorious United States would have amounted to the potential of assuming posts of power in the post-Hussein regime. Not joining an anti-Hussein organization or activity carried the advantage of possibly avoiding severe punishment, but it involved the risk of forfeiting political rewards (an opportunity cost is indeed a cost) if the regime crumbled. Readiness to rebel therefore depended on the probability of the collapse of the regime, because there was little doubt that it would severely punish the rebels if it survived. The Kurds who rebelled generally benefited because the Hussein regime's forces were, at least initially, successfully kept away from their region, but the Shia who rebelled suffered harsh repercussions. It only makes sense to join an organization if its star is rising vis-à-vis its rivals in one's neighborhood, if not on the regional or national level. Conversely, an organization is not worth joining when its rivals seem likely to control one's village for a long time, regardless of how wild its threats and grandiose its promises.

Organizations recruit based on their performance, their potential, their ability to punish nonparticipants and to provide meaning and rewards to participants, and their capacity to protect members from the negative sanctions that rival organizations would impose.[37] When some organizations are too weak to inflict punishment on defectors or those who join their enemies, they use the only cheap substitute available: the propagation of myths that defectors are cursed and loyalists are aided by supernatural intervention.[38]

A centralized organization with specialized branches and a safe haven, such as the state, has the great advantage of being able to coordinate the mobilization effort within the contested area.[39] An efficient centralized organization can also optimize the use of resources (including the ones needed to mete out costly sanctions) by directing them to where they are needed most to reduce inefficiency. Yet another advantage is that centralization allows for specialization in the provision of services that require a certain economy of scale to supporters (e.g., education, medical care, and irrigation projects). Such services are among the more potent positive sanctions available.

Some mature resistance and revolutionary organizations develop networks to collect taxes, recruit members, provide education, mete out (revolutionary) justice, and perform statelike functions in parallel to the state or occupier's apparatuses. The Communists in China and, to a lesser degree, in Vietnam managed to develop such statelike organizations as their safe havens grew and became more secure.[40] Some even believe that American anticolonialists developed such a countergovernment to British authority in the colonies: "They [the Committees of Correspondence and the Continental Congress] punished offenders, confiscated Loyalist properties, fixed prices, collected army supplies, fitted out privateers, recruited men."[41] This, however, is not something that organizations without a safe haven should attempt.

---

37. This argument is made by Tullock (1971), who writes: "The public goods aspects of a revolution are of relatively little importance in the decision to participate. . . . The important variables are the rewards and punishments offered by the two sides and the risk of injury during the fighting."

38. See McKenna (1998, 192–93) about how the Philippine Muslims made use of stories based on such beliefs to foster solidarity. The Mau Mau also made heavy use of such methods. See chapter 8 of this book on their use by the Taliban.

39. The French were among the first modern European colonialists to realize the importance of mobilizing the populations of their newly conquered territories, in this case in North Africa, through the use of institutions that provide positive sanctions in addition to punishing military raids (Beckett and Pimlott 1985, 4). See Kasza (1993) for a discussion of how single-party states use mass organizations to mobilize their populations.

40. Greene 1974, 72–73.

41. Beals 1970, 38–39. Tom Hayden (1966), a 1960s radical, referred to the model of the Constitutional Congress and urged "building institutions outside the established order which seek to become the genuine institutions of the total society" in the hope of replacing the U.S. government.

An organization needs to be safe from the intrusion of rival organizations for redistribution to work smoothly and for services to be provided regularly. Organizations that are subjected to continuous harassment are therefore better served by other structures that, while less efficient across the contested territory, make them less vulnerable. Weaker organizations are also less endowed with resources and therefore need to make their mobilization efforts less costly than they would be for centralized organizations. They also need to keep their cost of operations low once they do mobilize human and material resources. Burdensome bureaucracies and support personnel associated with centralization are clearly wasteful for weaker organizations because a higher proportion of members are involved in administrative or supportive roles in complex organizations. What structures would benefit them more?[42]

Decentralization and patronage are more efficient for mobilizing resources when the organization lacks a safe haven.[43] Such organizations cannot coordinate mobilization activities among their own subgroups and do not efficiently allocate resources to maximize their impact. They are also less capable of organizing specialized branches to provide large-scale positive sanctions to their loyalists, but this is a minor inconvenience because they are likely to lack the resources to provide such services anyway. They do, however, allow for simpler and cheaper mobilization, make the mobilization effort less vulnerable to the disruptive efforts of stronger rivals, and are more efficient at mobilizing resources and supporters on the local level, where cohesive groups create a sense of solidarity and loyalty that large centralized organizations generally fail to emulate.[44]

Olson (1971, 63) argues that a large group that is a "federation" of smaller groups enjoys the advantages of small groups. In this vein, Herbst (1968, chap. 1) shows that productivity among coal miners increases when autonomous small groups of workers are empowered to organize their work

---

42. See chap. 7 of Bedeian (1980) for a review of the management literature on this issue.

43. Formal dynamic models by Kowalewski and Hoover (1995, chap. 8) support the argument that having more than one organization benefits the mobilization efforts of state rivals. They argue that a single organization gets fewer concessions and musters less support than an "industry."

44. The reverse correlation between group size and efficiency has been deductively explained by Mancur Olson (1971, chap. 1). Support for this hypothesis has been produced by clinical psychologists, sociologists, and management scholars. See also Hardin (1982, chap. 3) for similar results with particular emphasis on optimally sized groups. Michael Taylor (1988, 67–68) adds to Olson's argument by emphasizing that collective action is more likely to succeed in a community whose members: (1) have beliefs and values in common; (2) have direct and many-sided relations; and (3) practice "generalized" as well as merely "balanced" reciprocity. Laitin (1993, 20) argues that mobilization and loyalty work best within small autonomous social groups.

patterns independently of management instead of having specialized groups perform specialized operations under constant monitoring. Herbst finds that small groups generate internal cohesion, pride, internal discipline, and excellent results in settings that do not require coordination among such groups and allow for easy monitoring of output.[45] Management exerts control over the autonomous small groups by monitoring their output instead of enforcing a specific activity and interaction pattern. These findings have been duplicated and are widely accepted by business-management scholars. The two alternative ways of organizing work available to British coal miners are also available to many revolutionaries, and I believe that Herbst's results are just as valid in revolutionary settings.

Noncentralized organizations can mobilize on the cheap because their local leaders are more responsive to local needs, can better leverage kinship ties, do not have to exchange mobilization-related information with a central leadership, can better estimate the need for costly positive or negative sanctions, and do not require costly support personnel. They should do well so long as their subgroups muster enough resources to apply necessary local sanctions. They are less vulnerable to the interference of rival organizations because the disruption of mobilization in one region does not impede it elsewhere.

To sum up, fragmented groups are obviously the least advantaged for mobilizing human resources. Organizations with a safe haven are best served by a centralized structure with the necessary specialized branches. Organizations without a safe haven would benefit more from a noncentralized structure. The three noncentralized structures—decentralization, patronage, and multiplicity—are likely to behave fairly similarly from a mobilization standpoint. I would expect patronage-based organizations to be slightly more cohesive and to have the lowest mobilization costs, however, because they are often based on strong clan ties. Rare indeed is the rural Chechen or Afghan who would not have joined the organization his clan leaders have chosen. Governance boards are likely to increase the mobilization capabilities of decentralized organizations by clearly articulating its position and explaining its actions. More important, they make specialization possible within the context of decentralization, a feature that remedies one of the major shortcomings of decentralization for the purpose of mobilization. Redundant structures are likely to increase the thoroughness of mobilization at an increased overall cost to the organization.

---

45. For similar results based on the study of Japanese firms, see Ouchi 1980.

Control and Discipline

Control and discipline mechanisms that motivate organizational members to behave in ways consistent with organizational goals are critical for organizational welfare. As Michael Hechter (1987) convincingly argues, both dependence (see discussion on sanctions above) and control are necessary for the production of necessary solidarity within an organization. Lack of discipline among the rank and file wastes existing resources, causes rent seeking, and weakens the ability to mobilize new human and material resources by alienating potential supporters.[46] Decentralization without control can be very costly, as Terry Moe reminds us: "Tasks and authority are delegated to lower-level units in the expectation that they will use their specialized knowledge and productive capacities to contribute towards organizational ends; but the inevitable information asymmetries create incentive problems."[47]

Frequent are the revolutionary organizations that have lost popular support because of the rapes, murders, extortion, and personal settlement of scores performed by newly armed and poorly organized members. The Huk rebellion and the Algerian GIA provide prime examples of such behavior. Control is also essential to preempt any move by rivals to woo a portion of the organization's constituency.

An organization is best served by a structure that increases the cost of exiting from its fold. Barriers to exiting can be created through the development of specialized branches that cater to the needs of different segments of the organization's supporters and provide them with essential services. The Egyptian Muslim Brotherhood, for example, has student-focused branches that provide transportation, textbooks, affordable food, and other necessities in poor neighborhoods in Cairo.[48] Another barrier that suits centralized organizations is the threat of meting out grave punishment to defectors, a practice common in many armies and revolutionary organizations such as the ETA and the PKK.[49] Brutal measures, however, can lead to the organization's accelerated demise absent the appropriate organizational welfare structure:

46. Rent seeking is the act of asking for a good to be provided that would disproportionably benefit an interest group but whose total costs exceed its total benefits for the entire organization.

47. Moe 1984, 755.

48. Hechter (1987, 46) tells us that "the more dependent people are, the more tax they must pay for access to the same quantity of a given good. This variable degree of dependence is indicated by the opportunity cost of leaving the group, or what may be termed the members' cost of exit."

49. See Laitin (1993, 26) on ETA.

the government might woo segments of the organization's constituency by moderating its own stance and inducing the organization to brutally massacre defectors and their families to set an example for other potential defectors. Although the organization's response can temporarily stem defections from its ranks, it will alienate potential supporters who will not find it rewarding to join because of the lack of material rewards as well as a newly heightened awareness of the high exit cost. Both the carrot and the stick are necessary to preempt the conciliatory efforts of a crafty opponent.

Control is achieved by redundant structures, clan systems relying on internalized controls, specialized branches, or a centralized hierarchy. The first and third methods are costly, and the fourth one carries the risk of bureaucratizing the revolutionary organization and diverting it from its original goals, the predicament of today's Egyptian Muslim Brotherhood.[50] With bureaucratization comes deradicalization, and the challengers end up competing with the state by using political tactics within the restrictions imposed by the more advantaged state apparatus.[51] The advantage of challengers lies elsewhere—in their efficiency, zeal, dedication, and organization in small cohesive groups. Efficiency can be lost if bureaucratization is carried too far and the revolutionaries become less differentiated from the state too early, prompting the development of fringe groups that want to reclaim the zeal, efficiency, and autonomy of the early days.

One of the most vexing challenges that faces the leaders of centralized organizations, including governments facing stiff resistance to their rule, is to keep the allegiance of the heads of their most potent specialized branches—the military and intelligence services—and to maintain control along the entire chain of command. A government's challengers can attempt to damage organizational ties and mechanisms of control within the state organization the same way the government often tries to manipulate the structure of their own organizations. A head of government can have his choice of strategies and policies considerably restricted if he is not sure of his ability to control specialized branches in the face of a serious challenge. The lower one goes down a centralized state's organizational hierarchy, the more one

---

50. Two other problems that generally arise from the implementation of rigid control systems are (1) selective attention to standards, i.e., maximizing the proxy that measures performance and not overall organizational interest, and (2) strategic measurementship (the manipulation of measurements) by the people whose performance is being evaluated.

51. The same argument is made by Michels (1949, 365–76) for European leftist parties. His description of the transformation of those previously revolutionary parties into conservative bureaucratic organizations could be used with little modification to describe what has been happening to the Egyptian Muslim Brotherhood.

finds a readiness to defect if the challenge to the regime is serious enough.[52] Lower-ranking soldiers and functionaries are normally held less accountable for the actions of the regime, are not as easy to recognize as their superiors once they defect, and have less of a sunk cost to forgo than those who have risen higher up the organizational ladder. One rare way in which resistance to foreign occupation differs from rebelling against an indigenous regime is that the organization of the powers that be is more cohesive in the first instance than in the second one because its members simply cannot defect to the colonized population.[53] The organizations of occupiers are less vulnerable than those of indigenous incumbents when they are staffed by individuals who do not share a common layer of identity with the occupied. Still, the occupier often raises troops among the indigenous population, and they may be convinced to shift loyalty as entire units or as individuals. In some cases, they can be persuaded to join or assist challengers (e.g., some French Communists in Algeria and Central Asian Soviet troops in Afghanistan).

The classic model of the redundant revolutionary organization is the Chinese Communist Party (CCP) before 1949. It featured redundant horizontal and vertical specialized branches: an independent organization of political workers alongside the military structure (vertical redundancy) and large number of overlapping associations for peasants, women, young people, workers, teachers, merchants, and cultural workers (horizontal redundancy).[54] The political officers helped indoctrinate the troops and supervise their activities, among other responsibilities. They could communicate directly with the party leadership and had every incentive to demonstrate their usefulness by reliably monitoring the troops.[55] The mass associations ensured the loyalty of the peasants in party-controlled areas by entangling them in a web of relationships that benefited them by solving collective-action problems but that were also costly to exit. This noncompetitive Chinese Communist redundant system was very successful for the purposes of maintaining control and discipline, but there is another less notorious type of redundant organization that is just as good while cheaper to maintain.

---

52. This can be seen, for example, in the readiness of lower-rank Syrian and Egyptian clerics from state-sanctioned religious establishments to defect when the Islamist challenge to the state becomes intense. Higher-ranking clerics, who often defended government-imposed laws, tend to remain loyal as long as possible (Sivan 1985, 54–66).

53. Mao, Castro, Trotsky, Ayatollah Khomeini, and other revolutionaries worked hard to cause defections in the regime's ranks (Russell 1974, 81–88), but resistance fighters rarely follow such a strategy with the troops of the occupying power because they understand that it can't be successful.

54. See Johnson (1962, 79–91) for more on this organizational characteristic.

55. Rice 1988, 75.

Loyalty can be maintained on the cheap in settings featuring multiple patron-client hierarchies. Discipline is bidirectional and competitive in this case: party leaders (patrons) compete for the loyalty of followers by maintaining a hard line and acquiring and distributing more goods, while field commanders (clients) prove that they deserve the goods by performing more efficiently than others on the battlefield. The party leader risks losing his client commanders to other patrons if he compromises with the state or occupier or proves to be a poor acquirer and distributor of necessary goods. If he loses too many field commanders then his prestige will diminish and his patronage system will crumble. If the field commander fails to mobilize his fighters for efficient resistance then he risks losing part or all of his allocation of goods from his patron. Further, his threats of defection to another patron will become less credible. The field commanders are efficient at mobilizing the rural population in their areas because of strong kinship ties and binding small-group dynamics. In short, the dynamics of a competitive redundant patron-client system produces efficient mobilization and a bidirectional imposition of discipline at little cost because such organizations are generally based on preexisting social-structural patterns. Further, this organizational structure, as well as some others, relies on a clan system to impose discipline on the rank and file.

One of the distinct advantages of the clan system is that it is inexpensive—there is no need for a bureaucracy or regional redundancy to ensure control over the rank and file. Another advantage of this method of control is that it promotes unit cohesion and camaraderie and increases personal commitment to the cause. It also helps the organization to survive in highly hostile environments where secrecy and cohesion are particularly valuable.[56] The major drawbacks are the difficulty of coordinating actions among the different groups and of recruiting from outside the clan.

Efficient control requires monitoring to avoid cheating, which disturbs the organizational incentive system.[57] An organizational subunit that deliberately sends information that it did (or will) perform better or worse than it knows it did (will) engages in cheating. Subunits cheat in the hope of getting more rewards (either absolutely or relatively to other subunits) or of being burdened with fewer responsibilities. Excessive cheating can wreak havoc in a centralized organization because it reduces the ability of the center to allocate resources and assign responsibilities in an efficient manner. Centralized organizations therefore need to develop monitoring organizational structures that

56. See Wilson (1978) and Ianni (1972) on how such an organizational structure assisted the Mafia.

57. For a discussion of cheating in a corporate environment of reward systems and incentives, see Burton and Obel (1984, chap. 6).

parallel the rest of the organizational structure, a feature that the patron-client organizations naturally have. Moreover, control in patron-client organizations is achieved on the cheap, which is an important consideration because the cost of monitoring plus the cost of successful cheating that takes place in spite of it should not exceed the cost of cheating without monitoring. Centralized organizations, however, normally have more latitude in meting out sanctions to cheaters: while patrons can punish clients by reducing their allotment of resources to just above the level at which they might defect, centralized organizations are likely to have specialized branches that inflict torture, death, or other penalties on those deemed to be pilferers, defectors, or traitors.

One way to reduce the cost of control consists of imbuing organizational members with shared, internalized beliefs and norms that provide them with meaning and guidance. To do so generally requires one or more specialized educational branches of the organization to continuously remind them of their goals, responsibilities, and beliefs. The commissars and political operatives of Communist organizations in China and the Soviet Union represent the epitome of such a specialized branch. Religious leaders often play a similar role among religiously motivated troops, such as the Taliban. What some game theorists dub as "cheap talk" is frequently used to reduce the cost of organizational control.

Governance boards also reduce the cost of control because the different organizational branches need to conform to their guidance if they don't want to lose their representation in the public eye. In addition, the authority of governance boards is often grounded in religious or ideological dogma, themselves factors that reduce the cost of control.

Another way for the principal to reduce the cost of monitoring cheating in both centralized and decentralized organizations consists of finding a reliable and easily measurable proxy for the effort (private and unobservable information) exerted by the agent. The outcome of the effort (recently gained territory, increased number of recruits or captured weapons) is normally the best measurable proxy but is often misleading under the adverse conditions that generally govern the lives of overwhelmed revolutionaries and resisters. Afghan field commanders in a remote area used the number of casualties (often the field commander's relatives) they lost in their assaults on Communist fortifications to illustrate to party leaders the amount of effort spent. Although such a proxy might seem to provide the wrong incentives at first, important factors make it a relatively efficient measurement of effort. Even if he were an amoral being, the field commander would not squander the lives of his kith and kin to increase his allocation of weapons and supplies from the party's headquarters, because he would soon lose the support of his followers.

In addition, those commanders could show little for their tireless and necessary circling of well-defended Communist fortifications because there was no one but other mujahideen to recruit and their weapons were inadequate to storm the forts. It was not wasteful to encircle and attack the fortifications, though, because such attacks helped sap the morale of their Communist defenders. The body count was the easily monitored proxy to solve the collective-action problem among the different field commanders in the area and to resolve the monitoring problem for the parties that acted as their patrons.

Excessive control in any organization can stifle creativity, inhibit initiative, and squander precious resources.[58] There is generally no fear of excessive control over organizations in fluid revolutionary situations, but excessively despotic leaders do occasionally make this issue a relevant one. Excessive control, by definition, occurs in highly centralized organizations where micromanagement can tax the leadership, reduce its ability to make good decisions, and gradually weaken the entire organization. Subordinates get penalized if they act out of line with the leadership's instructions even if those instructions are not suitable for the locale where they are trying to foster their organization's influence. Needless to say, local leaders will also not experiment with innovative tactics for fear of reprisals. Noncentralized organizations are, of course, not likely to suffer from the downsides of excessive control.

In brief, fragmented groups do not dispose of mechanisms of control. Centralized ones are generally better equipped than noncentralized ones in this respect but are also subject to greater costs of control, to risk of excessive control, and to the disruption of their intricate control mechanisms absent a safe haven. All organizations can increase control and discipline by developing redundant or specialized structures, as well as a governance board in the case of decentralized organizations. Clientage ties provide efficient bidirectional discipline inexpensively.

Resilience

Resilience is both an attribute and a goal of rival organizations. Some of the more dramatic endings of colonial conflicts of the twentieth century happened when internal fissures within the occupying power's structure were

58. AT&T, IBM, and General Motors provide textbook cases of corporations that stifled initiative and creativity through excessive control in the corporate world of the 1980s and 1990s (Flamholtz 1996, chap. 9).

exacerbated by seemingly endless resistance. Such was the case, among many others, with the Israeli withdrawal from Lebanon, the French withdrawal from Algeria, and, as Harry Summers convincingly tells us, the U.S. departure from Vietnam.[59]

Summers (1982) argues that it is the structure of the U.S. political system that made the United States less resilient than its foes in Vietnam, despite numerous battlefield victories. A U.S. president can start a war in his capacity as commander in chief of the armed forces (restrictions by the legislative branch were even weaker in the 1960s than after the War Powers Act was passed in 1973) even without declaring war, which would require congressional cooperation. If the war drags on and generates public discontent the way the Vietnam War did, then Congress, which does not have a commitment issue, can force the termination of the conflict by forcing the hand of the president over a period of time. Summers concludes that the North Vietnamese centralized structure explains its ability to outlast the United States in this conflict. Lenin also thought that no revolutionary movement could be durable without a centralized organization that provides a stable leadership to maintain continuity.[60] I argue in the rest of this section that this is true only in part, and definitely not when the organization is still weak vis-à-vis the state.

Resilience is the absolute opposite of strategic flexibility in revolutionary and resistance conflicts. It involves the ability to maintain a confrontational strategy longer than one's opponent, until the opponent's internal structure implodes (revolution) or it opts to withdraw (the end of occupation). The powers that be can adopt two shortcuts to impede the ability of rival organizations to resist: dismantle their structures or decapitate them. Centralized organizations without a safe haven are extremely vulnerable to both dismantling and decapitation, as the experience of the FLN's Armée de Libération Nationale (ALN) during the Algerian War of Independence shows.

The ALN organized differently in Algiers and in rural areas. The ALN was operationally decentralized outside Algiers, where it remained functional until the end of the war despite intense losses, isolation, and the commitment of immense French military resources. Under the influence of Leninist organizational thinking, the ALN in Algiers adopted a strictly pyramidal centralized structure. This centralized structure allowed it to execute some impressive high-profile operations, but ultimately it led to its defeat in the notorious Battle of Algiers. The French learned of the pyramidal

59. Merom (2003) makes this argument for Israel and France's experiences.

60. See Friedland et al. (1982, chap. 7) for a summary of Lenin's ideas on this issue.

structure and used it to guide their interrogation and persecution efforts. They soon started to fill the empty spaces in the organizational chart and ultimately caught the man at its head, Saadi Yacef.[61] The ALN's activities in Algiers never resumed after the capture of Yacef.

The Philippine Huks committed the same organizational mistake in Manila where much of their leadership, members, and records were rounded up one night in September 1950.[62] The highly centralized Islamic Jihad was crippled for years after its founder and leader, Dr. Fathi Shikaki, was shot to death in 1995 while the decentralized Hamas kept fighting.[63]

Highly centralized organizations are also vulnerable to treachery by their leaders, such as the Malayan Communist Party (MCP) leader Lai Tek.[64] Lai Tek was an agent of both the Japanese and the British and became the absolute strongman of the MCP with the help of his patrons, who eliminated all his rivals at his request. By the time he was uncovered and fled with much of the money in the MCP's possession, the MCP has lost most of its able cadres and limped along to its final defeat under the leadership of young, inexperienced leaders. Not surprisingly, the first thing the party's rank and file considered after the humiliating discovery of Lai Tek's treachery was decentralization. The rivals of a centralized organization need not recruit its top leader—a single individual in the higher ranks could suffice. A crude manuscript by the previous assistant and driver of Elie Hobeika (a post–civil war government minister in Lebanon and once the second in command to Bashir Gemayel, the head of the Maronite Forces Libanaises) documents how Hobeika often sabotaged the activities of the Forces Libanaises, impeded their relations with Israel, and might even have assisted in assassinating Gemayel after becoming a Syrian agent.[65]

Absent a safe haven, decentralized structures are more resilient than centralized ones because the violation of the integrity of any one of their branches has little effect on the ability of other branches to function and

61. A dramatic rendering of the Battle of Algiers is provided in the famous French movie carrying the same name. Note the scene in the movie featuring the *organigramme* I mention in the text. More information on this issue is found in Yacef (1982, 90) and Pellissier (1995, 110, 134–35, 232–23).

62. Chaliand 1982, 19 and 96.

63. Tracy Wilkinson, "Islamic Jihad Admits Role in Blast," *Los Angeles Times*, November 8, 1998, 16.

64. For a good account of the effects of Lai Tek's treachery, see the thorough study by Stubbs (1989, 54–59) of the Malayan conflict.

65. This crude volume by Robert Hatem (1999)—who is a confessed war criminal, assassin, thief, and kidnapper—is nevertheless compelling and credible. Hobeika was rewarded for his loyalty by the Syrians with ministerial posts at the end of the Lebanese Civil War but was assassinated in January 2002.

because their leaders are less useful to target. They are also less capable of shifting toward an accommodationist strategy than a centralized structure with strong control over the rank and file, if such becomes the wish of the leadership. Patronage-based organizations are the most resilient of all because of similar reasons and because of the strategy lockup feature I introduced in the strategy section and discuss in chapter 6. Depending on their number and size, multiple small organizations can be as resilient as a larger decentralized organization. Specialization without a safe haven weakens resilience because the successful targeting of any specialized branch could hamper the activities of the entire organization. Redundancy increases resilience because it allows the continuation of organizational operations even when part of the structure collapses. A governance board increases the resilience of a decentralized structure by making it even less useful to capture or assassinate its leadership.

Foreign Aid

Outside aid can be so important for some organizations at war that withholding it sometimes leads to the collapse of insurgencies. Such a collapse was, for example, the lot of the Democratic Party of Kurdistan (PDK, then the only Kurdish secessionist party in Iraq) after Iran withdrew its support in the wake of the March 1975 Shatt al-Arab agreements with Iraq.[66] Kurdish resistance collapsed after a major Iraqi army offensive, and Mullah Barazani fled to Iran and declared the end of the conflict. Resistance only resumed after new parties formed (Jalal Talabani's Patriotic Union of Kurdistan [PUK] and a Communist splinter group from the PDK) with Syrian support. Another example is the collapse of the Dhofar revolt following the 1975 withdrawal of South Yemeni support. Insurgents in both cases relied on a single outside backer whose policy shift led to their organizational collapse. State apparatuses are also vulnerable to the same dynamics, as the collapse of the Afghan Najib regime soon after the Soviets ceased their supply effort demonstrates. The effects of aid cessation are softened if the insurgents have two or more backers, as was the case for the Sahrawi Polisario when Libya withdrew its support after the 1984 Oujda agreement with Morocco. The Polisario had another backer in Algeria, whose consistent support allowed it to survive the withdrawal of Libyan aid.[67] The Algerian civil war

66. *Keesing's Contemporary Archives*, 27053–4.

67. Neuman 1986, 51, 84–85, and 102–4.

and the desire of the Algerian junta for rapprochement with Morocco led in turn to its sharp reduction of aid to Polisario, which was left with its weaker historical backer, Mauritania. And while Mauritanian support was hardly sufficient to allow the perpetuation of the Sahrawi organization as an effective fighting force, it protected it from immediate collapse. An organization is more likely to survive long enough to achieve its goals the more sponsors it has, but how is the number of sponsors related to organizational structure?

The key to answering this question is to understand what a sponsor of a warring organization wants to achieve with the resources it gives to it. Some of the more important goals of foreign donors to insurgents or the governments they challenge are: to weaken the government (or its own backers by proxy); to extend the donor's own geopolitical power; and to support ideological, ethnic, or religious kin. The first two, less altruistic, goals are generally accompanied by the desire to control the sponsored organization. And with the desire to control comes the pressure to centralize. It is much easier to control a centralized organization than any other structural type because of the ability of the leadership to direct the behavior of the rank and file as well as the expectation of holding the leadership accountable for the organization's actions. The premium backers put on control could also lead to a "one organization, one backer" arrangement where backers request full and exclusive loyalty to preempt the possibility of divergent goals with other backers.

Centralized organizations are therefore more attractive to potential sponsors. Supranational organizations are generally created and maintained to produce the photo ops necessary to placate donors by giving the illusion of unity and centralization. The downside of centralization is that it makes the organization vulnerable to pressure from its sponsor over its leader, who needs the donated resources to maintain influence within the organization and society. Because the leader of the centralized organization has the control apparatus to steer the organization in the direction he desires, it is not uncommon to see such organizations be reduced from revolutionary and resistance organizations to tools that exclusively foster their backers' interests (e.g., many Palestinian organizations that were based in Syria). This will not be the case if the centralized organization is the state, because it, and its backers, will likely have convergent goals: the state's survival and the elimination of all its rivals.

Conversely, decentralization makes an organization less appealing to potential backers but more immune to their control and manipulation because of its weaker control over local strategy and execution. A governance board, with its public image as lacking control over the different branches of the decentralized organization, reduces even further the influence of sponsors who find themselves giving money to a cause without being able to request accountability or force execution. Patronage-based parties are the least vulnerable of all to being controlled by sponsors because of the strategic lockup feature: the patron cannot redirect organizational strategy once it is focused on resisting the government, no matter what he or his sponsors desire.

The multiplicity of resistance organizations generally helps to increase their cumulative sources of exogenous support.[68] Sponsors are more likely to find an organization to their ideological taste and over which they can hope to exert influence when there are multiple organizations. This should result in more overall outside aid to the challengers of the powers that be than if they were represented by a single organization. It is indeed no coincidence that Afghanistan and Lebanon during its civil war, with their multitude of armed organizations, became awash with weapons. Whether each of the organizations in a multiorganizational setting becomes the tool of its sponsor(s) at the expense of the cause it is supposed to advance depends on its own structure, with centralized organizations being more vulnerable than decentralized ones and patronage-based ones being the least vulnerable of all.

Intraorganizational Cohesion and Competition

Organizations are arenas of political competition where members and groups form coalitions that jostle for influence and resources, if not outright control, and intraorganizational rivalry is shaped by structural incentives.[69]

Competition within an organization takes place among interest groups. Members of an interest group have the interests of the group as well as their own and those of the organization to advance. All is for the better for the organization if the three interests coincide, but intraorganizational competition can become destructive if they do not coincide. It is therefore very important for organizations that are likely to have interest groups to create incentives that make their competition helpful for the achievement of overall organizational goals. How does organizational structure affect those incentives?

Centralized organizations are not conducive to the development of interest groups and therefore have only to worry about aligning personal and organizational interests. Specialized branches within centralized organizations, however, could lead to the development of interest groups and the urgent need to develop incentives similar to the ones available in other types of

68. For an illustration, see Gerlach and Hine's (1970, 136–37) description of support for black empowerment organizations in the 1960s.

69. For more, see Bacharach and Lawler (1980, 75 and 214) and Pfeffer (1981, chap. 3).

structures to preempt turf wars that impede coordination within the organization. All other structural types feature groups that potentially could become competitors for organizational resources. The more decentralized the structure, the more independent the subgroups and the more likely they are to try to increase their power at the expenses of other subgroups or of the entire organization. Interest groups promote cohesion *within* the competing groups while promoting rivalry *among* them. The best way to make their competition beneficial for the entire organization is to develop a reliable monitoring system that informs the top-tier leadership of the performance of the subgroups and that regulates the distribution of resources. Ideally, subgroups ought to be instructed to expect performance to drive rewards and the distributive system should be made transparent. Those measures, however, are difficult to implement. Competitive redundancy, which involves overlapping areas of organizational work among the subgroups, facilitates the process by providing clear standards: the performance of the best subgroup becomes the benchmark set for all others. Governance boards in decentralized organizations only increase intraorganizational cohesion. Patronage-based organizations are based by definition on the exchange of resources in return for loyalty and adequate performance and are therefore well suited to creating healthy beneficial competition—until a client becomes too well endowed with the needed resources or the patron is too deprived of those same resources. The same does not apply to multiorganizational settings because competition among different organizations is not regulated by a patron or a central authority and can therefore degenerate into a Hobbesian conflict. In addition, one is likely to find less cohesive organizations in competitive multiorganizational settings, if only because of the pull factor created by organizations trying to woo adherents from others.

Generation, Distribution, and Preservation of Knowledge and Information

Resisting and governing require a complex set of skills (knowledge) that are acquired, developed, learned, and transmitted to others within the organization.[70] The learning of skills is formally or informally institutionalized in

70. Organizations in the modern economy can gain or lose their competitive edge depending on their ability to successfully manage, distribute, use, and act on knowledge (Nonaka and Takeuchi 1995, among others). The first and second U.S.-Iraq Wars showed that information and the ability to quickly utilize it have become an essential ingredient of modern warfare. The same applies to revolutionary and resistance conflicts.

revolutionary organizations and state apparatuses by using one or more of three mechanisms. The first one consists of learning in small groups: the experienced members in a small group initiate and teach the new recruits. The second method consists of the use of regular or frequent meetings of individuals of comparable rank and status so they can share their experiences and knowledge.[71] The third approach consists of using specialized trainers to centrally instruct recruits and mold them into the type of organizational members the leadership desires. Centralization of learning helps the specialized trainers to synthesize a broader range of experiences, tap sources of knowledge from outside the organization, and achieve economies of scale. Although only centralized organizations with specialized branches can use the efficient third approach in a safe haven, vulnerable groups without a safe haven can make efficient use of the first two. The first two approaches could even prove to be superior in large territories requiring specialization in local conditions, innovation, or when organizations are vulnerable and cannot afford to have training bases. Further, decentralization of learning protects the organization from rigid misguided indoctrination if such is the nature of the thinking of its leadership. Rivals of a centralized organization can seriously damage its ability to train new recruits if they destroy its training facilities, but they can only do the same to an organization that relies on the first two methods by destroying all of its small groups—that is, the entire organization.[72] This is another reason why the transition to a centralized structure should only be undertaken when the organization acquires a safe haven.[73] A quote from Giap that describes training activities during the early days of resisting the French illustrates this point:

> We came to Lam Son just when the popular movement was developing strongly. Each monthly military training course organized by the Inter-Provincial Committee drew in from fifty to sixty persons. The

---

71. I assume that groups that meet do it as frequently as required by the activities they engage in. This is of course not always the case (Janda 1980, chap. 9).

72. For an illustration of such circumstances, see Kerkvliet's (1977, 206 and 217) account of how the Huk could only train in a decentralized manner.

73. Some of those arguments have been made by Che Guevara (1961, 148):

> The fundamental training of the soldier of liberation is the life itself with the guerrilla band, and no one can be a chief who has not learned his difficult office in daily armed exercises. Life with some companions will teach something about the handling of arms, about principles of orientation, about the manner of treating the civil population, about fighting, etc.; but the precious time of the guerrilla band is not to be consumed in methodical teaching. This begins only when there is a large liberated area and a large number of persons are needed for carrying out a combat function. Schools for recruits will then be established.

> third course, held first in Kim Ma district, had to be shifted to another place before it was destroyed by the enemy. . . . Later Uncle [Ho Chi Minh] deemed it necessary to organize mobile training groups moving from one locality to another, short-term training courses of a few days for even two or three persons.[74]

Beyond knowledge (communication, military, organizational, and other such skills), organizations manipulate more perishable operational information. Information is needed to determine the best use of resources and to achieve effective coordination and adaptation. It is not freely available to everyone, and even the necessary minimum of information often is not available to decision makers quickly enough to be useful.[75] It is therefore important for organizations to develop mechanisms to collect information from where it can be found within the organization, the society, or other sources, such as sponsors, and transmit it to the decision makers who need it. Two such mechanisms exist. The first consists of having the dispersed information transmitted to a centralized coordinating leadership that decides on all matters of strategy and tactics. The other approach consists of developing a more decentralized system that involves less movement of information by leaving at least some of the calculations and decisions to those with whom the relevant information already resides.[76] Perhaps Friedrich Hayek's discussion of capitalist and communist markets will better convey how these mechanisms work than my words ever will:

> Which of these systems [central planning or competitive markets] is likely to be more efficient depends mainly on the question under which of them we can expect the fuller use will be made of the existing knowledge. And this, in turn, depends on whether we are more likely to succeed in putting at the disposal of a single central authority all of the knowledge which ought to be used but which is initially dispersed

74. Giap 1970, 60–61.

75. The insightful Jacob Marschak (reported in Burton and Obel 1984, 129) tells us that "the workings of an organization might be better understood if, instead of the usual organizational chart, one could have the description—if only very rough—of 'who does what in response to what information.' "

76. Rosa Luxemburg adopted this view in her critique of Lenin's arguments for the extreme centralization of leftist parties ("Organizational Questions of Russian Social-Democracy," 1904). Luxemburg reasoned that the degree of centralism advocated by Lenin would be disastrous for the emerging socialist movement in Russia because its conditions required flexibility, initiative, and experimentation, all of which require a certain degree of decentralization. She also argued that such centralization would give an advantage to "bourgeois intellectuals" whose organizations are structured in a way that facilitates such operations.

> among many different individuals, or in conveying to the individuals such additional knowledge as they need to enable them to fit their plans in with those of others.[77]

The trick with the first approach is to make timely decisions while keeping the cost of communication from becoming prohibitive, avoiding information overload, and preserving the integrity of the information itself (information is more likely to get distorted, edited, and impeded the further and higher it goes in a centralized hierarchy).[78] The challenge in decentralizing the information flow is to ensure that the separately made decisions yield a coherent and coordinated result. Decentralized organizations respond better than centralized ones to the problem of information overload and confusion.[79] Decentralization decreases the individual cognitive workload for the top-tier leadership and allows managers, cadres, or other midlevel leaders and managers to comprehend the issues, which improves the quality of upward communication and responsiveness to unpredictable change.[80] Because it is more costly, the first option suits organizations with extensive resources while the second option is the only one available for fledgling, resource-deprived organizations.[81] More important, centralization of the flow of information only makes sense when the organization has a safe haven. Events during the ill-fated Huk rebellion illustrate why this is the case:

> The [Philippine] government's intelligence units simultaneously raided twenty-two Manila homes and apartments and captured six officers in the HMK-PKP's [Huk] national leadership. Among them was PKP general secretary Jose Lava. Government soldiers also arrested over a hundred others and took hundreds of documents that later assisted their anti-Huk campaign. When other Regional Committee and national

---

77. Hayek 1945, 519.

78. For a discussion of how information overload and decision-making processes affect the Hayek thesis, see Jensen and Meckling (1995). Arrow (1974, 68) disagrees: "Since transmission of information is costly, in the sense of using resources, especially the time of individuals, it is cheaper and more efficient to transmit all the pieces of information to a central place than to disseminate each of them to everyone."

79. For example, see Hatch 1997, 168–69.

80. This point is developed and argued by a number of management scholars (Mamdouh 1990; Hedberg 1981).

81. This is not to say that decentralized information processing cannot be useful. Callwell (1976, 54), the experienced British colonial officer, wrote that information flows fairly efficiently in traditional societies to the point where "the regular [colonial] army is being watched in all its operations and cannot prevent it. The enemy has no organized intelligence department, no regular corps of spies, no telegraphs—and yet he knows perfectly well what is going on. He sees his opponent's hand."

> leaders at the general headquarters camp in the mountains of Laguna heard about the arrests, their feeling was the one "that divers have when their air hoses are cut deep down in jagged caverned coral reefs, or that men have in mines when the tunnel behind them caves in."[82]

Organizations without a safe haven are better served by decentralizing information as well as power over decision making, while those with a safe haven benefit from centralizing information to complement their centralization of decision making.

Information does not only flow along the lines of the formal organizational structure. Informal communication networks that facilitate learning and bolster or undermine organizational ties can exist within and across organizations. This phenomenon has long been observed by management scholars, and it is just as pervasive in insurgent and governing organizations. For example, Afghan field commanders from different parties in the same region maintained close ties that they cultivated through personal contact and regular group meetings during the Soviet occupation. Those ties provided each of them with information about how other parties reward their field commanders for their services and the opportunity to share experiences. The knowledge gained from being part of this informal (from the standpoint of the parties) network gave the field commanders more leverage in their relationships with their patrons than they would have had otherwise. The ties they developed also made the threat of defection to another party more credible if they needed to make such threats. Centralized organizations generally prohibit such contacts to maintain strict control over their rank and file.

Finally, a discussion of organizational knowledge requires a reference to the learning curve. There is no doubt that humans learn from repetition, and that societies that are more frequently invaded without their resistance organizations being fatally dismembered are more ready for efficient resistance at the next opportunity. The Chechens and Afghans epitomize societies that preserve their long learning curves in their clan-and-tribe–based acephalous social structure and oral culture. The coming together under one regional—and sometimes ethnicwide or even nationwide—banner to resist the invader is an oft-practiced maneuver that was applied to resist previous invasions or, more frequently and on a smaller scale, in interclan or intertribal warfare. The large-scale jihads are engraved in societal consciousness through poetry and story telling, while the smaller mobilizations are frequent

82. Kerkvliet 1977, 218.

enough to almost become an automatic societal reflex. Centralized organizations, on the other hand, need to create specialized branches to take full advantage of the historical learning curve.

To sum up, organizations with a safe haven would benefit from adopting centralized structures with specialized branches to process information and spread the knowledge necessary to perform organizational tasks among the rank and file. Redundancy within centralized structures makes the manipulation of information more reliable at an additional cost.[83] Organizations without a safe haven are better served by the use of small groups—through decentralization, clientage, or the multiplicity of small independent organizations—that are more efficient for processing locally generated information and acting on it. Governance boards are associated with extreme decentralization and help weaker organizations by keeping both information and decision making localized. Fragmented groups cannot process information unless they can somehow benefit from technologies (such as the radio or the Internet) that allow for it.

---

83. Bendor (1985, 254–56) argues that the existence of redundancy (whether passive or competitive) increases the load on the managers at the higher level but also forces them to give attention to a wider set of topics. Ries (1964) makes the same point while discussing the organization of the U.S. armed forces and its effect on the executive branch.

Chapter 4

The Gist of the Organizational Theory

> Bigeard [the lieutenant-colonel of the 10th French Division Parachutiste in charge of subduing Algiers during the Algerian War of Independence] intended to use the large blackboard he installed in his office to draw the organizational structure of the FLN in Algiers. It still consisted of empty rectangles. The names that were to fill them came little by little.
>
> —Pierre Pellissier, *La bataille d'Alger*

The organizational theory of group conflict assumes that societal groups, civilizations, religions, and nations do not engage in conflict or strategic interaction—organizations do. Its underlying principle is that the distribution of power within organizations (what we call structure) engaged in conflict creates incentives that motivate the individual behavior of organizational members in ways that affect each organization's ability to outlast its rivals and to win the conflict.

How each generic organizational structure performs the eight essential organizational processes with and without a safe haven, based on the discussion from chapter 3, is summarized in figure 4.1. The plus and minus signs describe the degree to which a structure facilitates or hinders a process, and a zero sign indicates that it doesn't benefit or hinder the process. A favorable structure does not guarantee the proper execution of a process but is essential for its proper execution—it is necessary but not sufficient. Structures, however, are normally created with a functional purpose in mind and it takes little imagination to find functions for them when they are available. And because the eight processes are essential for organizational success and survival, the odds are that the organization will do what its structure permits to improve performance. Scores in figure 4.1 are therefore likely to indicate not only a structure's potential to perform but also to provide a good approximation of its actual performance. Cumulative scores could theoretically vary

Processes	Organizational structure: Centralization	Decentralization	Patronage	Multiplicity	Fragmentation
Strategy	+ / –	– / +	– / +	– / +	– / –
Coordination	+ / +	– / +	+ / +	+ / –	– / –
Mobilization of resources	+ / –	0 / +	– / +	– / +	– / –
Control and discipline	+ / +	– / +	+ / +	+ / +	– / –
Resilience	+ / –	– / +	– / +	– / +	– / –
Foreign Aid	+ / 0	0 / +	+ / +	+ / +	– / –
Intraorganizational cohesion and competition	+ / +	– / –	+ / +	+ / –	0 / 0
Generation and preservation of knowledge	+ / –	– / +	– / +	– / +	– / –
Total Score	+8 / -1	-6 / +6	0 / +8	0 / +4	-7 / -7

Key:
- \+ Organizational structure allows good performance of process
- **0** Structure is irrelevant or has little effect on process
- – Structure impedes execution of process

(Each cell: With safe haven / No safe haven)

Which simplifies to...

	Centralization	Patronage, Multiplicity, or Decentralization	Fragmentation
Safe haven	Good Fit	Bad Fit	Bad Fit
No safe haven	Bad Fit	Good Fit	Bad Fit

FIGURE 4.1. How structure influences organizational processes in territorial conflicts

between −8 (a structure hinders the execution of all essential processes) and +8 (it allows for and encourages the beneficial execution of all processes). A score close to zero indicates that, on balance, a structure hinders the execution of as many processes as it assists. A higher score indicates that the structure is more likely to make a good fit with the availability or absence of a safe haven; a lower one indicates that it is less likely to do so. Cumulative scores imply that patronage-based and decentralized organizations are the most beneficial absent a safe haven. Centralization is the only adequate structure for organizations with a safe haven.

I do not include scores for generic structures with governance boards, specialized branches, and redundancy in figure 4.1 for purposes of simplification, but their effects deserve to be discussed.

A decentralized organization without a safe haven should develop a governance board, a low-cost structural addition, to dramatically improve its performance and enjoy the benefits of specialization without becoming more vulnerable. Adding specialized branches to a vulnerable centralized organization would make it even more vulnerable because of increased reliance on coordination. Conversely, competitively redundant and specialized structures improve the performance of centralized organizations with a safe haven by increasing their reliability and effectiveness. Redundant structures are likely to improve the performance of an organization without a safe haven, too, by making it more resilient. Redundancy is inherent in patronage and multiplicity, and contributes to their higher scores absent a safe haven.

Only centralized organizations enjoy a boost in performance if they gain a safe haven for some reason. This normally happens because of exogenous factors (e.g., the tsarist regime's debilitating loss to Germany in World War I or a dramatic infusion of outside aid) rather than their successful performance, because of the general disadvantages inherent in the centralization of vulnerable organizations. Other structures become a liability after the organization gains a safe haven. The larger the drop in score that comes with the acquisition of a safe haven, the more urgent the need to centralize as the old structure becomes a hindrance.

In brief, centralized organizations are generally more effective than noncentralized ones but are more vulnerable to the attempts of rivals to disturb their operations because of their dependence on coordination among their different specialized branches. An organization (such as the state, an occupier, or a strong insurgent group) that controls a safe haven that protects it from the easy disturbance of its operations by rivals must therefore adopt a highly centralized and specialized structure. Organizations that do not have such a space must adopt a noncentralized structure to increase their odds of outlasting their rivals. To have a safe haven is not essential to win the conflict, but it is essential for the organization to organize properly based on whether it has such a haven. An organization that suddenly gains control of a safe haven must therefore transform itself into a more centralized structure to take the strategic initiative beyond its turf and increase its odds of survival by the end of the conflict.

Structural Choice as Strategy

Choosing a structure is perhaps one of the most important strategic decisions that organizational leaders make. Decision makers have to pick a structure that best fits the availability of a safe haven and that allows them to perform better than their rivals at the lowest cost, if resources are scarce. The scores from figure 4.1 suggest dominant strategies and a resulting Nash equilibrium–centralized structures with competitively redundant and specialized branches for organizations with safe havens and patronage-based structures for ones lacking safe havens. This would assume that resources are abundant, that internal dissension doesn't exist, that organizational actors are aware of all their options but are not interested in maximizing their own influence within the organization, and that organizational restructuring is seamless. Such factors, however, frequently limit structural choices. Observable structural equilibria therefore markedly differ from the ones predicted under ideal conditions.

One frequently observed equilibrium is "centralized, fragmented" because the creation of organizational structures from scratch is a costly and daunting challenge for vulnerable and fragmented politicized groups. The state or occupier can improve its structure to become as efficient as possible at keeping challengers fragmented because of the challengers' inability to impede its development. This equilibrium is observed under most dictatorial regimes that develop overlapping and specialized coercive and intelligence branches whose job is to keep an organized challenge from emerging.

Another equilibrium frequently found in countries with intricate social structures is "patronage, patronage." This equilibrium is particularly stable because patronage-based structures diffuse power so effectively that it is very hard to centralize them. The existence of alternatives—there are often more than two organizations in the tribal settings favorable to the natural development of patronage-based organizations—weakens the hand of patrons. And, paradoxically, a patronage-based organization loses many operational advantages when it acquires a safe haven and gains strength, giving other similarly structured organizations the chance to regain power in a long-term cycle. In chapter 7 I illustrate the dynamics of this equilibrium in the context of Afghan conflicts. A radical social movement or organization, such as the Taliban whose rise I explore in chapter 8, sometimes temporarily dismembers a patronage-based system and interrupts the cycle.

Yet another common situation is "centralized, centralized." Once an organization is centralized, it is unlikely to ever restructure, no matter what the damage. The reason is that restructuring could only take away from the power of the centralized organization's leader, and he is therefore likely to resist it stubbornly. The leader's preferences are decisive within the organization because he already wields the most power, and a weak organization's vulnerability makes it risky for internal dissenters to disturb its operations by mounting an internal challenge. Generally accepted but flawed arguments, misperceptions, and the desire to emulate the structure of the dominant organization often facilitate the efforts of the leader to keep the organization centralized.

The ideal equilibrium "centralized, patronage" is fairly common in colonial conflicts. Colonizing powers naturally keep the centralized coercive institutions that allowed them to embark on their colonizing ventures. Their highly centralized structures are generally unimpeded by factionalism because their members are brought together by the common pursuit of gains at the expenses of the occupied. The degree of centralization often reflects the preparation and professionalism of the occupier. Colonized societies often feature tribal structures, many of which are based on patronage ties. Such societies generally offer protracted resistance and force the occupier to refine its structure even further. Patronage-based resistance is indeed capable of exhausting all but the most centralized, specialized, powerful, and well-integrated incumbents. In chapter 6 I illustrate the resilience of patronage-based resistance to occupiers through the study of the Soviet occupation of Afghanistan.

The Organizational Theory for the Strategist

So what should the powers that be and their rivals do? The leaders of an organization must have two clear goals: to develop their own organization so they can execute key operations as well as possible and to hinder the ability of rival organizations to do the same. This is so because, unless the extremely rare negotiated settlement is reached, interaction in the types of conflicts I consider is a zero-sum affair. Victory consists of fragmenting all opposition to the point where challengers cannot provide organized resistance and have to overcome the daunting hurdle of creating organizations from scratch under constant harassment to ever do so again.

Factors to Consider

The most important factors organizational leaders need to consider before deciding on how to organize are the availability of material and human resources and a safe haven. Resources are important not only because they allow for the execution of processes but also because restructuring is a costly process. Restructuring is costly because it is likely to generate intraorganizational conflict between reformist leaders and those who will inevitably lose power and influence within the organization once it is implemented. They will have to be either compensated with costly concessions or be purged, another costly activity that leads to a loss of membership and distracts the organization from its primary goals. Other costs can take more subtle forms such as the expression of dissatisfaction through pilferage, shirking, and sabotage. Just like their corporate counterparts, organizations involved in politicized conflicts must consider beneficial restructuring to be a tradeoff between painful short-term sacrifices and a debilitating long-term descent into the status of has-beens.

Resources are also important because some structures are more costly to maintain than others. The more centralized the structure, the higher the administrative overhead, as numerous studies in the business management and public administration literatures convincingly show. Specialization also increases cost by adding the need for the development of organizational staff to manage coordination and the heavy load of information management. Redundancy increases reliability at an additional cost for obvious reasons but could reduce it incrementally by increasing efficiencies that result from intraorganizational competition. Patronage-based structures have two cost-reducing features: they reward performance in a marketlike arrangement that reduces inefficiencies, and they reduce the need for staff to a small monitoring and logistical group.

In this book I address what the more significant organizations need to do, but it is worth noting that tiny organizations created from scratch are best served by a highly centralized structure that facilitates control, flexibility, and cohesion—attributes essential to preserve stealth vis-à-vis the prevailing organization. And if such an organization manages to elude the heavy hand of the powers that be long enough to grow and engage in more visible activities, then it needs to evolve into a decentralized or patronage-based structure.

Starting points (how the organization is structured at the moment) are important because not all restructuring efforts are equally costly. It is easier and less costly to centralize a decentralized organization than a patronage-based one. And it gets harder to centralize if there are rival organizations, because disenchanted followers can then defect to other organizations offering them more relative power. The two most daunting efforts are to start organizations from scratch and to decentralize a centralized organization. A decentralized organization must immediately adopt a governance board, a low-cost structural addition that bestows considerable advantages. The development of specialization requires extensive learning because organizational members will need to develop new skills—those pertaining to the specialized tasks as well as those necessary to enable necessary coordination. Developing redundancies in structures to which they are not inherent (such as patronage) is a costly effort that only well-endowed centralized organizations can afford.

Organizational leaders are sometimes pressured by particularly influential outside sponsors to adopt centralized structures, even when it is not in their interest to do so. This rarely happens, however, because sponsored organizations are too vulnerable, their leaders are not willing or able to restructure them, the sponsor is not sophisticated in such matters, or the organizational leaders leverage information asymmetry to do what they want anyway. This, of course, does not apply when an occupier is capable of imposing its will on indigenous organizations it sponsors and controls, such as in the relationship between Israel and the South Lebanon Army between 1982 and 2000.

The management of intense factionalism is one of the more important considerations driving the structural choices of organizational leaders. Redundant or specialized substructures are not factions because, while they might produce an esprit de corps, they do not mobilize organizational subgroups against others. The Green Berets or the Defense Intelligence Agency are examples of specialized substructures, while the two wings of the communist People's Democratic Party of Afghanistan, Khalq and Parsham (chapter 6), are archetypical factions. Ideally, nonsanctioned networks and exclusive solidarity groups should not exist within politicized organizations. But they do, and their existence can cause painful structural compromises. Centralized organizations will lose many of their advantages if factions take control of their specialized branches, because their rivalry will likely impede coordination. Organizational leaders must therefore dismantle factions as soon as possible and at any cost. Less centralized organizations do not require high levels of coordination and can therefore manage factionalism through regional or functional segregation until they acquire the resources to eliminate it.

Factions generally emerge on the basis of ethnicity, severe disagreements on watershed policies, in support of charismatic figures dissatisfied with the distribution of power within the organization, or any combination of the above. Each of those types of factions should be dealt with differently. Members of identity based factions can be diffused throughout the organization, controlled through redundant structures of ideological officers (e.g., commissars, mullahs) that also disseminate a unifying ideology, or be separated from their most influential leaders. Dissatisfied charismatic leaders must either be accommodated on the condition of demobilizing their followers or be excluded from the organization. Dissension over policies can be preempted by the creation of strong control mechanisms, such as the ones described in the discussion on control and discipline in the previous chapter.

How to Restructure

Organizations are likely to restructure just enough to gain an edge over the competition because restructuring is costly and can temporarily weaken the organization before it helps improve its performance. But once an organization restructures successfully, others might imitate its structural innovations or, if more savvy, choose a structure that makes a good fit with their own control of a safe haven. If restructuring is successful, then structural escalation will likely continue until one or more rival organizations reach their optimal form, meet insurmountable hurdles to restructuring, are eliminated, or simply misjudge their needs.

How should vulnerable organizations be structured to make it easier to centralize when, and if, they acquire a safe haven? It is less costly and difficult to centralize decentralized organizations, particularly those with governance boards, than patronage-based ones. Governance boards facilitate centralization because they provide direction for the entire organization, provide a focal leadership, and, most important, allow for the existence of specialized branches within the decentralized organization that can readily assume their roles in the more centralized structure. This advantage might be enough justification for some to adopt the otherwise less advantageous decentralized structures over patronage-based ones early on in the conflict.

How Organizations Impede Their Rivals' Performance

Decentralized, patronage-based, and multiple organizations weaken a centralized one by performing essential operations more effectively on the periphery of its safe haven. They are quite capable of taking advantage of local opportunities, but they are generally not well equipped to disturb core operations (e.g., coordination or information management), to manipulate the state's structures, or to implement sophisticated strategies. Their main goal is to endure—to be resilient—and weaken the state or occupier by draining its resources and support. Conversely, centralized organizations must use their ability to coordinate and execute complex strategies to take advantage of structural weaknesses in their rivals' organizations. They are fortunate if rivals without safe havens are centralized, because they can easily disturb their execution of essential operations. It therefore makes sense for the state or occupier to induce its weaker rivals to adopt disadvantageous centralized structures that it can defeat more easily.

Complex Organizations

The generic organizational structures I discuss above do not cover the entire gamut of the possible ways to organize. First, there might be other organizational patterns and components I failed to notice or that do not exist in the cases I researched. Second, and probably more significant, organizational innovators can combine the above structural components and patterns to form complex organizations that perform differently from the generic types. Improvising complex organizations to fit a situation in flux is risky, as evidenced by the stellar successes and the dismal failures of some organizational innovators. The organizational model created by Mao, improved by Giap, and later adopted by the Afghan military leader Ahmad Shah Massoud proved its enduring success. Lenin's innovative two-tier organization was also a resounding success under the unique circumstances of the Russian Revolution. But the adoption of a mixed centralized-patronage structure by the Najib regime in Afghanistan proved to be a fatal mistake. Other structural innovations are possible and are only limited by the organizational entrepreneur's imagination, skill in such matters, and willingness to dangerously venture beyond the tried and proven.

So how do the above three examples of complex organizations (Mao's, Lenin's, and the Najib regime's) perform in comparison to the generic structural types? Chapters 6 and 7 provide an account of the performance of the Najib regime's organization. The classic Mao and Giap organizational type consists of a multilayered structure formed of local groups on the village level for local mobilization and defense and regional operational groups. A third component is later added in the organization building process to take the strategic initiative: a centralized mobile force that complements, rather than replaces, the local and regional groups. The entire structure is flanked by a parallel network of political commissars that helps the leadership increase its control over the organization. As the organization centralizes, the leadership effectively graduates from providing strategic guidance (like a governance board) to actively managing the organization. It also makes use of redundant civic organizations that address niche needs and provide the positive incentives necessary to maintain popular support.

The Mao/Giap organizational structure is attractive because it improves on the advantages of decentralization with a governance board by using redundant vertical control mechanisms that enhance control and organizational cohesion when the organization is still vulnerable. It also facilitates the transition to a centralized structure when the time comes. And since the emerging centralized structure complements but does not replace the decentralized layers of the organization, it can survive by reverting to its original form if the transformation is initiated prematurely.

Lenin believed that a centralized organization could effectively confront the tsarist regime but would fail to mobilize the larger following necessary for its long-term success.[1] He further reasoned that a wider, less centralized organization can mobilize a broader segment of supporters but will be incapable of sustained and efficient (secretive) confrontation. Lenin thus decided to adopt a two-tiered organizational structure composed of a highly centralized core of professional and dedicated revolutionaries with a high readiness to sacrifice for the cause (a vanguard group) and a separate broad workers' organization that was only expected to play a nonconfrontational supportive role. The dedicated centralized organization allowed Lenin to adopt any strategy he deemed convenient and would be ready and able to take action when the opportunity offered itself, if it managed to maintain the integrity of its structure and to avoid decapitation. It also shielded the broad workers' organization from repressive tsarist responses to revolutionary acts. Recruitment into the broad popular organization was easier because its members did not have to suffer from repression and were not expected to adopt the extreme ideology of the vanguard.

The success of the Bolsheviks owed much to the ineptitude of the tsarist regime, its debilitating defeat by Germany, and the erosion of its power by a multitude of decentralized opposition organizations. Their organizational structure proved its worth when the state was weakened by Russia's military defeat, thus providing rivals with safe havens. Lenin's rivals could not take advantage of the tsar's weakness as well as he did

1. Lenin (1967, 1:122–200) discusses these issues in "What Is to Be Done."

because they led decentralized organizations that were incapable of prompt coordinated action.

The odds are that this structure would have been less useful absent those particular circumstances, but organizational genius consists of adopting the right structure for the situation. Conversely, it is strategically unwise to adopt a once successful structure in a completely different environment, a mistake many ambitious Communists and some noncommunists who hoped to emulate Lenin's success have paid for dearly.[2]

There will be considerable room for structural innovation in the future because the conflict environment is likely to be transformed by changes in transportation, communications, and weapons technology much faster in the coming decades than during previous ones. Transnational networks coordinated through recently developed communication technologies have already become a common way to organize militant groups (Arquilla and Ronfeldt 1996, 2001). The future will no doubt produce many surprises in this field.

---

2. The Afghan Islamist Gulbuddin Hekmatyar, for example, told a journalist in 1984 that he had adopted the tactics of Leninism but that he was going to use them for advancing the ultimate good cause (Islam), instead of the ultimate evil (communism). Reported by David Isby, "Afghanistan—Civil War Next?" *Jane's Intelligence Review* 4, no. 10 (1984): 463.

Part Two

Explaining the Outcomes of Afghan Conflicts

CHAPTER 5

The Soviet Withdrawal from Afghanistan

> Though my soul will go to God, my spirit will remain in Afghanistan. My last words to you my son and successors: never trust the Russians.
>
> —Abdul-Rahman Khan, amir of Afghanistan, 1880–1901

The Soviet withdrawal from Afghanistan was generally viewed as a devastating blow to Soviet foreign policy. Some observers of the course of events in Afghanistan marveled at the capacity of poorly equipped and trained rural Afghans to trounce the Soviet military, and some even credited the unruly tribesmen with striking the blow that ultimately led to the demise of the Soviet Union.[1] In addition to signaling Soviet weakness to enemies, allies, satellites, and republics, the Soviet withdrawal allowed some Afghans to support Islamic and ethnically oriented groups under the Soviet yoke; demonstrated how weak, unmotivated, and badly organized the Red Army was; caused the Soviets to cede strategic ground that included airfields some three hundred miles away from the Persian Gulf; and proved an embarrassment to General Secretary Gorbachev who had to retreat from every condition he set for the Soviet withdrawal by the time the last Soviet soldier left Afghanistan in February 1989.

The Soviet withdrawal has been variously attributed to international (particularly U.S.) pressure on the Soviet Union; the weakness of the Soviet economy; the development of New Thinking in Moscow; the supply of weapons

1. This is the thesis that Anthony Arnold develops in *The Fateful Pebble*. The Afghan mujahideen and their supporters also make similar arguments. See Khan (1993, 293 and n. 8) for a list of academics and politicians who made this claim.

to the Afghan mujahideen ("those who strive in the way of Allah"—the resistance in this book) including the vaunted Stinger antiaircraft missiles; and the mythologized Afghan fighting spirit and fierceness once popularized in the West by Rudyard Kipling's ballads:

> When you're wounded and left on Afghanistan's plains,
> And the women come out to cut up what remains,
> Just roll on your rifle and blow out your brains,
> And go to your Gawd like a soldier.[2]

And ingrained in Pushtun oral culture through sayings such as:

> I sacrifice my wealth for my head, but my head for my honor.
> The brave man has no faults, and the true coward no shame.
> When a son and brother have been murdered, who will restrain his hand?
> Young love, if you do not fall at Maiwand; By God! Someone is saving you as a token of shame![3]

The most popular argument, however, is that the Soviets withdrew from Afghanistan because their increasing economic difficulties motivated them to improve their relations with the West, China, and Muslim countries. Although all these factors are likely to have influenced the Soviet decision to withdraw, what ultimately caused the Soviets to leave Afghanistan was their failure to control the country well enough to take advantage of its strategic assets, a failure that resulted from a seldom appreciated but critical element: the structure of their own institutions and the organization of the Afghan resistance. My argument proceeds in two stages. I first show in this chapter that the Soviets would have withdrawn from Afghanistan regardless of the turn their relations with the West or China would have taken, because of the elusiveness of their goal of controlling the country well enough to justify their losses. I then argue in the following chapter that the structure of the Afghan resistance was such that it locked the mujahideen in a confrontational strategy and gave them the resilience to keep the cost of Soviet occupation high, to prevent the Soviets from benefiting from the strategic advantages they hoped to acquire by occupying Afghanistan, and to take

---

2. "The Young British Soldier."

3. According to Afghan lore, the Pushtun heroine Malalay held her veil as a standard and shouted this couplet to encourage the fighters at the battle of Maiwand (July 27, 1880) where the Afghans trounced the British (Ahmed and Hart 1984, 276).

advantage of developments in international relations. But how do others explain the Soviet withdrawal?

Competing Arguments

The two most popular lines of academic arguments to explain the Soviet withdrawal from Afghanistan are a domestic one that associates the withdrawal with the change of leadership in Moscow and the rise of New Thinking, and a systemic one that presents it as a sideshow to the evolution of U.S.-Soviet relations.

Domestic arguments to explain the Soviet withdrawal were developed by those interested in Soviet institutions, such as Sarah Mendelson (1993a, 1993b, and 1998), whose research consisted mainly of interviewing Soviet officials, and UN negotiator Diego Cordovez and journalist Selig Harrison (1995), who witnessed the Soviet change in attitude through the years without necessarily being exposed to the Soviet leadership's decision-making process. They were encouraged by statements, such as the following quote from Gorbachev and Soviet foreign minister Eduard Shevardnadze ascribing their dramatic policy shifts to their new thinking:

> The new political thinking has given us a new scale of values and new criteria for our conduct. We have declared that we will be guided by universal human values. . . . There are universally recognized instruments to give us our bearings, mainly the United Nations Charter, and the declaration, covenants, conventions and resolutions ratified and observed by most of the world's countries. . . . For years, over a hundred United Nations members condemned one Soviet action. What more did we need to see that we were at odds with the world community, violating international norms and universal human interests? . . . I am referring, of course, to the stationing of Soviet troops in Afghanistan. We have to draw a lesson from the fact that we also blatantly violated our national legislation, along with the standards and ethics of our Party and society.[4]

Mendelson argues that the withdrawal from Afghanistan

> resulted because the Gorbachev coalition gained control of political resources and placed what had been misfit ideas about both domestic

4. Shevardnadze 1989, 44–45.

> and foreign policies squarely on the political agenda. The Gorbachev coalition shifted the internal balance of power in favor of reformists and "new thinkers" through a series of political strategies previously unused by Soviet political elites attempting reform. Specifically, they actively encouraged the growth and empowerment of new constituencies pushing reformist, accommodationist beliefs, and simultaneously disempowered old constituencies advocating status quo agendas. . . . The leadership's mobilization of ideas and experts changed the internal balance of power and created the conditions necessary and sufficient for change in foreign policy, including the withdrawal from Afghanistan.[5]

My own argument benefits from Mendelson's well-conducted research that details how Gorbachev consolidated power before he was able to order the withdrawal. The only problem I have with her argument is that it tells only part of the story: she is ignoring the other relevant parties to this strategic interaction.

Cordovez and Harrison build on the work of Soviet specialist George Kennan who believes that reversals in Soviet foreign policy under Gorbachev stemmed from domestic factors by arguing that

> despite the widespread stereotype of a Soviet military defeat, Soviet forces were securely entrenched in Afghanistan when the Geneva Accords were finally signed on April 14, 1988. The Red Army did not withdraw in the wake of a Waterloo or a Dien Bien Phu. Confronted by a military and political stalemate, Gorbachev decided to disengage because the accords offered a pragmatic way to escape from the growing costs of the deadlock and to open the way for improved relations with the West. Perestroika was the indispensable prerequisite for the withdrawal, and diplomacy, reinforced by military pressure, made it happen.[6]

There is something appealing about the concept of new noble ideas changing the world we live in for the better, but leaders of occupying powers normally begin exuding empathy and expressing willingness to let colonized populations determine their own destinies after the occupying power is faced with stiff and costly resistance. It does not take a Dien Bien Phu, let alone an irrelevant Waterloo, to exhaust an occupier; years of harassment,

5. Mendelson 1998, 4.

6. Cordovez and Harrison 1995, 4–5.

the demoralization of the military and the population, and the regular flow of body bags often suffice. The Geneva Accords (and this is not a statement about Cordovez's abilities as a mediator) did not offer Gorbachev anything of value and were, as I show below, nothing more than a face-saving formality. Both Cordovez and Harrison were disposed to adopt a New Thinking explanation because they were influenced by the statesmen and diplomats Harrison interviewed and Cordovez negotiated with. What they failed to probe were the reasons behind the emergence of this new thinking. It is not success but failure that normally spurs new thinking. Gorbachev's New Thinking was nothing more than a dignified excuse to explain the retreat and failure of Soviet interventionism without losing face or damaging the delicate pride of the population of the waning superpower. It didn't cost Gorbachev a thing to pretend to be motivated by ethical considerations when it only made sense to withdraw, even by "old thinking" standards, and cheap talk was one of the few resources still available to him by then.

Systemic arguments to explain the Soviet withdrawal remain some of the more popular ones because of their simplicity and their appeal to many Western scholars and policymakers. They were developed by observers immediately after the withdrawal, when information on decision making in Moscow was still scarce and the end of the cold war was the focus of pundits, journalists, and academics alike.[7]

At the heart of the systemic explanation is an implicit assumption that the confrontation in Afghanistan is best considered as one between the two superpowers. The argument runs as follows: while the Soviet involvement was evidently direct, the U.S. effort was essential to the perpetuation and intensification of the resistance. As admirable as Afghan tenacity, courage, and sacrifices have been, it should not be forgotten that the United States organized the flow of weapons to the ill-equipped mujahideen and that U.S. guarantees of the security of Pakistan gave this country the strength to train, organize, and assist the Afghans. The intensity of the U.S. involvement in the conflict is indicated by the fact that, by 1984, the CIA station operating from Islamabad became the largest agency operation in the world outside the Langley, Virginia, headquarters.[8] The two billion dollars worth of weapons that the CIA poured into Afghanistan and U.S. mobilization of the Arab Gulf states and Egypt behind the Afghan cause ultimately inflicted the

7. Variants of this argument have been developed by Rubinstein (1988), Parker (1991), Halbach (1990), Rogers (1992), Hauner (1991), Rubin (1995b), and Blacker (1993).

8. Lohbeck 1993, 52.

"bleeding wound" to the exhausted Soviet body.[9] Perhaps the most obvious indication of how U.S. intervention was critical to the effort forcing the Soviet retreat was the spectacular rise in the number of downed Soviet jets and helicopters after the CIA supplied the Afghans with Stinger missiles.[10] The United States was not the only country supporting the mujahideen: Iran and China also contributed resources to make the protracted Soviet engagement as bloody and costly as possible.[11]

Another thread of the systemic argument notes that the Soviet economy had slackened since 1979, when Leonid Brezhnev and his clique, confident in a growing economy and a powerful military, decided to invade Afghanistan. The Soviet economy declined because of the allocation of enormous resources to the military in the relentless arms race with the United States, costly foreign policy commitments such as the occupation of Afghanistan, and overall Soviet mismanagement of the economy.[12] The rise of Gorbachev allowed the official Soviet recognition of this harsh economic reality and the subsequent readjustment of Soviet foreign policy. The "new thinking" (the ideological justification given by Gorbachev to explain the downsizing of Soviet global ambitions) only reflected the Soviet loss in the war of economic attrition with the United States and Gorbachev's newly acquired awareness of his country's need for Western money and the necessity of reducing the military budget.

As bitter as a withdrawal from Afghanistan might have seemed to the Soviets, it was the least the Soviets could do to improve their image in the West, China, and other countries they were courting. The Soviets needed to improve their relations with the West and China before they could downsize their military and reduce military expenditures. The Soviets also needed the West and

9. Gorbachev used this term to indicate, for the first time, that he was rethinking the Soviet involvement in Afghanistan (*Pravda*, February 26, 1986, 8). For a yearly breakdown of U.S. aid to the Afghans, see Goodson 1990, 333.

10. Some observers estimate the number of downed Soviet jets and helicopters to have risen tenfold after the introduction of the Stingers in 1986. Others (Cordesman and Wagner 1990, 176) note that Stingers accounted for less than 50 percent of Soviet aircraft downed in Afghanistan.

11. Iran armed and trained the Shia in the center of Afghanistan, and China directly equipped some Tajiks and supplied Peshawar-based parties with U.S.-purchased weapons.

12. Shevardnadze revealed in 1990 that the Soviet occupation of Afghanistan had cost the USSR eight billion rubles for every year of the war, while other Soviet sources put the cost at $7.5 billion. For the Shevardnadze figure, see *Pravda*, July 5, 1990, as reported in Sakwa (1991, 336). See Rogers (1992, 223) for the other figure. Yet other sources (Rubin 1995b, 29, 160 n. 30) put the cost at $5 billion yearly. This is more than 10 percent of the 1989 Soviet defense budget of 77.3 billion rubles, which constituted anywhere between 15% and 25% of the Soviet GNP. This means that the occupation of Afghanistan cost the Soviet Union anywhere between 1.55% and 2.6% of a GNP that was worth between $1.3 trillion and $1.73 trillion (25–33% of the 1989 U.S. GNP of $5.2 trillion). Some data are from Sakwa (1991, 272 and 335). See also *Far Eastern Economic Review*, July 3, 1989, 17.

the capital-rich oil-producing Muslim countries both as markets and as sources of capital that would enable the restructuring of the Soviet economy. The Soviets, some realists argue, would have been capable of remaining in Afghanistan if their occupation were not linked to the overall credibility of their foreign policy reforms. The Soviets claimed to have lost no more than fifteen thousand troops in the war, less than a third of U.S. deaths in Vietnam, and could have sustained the same casualty rate for a few more years.[13] Further, while the economic cost of the occupation was high, the Soviets poured some $10 billion in economic and military aid to the Najib government from their withdrawal until the fall of Kabul, a possible indication that Moscow was willing and able to sustain this level of spending but simply had to leave in order to improve relations with other states.[14] Another indication that the Soviet withdrawal was caused by developments that are only remotely related to what was taking place inside Afghanistan is that the USSR started a campaign of courting Islamic countries following the February 8, 1988, declaration by Gorbachev in which he set May 15 as the date for the beginning of the Soviet withdrawal. Trips by ranking Soviet emissaries to Pakistan, Iran, Egypt, Saudi Arabia, and other Gulf States resulted in a marked improvement in relations between some of these countries and the USSR.[15] The withdrawal also fulfilled one of three Chinese conditions for the improvement of relations with the USSR.[16]

Yet another element that suggests that the Soviet withdrawal should only be understood in the broader context of Soviet-American relations is that the USSR was scaling back its involvement in several less-developed countries by 1987. Examples of such disengagements include Soviet reduction of economic and military support for Vietnam while encouraging Vietnamese withdrawal from Cambodia, encouraging a peaceful settlement in Angola,

---

13. In fact, the Soviets underreported their losses, with later evidence suggesting that they lost around thirty-five thousand troops. The official number of Soviet casualties was contested by several analysts during and immediately after the war. Arnold (1993, 190) and Goodson (1990, 27), for example, argue that Soviet deaths could have been as high as fifty thousand. See V. Izgarshev, "Afganskaia bol" (Afghan pain), *Pravda*, August 17, 1989, 6, as reported in Mendelson 1998, 26.

14. Arnold 1993, 184–90.

15. Halbach 1990, 289. Pakistani media broadcasted favorable coverage of Gorbachev's "courage" in redirecting Soviet foreign policy, and Ayatollah Khomeini even suggested an alliance between Iran and the USSR against the Great Satan. Rais (1994, 136–37) discusses the rapprochement between Iran and the USSR in the wake of the Soviet withdrawal from Afghanistan.

16. The other two being a reduction in Soviet troop strength along the Sino-Soviet frontier and the withdrawal by Vietnam—Moscow's Southeast Asian ally—of its military contingent in Cambodia. For a discussion of these conditions, see Coit D. Blacker and Brian A. Davenport, *The Beijing Summit of 1989 and the Normalization of Sino-Soviet Relations*, Pew Case Studies in Diplomatic Training (Los Angeles: Center for International Studies, University of Southern California, 1991), 5–13.

and reducing arms shipments to Syria and general aid to Mozambique's Marxist government and Castro's Cuba.[17]

Despite its elegant simplicity, the systemic argument is simply not convincing.

A Better Explanation of the Soviet Withdrawal

The Soviets did not withdraw from Afghanistan because of their relations with the West but because they simply were not able to benefit from the advantages they hoped to enjoy from occupying the country, thus making their losses for a strategically useless and costly occupation unjustifiable.

When the Soviets invaded Afghanistan in December 1979 they probably hoped to establish and consolidate a loyal regime in Kabul so they could achieve (or not lose because of what they perceived to be the Afghan strongman Hafizullah Amin's desire for rapprochement with the West) several strategic advantages.[18] These goals might have included getting closer to warm water ports and within striking distance of the Persian Gulf, to encircle China and Iran, and to prevent a potentially hostile Afghanistan from allying with the United States or China in a bid to completely encircle the USSR.[19] It is impossible to know for sure the exact intentions of the four key Politburo leaders who made the decision and what "losing Afghanistan" really meant to them, because precious little is known about their secretive deliberations on

---

17. Katz 1989, chaps. 4 and 5.

18. The most comprehensive analysis of the reasons behind the Soviet invasion is provided by Garthoff (1994, 977–1075). Many other works discuss Soviet motives for the invasion of Afghanistan: see, for example, Collins (1986, chaps. 7 and 8), Saikal and Maley (1989, chap. 5), and Klass (1990, chap. 7). See Roy (1991, 13) on how the way Soviet troops were deployed in Afghanistan reflected the desire to "glean geo-strategic benefits from the invasion." The Soviets entered Afghanistan with antitank and antiaircraft weaponry as well as nuclear-biological-chemical detoxification units, all of which were unnecessary and useless to suppress the resistance. They also fortified and expanded the Shindand air base in southwest Afghanistan, not a necessarily logical location to place anti-insurgency assets. The base, however, placed Soviet bombers within close range of the Persian Gulf. Cordovez and Harrison (1995, 49) argue that "the Soviet invasion was clearly not the first step in the expansionist master plan of a united leadership. Rather, it was the reckless last act of a narrow Stalinist in-group that was starting to lose its grip even in 1979." They also argue in chapter 1 that Soviet leaders decided on the invasion after being successfully manipulated by Amin rivals, notably Babrak Karmal, and fearing that Amin would "do a Sadat" (meaning a turn to the West).

19. Many scholars contest one or more of these short and long-term goals so I mention all possible objectives. The decision to invade was made at most by five people (Brezhnev, Suslov, Andropov, Gromyko, and Ustinov), and it is therefore very hard to tell what their exact goals were. It is certain, however, that one of their goals was to strengthen Communist rule in Afghanistan and to remove Hafizullah Amin, the Communist leader they suspected of tilting toward the West, and to replace him

the issue during the six weeks preceding their December 12 decision to invade.[20] As resistance stiffened in Afghanistan, the Soviets might have added the goal of insulating their own Muslims from the rebellious Afghan influence.[21] Achieving these strategic goals could have justified spending billions of dollars and losing a few thousand soldiers a year, as shown by the long Soviet stay preceding Gorbachev's turnabout. It made little sense, however, to continue squandering such resources without achieving the desired strategic advantages. Perhaps the best evidence that Gorbachev was thinking along these lines is that the two years after he came to power as general secretary of the Communist Party of the Soviet Union (CPSU) in March of 1985 were two of the bloodiest of the war—only surpassed by 1984 in terms of Soviet casualties, although not in terms of Afghan losses.[22] Gorbachev was reported to have given his generals one or two years to eradicate the Afghan resistance, with the understanding that he would seek a diplomatic solution that included a withdrawal if they failed.[23] Only when the failure of the Soviet generals became apparent did Gorbachev and the rest of the Politburo decide, on November 13, 1986, to negotiate the withdrawal of the Red Army from Afghanistan.[24]

The main reason why Afghanistan became strategically useless was the resilient resistance of the mujahideen. This resistance restricted the movement of the Red Army and its area of control within Afghanistan. Afghanistan could not effectively be used as a springboard toward Pakistani ports or the Persian/Arabian Gulf when the Red Army's convoys were constantly harassed and its airplanes downed when accessing strategic airfields. The mujahideen, who

---

with the pliant Babrak Karmal. The Soviets achieved this goal almost immediately after the invasion when they assassinated Amin. See, inter alia, "Abstract from the Minutes N 172 of the Meeting of the Political Bureau of the Central Committee of the Communist Party of the Soviet Union, October 31, 1979," 53–56 of *Journal of South Asian and Middle Eastern Studies* 17, no. 2 (1994), as well as the rest of this journal dedicated to the analysis and documentation of the Soviet decision to invade Afghanistan.

20. See Garthoff (1994, 1012–1031) for additional details.

21. See Klass (1990, chap. 11) for a discussion of the effects of Afghan resistance on Islamic revival in the Soviet republics.

22. Official Soviet sources state that their yearly casualties peaked in 1984 with 2,343 dead. Rates for subsequent years were 1,868 in 1985, 1,333 in 1986, 1,215 in 1987, 759 in 1988, and 53 in 1989. Many works chronicling military operations in Afghanistan also note the increase in Soviet military activity after the ascent of Gorbachev in 1985–86. New sources (Russian General Staff 2002) confirm what seasoned observers long suspected—that the Soviets reported only a fraction of their casualties, around half.

23. This episode is mentioned in several secondary sources, e.g., Rubin (1995a, 146) and Arnold (1993, 137–38).

24. Gorbachev's (1995, 138 and 171) description of the Soviet occupation of Afghanistan in his memoirs as "a hopeless military adventure" and a "damaging and costly war" implies that he was concerned with its costs and benefits. For a discussion of the date of the withdrawal, see Maley 2002, 130–33.

could conceivably greatly facilitate Pakistani, Iranian, or other counterattacks from their areas, were in control of much of the countryside. And a demoralized army that could not control Afghanistan was not able to embark on more substantial and demanding missions such as an invasion of Iran or Pakistan. The same restrictions apply to the strategic goals of encircling rival China and hostile Iran: a continuously harassed and demoralized army would not be an impressive one on any country's borders. As for preventing a hostile Afghanistan from allying with Moscow's enemies, it is likely that the Soviets realized by 1986 that the Afghan resistance parties were so unruly and decentralized that, even if Kabul fell to them, they were unlikely to become anyone's effective ally.

The Soviets provided the Najib regime in Kabul with up to four billion dollars a year after they withdrew.[25] It is something of a puzzle why, until its own collapse, the cash-strapped USSR continued to subsidize heavily a fragile regime with poor prospects for survival. The Soviets probably wanted to keep the Afghans busy as long as possible to prevent them from exporting their Islamic zeal to their own Muslim-majority republics. Substantial numbers of Turkmen, Uzbeks, and Tajiks (some estimate the number of their descendants at half a million in the 1990s) fled Soviet-occupied lands to Afghanistan in the wake of the "Basmachi" revolt.[26] As resistance commanders in the north of Afghanistan gained confidence, assistance from Pakistan's Inter Services Intelligence (ISI), and military expertise, they and the descendants of the "Basmachi" performed incursions into Soviet Tajikistan and Uzbekistan, such as the March 1987 bombing of the Soviet Tajik town of Pyandzh. Armed with weapons and Korans, the Afghans had substantial influence over their coreligionists across the border, as demonstrated by the immediate spread of Islamist activities after the Soviet collapse, particularly in Tajikistan.[27] The links that the all-Union Islamic Renaissance Party (created in the former Soviet Union in 1990) developed with Afghan mujahideen a couple of years after its creation

---

25. Patrick Tyler, "Soviets Said to Be 'Pouring' Arms, Equipment into Afghanistan," *Washington Post*, February 9, 1990, 21. Testimony by General H. Norman Schwarzkopf, the U.S. commander for the Rapid Deployment Force in the Middle East. Similar estimates are reported in most studies of the issue.

26. "Basmachi" is a derogatory term meaning "bandit" that the Russians used to call the Muslim rebels in territories they conquered in the first forty years of this century. Regrettably, this term became the standard one in reference to these groups. See Akcali (1998, 274) for the figure.

27. Afghan Tajik commanders supported the Islamists who temporarily seized power in Tajikistan, for example. Islamist parties have formed in all the newly independent ex-Soviet republics that border Afghanistan. Afghan influence even reached Chechnya, as manifest in the declarations of Dzhokhar Dudayev, the first overall leader of Chechen insurgents. See TASS, April 19, 1987, reporting about mujahideen incursions into Tajikistan and Uzbekistan. See also United States Information Agency, *Afghanistan Chronology*, April 8, 1987.

also attest to such influence.[28] A leading authority on Soviet Central Asia in the West described the effect of a then possible Soviet withdrawal from Afghanistan in the following way:

> The effect of a complete Soviet withdrawal on Muslim society in Central Asia would be colossal. . . . It would be demonstrated [in that event] that Soviet might was not invincible and that resistance is possible. What are the Afghans for Central Asia? It is a small, wild and poor country. So then, if the Afghans could inflict (such) a military and political defeat, then that makes anything possible. And everyone in Central Asia knows that. I think that in Soviet Russia they know it too.[29]

And indeed they did. Public declarations by a number of Soviet officials, including Gorbachev himself, indicated that they were worried about the spread of the Islamist creed to their Muslim-majority republics.[30] Soviet foreign minister Shevardnadze requested U.S. assistance in stemming the spread of "Islamic fundamentalism" when he conveyed to Secretary of State George Shultz the Soviet decision to withdraw on September 16, 1987, leaving Shultz with the belief that "he was clearly worried about the Islamic republics in the Soviet Union."[31] Lesser Soviet officials were given early retirement because they implied that the Islamic resurgence would have spread to the Soviet Union if it weren't for intervention, and KGB officials publicly stated that events in Afghanistan were linked to CIA efforts to exploit Islam in Muslim Soviet republics.[32] Fiery statements by mujahideen leaders who declared their desire to free "the Muslim lands of Bukhara, Khiva and Khorezm" might well have fed this fear.[33] Their threats were reinforced

---

28. See Akcali (1998) for a study of the links between the IRP and the Afghan mujahideen.

29. The quote is by Alexander Bennigsen, Radio Liberty Research, RS 58/88, July 5, 1988, 6.

30. Bennigsen (Klass 1990, chap. 2) chronicles such declarations and indications of Islamic resurgence in Soviet republics after the start of the Afghan invasion.

31. Shultz 1993, 987.

32. Garthoff (1994, 1032) and Bradsher (1985, 157).

33. Borovik (1990, 10) quotes Hekmatyar as saying, "If the mujahideen persistently continue to fight, the day will soon come when the occupied lands of Soviet Central Asia will be liberated." Such statements were frequent. See also Akcali (1998, 276) for more such statements by Hekmatyar and Berhanuddin Rabbani. See, inter alia, the Rogers (1992) chronology for many instances of such declarations. See Cordesman and Wagner (1990, 70–71) for examples of mujahideen attacks on USSR territory. See Yousaf (1992, chap. 12) for a thorough account of ISI-supported operations in Soviet Central Asia. He interestingly reports that demand for Korans was stronger than for ethnically based motivational propaganda prepared by the CIA. Some sources mention that the CIA was motivating Hekmatyar's operations across Soviet borders (Rubin 1995b, 81).

by statements from Pakistani president Zia ul-Haq, the leading supporter of the Afghan jihad, who told the seasoned journalist Selig Harrison that "we took risks as a frontline state, and we won't permit it to be like it was before, with Indian and Soviet influence there and claims on our territory. It will be a real Islamic state, part of a pan-Islamic revival that will one day win over the Muslims in the Soviet Union, you will see."[34] Zia ul-Haq was not a man who limited himself to empty threats, as Brigadier Mohammed Yousaf of the ISI informs us in his revealing account of ISI-supported mujahideen actions across the Amu Daria River:

> The cross-border strikes were at their peak during 1986. Scores of attacks were made across the Amu from Jozjan and Badaksan Provinces. Sometimes Soviet citizens joined in these operations, or came back into Afghanistan to join the mujahideen. . . . In at least one instance some Soviet soldiers deserted to us. That we were hitting a sore spot was confirmed by the ferocity of the Soviets' reaction. Virtually every incursion provoked massive aerial bombing and gunship attacks on all villages south of the river in the vicinity of our strike.[35]

The earlier Soviet withdrawal of their Central Asian troops and their replacement with Slavic ones indicates that they were concerned with the potential for fraternization across the border.[36] Add to that the Soviet leaders' full awareness of the explosive growth of Central Asian populations—the Uzbek and Tajik populations trebled between 1959 and 1989 while that of the USSR as a whole increased by just 36.8 percent—and their fears become understandable. Those fears seemed well founded during the 1992–93 period when both Massoud and Hekmatyar trained and armed thousands of Islamist Tajiks and sent them back across the Amu Daria while providing shelter for tens of thousands of Tajik refugees.[37]

The Soviets only stopped their considerable military and economic assistance to the Najib regime when the Soviet Union itself was dismantled. The Najib regime collapsed soon afterward. This four billion dollars in yearly Soviet aid to the Najib government only ceased when the newly independent

34. Cordovez and Harrison 1995, 92. Quoted on June 29, 1988, in Islamabad.

35. Yousaf 1992, 200. The Pakistani-sponsored attacks were halted in May 1987 after the Soviets transmitted thinly veiled threats to the Pakistani Foreign Ministry (Yousaf 1992, 205).

36. Central Asian troops were mostly withdrawn in early 1980 after widespread refusal to fight, fraternization, trafficking in Korans, and other acts of sabotage of Soviet military efforts. Some Central Asian soldiers even defected to the mujahideen. See Akcali (1998, 275) for one brief account.

37. See Akcali (1998, 278–82) for a more detailed account of Afghan military support to Tajik Islamists.

Central Asian republics became a more logical buffer zone at Russia's borders, which might indicate that the Soviet Union had allocated those funds to prevent an upsurge within its own borders. The official independence of the southern Muslim-majority republics of the USSR made the allocation of precious money to shield them from Islamic influence an anachronism. The Soviets probably calculated that the best way to inhibit the growth of Afghan Islamic influence on their own Muslim populations was to keep the Afghans busy fighting a pro-Moscow government of their own, regardless of financial cost, instead of perpetuating the pathetic show of Red Army impotence. Today, the previous Central Asian republics are themselves Russia's buffer, with Russian troops guarding Tajikistan's borders and proxy or allied regimes keeping Islamist movements in check.

The Soviet withdrawal from Afghanistan was not necessarily part of a broader Soviet policy to disengage from third world conflicts. Although the Soviets reduced their support to some Marxist regimes, they maintained previous levels of support for regimes whose survival was strategically important, such as Nicaragua, India, and South Yemen.[38] Both Soviet arms transfers ($13.86 billion in 1985 to $19.3 billion in 1988) and economic aid ($3.1 billion to $7.3 billion extended, $1.3 to $1.6 billion drawn) to client states increased substantially in the four years that followed Gorbachev's ascension to the chairmanship.[39] The increases were markedly steeper for strategically important allies such as India, to whom the USSR extended almost four times more aid in 1988 than in 1987 ($4 versus $1.1 billion), and Nicaragua, to whom it allocated a dramatic sixty-fold increase ($1.25 versus $.02 billion).[40] Moscow's aid to Cuba ($4–$5 billion per year) and Vietnam ($2 billion) were also maintained after the Soviet withdrawal from Afghanistan, at least until the end of 1990. Afghanistan was strategically more important to the USSR than any of those states, and the Soviet withdrawal was a major foreign-policy setback.[41] The best indication that Afghanistan remained until the bitter end a critical concern for Soviet foreign policy is that the Kabul regime received 70 percent of all Soviet foreign aid in 1991, a much larger portion than the 10 percent it received in 1983–84, at a time when Moscow became incapable of fully meeting its aid commitments elsewhere.[42] This aid ran at

38. Katz 1989, 42–57.

39. From the *Handbook of Economic Statistics: A Reference Aid* (Washington, D.C.: CIA, 1989), 174.

40. Ibid., 175.

41. See Borer (1993) for one author's thorough analysis of the harsh repercussions of the Soviet withdrawal on Soviet influence.

42. Arnold 1993, 186.

a rate of $300–$400 million a month until the Soviets simply could not provide it anymore.[43] The Soviets financially and militarily disengaged last from countries of utmost importance to them. Because they withdrew their forces from Afghanistan before they substantially reduced aid to Nicaragua, Ethiopia, and South Yemen, it is reasonable to think that the military withdrawal is better explained by elements peculiar to the Afghan conflict and not to Soviet grand strategy.

The critic might wonder why the Soviets, if Afghanistan was so important to them, did not increase the number of their troops to squash the resistance. Despite Gorbachev's threats to raise the number of Soviet troops in Afghanistan up to half a million, the Soviets could not raise the number beyond 120,000. A dramatic increase was useless because the narrow Afghan infrastructure simply could not accommodate such reinforcements.[44] A large increase of Soviet troops would have been counterproductive, paralyzing their mobility and fighting efficiency. In addition, Moscow might have wanted to avert an increase of aid to the mujahideen by alarmed Western and Muslim countries.[45] To achieve better results, the Soviets could only improve the quality of their troops, and by 1986 they had already committed some of their best soldiers and aircraft to Afghanistan but still failed to subdue the resistance.[46] The Soviet military seemed resigned to its failure by 1988. Red Army generals did not oppose the withdrawal from Afghanistan, and some of them even seemed quite willing to be relieved of the mission to repress the Afghan resistance, despite the blow that the withdrawal was expected to give to the prestige of the Soviet military.[47]

The Geneva Accords did not lead to the Soviet withdrawal; they simply provided a face-saving timetable for a withdrawal made necessary by Soviet

43. In way of illustration, the *Washington Post*, September 2, 1989, p. 2, quotes a senior U.S. official who reports that between March and July 1989 alone the Soviets shipped to Kabul 550 SCUD missiles, 160 T-55 and T-62 tanks, 615 armored personnel carriers, and 1,600 five-ton trucks.

44. See Arnold (1993, 137) and McMichael (1991, 23) on the limitations imposed by geography and infrastructure in Afghanistan. Although mountainous terrain seemed to affect the outcome in this conflict, the statistical study in chapter 10 reveals that its impact cannot be generalized.

45. Hauner 1991, 111. Hauner also mentions Moscow's desire not to tarnish its image, but this is an unlikely argument considering the wide publicity already given to Soviet atrocities in Afghanistan.

46. Up to 20 percent of Soviet forces in Afghanistan were elite troops, a very high proportion (Cordesman and Wagner 1990, 137.) Yousaf (1992, 48) believes that the Soviets did not increase the number of their troops for political reasons.

47. Katz 1989, 26–28. McMichael (1991, 66–67) tells us that the mobile troops the Soviets used consisted of the elite Spetsnaz, highly trained airborne troops, and slightly less elite air-assault troops. The Soviets had little better to offer.

inability to defeat the mujahideen.[48] Although it is true that the Geneva Accords between the Afghan and Pakistani governments followed a U.S.-Soviet agreement over a formula for withdrawal, it should be remembered that this agreement resulted directly from Moscow's concessions. If the Soviets did not want to withdraw, the Afghan and Pakistani negotiators would simply have continued to snub each other in Swiss hotels the way they did for the six years that preceded the shift in Soviet policy. The Geneva Accords were flawed in the sense that the parties leading the fight against the Soviets, the mujahideen, were not signatories and immediately rejected the Accords.[49]

The Soviets, finally acknowledging the other significant party to the conflict, ultimately commenced direct talks with the Afghan mujahideen well after signing the Geneva Accords. In early December 1988, Yuli M. Vorontsov, the Soviet deputy foreign minister and ambassador to Kabul, met in Taif, Saudi Arabia, with a mujahideen delegation headed by professor Burhanuddin Rabbani.[50] If the Soviet withdrawal from Afghanistan had been the consequence of the evolution of Soviet relations with the United States then the Soviets would not have had to engage in negotiations beyond those concluded in Geneva. The Soviets needed to meet with their archenemy because the Afghan resistance could not be compelled to behave in accordance with the Geneva Accords that were signed by Pakistan and the United States on its behalf.[51] The Soviets had something to fear from the actions of the Afghan resistance for them to accept the humiliation of sitting across the table from those they all too often tried to portray as primitive bandits: the infiltration of their Islamic republics by Afghan Tajiks, Turkmen, and Uzbeks armed with weapons, Korans, and the confidence of the victor. They believed they could preempt such actions with the creation of a conciliatory coalition government in Kabul over which they could maintain some influence. It is not likely that the negotiations

48. Saikal and Maley (1989, chap. 2) also argue that the Geneva Accords were but a smokescreen for an inevitable Soviet withdrawal. Khan (1993) provides a convincing argument based on the negotiation process that the Geneva Accords offered Gorbachev a face-saving opportunity to free himself from the Afghan quagmire.

49. Incidentally, Iran also wasn't represented in the negotiations and declared its opposition to them.

50. Saikal and Maley (1989, 2), Halbach (1990, 288), and Rogers (1992, 198–200). See Duncan and Ekedahl (1990, 102) for reports by the Tehran news service IRNA of earlier attempts by the Soviets to contact the resistance.

51. See Yousaf (1992, 210–11) on how the relationship between mujahideen leaders and the Pakistani Foreign Ministry was strained because of lack of consultation on the Geneva negotiations and the leaders' desire to negotiate directly with the Soviets.

aimed at attenuating resistance attacks on retreating Soviet forces because the bulk of those forces had already left Afghanistan by then. It is also unlikely that the negotiations centered on the release of Soviet prisoners, the official reason behind the talks, because the number of such prisoners was not large enough to motivate the embarrassing Soviet acknowledgment of the mujahideen, and such an issue is generally not negotiated at this level of representation.[52] The negotiations failed: the Soviets had very little leverage because of their reduced military presence and the near-universal perception that the Najib regime would not long outlive the departure of the Red Army.

Another indication that the Geneva Accords were marginal to what was being decided by the interaction between the Soviets and the Afghan resistance was the gradual Soviet retreat from every demand or condition they set for their withdrawal, before and after the ratification of the Geneva Accords. The Soviets had started with the following list of demands to be met prior to their withdrawal: (1) a governing coalition dominated by the Communist government should be formed in Kabul; (2) Washington and Islamabad should stop their aid to the mujahideen; and (3) the Soviets should be guaranteed safe passage on their way out of Afghanistan. The Geneva Accords said nothing about the first issue, were murky and nonbinding on the second one, and could not possibly deal with the third one. The Soviets also steadily reduced the time frame for withdrawal from three years to the ten months the United States and Pakistan wanted, agreed to give a specific date to begin the withdrawal, and accepted to withdraw a larger portion of their troops at an early stage. The Afghan resistance groups, who immediately rejected the Accords, did not cease attacking Soviet troops until the very last days of the occupation, in spite of reported Pakistani and U.S. pressure.[53] Although the Pakistanis were willing to make concessions during the negotiations, the Afghan parties made none and did not feel bound by the agreement.[54] Furthermore, as already mentioned, the Soviets had to make the concession of directly negotiating with the resistance parties even after they had committed to withdraw. The mujahideen groups also rejected all efforts to share power with either the Communists or, at least in the case of the four Islamist parties, the previous king of Afghanistan, Zahir Shah. When

52. Rogers 1992, 197–98.

53. See Borovik (1990, 256) on Massoud's attacks on the withdrawing Soviets in late January 1989. Also, Rogers 1992, 33–34 and 47–48.

54. For a detailed account of the evolution of the negotiations in Geneva, see Khan (1993). See also Rogers 1992; Rais 1994; and Halbach 1990.

the Soviets threatened to suspend their withdrawal because of uninterrupted resistance attacks on their withdrawing troops, their threats were met with derision by the resistance and attacks continued unabated despite Pakistani and U.S. pressure on Afghan leaders.[55] Soviet capitulation during the negotiation process and continuing withdrawal in spite of the persistent disregard for the clauses of the Geneva Accords by the mujahideen strongly imply that the Accords and the negotiation process that led to them were irrelevant to the decision to withdraw.[56]

The Afghan resistance's resilience allowed it to take advantage of opportunities arising from the evolution of relations among the superpowers and other states, and from the deterioration of the Soviet economy. After successfully resisting Soviet control for seven years, the Afghans benefited from mounting anticommunist feelings in the U.S. Congress and received the infamous Stinger antiaircraft missiles that helped them reduce the effects of Soviet air superiority for the following three years.[57] The defeats of Islamists in Syria and Egypt, as well as the growth of Islamist activism in many countries during the 1980s, facilitated the infusion of considerable resources and manpower to assist the Afghans who had proven that they could effectively resist an atheistic superpower. Had the mujahideen failed to stand their ground, the Afghans would probably have been yet another completely subjugated people by the time support became available. It is indeed not a coincidence that Gorbachev argued at a Politburo meeting on November 13, 1986, that "we have been at war in Afghanistan six years already. If we don't change our approach we will be there another 20–30 years. . . . We need to wrap up this process in the near future."[58]

The Soviets withdrew from Afghanistan for a simple and straightforward reason: they were faced with a steadfast resistance that benefited from opportunities that emerged on the international scene during the protracted

55. Halbach 1990, 287.

56. In addition, several individuals who were close to Soviet decision making concerning the withdrawal have stated that the decision to withdraw had no connection to the Geneva Accord process (Mendelson 1998, 116.)

57. The Stingers did have a negative effect on Soviet morale, but the evidence as to their effectiveness is inconclusive. Some have argued that they forced Soviet pilots to fly high enough to be inaccurate or low enough to become accident-prone, but others have pointed out that Soviet tactics had already changed before their introduction. Many resistance commanders also reported that their Stingers were not very effective. See Mendelson (1998, 26 and 97–100) for a good discussion of the Stingers' role.

58. "Zasedanie Politburo Tsk KPSS (Session of the Politburo), Fond 89, Perechen' 11, document 56, November 13, 1986," 25; as reported in Mendelson 1998, 112. Also reported in Kakar 1995, 75.

conflict and prevented them from enjoying the strategic benefits they hoped to gain from occupying the country. The Geneva Accords were no more than a face-saving formality that was made necessary by the Soviet failure to subdue the Afghan resistance. Gorbachev did not sacrifice Afghanistan for the sake of improving relations with the United States, China, or the Muslim world; he simply tried to convince the world that he did.

CHAPTER 6

Resilience through Division, 1979–1989

When the organization becomes politically ordered, God is pleased. . . . This is indestructible.

—Ideological course lecture for mujahideen, Jamiat-i Islami, February 2, 1987, reported in "Education and Revolutionary Political Mobilization," by Farshad Rastegar

How did the Afghan resistance manage to be so resilient that it made the Soviet occupation of the country too costly and bereft of strategic advantages to maintain? The structure of the resistance locked it up in a confrontational strategy, and the patronage ties and the multiplicity of mujahideen parties also bestowed critical operational advantages under adversity and absent a safe haven. The multiplicity of locally specialized field commanders made it more difficult for the Soviets to co-opt them, and it allowed the mujahideen to effectively mobilize much of the rural population, to maintain local internal cohesion and discipline, to be less vulnerable to decapitation, and to coordinate well enough for defensive purposes through regional councils.

Conversely, the Soviets and their client regime failed to centralize their institutions well enough to efficiently subdue the resistance. Regime factions often sabotaged one another's operations, and the Soviet presence was so poorly coordinated that Soviet forces sometimes counterproductively attacked field commanders who were almost ready to defect from mujahideen ranks. The decision-making process in Moscow, however, had a cyclical tendency to become increasingly centralized as each general secretary of the Communist Party of the Soviet Union consolidated power. Gorbachev, who was to become the only general secretary after Brezhnev to live long enough to consolidate power, gradually appointed his supporters to all key positions and gave the army brass up to two years to end resistance in Afghanistan. Their failure showed that the Soviet occupation would remain costly and facilitated Gorbachev's decision to withdraw, a decision he was by then able to impose from above.

I begin by describing the organizational structure of the different contenders and then trace the processes that allowed the patronage-based mujahideen organizations to survive beyond their enemy's ability to maintain the occupation in spite of the lack of a safe haven within the contested territory and overwhelming Soviet strength.

The Organization of Rivals until the Soviet Withdrawal (1978–1989)

The decision-making process in the Soviet Union had a cyclical tendency to become increasingly centralized as each general secretary of the CPSU consolidated power. In December 1979, when the decision to invade Afghanistan was made, power over decision making on foreign policy was concentrated in the hands of four or five individuals. They made the decision while disregarding the advice of their military advisers, had it rubber-stamped by fellow members of the CPSU Politburo, and imposed it on its Central Committee, which submissively and unanimously approved it. The four decision makers were the almost-senile general secretary of the CPSU, Leonid Brezhnev; the dominant minister of defense, Dmitriy Ustinov; the minister of foreign affairs and yes-man, Andrei Gromyko; and the director of the KGB, Yuri Andropov.[1] They did not seek advice from regional specialists and brushed aside objections from the highest levels of the General Staff and the KGB, as well as experts from the International Department of the CPSU's Central Committee. Once they made the decision, they replaced all military and civilian Soviet officials and advisers in Afghanistan who did not support the invasion with more pliant subordinates to reduce the probability of the formation of interest groups that would hinder the operation.[2]

---

1. See, inter alia, Mendelson (1998, chap. 3); the dedicated issue of the *Journal of South Asian and Middle Eastern Studies* 17, no. 2 (1994); and Ekedahl and Goodman (1997, 184–94) for accounts of how the decision to intervene was made. Some (Cordovez and Harrison 1995, 49) argue that a fifth contributor to the decision-making process was Mikhail Suslov, the hard-line ideologue with influence over Brezhnev and his circle.

2. See Garthoff (1994, 1012–13) and Cordovez and Harrison (1995, 42) for more on personnel replacement.

Control over Soviet forces was also centralized under the CPSU and the Defense Council, which limited the Red Army's mobility and the decision-making ability of its units.[3] But, incredibly enough, and according to the well-informed Soviet journalist Artyom Borovik (1990, 247–48), it seems that the USSR failed to centralize its overall command in Kabul:

> One of our problems in Afghanistan, it seemed to me, was that the Soviet Union never had a central office in charge of the various delegations of its superministries: the KGB, MID [Ministry of Foreign Affairs], MVD [Ministry of Internal Affairs], and Ministry of Defense. The chiefs of these groups acted autonomously, often sending contradictory information to Moscow and often receiving conflicting orders in return. The four offices should have been consolidated under the leadership of the Soviet ambassador. But there were so many different Soviet ambassadors that none of them had enough time to become thoroughly familiar with the state of affairs in Kabul.

Yuri Andropov's short-lived chairmanship (November 1982–February 1984) and weak health did not allow him to centralize power well enough to implement a Soviet withdrawal from Afghanistan, though evidence suggests that he desired such a withdrawal because he believed that a military solution to the war was not possible.[4] Andropov, however, began the necessary consolidation and centralization process by giving his protégé, Mikhail Gorbachev, the job of changing personnel within the Central Committee to increase the number of like-minded reformist regional party secretaries.[5] Andropov's successor, Konstantin Chernenko, supported the continuation of the Soviet presence in Afghanistan but could not reverse during his fleeting chairmanship (February 1984–March 1985) the personnel changes that Gorbachev, still the senior personnel secretary of the party, implemented.

---

3. See Hemsley (1982, 2, 26, and 30) on the extreme centralization of Soviet forces. See also Roy (1991, 51–52) for how this centralization affected operations in Afghanistan.

4. See Kornienko (1994, 9) and Mendelson (1998, 73–76) for more details on Andropov and Afghanistan. Mendelson (1993b, 341) also reports "in 1983 . . . according to sources in Moscow, a high-level policy review concluded that the situation in Afghanistan could not be solved by military means." Cordesman and Wagner (1990, 47) report that Andropov told President Zia of Pakistan that the USSR wanted to leave Afghanistan. Cordovez and Harrison (1995, chaps. 4 and 5) provide more details on Andropov's desire to withdraw. The *Times* (Richard Owen, "The Afghan Cloud on Andropov's Horizon," *Times* [London], March 3, 1983, p. 4) noted that Andropov orchestrated "a spate of articles . . . publicly proclaiming what before was only whispered: that 'our boys' in Afghanistan are being slaughtered by rebels, and that the rebel forces are sufficiently powerful and skilled in mountain warfare to pin down both Soviet troops and armor" to create a sense of urgency about the need to deal with the problem.

5. See Gustafson and Mann (1986) on personnel changes.

Gorbachev, who succeeded Chernenko, probably wanted to withdraw Soviet troops as early as possible after he assumed the chairmanship but was willing to give the military solution a chance to make the difficult decision moot. He gave his generals one or two years (sources vary on the exact length) to subdue the Afghan resistance and consolidate the Afghan regime and went about centralizing the CPSU and the state's institutions under his control.[6] By the time a new Central Committee stacked with his supporters was elected at the 27th Party Congress in March 1986, Gorbachev, who also replaced much of the old guard in the Politburo with individuals close to himself, felt confident enough to become bolder in his initiatives. It was during this Congress that he made the famous "bleeding wound" speech. He also placed his supporters in the two institutions that strongly affected Soviet foreign policy: the International Department of the Central Committee (CCID) and the foreign ministry (MID) that was led by Eduard Shevardnadze from July 1985. Gorbachev already enjoyed the support of the KGB, his mentor's base of support, but his purge of hawkish military leaders and the minister of defense, and their replacement by more amenable individuals, had to wait for the convenient excuse provided by the daring landing of Mathias Rust's small Cessna aircraft in Red Square in May 1987.[7] He also reduced the influence of both institutions on decision making by diluting their role and representation in the Politburo. Centralization by the end of 1986 was such, Mendelson (1998, 357) tells us, that the decision to withdraw "seems in the end . . . to have been taken by a small group of men: Gorbachev, [head of the CCID Alexander] Yakovlev, and Shevardnadze."[8] This decision was likely made in November 1986, though some argue that it might have been made as early as October 1985 or as late as May 1987.[9]

The Kabul Regime

The People's Democratic Party of Afghanistan (PDPA)—renamed Watan (nation) in its last few years—consisted of two bitterly competitive rival factions when it gained power through a military coup d'état in April of 1978: the

6. See Sakwa (1991, chap. 8) for more details on how Gorbachev centralized decision making on foreign policy after he became chairman. See also Mendelson (1998, chap. 5) and Cordovez and Harrison (1995, 248).

7. Dmitri Yazov replaced Sergei Sokolov, who was defense minister after Ustinov's death in late 1984.

8. Sakwa (1991, 331–32) writes that "even after Shevardnadze had grown in the job, foreign policy was very much managed as a team but dominated by Gorbachev personally."

9. Maley 2002, 130–33.

mostly Dari-speaking Parshamis and the Pushtu-speaking Khalqis.[10] The two factions reunited in 1977 under Soviet pressure after ten years of being distinct rival organizations.[11] They continued to form important networks and interest groups within the structurally highly centralized PDPA until its demise in 1992, and their rivalry often resulted in purges, assassinations, and large-scale armed battles. The Khalqi Hafizullah Amin, the first effective PDPA ruler, centralized power in his own hands and eliminated both Parshami and Khalqi rivals.[12] The Soviet invaders, who probably saved the PDPA from imminent collapse, made Parsham dominant within all party institutions with their appointment of Babrak Karmal at the top post to replace Amin (whom they assassinated) and of Najib at the head of the secret services (KhAD). The Khalqis were given the leadership of the Ministry of the Interior and its powerful military-like police force (the Sarandoy), which became their enduring stronghold.[13] KhAD and the Sarandoy often feuded in bloody clashes. Khalqi officers dominated the army's officer corps, but the minister of defense and chief of staff were most often Parshamis during Karmal's era, except for parts of 1984 and 1985. High-level Soviet efforts to centralize the PDPA failed to reduce the formation of exclusionary interest groups, and some analysts even reported that Soviet officials and advisers in Afghanistan often espoused the factionalism of those they were supposed to turn into effective administrators or military officers.

The Soviets tried to model Democratic Republic of Afghanistan (DRA) institutions after their own, and Soviet officers and "advisers" reporting to Moscow made and implemented all important decisions, from writing Karmal's speeches to interrogating political prisoners.[14] Soviet advisers were reported to have outnumbered PDPA members at the beginning of the invasion and may have numbered more than ten thousand by 1984. They of-

10. Dari is the variant of Farsi that is the lingua franca of Afghanistan while Pushtu is the language of the majority Pushtun tribes. Most Parshamis were members of minority groups or urbanized Dari-speaking Pushtun, while Khalqis were Pushtun with stronger tribal ties. Parsham means "the flag" while Khalq means "the masses."

11. For a more detailed history of the PDPA, see, inter alia, Arnold (1983); Rubin (1995a); and Yunas (1998) for raw data on the PDPA.

12. See Giustozzi (2000, 3–6) for more information on the extent of Amin's purge of Parshamis who claimed to have lost two thousand of their own by the end of 1979. He also reports that by the time the Soviets invaded, the PDPA had lost half its members to internal purges, death, or defection.

13. See Kakar (1995) for more details on Khalqi concentration in the Ministry of Internal Affairs. He reports that most of the ministry's members were more precisely Paktia Pushtuns.

14. See Rubin (1995a, chap. 6) and Kakar (1995, chapter 3) for analyses of Soviet penetration of Afghan state institutions.

ten overruled Karmal himself when they disagreed with his decisions.[15] They even created more than fifteen "associations" that paralleled Soviet ones, such as the Democratic Youth Organization of Afghanistan modeled on the Soviet Komsomol, to better control the portion of the population within their reach.[16] Those associations or subfronts made up the National Fatherland Front (NFF), which claimed a membership of 700,000 but probably did not exceed 55,000 in 1984.[17] The NFF peaked at a paltry 116,000 members, then went into a steady decline, and was recognized to be a failure even by Najib himself in 1987.[18] The Soviet penetration of Afghan state institutions was so thorough that we could consider the Soviet and PDPA/DRA organizations to be one and the same for analytical purposes throughout much of the Soviet occupation, at least until 1987 when the Najib regime made serious efforts to make its institutions more capable of functioning independently. Soviet control of the DRA armed forces was also complete, as Giustozzi's synthesis of Soviet sources tells us:

> Soviet advisers were present down to battalion level and they were involved directly in the fighting. . . . Even Soviet sources sometimes accused them of taking the place of their Afghan colleagues, trying mechanically to apply forms and methods learnt in the USSR. In other words, more than giving advice they were giving orders. . . . Separate chains of command were retained, but in fact the tactical and operational levels were controlled by a single Soviet command structure.[19]

In addition to army, KhAD, and Sarandoy forces, the Kabul regime mobilized sections of the capital's population and most PDPA members in a generally ineffectual three-tiered urban militia force that was meant to both control the local population and provide a last-ditch defense in case the city's security belts collapsed.[20] The most motivated of the three urban militias were the Sepayan-i Enqelab (Soldiers of the Revolution) that recruited among dedicated party and youth organization members, gave them military training, and sent them to "pacify" territories after Soviet/PDPA offensives. The second tier was the Hauza-i Amniyati (District Security) that provided static and mobile protection for government facilities. Their function was

15. See Kakar (1995, 155) for examples.

16. See Yunas (1998) for a comprehensive listing of those "associations."

17. See Arnold (1985b, 48–49) and Giustozzi (2000, 143) for more details on the NFF.

18. Giustozzi 2000, 145–46.

19. Ibid., 66.

20. See Dorronsoro and Lobato (1989) for more details on the Kabul regime's militias.

redundant to that of the Khalqi Sarandoy, which the Parshami leaders couldn't completely trust with this function until 1985.[21] The third tier of the urban militia was the Geru-i Defa-i Khodi (Self-defense Groups) that provided local security and protection for lesser facilities and provided a mechanism to involve non-PDPA members.

The regime's rural militias were much more significant than its urban ones. They were recruited on a nonideological basis and played an increasingly important role after the Soviet withdrawal. Those militias acted as clients of the PDPA regime and were formed in one of two ways: the leader of a *qawm* (cohesive social unit) strikes a deal and brings with him his followers, or a political entrepreneur such as the Uzbek Abdul Rashid Dostum is given the resources and assisted in increasing his power base at the expenses of mujahideen parties.[22] Many rural militias were formed in the birthplaces of important PDPA leaders like Nur Mohammad Taraki's village, Sourkhaly, in Ghazni Province.[23] The rural militias were officially put under the umbrella of the ostensibly apolitical NFF to make it easier for qawm leaders to join, but it was well known that the NFF was under direct PDPA control. To increase the involvement and size of those militias was a central Soviet and PDPA strategy.

The Soviets replaced the ineffectual Karmal with Najib (whom they perceived to have a better chance of surviving absent Moscow's micromanagement and who was better disposed to accept Soviet disengagement) in May 1986.[24] Their imminent withdrawal but uninterrupted generous financial and military aid led Najib to expand state patronage to complement his weak and factionalism-ridden centralized state apparatus. The regime offered money and weapons to tribal and ethnic groups it dubbed as "militias" in return for loyalty.[25] The most significant militia groups that the regime managed to attract as clients were Abdul Rashid Dostum's Jawzjani Uzbek militia and Sayyid Mansur Nadiri's Ismaili Hazara group. Najib's dependence on the Moscow-financed patronage system became even more pronounced when Khalqi officers proved unreliable during the failed March 1990 coup d'état led by Khalqi defense minister Shahnawaz Tanai. Najib continued to lavish on those militias whose loyalty was essential to his survival weapons and

21. Ibid., 98.

22. Among Afghans, the word *qawm* designates a solidarity group that is based on ethnic, religious, or even professional ties. The tribal system produces only a particular type of qawm.

23. Giustozzi 2000, 52.

24. See Cordovez and Harrison (1995, chap. 8) for additional details.

25. The PDPA regime began patronizing tribal groups as early as 1982, but Najib definitely increased the pace. See Yunas (1998, 673–87) for the translation of relevant official decrees.

currency to the point where they became major contenders for power by the time his regime collapsed with the cessation of Soviet aid.

The Resistance

Islamist Afghan resistance groups started forming in the mid-1970s as a counterweight and direct reaction to the Marxist groups that were co-opted by Mohammed Daoud, a member of the royal family who overthrew the Afghan monarchy and proclaimed himself president in 1973.[26] When the Marxist PDPA ultimately turned against Daoud during what came to be known as the Saur "revolution" in April of 1978, those among the Islamist and traditional Afghan leaders and activists who survived assassination and capture fled to the countryside or to Pakistan. Efforts by the newly established Communist government to impose agrarian reforms in the countryside almost immediately led to impromptu local revolts on the village level in different parts of Afghanistan. Since many of the Islamic and traditional figures that fled the capital were either respected for their religious credentials and charisma or renowned for their descent from revered families, they became figureheads for a revolt that they could not necessarily direct or control.

By the time the Soviets invaded Afghanistan in December 1979, embryonic party apparatuses that dealt with matters of public relations, refugee welfare, and logistical support surrounded the major Peshawar-based resistance figures. The party apparatuses became instrumental to the allocation of weapons and other commodities to the otherwise independent mujahideen groups they sponsored inside Afghanistan as the flow of weapons through Peshawar increased. Most mujahideen groups inside Afghanistan (except for the Shia, some leftists, and few other exceptions) became affiliated with seven parties because the Pakistanis decided to only channel weapons and funds through those Peshawar-based organizations.[27] The rural mujahideen were organized into numerous groups led by field commanders and largely cemented by family, clan, tribal, or ethnic ties. Except for the occasional defection of a field commander from one party to another or to the government, the composition and structure of Afghan parties remained largely unchanged from 1980 until the Soviet withdrawal in February 1989. There were seven substantial Sunni parties (four led by Islamists and three by traditionalists) in addition to a number of Shiite parties in the central region of Hazarajat. Table 6.1 lists the

---

26. For more detailed accounts on the organization and history of Afghan parties, see, inter alia, Brigot and Roy (1985), Roy (1990), Kakar (1995, chaps. 4 and 5), and Rubin (1995a).

27. See Yousaf (1991, 66) on how General Akhtar Abdur Rahman of the ISI executed this policy.

most significant mujahideen organizations, and appendix B provides brief descriptions of Afghan resistance parties and biographies of key participants.

With the single exception of Hekmatyar's Hizb, Afghan resistance parties (called *tanzimat*, plural of *tanzim* or organization) were noncentralized and consisted mostly of three distinct components: the party leader, the bureaucracy, and the field commanders and their mujahideen.[28]

The party leader was a widely respected figure that derived charisma from religious scholarship (in the case of the Islamists) or lineage (the traditionalists).[29] The leader of a party was, in most instances, the only public figure visible to the outside world. His reputation, political skills, relation to Pakistani power brokers, and perceived integrity affected the amount of outside aid the party received. The party leader also influenced the composition of the party because many field commanders were drawn to (or driven away from) party leaders because of ethnic, sectarian, or ideological affinity. Party leaders negotiated in the name of the resistance and unsuccessfully attempted to develop a political system by dividing power among themselves under pressure from their sponsors. Despite the widespread support that these leaders enjoyed among Afghans during the jihad, their claim to power over matters of policy was increasingly challenged by field commanders in the later years of the conflict. Each leader had the final say over the allocation of resources among his field commanders, and all of them made full use of their monopoly over this type of decision, except perhaps for Burhanuddin Rabbani, who was said to make an effort to build a consensus within his party on major decisions.[30]

The Peshawar-based bureaucracies of the resistance parties were less developed than one would expect to find in such a long conflict. The centralized Hizb, and to a lesser degree the Jamiat and Ittihad, had bureaucracies with specialized branches but the traditional parties simply featured vestigial "committees" named after generic ministerial portfolios.[31] Although the bureaucracies

28. The names of some of the parties—Ittihad (unity) or Jamiat (society)—refer to a diffuse type of structure, while the term *hizb* (party) implies a more unified structure. Terms adequately reflected reality.

29. Even the followers of "Engineer" Hekmatyar liked to point out that he wrote some forty booklets on religious matters. This number might have been an exaggeration. Some of the traditionalist leaders lost popularity when it became known that they lived a life of luxury while their commanders suffered at the front.

30. Rastegar 1991, 153. Hekmatyar's Hizb held elections during which those with the longest history of membership selected the leader and key officials from among themselves. There is little doubt though that Hekmatyar centralized power in his own hands despite those elections.

31. The Hizb, for example, ran a sprawling network of five hundred schools that taught 43,500 students in 1986, according to its own sources.

Table 6.1. Significant mujahideen parties during the Soviet occupation

ORGANIZATION	LEADER	STRUCTURE	EXTERNAL SUPPORT	MAJOR COMMANDERS	ETHNIC COMPOSITION	IDEOLOGICAL ORIENTATION
Hizb-i Islami	Gulbudin Hekmatyar	Highly centralized . with specialized branches Some clients	USA/Pakistan, Saudi Arabia, China, independent Islamists, Iran until 1985, Egypt early	Bashir, but mostly minor independent commanders	Probably the most ethnically diverse party, but with a Pushtun majority	Islamist, pragmatist
Hizb-i Islami	Yunis Khalis	Client field commanders with personal loyalty to Khalis	USA/Pakistan, Saudi Arabia, independent Islamists	Abdul Haq (Kabul), Haqqani (Khost), Mullah Malang	Pushtun in the south of the country and north of Kabul	Traditional Islamist
Ittihad	Abdul Rasul Sayyaf	Client field commanders	Saudi Arabia, independent Islamists, USA/Pakistan	Only mid- and small-scale commanders	Mostly Pushtun	Purist Islamist, Salafi
Jamiat-i Islami	Burhanuddin Rabbani	Efficient Peshawar-based bureaucracy and client field commanders	China, France, USA/Pakistan	Massoud, Zabihullah, Ismail Khan, and several others	Mostly Tajik, but also some Uzbek, Sunni Hazara, and Pushtun	Moderate Islamist
Ahl-al-Kitab-wal-Sunna	Jamil al-Rahman (until 1991)	Regionally based, centralized	Saudi Wahhabi groups and Saudi Arabia	N.A.	Kunar and Nuristan Pushtun and Nuris	Wahhabi, purist Islamist
Harakat-i Inqilab-i Islami	Muhammad Nabi	Clientage	USA/Pakistan	—	Pushtun	Sufi, traditional

Jabha-i Nejat-i Milli Afghanistan	Sibghatullah Mujaddedi	Small/clientage	USA/Pakistan	—	Pushtun	Secular with Sufi Naqshbandi tendencies, royalist
Mahaz-i Milli Islami	Pir Sayyed Ahmad Gailani	Small/clientage	USA/Pakistan	Haji Abdul Latif	Pushtun	Qadiri Sufi, royalist
Shia parties						
Shura-i Ittifaq Islami	Ayatullah Sayyed Baheshti	Small party, some 3,000 members	Independent from Iran	Sayid Muhammad Jaghlan	Hazara + other Shia	Traditionalist Shia
Sazman-i Nasr	Shaikh Karim Khalili	Centralized, some 5,000 members	Iran, but often strained relations	Mir Sadiqi Turkmani, Abdul Ali Mazari	Hazara + other Shia	Iran-style Shia funda mentalist
Harakat-i Islami	Shaikh Asif Muhseni	Small party, some 3,500 members	Iran	Qari Taj Mohammad, Muhammad Anwari	Hazara + other Shia in Kabul and Kandahar	Moderate Shia
Sepah-i Pasdaran	Akbari and Saddiqi	Decentralized, some 3,500 members	Iran	—	Hazara + other Shia	Radical Islamist
Hizballah	Shaikh Wusoqi	—	Iran	Qari Ali Ahmad Darwazi	Hazara	Iran-style Islamism
Hizb-i Wahdat	Abdul Ali Mazari then Karim Khalili	A unity party formed of all Shia parties in 1988	Iran	Many of above	Hazara and some other Shia, particularly Quizilbash	Moderate Islamism, Hazara nationalism

managed public relations, published magazines, coordinated activities with relief agencies, and arranged itineraries for visiting journalists, their most important function was to organize the supply and distribution of weapons to the different commanders the party sponsored. In general, those who formed the Peshawar bureaucracies were more intransigent on the issue of compromise with the Soviets or the Kabul regime than either party leaders or field commanders. Both the Hizb and the Jamiat also had a stratified system in their bureaucracy that gave the earlier adherents (mostly those who joined prior to 1975) the higher posts, which guaranteed the ideological purity and steadfastness of their bureaucracies.[32] Interacting with Arab volunteers in Peshawar also helped to radicalize the bureaucracies of the four Islamist parties.

Field commanders were the actual leaders of mujahideen groups. They defended the villages, harassed Soviet and government posts, downed Soviet planes, or surrounded government-held towns. The resistance had thousands of field commanders who led groups that ranged in size from half a dozen up to several thousand individuals.[33] Most field commanders claimed to follow one of the Peshawar-based parties from which they received a portion of their weapons, ammunition, and other supplies. Field commanders were usually geographically limited, behaved independently from the Peshawar apparatuses, coordinated with commanders from other parties, and may even have clashed with commanders from their own parties.[34] Some influential commanders had a relationship of patronage with lesser commanders that mirrored their own relations with the Peshawar party they followed.

Party leaders rarely intervened in the commanders' military activities when they were directed against the Soviets or the Communist regime. Hekmatyar's Hizb was the only exception. This general rule of conduct was not observed when a resistance attack needed to be staged for an outside

---

32. Ibid., 151–57 and 189–91, for more on the structure of the Hizb's elaborate educational network.

33. Yunas (1998, 784–846) has lists from 1984 that the main parties compiled of their own commanders. Mohammad Nabi Mohammadi's party listed 208 commanders; Sebghatullah Mojaddedi, 419; Sayyed Ahmad Gailani, 211; Abd Rab al-Rassoul Sayyaf, 394; Hekmatyar, an incomplete list of 84; Yunis Khalis, an incomplete list of 32; and Rabbani, an incomplete list of 77. While parties tended to inflate the number of their commanders, it is reasonable to estimate that the resistance had at least a thousand and maybe up to twenty-five hundred of them. Yunas lists 125 commanders in the area surrounding Kabul with followings ranging from tiny groups of six (from other sources) to 2,250. Kakar (1995, 263) mentions four thousand commanders. Giustozzi (2000, 242) estimates that there were at least six thousand commanders, a third of which had no affiliation with a party, in Afghanistan "by the second half of the 1980s."

34. In tune with my observations in chapter 2, Roy (1991, 60) tells us that the Afghans kept the traditional pattern of patron-client relations but with different types of people playing the roles of patrons and clients than before the conflict began. See also Kakar 1995, chap. 8.

audience under the auspices of Pakistani intelligence (e.g., the 1989 attack on Jalalabad). Party leaders sometimes also attempted to pressure their field commanders to engage in military action during instances of rivalry among parties, but most commanders valued relations with commanders from other parties in their region and often rebuffed their leaders. Some commanders, particularly among the relatively few Hizb clients, were reported to have switched parties in protest over pressure to attack other parties.[35] The commanders needed the party leadership to maintain a steady supply of weapons, ammunition, and other necessary supplies, and the leader needed to have the allegiance of capable commanders to justify additional outside aid and to gain more influence in Afghan politics. If a party leader was not forthcoming in allocating resources to his commanders, he risked losing them to more generous providers.[36] Many factors affected a party leader's leverage over the behavior of field commanders, but generally (once again with the exception of the Hekmatyar's Hizb) field commanders from different parties often cooperated when their leaders in Peshawar bickered.[37]

The one resistance party whose commanders are not well described by the above sketch is Hekmatyar's Hizb. The Hizb was highly centralized and well organized. Its structure was hierarchical: commissioned officers were trained in the party's military academy and filled the role of field commanders. The officers were assisted and kept in check by religious commissars with madrassa (religious school) training.[38] But while the Hizb was the only Sunni Afghan party featuring this centralized structure, it also maintained patronage ties with several field commanders. The Hizb drew much of its manpower from the refugee camps where the disruption of the clan structure made affiliation with a centralized party appealing.[39]

---

35. Mansur (1995, 26–8) reports interviewing two such commanders (Bilal Niram from the Kabul area, who joined Mujaddedi, and Qazi Rahimi from Meydan, who joined Sayyaf) who left the Hizb because of their refusal to carry out orders to assassinate commanders from other parties. It should be noted, however, that Ahmad Mansur, an Arab reporter, is particularly hostile to Hekmatyar and supportive of his rivals for reasons I do not know, and his information might therefore be unreliable. Edward Girardet also said in a September 26, 1981, article in the *Christian Science Monitor* that two Hizb commanders defected to Jamiat because "they wanted to fight Russians not other mujahideen." Girardet does not hide his admiration for Hekmatyar's rival Massoud.

36. There are many sources mentioning commanders who switched parties. See Jalali and Grau (1999) for interviews with a large number of field commanders that mention defections. See Yousaf (1992, 131) for an example of defection from Hekmatyar's party caused by disagreements over weapons allocations.

37. See Isby (1989, 43) and Hyman (1984, 21) for examples of Hizb conflicts with other parties inside Afghanistan.

38. McMichael 1991, 165.

39. Roy 1990, 111–12.

One particularly successful field commander, and the one with the largest following, was Ahmad Shah Massoud, who gradually built the infrastructure of a parallel state in the Panjshir and neighboring valleys.[40] His organization was highly centralized and tightly controlled but supplemented the local social structure and tried not to disturb it.[41] It advocated respect for democracy and Islam and was led by several specialized committees: the military affairs and logistics committee, the economic and taxation committee, the culture and propaganda committee, the intelligence committee, and the judicial committee. Unlike their namesakes in most parties, the committees were fully functional and built the infrastructure of a state, including a prison that held DRA POWs as early as 1979, a radio station, schools, a library, and a hospital run by French doctors and nurses. Massoud also developed a structured military force made of three types of units: the *motaharak* or mobile groups, the *matanga* or regionally stationed groups, and the *zarbati* or striking force:

> While the *matanga* were organized in a four-week cycle of one week as fighters and three weeks as farmers, the *motahraks* [*sic*] were full-time fighters receiving subsistence allowance as well as rations. Their families cared for by the resistance and entitled to indemnity in case of the fighter's death or incapacity, the *motahraks* had no other responsibility except fighting the war. The *matanga*, also called *sabbet*, were village-based units which functioned as a local militia sharing a small number of anti-aircraft guns among themselves for the defense of their respective areas. The *zarbati* were the striking force mainly operating outside the valley, harassing enemy positions and ambushing convoys.[42]

With the exception of Hekmatyar's Hizb, Massoud's troops were the only ones in mujahideen ranks to feature this degree of professionalism and mobility. Also like the Hizb, Massoud's troops were kept in check by a parallel hierarchy of political commissars and mullahs.[43]

---

40. We have more information about Massoud than any other field commander because he led the most mujahideen and was the only one among them to create local government. His French education and intellectual sophistication also endeared him to French writers and journalists and attracted the services of French volunteer medical organizations such as Médecins sans Frontières that provided considerable information on events in Panjshir. For more information on Massoud's organization, see Girardet's series of articles, *Christian Science Monitor*, September 23–26, 1981. See also Roy 1989, 55–59.

41. Yusufzai 1985, 123.

42. Ibid., 109.

43. Ibid., 110. Massoud is said to have studied the writings of Mao, Giap, and Lenin, and the way he structured his organization definitely reflects the Giap and Mao models.

Some of the small Shiite parties were highly centralized while others followed the Sunni patronage pattern. The number of Shiite parties (a half dozen or more) in a small population (two million) made the Hazara community, the ethnic group that includes the majority of Afghan Shia, one that featured a highly fragmented resistance structure regardless of the structure of each party.

The leaders of the resistance parties were divided along three axes: traditionalists (royalists) versus Islamists, Sunnis versus Shia, and Hekmatyar versus the rest.[44] The traditional versus Islamist divide hardly mattered for most field commanders who already ran their own affairs and did not care who would ultimately govern Kabul, so long as the central power did not undermine their local autonomy or attempt to impose a new belief system. The divide between Sunni and Shia became more salient on the ground when Iran increased its support for the Afghan Shia and the ancient animosity between Pushtun and Hazara was revived. The Hekmatyar-versus-rest divide was the direct result of party structure: the Hizb's near-absolute control over its salaried commanders' actions often prevented cooperation with other commanders in regional operations. Moreover, Hekmatyar was the only Peshawar leader capable of backing his national ambitions with action by loyal and organized forces on the ground. Such forceful actions did not go unnoticed by the other leaders, who perceived Hekmatyar as a dangerous and powerful rival.

The Peshawar leaders were only ephemerally capable of uniting under international pressure. Their councils and transition governments always proved to be no more than fora for debate. Yunas (1998, 889–968) lists fifteen mujahideen attempts to create supraorganizational institutions, most of which were formed to please outside parties—religious leaders, Arabs, Pakistan, the United States, and Iran (for Shiite groups).[45] They all failed, many of them within months and some immediately after their formation. The only long-lasting Sunni mujahideen arrangement, the Islamic Unity of the Afghan Mujahideen, was created in 1985 to please the foreign supporters of the jihad and never took the shape of an organization that effectively increased coordination among its members.[46] This nominal union lasted until Pakistan and Saudi Arabia encouraged the creation of the similarly ineffectual Afghan Interim Government in Rawalpindi to coincide with the withdrawal of Soviet troops. Moreover, any union by the Peshawar leaders would

---

44. See Tarzi (1991) for a study of these cleavages.

45. See Kakar (1995, 92–93) for discussions of those unions.

46. See Yousaf (1992, 39–40) for an account of how this ineffectual union was created.

have been inconsequential on the battlefield because, again with the exception of the Hizb, no party was able to impose changes in tactics, strategy, or organization from above. And the Iranian experience with the Shiite groups was just as discouraging.[47] The most the Iranians could achieve in the way of uniting the Hazara until the formation of Hizb-i Wahdat in 1988 was a 1985 cease-fire agreement.

How Organizational Structure Increased Mujahideen Resilience

When scholars explain the puzzle of the resilience of the Afghan resistance to Soviet occupation, they generally ascribe it to Afghan culture, the ruggedness of the Afghan landscape, and the availability of weapons.[48] The Afghans' attachment to Islam and their code of honor—*pushtunwali* in the case of the Pushtun—was evidently a highly effective motivational force, and while it could be considered a necessary condition for resilience, it certainly was not a sufficient one. The colonization of countless tribal Muslim societies, including those of neighboring Central Asia, by non-Muslim powers in the past two centuries is proof enough that this is so. The ruggedness of the Afghan terrain was very useful to the mujahideen, but they were no less resilient in desert areas (e.g., around Kandahar) and plains (south of Jalalabad) than in the rest of the country.[49] As for weapons, Afghan resistance started well before international arms shipments arrived to Peshawar, and up to 1986 many field commanders had greater numbers of weapons captured from the Communist government and the Soviets than imported arms.[50] Kakar (1995, 147) illustrates with an example from the province of Logar what many other sources confirm to have taken place in much of Afghanistan:

47. Emadi 1990, 102.

48. See, for instance, Hauner (1991) and Roy (1990).

49. See Kaplan (1990, chap. 6) and Kakar (1995, 125).

50. See, for example, Farr and Merriam (1987, chap. 3) who believe that, at least up to 1986, most of the mujahideen's weapons were either captured in battle, traded by Soviet soldiers, or provided by defecting regime troops. J. Collins estimates that in 1985 no more that 30% of weapons in areas bordering Pakistan and practically none in the inside areas were imported (Brigot and Roy 1985, 58). These opinions are also shared by Cordesman and Wagner (1990, 146). Bradsher (1999, 208) also reports that "a resistance leader estimated that in the early years 80 per cent of mujahideen weapons and ammunition came from defections and mutinies or were captured, but this later dropped to only 30 or 35 per cent." See also McMichael (1991, 27–29) for anecdotal evidence on how the mujahideen got their weapons from the government troops and the Soviets. McMichael estimates that this source of weapons was the most reliable throughout much of the conflict.

> To acquire weapons, the mulla [*sic*] commanders of Logar, particularly of the Mohammad Agha front, would ambush enemy forces when they were in their locality. In addition, troops from the Kabul regime sometimes assisted them by defecting, bringing their advanced weapons with them. The commanders would submit such weapons to their headquarters as spoils, in contrast to the tribes of Paktia, who either quarreled over weapons or received some concessions from the regime in return for weapons. The Logaris were successful in acquiring weapons from the regime forces. During the twenty months following the Soviet invasion the Kabul regime lost 25,000 Kalashnikovs to the mujahideen in Logar.

The two billion dollars in U.S. funds earmarked to the mujahideen over ten years of Soviet occupation included shipping costs, defective and ill-suited weapons, camouflaged aid illegally sent to the Contras in Nicaragua, weapons diverted to the Pakistani Army's depots, and weapons resold on the international market.[51] Some estimate that diversion by Pakistan and reselling alone accounted for up to half the total amount.[52] Transportation costs from Pakistan to Afghanistan were also staggering with mortars, for example, costing $1,100 apiece to transport to Mazar Sharif, and their projectiles costing another $65 each.[53] Much of this aid also reached the mujahideen after 1986, seven years after they began their resistance.[54] The distribution of weapons to the different field commanders also left much to be desired: while the Pakistani ISI stocked the arms depots of the Hizb quite well, other parties were only supplied with a trickle.[55] Further, as much as a third of the weapons that found their way into Afghanistan were lost to Soviet ambushes of supply caravans.[56] Also, if the quality of weapons was decisive, then the

---

51. See Hyman (1992, 241–44) for a listing of the extensive leaks in the arms pipeline to the mujahideen. Rubin (1995a, 198–99), Cordesman and Wagner (1990, 20–21 and 147), and many journalists report on Pakistani diversion of weapons sent to the Afghans. Karp (1987, 38) reports that only three out of each four Stingers or Blowpipes sent to the mujahideen reached them. See Yousaf (1992, 86–89) on defective and useless weapons.

52. See Kakar (1995, 148) for a short discussion of this issue.

53. Yousaf 1992, 106. It cost $30,000 to transport a multibarrel rocket launcher and accompanying ammunition to northern Afghanistan (126).

54. The United States allocated $30 million to the mujahideen for 1980 and $50 million for 1981. U.S. yearly military aid exceeded $100 million for the first time in 1985 and reached $630 million in 1987. These figures are from Rubin (1995a, 180–81) who lists them by the fiscal year during which they were budgeted. Others (e.g., Cordovez and Harrison 1995, 157) report similar figures.

55. See table 9.1 in Rubin (1995a) for a breakup of the skewed distribution of weapons among the resistance parties.

56. This is a personal assessment made by Roy (1991, 22). He believes that the one-third attrition rate was reached, and peaked, in 1986.

Afghans should have lost to the Soviets at a very early stage of the confrontation when they had no better than World War I–vintage rifles—mostly local imitations of the venerable Lee-Enfield.[57] This, of course, did not happen: eyewitnesses looking for evidence of outside aid report as late as September 1981 that almost no outside weapons reached, among other places, the Panjshir Valley where the resistance was vibrant and the mujahideen mostly used captured weapons.[58] By the time the vaunted Stingers were introduced to Afghanistan in 1986 and began to be militarily relevant in the spring of 1987, Gorbachev had already described the occupation as a "bleeding wound" and the Soviet generals failed to meet the deadline he purportedly set for them to subjugate the resistance.[59]

The source of the resilience of the Afghan resistance was its structure, which reflected, in part, the intricate Afghan clan and tribal social structure. I show below how this structure locked the Afghan mujahideen in a confrontational strategy and helped them endure by adequately performing all the vital processes necessary for the maintenance of vulnerable organizations without a safe haven. The Soviets were given a cyclical opportunity to disengage from Afghanistan whenever a new general secretary centralized power and failed to structure their institutions in Afghanistan and those of their Kabul protégés to effectively counter the advantages of the resistance. Ultimately, the resistance's resilience and tenacity led the Soviets, who lost faith in their military ability to subdue the mujahideen at a reasonable cost, to withdraw from Afghanistan.

Strategy

One of the most puzzling aspects of the Afghan conflict is the inflexibility of the Peshawar-based leaders of the resistance. Afghan leaders remained firm, even when the United States and Pakistan occasionally pressured them to

---

57. See Brigot and Roy (1985), among others, for a study of weapon availability to the mujahideen.

58. Edward Girardet, *Christian Science Monitor*, series of articles, September 23–26, 1981.

59. For the text of the "bleeding wound" speech, see in particular the "Report to the 27th Congress of the Soviet Union, 25 February 1986" (Gorbachev 1986, 77). Some, like Klass (1988, 931), believe that Gorbachev meant that the "bleeding wound" was Afghanistan's and not the Soviet Union's, but his other statements imply that such wasn't the case, or that he was simply using double talk and letting each audience impute whatever meaning it wanted to his words. Others, like Yousaf (1992, 48), tend to see the "wound" as a Soviet one. Also note that Massoud, the most successful commander, never received Stingers from the ISI during the Soviet occupation (McMichael 1991, 91). Cordovez and Harrison (1995, 198) also point out that Stingers had little effect on Soviet decision making. Shevardnadze (1991) even argued that the Stingers made withdrawal more difficult because Soviet generals did not want to appear to have been defeated by U.S. technology.

accept and abide by the Geneva Accords after their ratification.[60] Afghan commanders continued to attack Soviet troops until the last day of their presence on Afghan soil in spite of Soviet threats to halt the withdrawal if the attacks did not stop and U.S. and Pakistani pressure on resistance leaders.[61] They also refused to enter into a coalition government with the Kabul regime despite more such pressure. This puzzling inflexibility, which meant that the Afghan resistance parties could not be co-opted or deterred by their enemies nor be manipulated by their powerful sponsors, was a direct consequence of the structure of the resistance.

Figure 6.1 describes the two-level game that every Peshawar-based resistance party leader played when he considered a strategic policy change (e.g., to compromise or accept the Geneva Accords). The first level of the two-level game was played among the different party leaders. Utility is measured in terms of mustering the support of field commanders inside Afghanistan because a party leader's prestige and influence were proportional to the number and strength of commanders whose allegiance he was able to claim. Field commanders had an inherent interest in the continuation of the jihad because their stature, economic interests, and raison d'être depended on being needed field commanders.[62] More important, field commanders wanted to preserve local autonomy from the intrusive Kabul regime and its Soviet sponsors, and the perpetuation of the resistance was essential to maintaining it. If a Peshawar-based leader opted for compromise, he was likely to lose the support of field commanders who staunchly disagreed with his policy and would therefore defect to other parties who were more than happy to welcome them. Agreement among all party leaders to jointly compromise with the Soviets or their client regime in Kabul was virtually impossible because they did not even have an incentive to devise a way to develop cooperation in this deadlock game. Unlike what one observes in prisoners' dilemma games, the Nash equilibrium in deadlock is Pareto optimal—the leaders become worse off by cooperating. The first game is a deadlock instead of a prisoners' dilemma because field commanders could choose to become unaffiliated with any party if all party leaders simultaneously chose to compromise with

60. See Khan 1993, 2 and 190–93.

61. See Rogers (1992, 47–50) for U.S., Pakistani, and Soviet attempts to pressure and cajole the resistance not to attack the withdrawing Soviet troops.

62. Dorronsoro and Lobato (1989, 103) argue that this is indeed the case because most field commanders belonged to new Islamist elites, not traditional notables. It is my impression, however, that most of the mujahideen commanders who were traditional notables were subject to the same dynamics and therefore defined themselves in the same way vis-à-vis their parties.

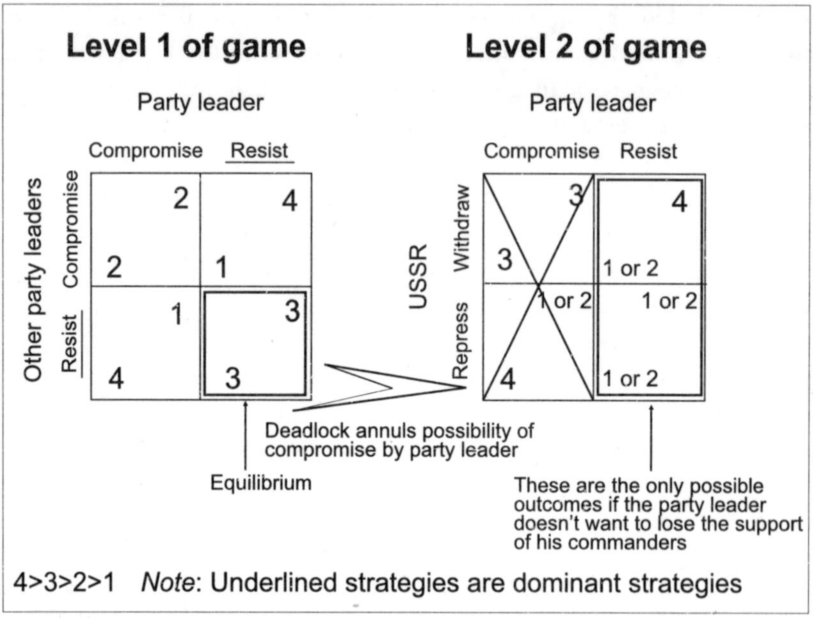

FIGURE 6.1. A two-level game that illustrates how patronage ties created a strategic lockup for Afghan mujahideen parties

the Soviets, thus weakening all parties and making them irrelevant negotiating partners. The equilibrium for the first level of the game is that no party leader will ever compromise with the Soviets.

The first level of the game restricts the second one. The inability of party leaders to compromise because of the limitations imposed on them by the structures of their parties meant that resistance continued until the Soviets withdrew, regardless of the cost of the confrontation to the Afghans. The deadlock persisted even when compromising with the Soviets seemed better than continuing to resist—such as when the Soviets committed large-scale atrocities, the Soviets made offers to one leader to woo him from the pack, or sponsors encouraged compromise. In brief, the Afghans could not be deterred or coerced, and the Soviets could only choose between an unending debilitating conflict and unconditional withdrawal. Soviet preferences obviously changed over time. Before the end of 1986, when they still hoped to obtain the strategic advantages they thought the occupation would bestow on them, they preferred repressing the Afghans (value = 2) to withdrawal (value = 1). When the Soviets realized that they could not benefit from their occupation because of Afghan resistance and that there was no hope of having this resistance end, they switched preferences (repression = 1, withdrawal = 2).

The above analysis applies to the majority of Afghan parties that were based on ties of clientage. If correct, then we should expect the one party with a centralized structure, Hekmatyar's Hizb, to behave differently. Another expected exception would be the highly centralized and large Massoud group. The facts confirm the predictions: the only two major organizations that made deals with Communist figures were Hekmatyar's Hizb and Massoud's group.[63] During ten years of conflict, none of the leaders of patronage-based parties followed a consistent compromise policy with the Soviets. The traditionalists lost large numbers of field commanders and had to rejoin the fold when they appeared to soften their position for a while, both in 1980 and 1987.[64] This dynamic became apparent once again when, on February 23, 1988, the seven major Sunni leaders proposed an interim government that, for the first time, allowed some ministerial posts to go to officials from Kabul. Soon afterward twenty-one mujahideen field commanders condemned compromises in Geneva and pledged to continue fighting regardless of any pact. Party leaders then had to adopt the uncompromising attitude of their field commanders.[65] And only Hekmatyar and Massoud allied themselves with components of the Kabul regime in separate efforts to bring it down—Hekmatyar with Khalqis such as Defense Minister Shahnawaz Tanai and Massoud with the Uzbek militia leader Dostum.

Military operations provide additional evidence to support this argument. The summer of 1986 saw some of the heaviest fighting of the war in all parts of the country, with the exception of the Panjshir Valley, where Massoud negotiated a truce between his forces and the Soviets.[66] This truce was a repetition of the unprecedented 1983–84 truce that Massoud signed with the Soviets without DRA involvement and that officially was to last six months but endured for a year.[67] Although Massoud needed the truces to expand his influence and prepare for future battles, they allowed safe passage for Soviet convoys to Kabul and allowed the Soviets to focus on other resistance groups, causing resentment among commanders in other regions of Afghanistan. In addition, mujahideen attacks on Soviet forces intensified all over Afghanistan as they retreated. Attacks persisted despite Soviet threats to halt the withdrawal if they did not cease and U.S. appeals to the mujahideen to desist.[68] Only

63. See, for example, Rubin 1995a, 151.

64. Kaplan 1990, 191.

65. Cordesman and Wagner 1990, 78 and 82.

66. Lohbeck 1993, 175.

67. Kaplan 1990, 41; Cordesman and Wagner 1990, 47; Yusufzai 1995, 106–13.

68. Cordesman and Wagner 1990, 86 and 89.

Hekmatyar's Hizb and Massoud were able to rein in their forces, presumably as part of private deals they made with the Soviets.[69]

The United States, Pakistan, and Iran often pressured the Afghan parties to unite in an indication that they understood that centralizing authority was the only way to put the resistance in line with the policies of its sponsors.[70] Further, both Pakistan and Iran channeled most of the aid they disbursed to centralized parties they could influence at the expense of larger and more effective, but less pliant, parties.[71] The U.S. embassy also exerted intense political pressure on the resistance parties to form a working coalition. These attempts at unifying and centralizing the resistance failed, however, and the Afghan resistance remained by and large insensitive to outside pressure until the Soviet withdrawal. This independence from the influence of sponsors also kept the Afghan parties from being used as tools for projecting influence inside Afghanistan and being used against one another. The only organization that did play this role was the centralized Hizb, which was party to almost every intermujahideen clash that was reported in accessible sources. The CIA and ISI also attempted to force coordination and the centralization of resistance fronts. Field commanders all too often resisted this pressure and kept coordination confined to territorial defense, when their interests converged.[72]

In brief, the structure of the Afghan resistance generally locked it into a perpetually confrontational strategy that made it by and large immune to being co-opted or deterred by its foes and from being manipulated by its powerful sponsors. Conversely, the power structure in Moscow allowed Gorbachev to switch strategies once he centralized power in his hands. The inability of the Kabul regime and its Soviet backers to mollify the Peshawar leaders led them to focus on their field commanders by attempting to execute divide-and-conquer, co-optive, and hearts-and-minds strategies.

The Soviet divide-and-conquer strategy had mixed results in Afghanistan. The only ethnic groups the Soviets were able to co-opt through the formation of centralized ethnic organizations were the minority Uzbeks, Quizilbash, and Ismailis. The Hazara, through their many political parties,

69. Lohbeck 1993, 250–51.

70. See Rais (1994, 195–200) for a history of mujahideen failed attempts at unity under foreign pressure. See also Rubin (1995a, 223–25).

71. Hekmatyar's Hizb in the case of Pakistan and the Organization of Islamic Victory (Sazman-i-Nasr or Nasr) in the case of Iran. See Rubin (1995a, table 9.1) for a breakdown of Pakistani aid among Sunni parties.

72. Lohbeck 1993, 259–64 and 276.

enjoyed de facto self-rule. The Tajiks, mostly under the influence of the centralized organization of Massoud, opted for resistance. Some Pushtun clans were successfully co-opted by the Soviets but often switched sides while the absolute majority was unequivocally on the resistance's side.[73]

Afghan historian Hasan Kakar (1995, 180–81) reports that Soviet ambassador Ahmad Fikrat J. Tabeev was the likely initiator of the Soviet divide-and-conquer strategy in Afghanistan. Execution was entrusted to Hazara Politburo member and prime minister Sultan Ali Kishtmand who, again according to Kakar, wrote in an internally circulated booklet titled *Samara-e-Dosti* (Fruit of Friendship) that "non-Pushtun ethnic minorities could be made oversensitive to each other and . . . could be persuaded to form an anti-Pushtun front." Divide and conquer was implemented through the Ministry of Tribal Affairs and received a large nonaudited budget.

Divide and conquer was most successful among the Uzbeks because of the ability of Abdul Rashid Dostum to efficiently build his Jawzjani militia as a Kabul client and effectively eliminate most Uzbek mujahideen commanders who were quite active during the early stages of the conflict. Dostum's relationship with Kabul (under direct Soviet control or that of Najib's regime) was strictly one of patronage and lasted as long as he was paid for his loyalty. The Uzbeks were more responsive than larger groups to developing ties of patronage with Kabul because they had been marginalized by the central power throughout Afghan history and had been given an opportunity to develop a strong independent presence through this relationship, and perhaps because

> with very little religious consciousness or education, their cultural reference lay outside Afghanistan's borders, as they felt they belonged to the Turkic civilization of Central Asia. Only the Muhajerin (who fled Bolshevism in the thirties) had a high political awareness, and joined the ranks of the resistance in greater numbers.[74]

Despite their brief attempt to control the city of Kabul after the collapse of Najib's regime, Uzbeks, who number some 6 percent of the population, could not reasonably hope to themselves become the central power. They therefore preferred a colonial power that allowed them to gain regional autonomy over the emergence of yet another potentially hostile Pushtun government in

---

73. I do not discuss the success of divide and conquer among Aimaqs, Balush, and tiny ethnic groups such as the Kirghiz, Kazakh, and Afghan Arab tribes because of the lack of reliable information.

74. Dorronsoro and Lobato 1989, 101. For more on the Uzbek Muhajerin to Afghanistan, see Shalinsky 1979.

Kabul. The daunting terrain between Peshawar and Uzbek areas made the supply of weapons and other resources to Uzbek clients of mujahideen parties difficult and, consequently, the patronage ties less appealing.[75] It also disadvantaged the many Uzbek commanders who joined the resistance in their attempt to resist Dostum and the Soviets. Regime declarations about giving rights to minorities also eased the transition of many Uzbek areas to Dostum's control. But perhaps the greatest facilitating element for bringing large sections of the Uzbek population to the DRA's side was the centralized structure of tribes in the northern areas:

> [The DRA government] discovered that it was much easier to attract the leaders of hierarchically structured tribes. . . . Furthermore, they were much more capable of changing the attitude of the members of their tribe. On the other hand, the closer the tribal structure was to "democratic" (in the form of the *qawm*) as the border tribes of the East were to a considerable extent, the more government efforts tended to be useless, since even when the notable was drawn onto Kabul's side, his followers could perfectly well choose another notable and continue their fight against the regime.[76]

The other two ethnic groups that were generally successfully induced to support the Kabul regime were the tiny Shiite Quizilbash and Ismaili communities. The Quizilbash are descendants of Persian bureaucrats who resided in the larger cities of Afghanistan where government control was very strong, and therefore had little choice in casting their allegiance. Afghan Ismailis numbered some 150,000 to 180,000 or around 1 percent of the Afghan population and were generally suppressed by Afghan rulers and governments throughout Afghan history. Their numbers, rural location, and poor economic situation never allowed them to play a significant role on a national level.[77] Their alienation led many of them to join extreme leftist and Maoist groups such as Shula-i-Javid and the PDPA before the Saur "revolution." And while some Ismailis did resist Kabul and created a liberated zone in Shibar under Noor Muhammad, most of them heartily supported the regime and the Soviet occupation because of their past suffering

---

75. A December 16, 1991, Reuters wire reports that Uzbek militiamen openly said that they switched to the regime's side because economic help from mujahideen parties wouldn't reach them anymore and that the DRA offered to substitute for such aid. They declared their intention to remain good regime clients so long as DRA assistance continued.

76. Giustozzi 2000, 128.

77. Much of the information on Afghan Ismailis is from Emadi 1993b.

under Pushtun regimes, and possibly because of the secret prodding of the Agha Khan, the sect's worldwide leader. Ismailis were given some positions of power for the first time in Afghan state history and were allowed to form a client militia under the Nadiri clan's leadership that controlled strategic sections of Kabul's northern supply routes.

The Shiite Hazara generally eliminated government presence from their rugged mountainous territory by September 1979 at which time a grand assembly of some twelve hundred Hazara dignitaries met in Bamyan to decide how to administer their newly liberated lands.[78] After that, the Soviets and the Kabul regime made little effort to regain control over the Hazarajat. The Soviets had little interest in the Hazarajat because the Hazara were both geographically and ethnically contained in the inaccessible and forbidding terrain of central Afghanistan: the Hazarajat was well encircled by the Soviet road and garrison network and historical enmities made Hazara cooperation with Sunni mujahideen unlikely. The challenge of manipulating the multitude of Hazara groups soon became an Iranian concern that culminated in the 1988 establishment of Hizb-i-Wahdat under Abdul Ali Mazari. Iranian efforts were facilitated by the early PDPA elimination of leftist Hazara elites belonging to Maoist parties, Iranian control and indoctrination of the Hazara refugee population within its borders, and the steady decline of the traditional landlords who couldn't keep up with Iranian-financed organizations. Overwhelming Iranian influence, several years of near independence, and resentment of historical mistreatment by successive Kabul regimes made the possibility of secession both desirable and seemingly realistic for the already autonomous Hazara, thus diluting the potency of any divide-and-conquer efforts by the Kabul regime. Even though the Hazara were represented in the PDPA—notably by the Parshami Sultan Ali Keshtmand, prime minister between 1981–88—they could not reasonably hope to control Kabul to the exclusion of their historic Pushtun enemies, despite their Sisyphean attempt to control portions of the capital before the rise of the Taliban. Hazara preferences (secession or already established autonomy > risky and unlikely control of center > colonial control > Pushtun control) therefore would have made any government divide-and-conquer initiative, if attempted, unsuccessful in Hazarajat.

The most serious challenge to Soviet and government rule came from the two largest Afghan ethnic groups: the Pushtun (some 40–45 percent of the population) and the Tajik (some 30–35 percent). The Pushtun have always been the dominant political group in the country and the term "Afghan" is

78. Some of the information in the paragraph is from Emadi 1997 and Harpviken 1996.

colloquially used to mean Pushtun. Because of their numbers and the shared Sunni Hanafi faith, Tajiks have historically been given prominent representation and allowed reasonable influence by the Pushtun. The Tajiks therefore do not share the fear of Pushtun central power one finds among the Hazara, Ismailis, or even the Sunni Uzbeks. The Tajiks are also concentrated in the area north of Kabul, putting them within easy reach of the center of power during those brief historical episodes when the Pushtun left a tempting vacuum while engaged in internecine rivalries, namely during the Basha-i-Saqao episode, after the collapse of Najib's regime, and after the 2001 U.S. invasion. The Communist regime and Soviet presence therefore did not appeal to Tajiks as an equalizer the way it did to smaller minorities because they did not suffer under Pushtun dynasties. Secession was not an option because Tajik nationalism would have had to be linked to Soviet Tajikistan, which was under the yoke of the very power from whose grip they were trying to escape. All those elements made divide and conquer unappealing to the Tajiks as a whole.

The Pushtun as a group were obviously the least likely candidates to accept the PDPA/Watan regime or the Soviets because they felt they lost the most from the assumption of power by the first and the invasion of the second. Rhetoric from Kabul about giving minorities (or "nationalities" in the adopted Soviet lingo) their rights, and the mostly minority-dominated and Dari-speaking membership of the ruling (after the Soviet invasion) Parshamis alienated rural Pushtun.[79] The Ghilzai and Eastern Pushtun dominated six of the seven Sunni mujahideen parties and had little affinity with the Parshami leaders in Kabul. Members of the powerful Durrani tribal confederation that provided all of Afghanistan's kings felt even more cheated and alienated by the Kabul regime that replaced the Durrani Daoud. Secession was also meaningless from what has been a mainly Pushtun empire.

The Nuristanis have been closely associated with the Pushtun since their conversion to Islam in the late nineteenth century and therefore would not be responsive to the central power's divide-and-conquer efforts for similar reasons.

The factors that affected the success of Soviet/PDPA divide and conquer, the expected results, and what actually happened are summarized in table 6.2. Only the smaller ethnic groups were responsive to Soviet and PDPA divide-and-conquer efforts. For the more numerous Tajiks and

79. Giustozzi (2000, 36) reports that in 1989, Pushtun made up 37.7 percent of the two hundred thousand PDPA members while Tajiks accounted for 47.7 percent, roughly in inverse proportion to their percentages in the Afghan population. The ethnic composition of the PDPA up to 1988 is described in tables on pages 256–57. Notice the gradual increase in the proportion of non-Pushtun membership.

Table 6.2. Summary of factors that affected the Soviet divide-and-conquer strategy: expected results and actual outcomes

	FACTORS AFFECTING SUCCESS OF D&C				RESULTS FOR D&C	
ETHNIC GROUP	FEAR FROM OTHERS IN CENTER	SIZE AND DISTANCE	COST OF SECESSION	PERCEIVE CENTER TO BE NEUTRAL	EXPECTED	ACTUAL
Uzbek	High	Small/far	High	Somewhat	Score: +++? D&C works	worked
Quizilbash	Moderate	Tiny/near	Impossible	Yes	Score: ?+++ D&C works	worked
Ismaili	High	Tiny/far	Impossible	Yes	Score: ++++ D&C works	worked
Hazara	High	Medium/near	Low	Somewhat	Score: +?–? D&C fails	failed
Tajik	Low	Large/near	High	No	Score:–––– D&C fails	failed
Pushtun	Low	Large/near	High	No	Score:–––– D&C fails	failed

Note: Each factor affecting D&C success is assigned a code: +, helps D&C; –, hinders D&C; ?, unclear.

Pushtuns, the central power had to resort to another more piecemeal strategy: co-option.

The Soviets and the Kabul regime tried to co-opt many of the more important Pushtun and Tajik field commanders or tribal leaders, with little success. They would offer the khan or commander salaries for his followers, weapons, ammunition, food, and immunity from government attacks and bombardment in return for loyalty and keeping the mujahideen out of his area of control. Although such a strategy seemingly would be eased by the need to co-opt a single individual (the commander or the khan), it generally failed because of the dynamic that resulted from the structure of the resistance.[80] There were so many commanders (thousands within Afghanistan and at least dozens in most provinces) that each of them would have had to deal with the enmity of all others if he were co-opted by the Soviets. This makes the offer of the government seem inferior to that of the resistance parties: while the government's positive sanctions might have been more generous than those of the impoverished mujahideen parties, its potential negative sanctions were less daunting than having all other commanders make an example of the new co-optee. Particular windows of opportunity

80. On a contrary note, Arnold (1985b, 41) mentions that even the assumption that co-opting a malik or khan (traditional leaders) suffices to co-opt his group is debatable.

provided by the weakness of the resistance in certain areas and the desperate need for food or weapons did lead to the temporary co-option of some commanders and khans, such as the head of the Karokhel tribe, Hasan Khan, who controlled a large area east of Kabul in the early 1980s.[81] He protected government facilities and kept the mujahideen at bay but maintained open channels with them and gave them a portion of the supplies he received from the government. When resistance groups built and consolidated their presence around his area, they pressured him to commit to one side. Hasan Khan consequently evacuated his three thousand tribesmen and their weapons toward the Pakistani border in August of 1984, after destroying almost all the electric pylons leading to Kabul.[82] Another such defecting co-optee was Arbab Ghani Teymuri, who protected traffic in the vicinity of Herat for the government for two years until the autumn of 1987, when he defected with his two thousand men to the resistance.[83] Yet another was Haji Qandahari of the Ahmadkhel, who took weapons from the Soviets but clashed with them when they performed operations in his area in November 1981.[84] Yet another was Ashar Khan in Herat Province, who joined the mujahideen in 1989 after they moved too close to his base.[85] Commanders who chose to be co-opted anyway generally lived in fear for their lives and might have been prevented from even visiting their villages, like Ismatullah Ansari, who is from around Mazar, discovered after his 1985 defection.[86]

The PDPA achieved its most lasting successes in co-opting qawm leaders and khans before 1984 and in northern provinces (from Herat to Badakhshan),

81. Yusufzai (1985, 109) mentions other resistance commanders that were won over by the DRA and used to harass the resistance: Maulvi Afzal in Nuristan, Juma Khan in Andarab, Ismatullah in Kandahar, and Sher Agha Chungar in Herat.

82. Afghan Information Center, *Monthly Bulletin* 42 (September 1984), 2–3.

83. "Afghan Militiamen Defect with Government Weapons." *Jane's Defense Weekly*, January 9, 1988. Alex Alexiev (1985, 35) reports that parts of the Ahmadzai, Waziri, and Shinwari tribes were also at least temporarily co-opted by 1984.

84. Kakar 1995, 176–77. See also the Malik Qays example.

85. Giustozzi 2000, 217.

86. Ibid., 75. The mujahideen regularly assassinated those who joined government militias. One example is the Herati Sher Agha who defected from Nabi's Harakat in 1981 and was assassinated in 1983 (Dorronsoro and Lobato 1989, 104; Giustozzi 2000, 33.) Another Herati, Sayyed Ahmad, was assassinated in 1990, a couple of years after he unambiguously joined the government side. Yet another was the Mangal tribe notable Din Gol Mangal who was executed in Pakistan after refusing to stop collaborating with the regime. Mujahideen also assassinated twenty-seven senior members of the NFF in the one month following its founding congress (Giustozzi 2000, 143.) My argument is consistent with an interesting analysis by Anthony Arnold (1985b, 41).

where and when the resistance groups were the least established and the social structure less pervasive or more centralized than in Pushtun areas.[87] Another reason for this regional concentration is that this area had regional minorities uneasily embedded within already hostile regional majority groups. Regional minority groups preferred being backed by the more mobile Soviet troops than by remote mujahideen parties when balancing commanders from regional majorities belonging to Jamiat.[88] Juma Andarabi (of the Andarab Valley close to Massoud's Panjshir) is a case in point: he first joined Hekmatyar's Hizb, among other reasons, to balance Massoud's power. As Massoud's influence increased, Juma defected to the government and made it his sole mission to harass his Panjshiri neighbor. The Balush and Pushtun government militias in the mainly Persian-speaking zones of Badghis and Herat provinces provide additional examples. Yet another example is Rasul Pahlawan of Faizabad who was part of Mohammad Nabi Mohammadi's Harakat but defected to the Kabul regime in 1982 after violently clashing with Persian-speaking commanders of Jamiat.[89]

Overall, however, the results of the government's co-optive efforts were mediocre, as the Kabul regime's prime minister in 1988–89, Mohammad Hassan Sharq, who terminated special allocations of local autonomy in return for loyalty in northern Afghanistan, writes in his memoirs: "Until the end of my office no known commander submitted, nor was any known refugee willing to negotiate. If a known commander received a government emissary it was to tell him that they were unwilling to negotiate but willing to fight to the end."[90]

The failure of co-optive efforts happened in spite of DRA efforts to move, or appear to move, to the political center. Karmal, for instance, made a November 1985 public speech in which he said that the PDPA should not monopolize power, private agriculture should be encouraged, tribal self-government should be allowed, Islam should be respected, and Afghanistan should be more neutral in its foreign relations.[91] The broad-based 1987 Soviet-backed co-optive effort of the Kabul regime similarly failed, despite even greater efforts to appear closer to the political center. Najib re-added

87. Dorronsoro and Lobato 1989, 99–101.

88. S. B. Majrooh, a leading Afghan observer of the conflict, noted this dynamic. Reported in Giustozzi (2000, 204).

89. Dorronsoro and Lobato 1989, 102.

90. Sharq's memoirs were printed in a limited Dari edition. This quote is from Kakar 1995, 263.

91. Giustozzi 2000, 56.

"Allah" to his name, renamed the PDPA the Watan (Nation) Party, reversed unpopular reforms, proclaimed his respect for Islam and modified the constitution to say that Afghanistan is a Muslim state, declared a cease-fire and amnesty, appointed some nonparty figures to the cabinet, and did away with Communist symbols, with Moscow's blessings, in an effort to make his regime's norms more acceptable to potential co-optees. The policy generated little response from mujahideen party leaders and their field commanders, an indication that ideology and policy played a much smaller role in mobilization than positive and negative sanctions.

Finally, two more structural factors hampered the DRA regime's co-optive efforts: its own factionalism and its poor control mechanisms. They impeded necessary coordination and allowed for corruption and pilferage of resources allocated for co-optive efforts, as Giustozzi (2000, 135) tells us by drawing on Soviet sources:

> Factional infighting and disagreements within the Afghan state made the conduct of a unified strategy impossible. A Soviet scholar complained in 1984 that some Parshami leaders favored the use of force against the tribes, in order to get rid of them once and for all, and they therefore did their best to undermine the activities of the Ministry [of Tribes and Nationalities] and the prestige of Minister Laeq himself. Certainly, the dispatching of vital goods to the tribes was often interrupted. . . . Karmal himself often complained about this: the goods destined for the tribes often did not go farther than the provincial center, or were sold on the black market. It was decided that it was necessary to take effective measures in the border provinces, to be implemented as soon as possible. . . . But one year later the new president Najibullah was still complaining that the governmental departments had violated the protocols with the tribes. In some cases it was the Red Army that caused trouble, as with the Zazay in 1981, when it entered the tribal territories, violating the accords and causing the militias to rebel.

Yet, the Soviet and DRA co-optive strategy was, and could only be, much more successful than their hearts-and-minds approach.

Hearts and minds was a strategy beyond the pale of those realistically available to the DRA and the Soviets. One structural reason is that neither achieved the prerequisite degree of effective centralization necessary to implement such a strategy. Another reason was that it was very difficult for the Kabul regime and its sponsor to differentiate among active fighters, passive supporters, genuine neutrals, and government loyalists, because of their poor penetration of rural society and the strong overlap between society and resistance groups. It was also virtually impossible for the Soviets to isolate resisters from the rest of society where the mujahideen were well enmeshed within the tribal and clan structure. Finally, the Soviets were too inept at meting out positive and negative sanctions to affect anyone's behavior, even if they managed to isolate the mujahideen from the rest of society. Interestingly, a hearts-and-minds strategy only had the potential to work against Hekmatyar's Hizb, most of whose troops were drawn from the refugee camps and therefore did not enjoy strong ties with the population in areas where they operated. This explains why Radio Kabul's broadcasts and other regime propaganda tools did their best to convince listeners that the Hizb *was* the resistance (the Hizb and Hekmatyar were mentioned more than anyone else besides regime and Soviet figures) and that it planned to bring a way of life that would trample on the interests and affinities of all Afghans if it came to power.

One example of how the DRA hearts-and-minds strategy was impeded by the lack of requisite coordination among its organizational components is provided by the experience of Sayyid Jagran, the commander of the shura in control of Jaghori District in Ghazni Province. He had expressed his desire in 1982 to cease hostilities with the regime but changed his mind when the DRA's air force, which was either not informed of his conciliatory move or was dominated by a faction that wanted to sabotage a possible cease-fire, bombed his positions.[92]

To sum up, the Afghan mujahideen were stuck in a confrontational strategy vis-à-vis the Soviets and the Kabul regime because of structural reasons, while the Soviets had cyclical opportunities that peaked when a new general secretary centralized power in Moscow to shift to an accommodationist strategy. The central power was also severely limited by structural factors (lack of centralization on its part as well as the resistance's structure) from satisfactorily implementing more sophisticated strategies but did meet some success in areas where the resistance or society did not follow the general structural patterns that favored the mujahideen.

Coordination

Soviet forces were fairly well coordinated during the last years of the conflict, as demonstrated by their well-organized operations and effective artillery and air support. More broadly, however, the Soviets never centralized the arms of their different intelligence and political agencies in Afghanistan

92. Ibid., 175.

well enough to achieve better levels of coordination. The largest impediment to full coordination was the identification of different Soviet agencies with rival PDPA branches they supervised and directed. Yet coordination among different Soviet offices was remarkably better than among the different PDPA branches, which were so riddled by factionalism that "militia villages were attacked without the army intervening, in spite of its ability to do so."[93] Air operations, which were centralized in Kabul, often provided air support a day late.[94] On January 17, 1984, Babrak Karmal candidly admitted in a speech that the army, Sarandoy, and KhAD had not been cooperating well enough on the local level.[95] Giustozzi (2000, 77–80), relying on well-informed Soviet forces, best describes the PDPA/DRA's poor ability to coordinate the activities of its military and other organizational components. He tells us that in the early 1980s infantry divisions did not have contact with one another or with the divisional command. A late 1980 reorganization aiming at modeling the Afghan forces after the Soviet structure only showed improved coordination after the 1986 appointment of Najib as head of state. A 1983 initiative aimed to create headquarters at various levels to coordinate the activities of military, economic, and party officials:

> One of the main duties [of the headquarters] would be the coordination of army, sarandoy, KhAD and militia activities. The decision was implemented slowly, and in September 1984 such headquarters did not yet exist in most districts and subdistricts. Although some HQs (Kabul, Jowzjan, Badakhshan) were praised by Karmal for their effectiveness, in general "the organization and co-ordination of their activity was blunt and weak." Moreover, no organ existed in the capital "to exercise permanent administration and provide urgent leadership to the lower headquarters and to bring about a permanent coordination in the activity of ministries and offices in the solution of the problems of localities." Some members of the HQs made "privileged claims for themselves and for their departments and establishments" and guarded "their independence with jealousy," inflicting damage on the activity of the HQ.[96]

Substantial improvements in coordination could only be felt after mid-1987, and, even then, coordination among regime components only took

93. Dorronsoro and Lobato 1989, 104.

94. Cordesman and Wagner 1990, 122.

95. Yunas 1998, 604.

96. Giustozzi 2000, 78. The quotes are from two Karmal speeches, one made in March at the 13th Plenum of the PDPA and the other on September 21, 1984 at the 14th Plenum.

place on the regional level when all operational military units other than militias were finally subordinated to regional headquarters. Coordination on the national level remained elusive until the demise of the PDPA/Watan regime:

> Factional infighting within the party was probably responsible for the inability to create effective, nationwide coordination, as the existence of three armed forces was part of a checks and balances system. It is worth noting that Najibullah, who personally agreed to give the Supreme Command "guidance of all military operations," became resolutely opposed to such proposals (coming from Soviet advisers) after Defense Minister Tanai's attempted coup in 1990. It added to the paradoxical character of the situation that WAD [KhAD] and the Interior Ministry were only concerned with administrative, training and logistical matters and did not exercise any leadership over the activities of their units. Only the Special Guard, created in 1988 within the framework of WAD but largely independent of it, had its own military command, although this too was not able to direct its operations on a daily basis.[97]

Coordination among the mujahideen was also poor, and it mainly took place on the local level among neighboring field commanders. The Peshawar parties hardly coordinated their actions, mostly because they wouldn't have been able to impose their decisions on their field commanders anyway. Local coordination against regime and Soviet attacks often came naturally because of the convergence of interests that resulted from defending a common region. There were exceptions, however. A 1980 *Le Monde* article reports, for example, that a Hizb unit that wanted to save its few antitank weapons allowed a Soviet column that later crushed other mujahideen groups and committed massacres in Kunar to go through a convenient ambush site unmolested.[98] Of course, it could be that in this instance the pro-Massoud *Le Monde* was trying to undermine the Hizb, the main rival to his organization, but such failures to coordinate were known to happen.

Although coordination in defense was generally not a major issue for the mujahideen, their organizational structure definitely reduced their ability to coordinate when they had the opportunity to take the initiative. For example, local leaders who did not want to suffer from Soviet reprisals sometimes did not allow outside mujahideen commanders to wage operations from their region at critical junctures.[99]

97. Ibid., 80.

98. Mike Barry, *Le Monde*, May 25–26 1980, p. 5.

99. Jalali and Grau 1999, 47–48.

There were instances when the resistance enjoyed overwhelming local superiority but could not take the initiative because of poor coordination, such as their inability to take the isolated, seven-hundred-man garrison of Qalat when they attacked it with seven thousand men in the summer of 1988. This became an even greater problem after the Soviet withdrawal when effective coordination could have helped the mujahideen achieve great immediate gains.

Coordination was more likely to occur in areas that featured a dominant field commander. Other commanders were said to have attacked Soviet and DRA forces in their regions to relieve the pressure on Massoud during the brutal 1982 "Panjshir V" assault on his valley.[100] This might be due to Massoud's hegemonic position in his region and to his good use of one of the better tools of coordination available to the mujahideen: the commanders' shura (meeting or council).

Regional commander shuras emerged on all fronts in the latter part of the conflict, but the most significant among them were created under the auspices of powerful commanders such as Massoud, Ismail Khan, and Abdul Haq. The presence of a dominant figure in a shura maintained cohesion, particularly when the dominant commander made an example of renegade members. One example was Massoud's elimination of Juma Andarabi, the previous Hizb commander who switched to the DRA and harassed his forces, in 1983. Some other factors, such as proximity, which reduced information asymmetry, also facilitated regional coordination among field commanders.

In brief, the Soviets coordinated their military operations in Afghanistan fairly well but not as well as they should have. They also failed to coordinate their overall presence. The PDPA utterly failed to take advantage of its centralized structure to improve coordination because of factionalism. The resistance was not coordinated at all on the national level but achieved sufficient coordination on the local and regional levels for defensive purposes. It was hardly sufficient to allow it to take the strategic initiative, however, whether locally or nationally.

Mobilization of Resources

There were three distinct zones where the Soviets and the mujahideen competed in mobilizing the population and depriving the other side of support: the refugee camps where the resistance was unimpeded; the cities where

100. Yusufzai 1985, 104.

the Soviet and Kabul regime's control became largely uncontested after 1982; and the rural areas where competition was very intense.

In areas under its control, the DRA regime made efficient use of both positive and negative sanctions to involve the population in its institutions. The early years of Soviet occupation witnessed angry protests and constant nightly activities by resistance-minded city dwellers, but the Soviets managed to subdue resistance by 1982. The Soviets and DRA took good advantage of their safe haven to entangle the urban population in the multitude of overlapping organizations that made up the NFF. The PDPA also used its monopoly over jobs, education (albeit mostly ideological), foodstuffs, and other necessities to subdue the population. Its three-tiered urban militia system, while a failure from a military standpoint, did function well as a mobilizing device.

Just like its centralized rivals—the Hizb, and to a lesser extent the Jamiat, which recruited among the less clannish Tajiks—the Kabul regime had to build institutions to impart a sense of loyalty and organizational and ideological belonging to potential recruits to reduce the cost of mobilization.[101] The Communists, whose soldiers continued to desert in droves throughout much of the war, imported Soviet and other Communist teachers for their schools and even sent several thousand orphaned and poor Afghan children for long stays in the USSR to mold them into the kind of loyal and obedient cadres they desperately needed.[102] No wonder then that the destruction of government schools in rural areas was a priority for impromptu insurgents and that several resistance parties declared it legitimate to slaughter any Afghan who was part of the indoctrination program in the Soviet Union.

The mujahideen organizations were given free rein by Islamabad to mobilize the refugee population on Pakistani territory. Yet, only the Hizb, and to a lesser extent the Jamiat, were capable of effectively taking advantage of this favorable environment because of their centralized and relatively streamlined bureaucracies in Peshawar. They used positive sanctions such as the provision of education, shelter, and foodstuffs to attract refugees, but the general scarcity of those resources made their withholding akin to imposing negative sanctions. They both made use of education to reduce the cost of mobilizing the refugee population. Party-controlled schools promoted

101. See Arnold 1985b, 53–55, for a discussion of the effectiveness of the DRA's educational system and its scale.

102. Alexiev (1985, 34) and Rubin (1995a, 141). See also Giustozzi (2000, 38) for a discussion of the schooling the PDPA provided to its cadres and for a table (260) detailing desertion rates from DRA forces until 1990. Between 25,000 and 47,000 DRA troops deserted every year, with peaks in 1983 and 1988–89, just before the Soviet withdrawal.

political socialization, ideological indoctrination, organizational participation, and party loyalty.

Rastegar (1991) finds that the curriculum was geared toward the development of future and potential party members by increasing discipline and reducing the cost of control through the elevation of obedience to the *amir* (party leader) to the level of religious duty. Organizational matters were at the core of the curriculum, and teachers in Islamist schools borrowed organizational ideas from communist thinkers and integrated them into an Islamic ideological context.[103] Belief in God was equated with performing one's role in jihad and obeying one's amir—in other words, to scrupulously assuming one's organizational responsibilities.

Both Hizb and Jamiat also held courses for commanders on rest in Peshawar to upgrade their ideological, military, and organizational knowledge.[104] They also targeted different sectors of the refugee population they wanted to recruit through specialized and differentiated courses:

> As each program attends to the needs of a specific group, program diversity matches the capabilities and expectations of potential recruits and target populations with what is expected of them in the organization. For example, health or language courses may attract students less interested in ideology and politics. Yet it provides an avenue, sometimes the only one available, that in matching the students' interests provides contact with the student where gradually ideology is introduced. . . . Differentiation of educational programs also enhances the integration of new recruits by institutionalizing new behavior patterns along existing organizational roles and structures in the party.[105]

Other less structured mujahideen organizations were less capable of mobilizing the population of the refugee camps because the disintegration of the traditional social structure under the stress of displacement did not favor the development of patronage ties. Where they did excel, however, was in the rural areas of Afghanistan where the development or perpetuation of local resistance-minded solidarity groups in need of funding and weapons

103. Rastegar (1991, 184) quotes a Jamiat teacher explicitly advocating Lenin's views on organization: "I realized that they [the Marxists] have found the way to reach power. Although the political and economic ideas of Marxist-Leninism are aberrations, are not correct, are wrong, they [the Marxists] have realized the fundamentals."

104. Ibid., 191–93.

105. Ibid., 193.

lent itself to the development of sprawling patronage systems that mobilized much of the population in Pushtun and other areas.

The Afghan resistance parties were able to claim the support of most rural Afghans aside from the few qawms and ethnic militias that the government was able to co-opt. The structure of the Afghan resistance followed to a large extent that of the Afghan clans, tribes, and ethnic groups. The origin of this similarity can be found in the way the uprising started and the way the Peshawar parties adopted it. By developing a relationship of patronage with their field commanders, the Afghan leaders allowed the perpetuation of the cohesive prewar patterns of local loyalty, even if with new local and national elites:

> The combatants gathered in a *markaz* [a fortified base usually located away from areas of habitation and from where the mujahidin administrate the surrounding area] belong usually to the same *qawm* or the same religious brotherhood. Estranged from a civilian society, the garrison of mujahidin recreates something very similar to the village society. The changes in social status caused by the war do not imply the abandonment of the traditional conception of the exercise of authority: the newly promoted people adopt the way of life and behavior of the ancient notables (significantly the title of khan is attached to the name of commanders, which were in the past students with no prestige but who are today at the head of large fronts: Basir Khan, Ismail Khan, Bashir Khan). The sociological origin of the chief has changed from the past but not the behavior of the one who is now perceived as the new khan.[106]

It is not surprising that the problems we normally associate with collective action were not salient for the resistance, because relations within the clan and the tribe are some of the most resilient and robust to be found in any human society. Hekmatyar's Hizb mostly thrived where the social structure was dislocated (in the refugee camps and among urbanized groups) because its centralized structure was not needed where traditional ties were still strong. Massoud, the other organizational entrepreneur, was able to build a large centralized organization in the Panjshir mostly because qawm ties were largely diluted by 1979. Put simply, the Afghan parties were effectively able to solve the collective action problem by delegating the task of mobilization to local commanders. When this approach was not feasible, the Hizb's elaborate organization (and to a lesser extent Massoud's in the Panjshir) replaced

---

106. Roy 1989, 52.

the social structure and performed its mobilization function. The similarly centralized PDPA was also more successful in mobilizing supporters where the social structure was dislocated, mostly in Kabul and among migrant laborers on the periphery of cities.[107]

When both the Hizb and the PDPA reached the limits of their growth in areas where the social structure was dislocated, they both tried to develop patronage ties in rural Afghanistan, with limited success. This strategy was particularly damaging for the PDPA because it developed patronage ties more to prevent its clients from joining the mujahideen than to make good military use of their human resources. As for the Hizb, its persistent effort to centralize its structure and to strengthen internal control often led to the defection of disgruntled clients. The brutal punishment the Hizb's troops sometimes meted to defecting commanders also reduced its appeal to potential new clients. This hybrid structure was ultimately a wasteful failure for both the Hizb and the PDPA.

The leaders of patronage-based parties were generally incapable of imposing negative sanctions on defectors, but the PDPA (Soviets), Hizb, and major commanders used a large array of positive and negative sanctions in rural Afghanistan to attract followers and reduce support for their rivals. The Soviets, and later the Najib regime, tried to bribe local leaders to protect vulnerable facilities from mujahideen attacks. The regime also paid generous salaries to its security forces, whose loyalty was essential for its survival, and the mujahideen tried to balance this incentive by subjecting any KhAD agent they caught to the most vicious treatment they could mete out.[108] The Soviets also reduced areas where the mujahideen dwelt to rubble by destroying homes, laying mines in agricultural lands, and ruining irrigation systems. Thousands of Afghan villages were destroyed—fifteen thousand out of a total of twenty-two thousand by one, perhaps exaggerated, estimate.[109] Soviet soldiers also massacred villagers and raped women in areas where they suffered heavy losses to the mujahideen.[110]

There were also unintended unhelpful incentives that organizations on both sides created. The horrendous treatment Kabul's forced recruits endured

107. Dorronsoro and Lobato 1989, 100; Giustozzi 2000, 14–15.

108. Ibid., 49. See Yousaf (1992, 32) for the example of one mujahideen commander who earned the nickname "the Butcher" for slitting the throats of KhAD agents he captured.

109. Klass 1988, 941. See also Massoud's account in the *Christian Science Monitor*, September 25, 1981.

110. Kakar 1995, chap. 13; Rubin 1995a, 143. The rapes were a horrendous crime against the immediate victim but also the ultimate humiliation for the males of the family, which explains in part the later large-scale Taliban backlash that isolated women to "protect" them.

contributed to draft avoidance. These conditions were later somewhat improved to address the problem.[111] Different mujahideen groups often taxed the same villages at the beginning of the conflict, which drove some disgruntled local inhabitants to sometimes support a government presence instead.[112] The severity of this problem was later mitigated by the increase of aid channeled through the Peshawar parties.

In a creative twist on the incentive theme, the Soviets reportedly created fake mujahideen units in an effort to alienate the population from the true mujahideen.[113] One would assume that the fake units committed atrocities against mujahideen sympathizers who, the Soviets hoped, would then shift their support to the regime to avoid what they perceived as misdirected negative sanctions for loyalty.

Rates of desertion from the DRA's military forces support my argument that positive and negative sanctions, and not policy positions, drive mobilization. Giustozzi (2000, 84–85) compiled data from Soviet sources on yearly rates of desertion from the DRA's armed forces, and they show that they were largely unaffected by Kabul's efforts to moderate its policy after 1986:

> Although ideological motives might have played some role, the average deserter was more interested in avoiding the war altogether, rather than joining the other side. The level of desertions has been reported to have been higher when commanders announced forthcoming operations, during the peak of winter (barracks being very cold) and during summer (work being needed in the fields). The highest level of desertions (reaching at times 60–80%) appears to have been among Border Troops, who were active in areas that were both "hot" and close to the borders. The nearest thing to active opposition to the regime that had a significant impact on the proclivity to desertion was membership of one of the Pushtun "rebel" tribes, i.e., those more strongly involved in insurgency. . . . Finally, desertions were less common when troops were deployed in areas peopled by other ethnic groups. . . . The non-political character of most desertions is confirmed by the low sensitivity of the desertion rate to the overall political situation.[114]

111. See Giustozzi (2000, 92) and Rubin (1995a, 132) for more on this matter.

112. Kakar 1995, 145.

113. Giustozzi 2000, 99.

114. Ibid., 84–85.

Giustozzi's data do show a jump in desertions in 1989, the year the Soviets withdrew, which suggests that the perceived probability of an organization's ultimate success does affect its ability to recruit and keep its members.

To sum up, the structure of the resistance and its inclusion of both centralized and patronage-based organizations allowed it to mobilize much of the Afghan population in refugee camps and outside of the cities and the areas of the more successful Jawzjani and Ismaili regime militias. The mujahideen were able to mobilize much of the population at little cost because the close qawm ties that generally brought commander and follower together solved the intragroup collective action problem on the local level. Patronage ties also created little need for the loosely structured parties to develop extensive and costly bureaucracies. Experimenting with a dual structure (centralization with patronage) was generally wasteful of both Hizb and PDPA resources from a mobilization perspective but was acceptable so long as sufficient resources were available. Although the PDPA ultimately mobilized the populations of the cities and their surroundings fairly well, it failed to plant its institutions in the countryside long enough to expand the process. Even when it did, its brutal faction-riddled presence was no match for the more responsive and locally based mujahideen commanders in addressing local needs and applying sanctions effectively.

Control and Discipline

Both Soviet and DRA troops suffered from lack of good control mechanisms that could have reduced the very damaging defections and discipline problems they experienced. Soviet troops abused drugs and alcohol and often sold weapons and ammunition to the mujahideen in return for hashish, opium, or food.[115] They also engaged in looting, rapes, and other atrocities above and beyond those sanctioned by their leadership in areas where the application of negative sanctions was not desired. Central Asian troops, which made the bulk of the Soviet invasion force, often fraternized with the mujahideen and sometimes even defected to them. Soviet generals soon realized the severity of the problem and adopted two major changes. In February 1980 they began to send troops of Central Asian descent home, replacing them with troops from the European part of the Soviet Union with no ethnic or religious

115. See Borovik (1990, 158) and Yousaf (1992, 55–56) for anecdotal evidence on pilferage and sale of weapons by Soviet soldiers to the mujahideen. Borovik (36) also reports that Afghan Communist soldiers had good monetary incentives to defect: they could feed their families for a year with the price their personal weapons would fetch in the Afghan weapons market.

ties to the Afghans by June 1980.[116] In addition, in what might be thought of as an emulation of the resistance's structure, they increasingly relied on small cohesive elite units for aggressive operations.

Although most of the mujahideen fought with groups of kith and kin and under commanders who had earned their loyalty and shared their language, code of ethics, and faith, government troops had little loyalty to their institutions. This meant that the Kabul regime had to make a much greater effort to maintain control over its troops to avoid mass and individual desertions, such as the August 1988 defection of three thousand troops that allowed the mujahideen to occupy Herat after they declared an amnesty for deserters.[117] The PDPA had to adopt harsh negative sanctions to reduce defections, pilferage, and the sale of weapons to the mujahideen, but it never achieved satisfactory results. The only resistance party that resorted to negative sanctions to enforce control and discipline like the centralized Kabul regime was the similarly centralized Hizb.[118]

One additional structural mechanism all three centralized organizations tried to develop with varying success was a parallel structure of political or religious officers. The PDPA made it a priority to create parallel political organizations within the armed force. The army's political chief, Brigadier Gul Agha, was sacked in 1981 because he did not develop this parallel structure quickly enough. His successor, Brigadier Yasin Sadeqi, expanded the parallel structure by 1984 to include 86 percent of all army units, and he staffed this structure with political cadres formed in the PDPA's Social Sciences Institute and the Armed Forces Military-Political University.[119] In addition to using a parallel structure of political officers, the well-endowed DRA used another type of redundancy that the poorer Hizb and Massoud couldn't afford: military and security structures with overlapping authority. The DRA kept its different branches in check by giving KhAD, Sarandoy, some urban militias, and the elite Special Guard corps created in 1988 overlapping authority.

The leaderships of patronage-based resistance organizations had poor control over the behavior of their field commanders, but the multiplicity (redundancy) of field commanders in any one area generally ensured that they did what was expected of them anyway: to prevent the DRA and Soviets

116. McMichael 1991, 12.

117. Rogers 1992, 30.

118. See, for example, Rastegar 1991, 200.

119. Giustozzi 2000, 87–88. There were some twenty thousand such political workers by 1989 according to Giustozzi's sources (table 26, p. 265).

from creating a permanent presence in their area. There was a congruence of interests between leadership and commanders so long as there was conflict. Field commanders solved the control and discipline issue on the local level better than any centralized organization ever could have.

To sum up, all centralized organizations, the regime and resistance organizations alike, made use of the same expensive mechanisms to increase control. The regime's efforts were generally a failure, while Massoud was fairly successful and Hekmatyar achieved moderate success. Patronage-based organizations solved the control issue on the cheap so long as they didn't need their commanders to engage in any action above and beyond preventing the development of a DRA presence in their immediate vicinity, which was perfectly adequate when the resistance's goal was to outlast the Soviets.

Resilience

The multiplicity of Afghan mujahideen parties and their patronage-based structures deprived the Soviets of shortcuts to end resistance through the assassination of key figures, disarmament, dismantling, or by interrupting their execution of organizational processes.

The Soviets were well aware of the Afghan resistance's structure and knew that they had nothing to gain from assassinating party leaders.[120] Those who inflicted the actual damage on the Soviets were the field commanders, and Afghanistan had thousands of them. The party leaders were no more than public figures with little impact on the actual process of inflicting damage on Soviets troops and raising the cost of their occupation. The fact that not a single Peshawar-based party leader was assassinated during ten years of Soviet occupation, despite the KGB and KhAD's extensive activity in both Afghanistan and Pakistan, seems to support this argument. KGB and KhAD capabilities were demonstrated by the extensive acts of terrorism performed by these two organizations on Pakistani soil.[121] The KGB or KhAD may have been responsible for the assassination of Abdullah ʿAzzam, the head of

---

120. The same logic could not be applied to the DRA and Soviet side. The United States supplied ISI and the Afghan mujahideen with sniper rifles with the goal of helping them assassinate Soviet generals. ISI-trained Afghans also almost managed to assassinate Najib with explosives in 1985 when he was head of the hated KhAD (Yousaf 1992, 146).

121. See Cordesman and Wagner (1990, table 2.4) for a list of what are thought to be KGB/KhAD-sponsored terrorist bombings in Pakistan. This number increased from two in 1982 to 487 in 1986 and caused more than a thousand casualties in 1986 and 1987.

the Arab Islamists supporting the mujahideen, and Pakistani president Zia-ul-Haq in 1988.[122]

On the other hand, the Soviets frequently attempted to assassinate field commanders heading groups of various sizes. Not surprisingly, they made several attempts on Massoud's life.[123] They managed to assassinate the prominent Tajik commander Zabihullah, whose death led to the collapse of resistance in Balkh for several years.[124] They also assassinated Nik Muhammad Moalem, whose May 1989 death led to the collapse of jihad in Badghis Province. They also killed several field commanders in Faryab in 1982–83 with comparable results.[125] That they did not assassinate Hekmatyar could be because it suited them to have him be the prominent face of the resistance because of his lack of appeal to the tribes they were actively trying to co-opt. He also was the best protected mujahideen leader.

Also in contrast to their attitudes toward the Peshawar party leaders, the Soviets and their client regime decimated centralized radical Maoist organizations. They eradicated the pro-Beijing Shula-i Javid, SAMA, and Rahaye this way.[126]

Another advantage of the mujahideen's structure is that it generally allowed them to protect their weapons, a crucial resource, from efficient Soviet seizure or destruction. Although the Soviets did manage to destroy some important weapon and ammunition depots—notably in Nangarhar (November 1986), the Zhawara base in Paktia (March 1986), and perhaps the ISI's main Ojhri depot inside Pakistan in April 1988—the distribution of weapons among thousands of commanders made the disarming of the mujahideen an impossible goal.[127] It was also just as hard to stop the overall flow of weapons across the Pakistani-Afghan border because each party sent numerous caravans that meandered their way to the field commanders. The lack of complicated logistics and the redundancy of field commanders, parties, and supply lines that characterized the resistance made any effort by the

122. Brigadier Yousaf (1991, 104–5; 1992, 12) believes that the KGB and KhAD were behind the assassination of Zia. There is little doubt that the Soviets and the Kabul regime benefited most from the death of Zia and his top brass.

123. See Beatrice Bacconier, "Commander Massoud: The Lion of Panjshir," in *Libération*, May 2, 1984, and Yusufzai (1985, 115) for accounts of two attempts on Massoud's life.

124. Roy 1991, 21.

125. Dorronsoro and Lobato 1989, 101.

126. Emadi 1993a, 114.

127. McMichael 1991, 30 and 62.

Soviets to dismantle resistance organizations piecemeal in order to hinder their performance of necessary processes unrealistic.[128] The autonomy of field commanders meant that the military destruction of any resistance group did not affect the performance of others, even from the same party.

Foreign Aid

The structure of the resistance helped it to maximize outside aid and to diversify its sources while minimizing control by sponsors over its behavior. Conversely, the PDPA depended almost exclusively on Soviet support, was micromanaged by Moscow, and was vulnerable to Soviet aid cessation.

The diversity of resistance parties allowed outside sponsors interested in increasing pressure on the Soviets to find at least one party that they preferred to assist.[129] The Pakistanis channeled most U.S. aid to the Islamist parties; the Saudi state backed Abd Rab al-Rassoul Sayyaf in particular; the Saudi Wahhabi establishment backed Jamil al-Rahman's group and other Salafi "emirates"; the Chinese possibly supplied Massoud and sold weapons to Hekmatyar; Iran supported Hazara groups; Egypt originally had a preference for the royalist camp; and different Islamic transnational organizations mostly dealt with Sayyaf and Hekmatyar.[130] Even Libya (early in the conflict and despite its ties to the Soviet Union) and Iraq (during the first U.S.-Iraq War) provided aid to some groups.[131] The diversity of parties allowed the overall diversification of sources and guaranteed that, even if one or more suppliers of weapons had a change of heart, the supply of weapons would not be abruptly interrupted. Aid suppliers also had to calculate that if they withdrew their support from their parties of choice, then other parties less friendly to them might gain influence at their expense and perhaps ultimately be able to monopolize power after the fall of the Communist regime.

128. Some estimate that up to twenty thousand cross-border supply trips were attempted by mujahideen yearly (Giustozzi 2000, 101). See Yousaf (1992, 109–12) for more on the issue.

129. See Rubin (1995a, chap. 9) for an extensive analysis of the sources of outside support for the Afghan resistance.

130. Lohbeck 1993, 171. See Yousaf (1991, 87) for more details on Saudi aid to the mujahideen. See Roy (1995, 82–83) for descriptions of Salafi emirates that emerged in Afghanistan. The more important were Mawlawi Afzal's in the Barg-i Matal in Northern Nuristan, Jamil al-Rahman's in the Pech Valley in Kunar, and Mawlawi Shariqi's in the Argo District in Badkhshan, which was formed by Tajik and Uzbek muhajireen. See Emadi (1993a, 115) for more on Chinese aid.

131. See Garthoff (1994, 1030) on Libyan aid. The Libyans had confidentially informed the U.S. embassy of this aid, which became publicly known when the Iranian revolutionaries published the secret documents they captured from the U.S. embassy in Tehran.

The one sponsor with the potential ability to manipulate resistance parties was Pakistan, through the ISI. The ISI did perpetuate the seven-party system but helped the centralized Hizb more generously than others in what proved to be a long-term commitment that lasted until it shifted its support to the Taliban in 1994–95, well after the collapse of the DRA and under completely different circumstances. Pakistan's goal was to ensure the survival and resilience of the resistance in order to exhaust the Soviets who were at its borders. The fear of a Soviet invasion was both sincere and acute in Islamabad, as Brigadier Yousaf, who was in charge of coordinating Pakistani support for the Afghan jihad, tells us in his generally candid account.[132] The ISI also realized the difficulty of centralizing the resistance's structure after initially reducing the number of Peshawar parties from eighty to seven by 1982 and, consequently, accepted the multiplicity of parties.[133] Simultaneously, it gave Hekmatyar the lion's share of weapons and resources to make the Hizb a more potent centralized organization that functioned as the ISI's stick to discipline uncooperative commanders who couldn't be motivated by their own parties to follow ISI directions.[134] It is no wonder that the Hizb was involved in more interparty clashes than any other party. Pakistan could not have completely deprived parties besides the Hizb from aid because such a policy would have deprived large numbers of commanders, who wouldn't join the Hizb for a number of reasons, of necessary weapons. Periodic U.S. pressure also kept weapon distribution more balanced than the ISI might have desired. The multiplicity of parties also provided the Pakistanis with the option of incrementally adjusting the distribution of weapons among them as a reward mechanism without substantially damaging operations.

With the exception of the Hizb, the ISI could only confirm party leaders in their confrontational strategy, a strategy they couldn't veer from anyway for the reasons explained above.[135] It couldn't impose on them conciliatory moves like, for example, the accommodation of Moscow to avoid the postponement

---

132. Yousaf 1992, 25, 165, and 205.

133. The party system was a step up from the previous, even more fragmented, arrangement that lasted until 1983 and consisted of the ISI directly supplying field commanders (Yousaf 1992, 38). See also Weinbaum 1994, 76.

134. Roy (1995, 87) and others argue that Pakistan's disproportionate aid to the Hizb was motivated by a pro-Pushtun bias and Saudi worries about the possibility of Dari speakers siding with Iran.

135. One reason Hekmatyar's Hizb did not participate in some local battles is that its commanders were following the party leadership's orders based on Pakistani instructions. The Pakistanis might have felt the need to accommodate the United States or the Soviets. See Rogers (1992, 32–33) for an instance where Zia-ul-Haq and his prime minister, Muhammad Khan Junejo, felt the need to accommodate Moscow on the power-sharing issue and alienated most Afghan party leaders by applying pressure.

of the agreed-upon troop withdrawal. Nor could it impose on them the pursuit of aggressive military action without offering hefty financial and other incentives. One example was the ISI's failure to convince commanders around Kandahar to attack the city in July 1988 after the Soviets vacated the historic Afghan center of power, even though it offered considerable sums to those who would accept.[136] After giving up on mobilizing the Kandaharis, it made use of Hekmatyar's troops who, while numerically insufficient and mostly foreign to the area, it could reasonably control. Brigadier Yousaf, who was in charge of the distribution of military aid to the Peshawar parties and fostering coordination among them during his 1984–87 appointment at ISI, tells in his candid account how "to the Mujahideen I could issue no orders—an advantage taken for granted by my Soviet opponents. I had to achieve operational results by cajoling and convincing, not commanding."[137]

What makes this statement particularly significant is that it comes from one of two individuals who had complete control over the allocation of weapons and other resources to the seven parties.[138] This trade-off between control and effectiveness was acceptable for the Pakistanis so long as the Soviets were still at their borders but became less advantageous once the opportunity to take the strategic initiative emerged.

Things were quite different for the PDPA. Its very existence depended on Soviet aid and its Moscow-appointed leadership was under the complete control of their northern "advisers." Even though Kabul became operationally weaned from Moscow as the withdrawal date neared, it still depended on Soviet aid to finance its increasing reliance on client militias and to glue its factionalism-ridden membership together. Excessive Soviet control was not a major problem for the PDPA because the interests of the PDPA and Moscow generally converged during and after the Soviet occupation, but it was perhaps more of an issue for some PDPA leaders, such as Amin and Karmal, who were disposed of according to Soviet whims. Ultimately, however, the PDPA's dependence on one provider of aid contributed to its demise.

---

136. Rubin 1995a, 262.

137. Yousaf 1992, 2–3. See also p. 31 on how commanders sometimes politely ignored his advice.

138. Yousaf (1992, 102–104) confirms his bureau's control over allocations: "During General Akhtar's eight years as Director-General of ISI it was the policy, on which he rightly remained unmovable, that ISI decided who got the weapons, how many, and what types. By this I mean that, after the formation of the [mujahideen] Alliance, the detailed allocation to each party was our responsibility. It bears repeating. No one outside the ISI, including President Zia, had any say or control over the allocation of arms, ammunition and allied logistic stores from our warehouses at Rawalpindi and Quetta." The ISI needed that monopoly to have some leverage over the parties.

Intraorganizational Cohesion and Competition

Despite its apparent looseness, the patronage-based structure of most Afghan mujahideen parties kept intraorganizational conflict to a minimum while increasing beneficial competition. Although client commanders did not hesitate to defect to another party if they received better offers, their interests and those of the leaders of the party they belonged to at any moment were generally consistently aligned. This would remain the case so long as the client did not acquire too many resources or the patron did not become too deprived of the same. Things worked differently for the one centralized mujahideen party. The Hizb's centralized structure could not accommodate divergent views, which led to intraorganizational fissures that were reflected in the endemic splintering that plagued the party throughout its history. Defection was eased by the existence of other parties that gave greater autonomy to those who joined them. The most important splinter group from the Hizb was centered on Younis Khalis who opted to form his own party with the same name in 1979.[139] Qazi Muhammad Amin and a number of dissatisfied commanders left the Hizb in 1982, reportedly to protest Hekmatyar's refusal to join a mujahideen union (*ittihad*).[140] Jamil-al-Rahman defected to form his own Salafi Ahl-al-Kitab in Kunar. In July 1990, eight out of twelve Hizb Executive Committee members and five out of seven Supervisory Council members collectively resigned to protest Hekmatyar's failed alliance with the Khalqi Tanai. Although defections were common among the mujahideen, no resistance organization shrank as much as the once dominant Hizb over the length of the jihad.

No Afghan organization suffered from factionalism more than the PDPA. This factionalism originated in the party's formation from two competing groups under Soviet pressure and a history of intraparty purges that lasted well into the Soviet occupation. Members of persecuted factions (the Parshamis before the Soviet invasion and the Khalqis thereafter) often did not carry out party directions and even cooperated with the mujahideen.[141] Factional uprisings were not uncommon, and perhaps up to two hundred new subgroups and factions (like the extremist Khalqi Zarghounists, the post-1986 Karmalites, and the Kor and Kozha Jawzjani factions) emerged throughout the

139. This summary of dissension within Hizb ranks is from Mansur (1995, 29–33). I do not have redundant sources to confirm this information, which may be tainted by the author's hostility toward Hekmatyar.

140. Edwards 2002, 269.

141. See Giustozzi (2000, 82–83) for more details.

post-1979 life of the PDPA. The PDPA simply failed to subsume clan, ethnic, and other loyalties under its banner. Its indoctrination program was lacking and it failed to diffuse members of factions across the organization, allowing them instead to form entrenched rival centers of power that sometimes felt more threatened by each other than by the mujahideen.

Massoud's was the only one among Afghanistan's major centralized organizations before the Soviet withdrawal to achieve good integration through centralization. This is probably due to Massoud's management skills, the organization's regional concentration and hegemony, the lack of tribalism among its constituency, and its ethnic homogeneity. Much less effort is required to align the interests of a regionally concentrated, nonclannish, and ethnically homogeneous organizational membership than a diverse nationwide constituency. Massoud was lucky in that respect.

The structure of the resistance made it fairly hard for the PDPA to manipulate its components, and the only mujahideen party whose structure allowed it to try to manipulate regime factionalism was the centralized Hizb. Indeed, it tried to do so: the Soviets arrested some 450 of its supporters, including seventeen officers, in the DRA's armed forces and KhAD in 1981.[142]

In brief, the PDPA was never able to align the interests of its different factions with those of its leadership but was kept together because of the Soviet hegemonic presence and, later, centrally channeled Soviet-donated resources. The Hizb managed to align the interests of its members by excluding dissenting factions, whose exit cost was reduced by the availability of other less demanding resistance organizations, but its size was reduced as a consequence. The Massoud group took advantage of a favorable environment and its centralized structure to align individual and organizational goals and to preempt the development of factions. The patronage-based organizations had the interests of their leadership and existing field commanders aligned by definition because either side would have broken their ties of patronage in case of strong disagreement.

Manipulation of Knowledge and Information

The PDPA's ability to manipulate knowledge and information suffered from the intense factionalism that plagued its ranks. Its Soviet sponsors suffered from their own severe shortcomings in this area. On the other hand, the local specialization of the mujahideen; occasional training of their commanders in centralized Pakistani, Hizb, or Massoud training facilities; and regular

142. Ibid., 109.

regional meetings of commanders in the later part of the conflict allowed the efficient manipulation of knowledge and information for local resistance activities. And this was all the mujahideen needed so long as their main goal was to exhaust and outlast the Soviets.

The Soviet military was not particularly effective in capitalizing on its centralized structure to preserve knowledge, process it, and distribute it to where it could reduce the learning curve and improve the troops' efficiency, as McMichael (1991, 121) tells us:

> On the whole, there does not appear to have been a systematic comprehensive, command-wide effort to use training circulars, briefings, SOPs [standard operating procedures], operational notes, or manuals to keep the LCSFA [Soviet forces or Limited Contingent of Soviet Forces in Afghanistan] continuously informed about new tactical developments. It was up to individual units, more or less, to update their own procedures based on their own experiences. There are few indications of lateral flow of this kind of information between similar units. Many tactical lessons probably had to be re-learned over and over again, especially in view of the frequent change-over in personnel.

But personnel turnover was not the only factor that made learning more difficult for the Soviets than for the mujahideen—strict compartmentalization and poor coordination among specialized branches also made it challenging. While a resistance group under a field commander was self-contained as a fighting unit, the Soviets gave each officer a specific set of duties and forbade overreaching beyond specified responsibilities. This rigidity hindered operations because of the absence of good coordination, which was difficult in such a fluid and complex environment, and increased the complexity of skills to be learned well beyond what is reasonable. Ultimately, the Soviets identified this problem and encouraged their officers to be responsible for all aspects of combat to reduce the need for difficult coordination.[143] This largely explains the increased success of the 18,000–23,000 or so elite *spetsnaz*, airborne and air-assault troops the Soviets gradually introduced into the conflict. Such elite troops were organized in small autonomous groups and began to be given special training for Afghanistan in Soviet Central Asia three years into the invasion.[144] This imitation of the mujahideen's structure increased the number

---

143. See also Yousaf (1992, 55 and 125) for turnover in fighting units that were mostly formed of young conscripts with two-year tours of duty.

144. Cordesman and Wagner 1990, 120.

of skills that needed to be learned on the unit level but reduced the amount of coordination skills required at higher levels of command.

As for intelligence, Soviet reliance on signal intelligence inhibited their ability to collect data about the small self-contained mujahideen groups that rarely used radio communication.[145] Photo intelligence was also useless because of the lack of large detectable equipment in mujahideen possession. They therefore had to almost exclusively rely on human intelligence, which meant using the regime's brutal KhAD to collect information on the resistance. But the decentralization and local specialization of the resistance, as well as popular support, made it much more apt to engage in human intelligence than Kabul. Mujahideen groups did penetrate regime institutions and developed effective early warning systems.[146]

Further, and as Anthony Arnold (1985b, 50) tells us, the mujahideen's structure also inhibited Soviet and DRA efforts to collect data about them: "As with the party, the intelligence organs find it difficult or impossible to infiltrate the self-contained village units, where every citizen is personally acquainted with every other." Soviet journalist Artyom Borovik (1990, 81) also quotes an observant Soviet veteran of the conflict:

> To talk about the *dukhi*'s [ghost, mujahid] tactics, however, is to overgeneralize. Each band of rebels has its own style of fighting. And despite a common headquarters, each has its own interests and views on conducting combat operations. . . . During the years of war, the *dukhi* have learned our tactics thoroughly as well. They regularly exchange information about the commanders of Soviet and Afghan troops. . . . They know by heart all the peculiarities of how to use airborne troops and conduct combat operations in the mountains. . . . While planning their operations, they take into account all of the factors that complicate our work.

This anecdotal evidence also supports what some interviewees told me about the occurrence of regular regional meetings among field commanders from different parties. Those meetings were used by commanders to share experiences, insights, and knowledge; solve problems; and to learn what other commanders were getting from their parties in return for loyalty to improve their own negotiating positions. In addition to the more regular meetings among commanders of the same area, particularly powerful

145. Ibid., 107–12.

146. Ibid., 110.

commanders like Massoud occasionally held large-scale meetings that had a similar purpose:

> In September 1983 Massoud reportedly played host to some 130 resistance commanders from many provinces, where they discussed how to improve the fighting, to coordinate large-scale operations, and to organize the people. In the short-term their intention was to conduct joint operations simultaneously in many places, while the long-term aim was to receive arms inside Afghanistan directly from abroad instead of getting supplies through the squabbling political parties in exile. Later in the autumn, a similar meeting of commanders from northern Afghanistan was held in Ishkamish in Takhar province.[147]

The mujahideen shuras were just one mechanism to disseminate and analyze knowledge, ideas, and information. Training in the techniques of efficient resistance was generally conducted on the local level, but some facilities were available in Pakistan to provide training in skills that could not be developed locally.

Centralized training facilities could not reasonably be successful in a country as ethnically diverse and geographically forbidding as Afghanistan, and one mujahideen leader was reported to estimate that only 5 to 10 percent of all resistance fighters had any military training.[148] Massoud organized training camps for his mujahideen and others, but they were attended mostly by Tajik field commanders from northern provinces.[149] Those commanders in turn passed on what they learned to their followers, thus preserving their own influence and prestige.[150] Pakistani camps were probably only used to train a minority of mujahideen to use Stingers, larger weapons, and tactics, despite Pakistani exaggeration of their role.[151] The Pakistani officer in charge of the training program mentions that the camps became effective after 1984, five years into the invasion.[152] The only

147. Yusufzai 1985, 111.

148. Bradsher 1999, 208.

149. Hyman 1984, 20; Rais 1994, 203–4. In what I believe to be an exaggerated account, Edward Girardet (*Christian Science Monitor*, September 23, 1981) reports that Massoud's center graduated five thousand mujahideen from two-month-long courses by September 1981.

150. Yusufzai 1985, 110–11. Yusufzai also mentions an instance when Massoud sent his instructors in 1983 to help organize resistance groups along the Panjshiri model in Badakhshan, Kunduz, Takhar, and Samangan. The Soviets dropped leaflets warning local residents to expel the instructors or be punished by aerial bombing.

151. Brigadier Yousaf claims that eighty thousand mujahideen were trained in those camps.

152. Yousaf 1992, 28–29 and 116–17.

party with substantial training facilities was Hekmatyar's Hizb, which was also the only one that strove for a centralized organization. Sayyaf's small Ittihad had the only other independent substantial training facility, which he jointly ran with Arab volunteers in Sadda. The other parties did not need to bother with the creation of training facilities because essential knowledge was generated and perpetuated on the local level by field commanders and their followers. The field commander and other seasoned fighters had an inherent interest in teaching followers and peers the fighting skills acquired through experience because the family and kinship ties that linked them were strong enough to generate trust. The fighting experience of the field commander was strictly local and he was therefore able to specialize in the skills useful within his territory and adapted to his unique environment.

The learning process on the larger societal scale also favored the Afghan resistance. The Soviets drew the wrong conclusions, when they even bothered to try, from the lessons learned during the Russian, then Soviet, occupation of the Caucasus and Central Asia (Ewans 2005). On the other hand, the Afghans internalized their experiences with invaders through their acephalous social structure and their oral culture. The coming together under one regional, ethnicwide, or even nationwide, banner to resist the invader is an oft-practiced maneuver that was put into effect to resist the British and, more frequently and on a smaller scale, in interclan or intertribal warfare. The large-scale jihads are also engraved in the Afghan collective consciousness through poetry and storytelling while the smaller mobilizations are frequent enough to have become an automatic societal reflex.

In brief, the mujahideen did a better job than either the Soviets or the DRA at directing information to where it was needed simply because it was not necessary in their case for information to travel far. The Soviets and DRA simply failed to develop the essential skills to manipulate information and knowledge to be able to benefit from their centralization, strength, and mobility.

Bringing It All Together

In this chapter I have explained why the Afghan mujahideen were so resilient, a necessary condition for making the Soviet occupation costly and allowing the resistance to benefit from emerging opportunities on the international scene. How the different organizations performed critical operations, their structure, the availability of safe haven, the fit of structure with haven, and survival are summarized in table 6.3. The patronage-based

Table 6.3. How different Afghan organizations executed processes before the Soviet withdrawal

PROCESS	USSR	PDPA	HIZB	MASSOUD	PATRONAGE-BASED PARTIES
Strategy	Had cyclical opportunities to adopt conciliatory strategy. Limited D&C/ co-option potential, no H&M[a]	Can switch to conciliatory strategy. Limited D&C/ co-option potential, no H&M	Very limited ability to adopt conciliatory strategy	Limited ability to compromise	Stuck in confrontational strategy
Coordination	Moderately good coordination	Poor coordination	Satisfactory minimum coordination	Excellent coordination	Low coordination
Mobilization	Only effective in detribalized cities and adjacent areas		Mostly effective in detribalized refugee camps	Only effective in detribalized Tajik areas	Effective in *qawm*-dominated countryside
Control and discipline	Moderately successful control mechanisms	Poor control mechanisms	Moderately successful control mechanisms	Successful control mechanisms	Alignment of goals but poor control
Resilience	N.A.: Occupying power with over-whelming strength		Vulnerable to decapitation and weapon seizures	Vulnerable to decapitation	Not vulnerable to decapitation or other coun-terinsurgency shortcuts
Foreign aid	Depended on health of own economy	Depended on USSR and was controlled by it	Multiple redundant suppliers and logistics. Convergence of goals but no control by sponsors except in case of Pakistan and Hizb		
Intra-organizational cohesion	Affected by PDPA factionalism	Suffered from intense factionalism	Cohesive but expelled dissenters	Cohesive	Simple struc-tures prevented factionalism
Knowledge and information	Fair implementation of necessary information systems	Mediocre implementation of necessary information systems	Local information generally reached local decision-makers. Commander councils and centralized training facilities diffused knowledge that couldn't be locally generated.		
Structure	De facto decentralized because of intense factionalism. Competitive redundancy and specialization		Centralized and patronage	Complex Giap structure (both centralized and decentralized layers)	Patronage
Safe haven?	Yes		No	No	No
Good fit?	No		mixed	Yes	Yes
Survived?	Soviets withdraw, PDPA survives for three more years		Yes, but shrinks considerably	Yes	Yes

[a] D&C = divide and conquer; H&M = hearts and minds

mujahideen parties (no safe haven, good fit) survived as the organizational theory of group conflict predicts. The Hizb (centralized and patronage without safe haven) survived but shrank considerably over the course of the jihad. Massoud's choice of a Giap-like structure served him well absent a safe haven (good fit). The Soviets and their client regime did not take full advantage of what their structures allowed them to do. In fact, the PDPA's factionalism made it a de facto decentralized organization when it was meant to be a centralized one. The Soviets (bad fit) withdrew and the PDPA (bad fit) survived for three more years.

Centralized organizations generally faced similar challenges in performing essential operations and tried to remedy them with comparable structural and other fixes. The smaller size, ethnic homogeneity, and regional focus of the Massoud organization allowed it to best execute the processes facilitated or made necessary by centralization and specialization, while the PDPA and Hizb were less successful because of their geographic dispersion, factionalism, and larger size.[153] The simplicity of the structure of patronage-based parties spared them the challenges of complex management and organizational development in a hostile environment. The resistance's diversity and multiplicity of organizations allowed it, as a whole, to outperform the PDPA in executing all necessary processes except for coordination, which wasn't a priority so long as the resistance lacked a safe haven and was not ready to take the strategic initiative. The resistance's overall good performance allowed it to continue to be effective so long as its leaders adopted a confrontational policy. And it just happened that they were locked up in a confrontational strategy for structural reasons, namely the leaders' fear of losing uncompromising field commanders to more militant parties if they adopted a conciliatory strategy. The strategic lockup and the resistance's resilience made it clear to Gorbachev and his generals that it wasn't possible to benefit from occupying Afghanistan at a reasonable cost.

The Soviet withdrawal ushered in a new phase of the conflict that shifted the onus of taking the strategic initiative to the mujahideen, a task that required levels of coordination that patronage-based organizations could not provide.

---

153. See Roy (1995, 72–75) for more on how Massoud centralized and expanded his organization following the Giap model. Roy also argues that Massoud's task was facilitated by the availability of urbanized Panjshiris who returned to the valley.

CHAPTER 7

The Cost of the Failure to Restructure, 1989–1994

The Soviet withdrawal from Afghanistan gave the mujahideen the potential to take the strategic initiative by providing them with a safe haven in large areas of the countryside. On its own, the Kabul regime was reduced to defending the larger cities and most provincial capitals. Most of its border posts and lesser garrisons were either evacuated or captured by the resistance. Mujahideen parties were finally able to supply their commanders without fear of aerial bombing or ambushes by highly mobile Soviet paratroopers. Large campaigns like the eight massive assaults the Soviets conducted in Panjshir were a thing of the past. Much of the countryside, except for the Uzbek regions still in Dostum's hands and the areas controlled by the Ismaili and lesser militias, were under the control of mujahideen commanders who were patiently encircling the defensive belts of the main cities and launching the occasional brave but uncoordinated attack. Areas that did not border one of the security belts mostly experienced the government projection of power through the occasional, inaccurate, loud, but mostly symbolic launch of a SCUD missile. Mujahideen morale was high while that of members of the Kabul regime was sagging and the schisms that always plagued them were resurfacing in the absence of the cementing Soviet presence.[1]

1. See Giustozzi (2000, 34–35) for a discussion of the number of committed PDPA members in 1989. Soviet sources seem to estimate it at some thirty thousand to fifty thousand. See *Far Eastern Economic*

Although generous Soviet aid motivated the regime's clients to remain loyal, the Jawzjani and other militiamen began to demand greater compensation for their loyalty and the Ismaili militia increased its cooperation and double dealing with Massoud in preparation for anticipated changes in the balance of power.

Yet the Kabul regime survived for longer than three years. It ultimately fell not because the resistance parties overwhelmed it but because its patronage system collapsed with the cessation of aid from Moscow. The resistance endured long enough to see the central power collapse, but most resistance organizations unraveled as well. Only the two centralized mujahideen organizations, Hekmatyar's Hizb and Massoud's organization, were able to attempt sophisticated strategies such as the manipulation of segments of the state organization, but they tried to undermine each other as well. Their feeble efforts only succeeded after the cessation of Moscow's aid. They moved on to the next phase of the conflict to become the only serious contenders for power along with the similarly centralized Dostum and Wahdat organizations, until the rise of the Taliban. Curiously, the April 1992 breakup of Watan (the new and more politically neutral name of the PDPA) did not translate into a mujahideen victory, as most observers believed it would. It only heralded the demise of all patronage-based organizations, including Watan, in an environment that favored centralized ones from both sides. The 1989–95 Afghan conflicts allowed one type of organization that was better adapted to the new environment to survive at the expense of another, regardless of ideology, ethnicity, or religion.[2] It is ironic that what seemed to most observers to be an epic battle between two ideological camps produced an outcome where winners differed from losers not by their ideology but by the way they structured their organizations.

In this chapter I explain the outcome of Afghan conflicts in the period between the Soviet withdrawal and the rise of the Taliban. Along the way, I explain a number of puzzling developments following the Soviet withdrawal: the ability of the unpopular Najib regime to survive longer than anyone predicted; its sudden collapse in April 1992; the disintegration of all the Sunni mujahideen parties other than Hekmatyar's Hizb soon afterward;

Review, July 13, 1989, 18, for more on intra PDPA schisms: " 'Last August-September the [party] situation was desperate,' said a Soviet source. 'The Khalq leaders were openly talking about a coup; which Parchami leaders would be acceptable, which would be killed.' Around the October 1988 plenum meeting of the PDPA central committee, Najibullah arrested about 200 party opponents, putting major opponents out of action."

2. This chapter technically deals with two successive Afghan conflicts separated by the collapse of PDPA/Watan.

the increase in the autonomy of the local leaders who later ravaged the country; the failure of Hekmatyar to unify the Pushtun the way the Taliban later did; the consistent attempts of the ideologically related Hekmatyar and Massoud to undermine each other but not other mujahideen groups or parties; the inclination of only Hekmatyar's Hizb and Massoud's groups, but not others, to strike deals with segments of the regime's organization; the Iranian success in centralizing the Shiite groups and the Pakistani, U.S., and Saudi failure to do the same for the Sunni mujahideen; and the mujahideen's failure to take Jalalabad or Kabul before the regime imploded in 1992.[3]

I begin by describing events between 1989 and 1995. Next, I describe changes in the organizational structures of rival organizations and discuss their performance in the periods preceding and following the April 1992 demise of Najib's regime.

From the Soviet Withdrawal to the Rise of the Taliban (1989–1994)

The last Soviet soldier left Afghanistan on February 15, 1989.[4] The withdrawal produced euphoria among the mujahideen and their supporters. Virtually all observers and participants, with the exception of some diehard Soviet backers, predicted that the Najib regime would collapse within a year. U.S. confidence in the imminent collapse of the regime translated into an immediate and drastic reduction of aid to the mujahideen in the first half of 1989.[5] The collapse failed to materialize, however, because the Soviets poured immense resources ($3–$4 billion a year) to help their client regime survive. The United States and Saudi Arabia responded to Soviet aid by resuming supplies to the resistance in earnest to bring the 1989 aid total to some $1.3 billion.[6] The United States and Pakistan attempted to give the mujahideen the trappings of an alternative government by encouraging them to form the

3. Some of my arguments to answer those questions were either partly or completely made by other authors (Rubin 1995a, 1995b; Giustozzi 2000). These authors were not attempting to provide an explanation of all events based on a consistent theoretical perspective but found valid and convincing explanations for some events that make a good fit with my theoretical approach. I acknowledge previously made arguments and points of disagreement in other notes.

4. For more on events following the Soviet withdrawal, see Rubin 1995a. See Rubin (1995b) for more on diplomatic events and Giustozzi (2000) for how events affected the (D)RA.

5. *Independent*, June 20, 1989, 12.

6. Ahmed Rashid, "Highway Lifeline; Soviet Convoys Keep Kabul and Other Cities Alive," *Far Eastern Economic Review* 146, no. 43 (October 26, 1989): 22–23.

Interim Islamic Government of Afghanistan (IIGA) and supplying them with weapons that better fit the offensive role expected of them. The IIGA was for show, however, and the Pakistanis increased their support for Hekmatyar in the hope of bringing cohesion through the eventual domination of one loyal organization instead of the union of all parties. They still had to support the other parties, and later to provide aid directly to field commanders, because of the American desire to sideline the "extremist" Hekmatyar and Sayyaf.

U.S. and ISI strategists reasoned that one way to make the IIGA more relevant was to establish it in a major Afghan city. The ISI therefore orchestrated one of the conflict's major military disasters: the battle of Jalalabad. The mujahideen massed between five thousand and seven thousand men in the hills around Jalalabad in March 1989, but regime forces both outnumbered them and were ready to repulse the much-publicized and hyped attack. The attackers achieved immediate gains with sheer courage but were soon bogged down and even driven out from strategic positions they occupied. The mujahideen lost three thousand dead and wounded. It was clear by June that the battle for Jalalabad was lost.

The damage from the Jalalabad debacle was not limited to military losses and impact on morale; it also improved the regime's ability to retain supporters by demonstrating its unexpected resilience. The regime even managed to mobilize new supporters in areas where it posted particularly savvy administrators who made good use of the immense resources provided by Moscow, namely Brigadier Nurolhaq Olumi in Kandahar and Fazel Haq Khaleqyar in Herat. The regime's perceived resilience also weakened the cohesion of resistance parties, many of whose commanders increasingly preferred to free ride on the efforts of others and to focus on local affairs now that material incentives from their patrons mattered less or flowed less freely.[7] The Jalalabad debacle was so demoralizing that even the international press that was predicting the regime's end months earlier changed its prognosis and began criticizing mujahideen performance.

Another major battle raged around Kabul. It followed a different pattern than the battle of Jalalabad until the April 1992 collapse of the Najib regime. The mujahideen continued their patient ten-year-old encirclement of the city's defensive perimeters, which they occasionally attacked in brave but weakly coordinated regional operations. Although the mujahideen were never as close as they were in Jalalabad to capturing the city until the regime imploded, they did not suffer any debilitating setbacks either. It was theoretically

7. Giustozzi 2000, 178–85. Giustozzi's numbers, which might not be very reliable, reflect an increase in the numbers of "pacified" mujahideen groups after the Jalalabad disaster.

possible for the Kabuli mujahideen to have achieved decisive results with available resources immediately after the Soviet withdrawal, but, fortunately for them, they were not forced into the kind of sustained assault they simply were not organized to conduct effectively.

The departure of the Soviets, the failure of the IIGA, Pakistani bets on the Hizb, and the surprising resilience of Najib's regime led to a reduction of U.S. aid to the mujahideen in 1990 that was compensated for by increased Gulf State assistance until the Iraqi invasion of Kuwait ($280 million from the United States and up to $1.3 billion from Arab sources).[8] Hekmatyar and the ISI tried to take the initiative by developing a centralized conventional force they dubbed Lashkar Ithar (Army of Sacrifice) and attempting to manipulate intra-Watan schisms. Iran completed the unification of Hazara parties, thus creating Hizb-i Wahdat, and began supporting the Najib regime and Rabbani's Jamiat in an effort to counter Saudi and Pakistani influences.

Shahnawaz Tanai, defense minister of the DRA and the generally acknowledged leader of Watan's Khalq faction at the time, mounted a failed coup against the Parshami Najib on March 6, 1990. The coup took place in spite of Soviet mediation between the two men and after several lesser coups by Tanai supporters failed. Tanai failed to mobilize enough Khalqi officers to overwhelm the well-prepared Najib and requested help from Hekmatyar, who claimed in journalistic conferences to have been behind the coup and to have fully supported it. Hekmatyar gave refuge to Tanai and other fleeing Khalqi officers and was soon after ridiculed by leaders of other Peshawar parties. Although they cloaked their disapproval in terms of principles and ideology, it seems more likely that they disparaged Hekmatyar because he was the only one among them to have had the ability to manipulate the organizational segments of the regime.[9]

Tanai and other rebellious Khalqis joined Hekmatyar's Lashkar Ithar, and the ISI and Saudi Mukhabarat (intelligence) reportedly paid $15,000 a head to encourage commanders to support the centralized force's operations. The effort to increase the force met with strong resistance from the U.S. embassy, which took the side of the other Peshawar party leaders, who resented the encroachment on their party organizations, loose as they were.[10]

March 1991 saw an encouraging, though costly, mujahideen victory with the liberation of Khost, a small but well-fortified garrison town in Paktia

---

8. *Los Angeles Times*, November 19, 1989; *Far Eastern Economic Review*, December 7, 1989; *Christian Science Monitor*, June 20, 1990.

9. Kakar 1995, 271.

10. Rubin 1995b, 114–15.

Province. This military victory was achieved with ISI help and involved close coordination among mujahideen groups, including troops trained in defusing mines. Khost was insignificant in the larger scheme of things, however, and the mujahideen couldn't even agree on how to divide the spoils from the city.[11]

The first U.S.-Iraq War and the failed August 1991 coup in Moscow, whose discredited leaders were among the most dedicated supporters of Najib, led to a reduction of aid to both the Najib regime and to the mujahideen. A September 13, 1991, agreement between Soviet foreign minister Boris Pankin and U.S. secretary of state James Baker included a commitment to implement "negative symmetry" (the cessation of aid to both sides) effective at the beginning of 1992, and Soviet aid to Kabul ceased soon afterward.[12] The United States also ceased all weapon deliveries as promised by September 30, 1991 (the end of the U.S. budget fiscal year) but the mujahideen continued to receive some aid from Arab states and individuals.[13]

The failure of the August coup in Moscow signaled the beginning of the endgame and the urgent need for the different factions of the Najib regime to develop exit strategies. The only Hazara in the PDPA/Watan leadership, Sultan Ali Kishtmand, resigned and declared his support for Hazara national rights and regional autonomy. Khalqis intensified their contacts with Hekmatyar. The militias raised the price for their continued loyalty. Karmalists (the supporters of the removed president Babrak Karmal) among the Parshamis began negotiating with Dostum, while others, particularly among the numerous Tajik Parshamis, contacted Massoud. Several garrisons, including those of Herat and Kandahar, began negotiating with local mujahideen to prevent unnecessary bloodshed once the regime collapsed.

The centralized rivals of the regime were also preparing for the endgame. Massoud made good use of U.S.-supplied matériel to equip what had become his twelve-thousand–man Islamic Army; Wahdat consolidated its ranks; and Hekmatyar recruited as many fighters as he could find into his Army of Sacrifice, often sacrificing internal cohesion and good training. None of them could match in numbers Dostum's forty-thousand–strong

---

11. "What Khost Victory?" *Time*, April 15, 1991, 31.

12. "U.S.-Soviet Joint Statement on Afghanistan (Joint Statement and Commentary released by Secretary of State James Baker and Soviet Foreign Minister Boris Pankin)," *U.S. Department of State Dispatch* 2, no. 37 (Sept 16, 1991): 683. The regime continued to receive some assistance from New Delhi. *Time*, September 16, 1991, 43.

13. *Time*, June 24, 1991; *Washington Post*, October 1, 1991; see also *Far Eastern Economic Review*, October 3, 1991, 28, in which journalist Salamat Ali reports that Saudi Arabia provided the mujahideen with captured Iraqi weapons after the Gulf War, including some three hundred tanks.

force, or even Nadiri's Ismaili militia, which reportedly peaked at some eighteen thousand.[14]

Dostum openly rebelled against Najib in January of 1992, immediately after aid from the USSR ceased, and opened direct communication channels with both Massoud and the Ismaili militia.[15] Najib reacted by dispatching a force to quell the rebellion, but the force, under General Azimi, joined Dostum. They were joined on March 22, 1992, by Ahmad Shah Massoud, the Shiite Wahdat party under Abdul Ali Mazari, and the Ismaili militia under Sayyid Jaʿfar Nadiri (Mansur's son). Their alliance was assisted by Iran and was also joined by lesser commanders in the north of the country.

On March 18, 1992, Najib read on state radio and television a speech written for him by UN envoy Benon Sevan in which he announced his future resignation. He said his resignation would take effect once the United Nations established an interim government. Signaling weakness was never a helpful strategy in Afghanistan, and other significant players within Watan, the state apparatus, the militias, and among the mujahideen were in no mood to grant him the courtesy of a graceful exit. The Dostum-Massoud-Wahdat coalition first took over the strategic northern city of Mazar Sharif, where Dostum announced the establishment of an independent administration under his National Islamic Movement (Jumbish-i Milli-i Islami). More urgently for the beleaguered Najib, some Parshamis in Kabul under the leadership of Foreign Minister Abdulwakil defected and secretly invited Massoud to enter Kabul. Najib tried to flee from Kabul to avoid capture but was kept from reaching the airport by the renegade Parshamis and took refuge in the UN compound where he remained until hanged by the Taliban a few years later. Khalqis and some Pushtun Parshamis reacted to the possibility of a minority takeover of the capital by inviting Hekmatyar's forces to penetrate the city's defenses. But the pro-northern Parshamis had already armed the substantial Shiite population of Kabul that inhabited many areas from which the Hizb was to enter the city, and Dostum's and Massoud's forces moved in on April 25. A nimble Hizb-i Wahdat also took over the effort to mobilize the Shia of Kabul to achieve the till-then-unimaginable feat of controlling almost half of greater Kabul, mainly its southern and western sections.[16] The combined forces of the northern coalition drove Hekmatyar's forces and their Khalqi supporters from the sections of Kabul they occupied after several days of brutal combat.

---

14. Rubin 1995a, 160.

15. Rubin 1995b, 131 and n. 13.

16. See Harpviken (1995, chap. 10) for an account of how Wahdat entered Kabul.

The advancing forces of Dostum and Massoud gained control of large quantities of the fallen regime's military equipment.[17] Dostum seized the large stockpiles the Najib regime hoarded in Mazar Sharif as part of a contingency entrenchment plan that involved relocation from Kabul, and Massoud took over much of the weapons, including armor and airplanes, in the capital. Hekmatyar didn't fare nearly as well, mainly because the Hizb shared much of the spoils with regional commander shuras. Massoud, Dostum, and Hekmatyar also competed for the allegiance of complete units of the previous regime. Dostum gradually integrated the most effective northern units into his Jumbish, but Massoud took a little longer because of his insistence on creating a more cohesive organization controlled by loyal veterans from the jihad. Massoud did, however, control some of the better armored, missile, and air force units of the defunct regime.[18] Hekmatyar attracted Sarandoy and some KhAD/WAD units, but several militias that gave him their allegiance early on were either defeated by rivals, turned into independent drug lords and smugglers, or switched allegiance like so many field commanders had done before them.

In the meantime, Peshawar leaders, minus Hekmatyar, agreed to make Sibghatullah Mujaddedi president for two months, to be followed by Rabbani for four months. Afterward, they further agreed, the government would hold a shura that would select who would govern for the next eighteen months, at the end of which elections would be held. Massoud was the defense minister of the interim government, which arrived in Kabul on April 28 to proclaim the establishment of the Islamic State of Afghanistan. Hekmatyar expressed his disapproval of the new government and of its defense minister in particular by persistently bombing the capital, while Dostum and Massoud's forces remained independent from government control. Even worse, Sayyaf's Salafi forces were fighting Shiite Wahdat troops in the city's western and southern suburbs.

The disintegration of the Najib regime began a three-year period of bloody competition, alignment, and realignment among the centralized organizations, whose overarching goal was the partial or exclusive control of Kabul and their own ethnic spaces. The first coalition was formed by Massoud, Dostum, Wahdat, Nadiri, and their Parshami supporters to eject Hekmatyar and his Khalqi allies from Kabul immediately after regime components began executing their exit-and-preservation strategies of inviting their eth-

17. Ahadi 1995, 627.

18. Davis (1993) provides the best account of what happened to the units of the Afghan army after the collapse of the Najib regime.

nic kin to invade the city first. The first alliance was short lived, however, mostly because of its own success, the relative weakness of the Hizb (the only significant party attempting to mobilize the Pushtun), and regional politics now involving the newly independent states of Central Asia. On June 7, 1992, Massoud and Sayyaf's forces jointly attacked Wahdat's positions in Kabul, forcing the Hazara party into an unlikely alliance with Hekmatyar's Hizb, while Iran ironically supported the Rabbani government against fellow Shia for overarching geostrategic reasons.[19]

That year also witnessed the beginning of a serious Islamist outburst in Tajikistan.[20] The Islamist Tajik opposition obtained weapons and training in Afghanistan from commanders across the Amu Daria River. Their supporters and trainers included Massoud, Hekmatyar, Arab and Pakistani Islamists, and the always ambitious ISI.[21] This conflict was to simmer for several years and to involve Russian troops who reestablished Moscow's clients in Dushanbe and took up positions on the Tajik-Afghan border.[22] Much of Russia's policy in Afghanistan from this point on consisted of prolonging Afghan infighting to reduce the risk of an Islamist takeover in its new "near abroad." Attempts by Dostum's sponsors (Russia and Uzbekistan) to destroy the Tajik Islamist movement, which was closely supported by Massoud, accelerated the fallout between the two previous allies.[23] Those Afghans who needed Russian support claimed not to back the Tajik Islamists or even tried to impede their activities, like Dostum did. Interestingly, even Massoud officially distanced himself from the mujahideen of Tajikistan when he found himself with a dearth of allies.[24]

Yet, the Tajik Islamists mainly trained in Taloqan, an area under Massoud's direct control, and their troops were said to don his forces' uniforms.[25] Continuing cross-border attacks and rising Russian losses led Russia to increase its

---

19. Emadi 1997, 380–81.

20. See Rubin (1993–94) for more on Afghan influences on the Tajik conflict.

21. For more details, see Ahmed Rashid, "Point of Conflict: Russia and Islamic Militants in Tajik Proxy War," *Far Eastern Economic Review* 156, no. 22 (June 3, 1993): 24–25.

22. The August 1993 Moscow summit that brought together the leaders of the five previously Soviet Central Asian states and Boris Yeltsin mostly to coordinate to stem the development of Islamist challenges illustrates Moscow's preoccupation with this matter. See Vera Kuznetsova, et al., "Moscow Summit Addresses Tajik Border Crisis," *Current Digest of the Post-Soviet Press* 45, no. 32 (September 8, 1993): 13.

23. Rubin 1993.

24. "Massood Reviews History of Victory: Transcript of Sandy Gall's Interview with Ahmad Shah Massood, in Jabulseraj, on Monday, June 28th, 1993," *AFGHANews* 9 (November 1993): 7.

25. Rubin 1993–94, 85.

involvement in Tajikistan and to boost its border troops to fifteen thousand in mid-1993. Tashkent, Moscow, and Rabbani seemed to agree that the main Afghan supporter of the jihad in Tajikistan was Hekmatyar, who proudly assumed the responsibility to "teach the Tajik and Uzbek governments a lesson" by punishing them for supporting Dostum and Rabbani.[26] Hekmatyar, of course, wanted to increase the tension that the issue of the Tajik jihad caused in the relationship between Dostum and Uzbek president Islam Karimov, on the one hand, and the Tajik Massoud, on the other.[27]

In the last few days of 1992, Rabbani was chosen for a second term as president by what was widely perceived to be a biased and nonrepresentative shura of mostly Jamiat members. The poorly received election isolated Rabbani and Massoud. The only ally they gained in this period was Sayyaf, who abandoned Hekmatyar after January 1993 because of the Hizb's new alliance with his Shiite nemesis, Wahdat. Wahdat provided the Hizb with a foothold in the southern and western parts of Kabul. The shifts in alliances dispelled any lingering impressions that the conflict was one among ethnic groups. Attempts by Saudi Arabia and other outside parties to bring the rivals together in a coalition government during 1993–94 failed.

Dostum's relations with Rabbani and Massoud cooled when they refused him a seat in a new government, and he severed his alliance with them to join the Hizb in the early part of 1994. Dostum's Jumbish, the Hizb, Mujaddedi, and Wahdat allied in the Council for Coordination, which fought Massoud's force in Kabul without achieving substantial gains. The attacks gave the Rabbani government the opportunity to consolidate its presence in Kabul with some skillful maneuvering by Massoud's troops. The unlikely alliance was attributed to Uzbek and ISI brokerage.

The summer of 1994 witnessed a major attack by the Rabbani government on the increasingly weak Hazara in and around Kabul. Massoud managed to divide Hazara ranks by co-opting Harakat-i Islami, a substantial group under Ayatollah Mohammad Asif Mohsini that had once been part of Wahdat. Rabbani and Massoud's position still wasn't secure, however, because of the wide array of forces challenging them and a blockade of the capital by Jumbish and Hizb, so they tried to attract international support wherever they could find it. One out-of-character step by Rabbani was to visit the Tajik capital, Dushanbe, and the Uzbek capital, Tashkent, to appease

---

26. Boris Vinogradov, "In Tashkent, Afghan President B. Rabbani Promises to Block Arms Deliveries to Tajikistan," *Current Digest of the Post-Soviet Press* 44, no. 41 (November 11, 1992): 22.

27. Igor Rotar, "Practical Considerations Are Stronger Than Ideological Differences," *Current Digest of the Post-Soviet Press* 44, no. 42 (November 18, 1992): 16.

the Tajik, Uzbek, and Russian governments over the issue of continuing attacks by Tajik Islamists from bases in Afghanistan.[28] He did receive assistance from Russia and India, which both wanted to weaken Pakistan's longtime client, Hekmatyar. He also improved his ties to Saudi Arabia through his recent alliance with the Salafi Sayyaf and because of his aggressive attacks on the Shiite Wahdat party. Russia was also reported to support the secularist Dostum through Uzbekistan in an effort to extend the conflict and keep its "near abroad" safe from Afghan Islamist influence.

By the beginning of 1995, the persistent Hekmatyar was getting ready to finally deal a blow to his longtime rival Massoud with the help of his eclectic alliance and an expanded Army of Sacrifice. This was not to be—a new organization made an unexpected entry into Afghan affairs and swiftly disposed of Hekmatyar's forces. Hekmatyar's allies of convenience proved of little help to him when he was squeezed between Massoud's troops and those of the emerging organization, but the Taliban did not take long to defeat their first victim's unfaithful allies as well as most of his temporarily jubilant adversaries.

Organizational Changes

Rival organizations experienced important structural changes between the Soviet withdrawal and the rise of the Taliban. The Najib regime became increasingly reliant on patronage ties and made little progress integrating its different branches. Hekmatyar and Massoud developed their centralized structures to expand their zones of influence. Other mujahideen parties slowly dissolved; by the end of this phase of the conflict, most field commanders had little more than nominal allegiance to the Peshawar parties. Some commanders came together in regional shura councils, some of which were consolidated by the presence of prominent commanders who became regional patrons. Three short-lived autonomous "emirates" emerged to play important regional roles, one equivalent to those of important commanders, but they were soon eliminated by stronger centralized rivals. Dostum and lesser client militias used Najib's desperation to their advantage by extracting increasing amounts of resources from their patron and developing large centralized forces. The Hazara parties coalesced under Iranian pressure to form the centralized Wahdat party. The remainder of this section explains why and how those changes took place, and table 7.1 lists the more significant organizations before the rise of the Taliban.

---

28. Magnus and Naby 1995, 616.

Table 7.1. Significant organizational contenders during the 1989–1994 conflicts

ORGANIZATION	LEADER	STRUCTURE	EXTERNAL SUPPORT	ORGANIZATIONAL LIFE	ETHNIC COMPOSITION	IDEOLOGICAL ORIENTATION
Watan/DRA	Najib (ullah)	Centralized organization with redundant structures dominated by rival factions with an extensive network of patronage	Soviet Union/ Russia, India	Organization disintegrates in April 1992. Clients become independent and factions join Dostum, Massoud, and Hekmatyar	Khalqi faction made of mostly Pushtu speakers and Parshami faction composed of minorities and Dari speakers	Gradually tried to shift toward center to increase its ability to mobilize
Jawzjani militia/53rd Division/ Jumbish-i Milli	Rashid Dostum	Centralized organization with mobile formations and some patronage ties. Patronage ties increased after 1992	Uzbekistan, Turkey, India, Russia, Iran	A largely autonomous client of the DRA even when called an army division, then an independent organization	Mostly Uzbek but also some Pushtun and others. Post-1992 clients more ethnically diverse.	Secular, desired a loose federal state with a weak center
Hizb-i Islami	Gulbudin Hekmatyar	Highly centralized, Marxist-like structure. Calls its integrated mobile force Lashkar Ithar (Army of Sacrifice)	USA/Pakistan, Saudi Arabia, and Kuwait until Gulf War and Iraq after, independent Islamists.	Incorporates Watan's Sarandoy and other Khalqi units	Probably the most ethnically diverse party, but with a Pushtun Ghilzai majority	Islamist. pragmatist
Jamiat-i Islami	Burhanuddin Rabani	Its commanders became increasingly independent	China, France, USA/Pakistan	Gradually reduced to Massoud's and Ismail Khan's organizations	Mostly Tajik, but also some Uzbek, Sunni Hazara, and Pushtun	Moderate Islamist
Shura-i Nazar-i Shamali	Ahmad Shah Massoud	Highly centralized organization that used old Jamiat superstructure and Rabbani's presence to maintain ties to other commanders	Russia, India, USA, France, Iran	Last bastion resisting Taliban as of 2001. Rebounded with U.S. invasion.	The core organization is mostly Tajik but the umbrella group included a multiethnic coalition	Islamist, pragmatic

Hizb-i Islami	Yunis Khalis	All five patronage-based parties were debilitated by the increased independence of their commanders and the cessation of foreign aid. Only Sayyaf managed to develop a small mobile force that played an active role in the battle for Kabul.	Aid from the USA and Pakistan was gradually reduced and largely stopped by the beginning of 1992. Sayyaf and Khalis continued to get some help from Arab Gulf states and individuals.	The parties themselves became increasingly irrelevant but the leaders continued to play public roles for a while. The formation of regional commander councils weakened parties even further.	Pushtun	Traditional Islamist
Ittihad	Abd-Rab-al-Rassoul Sayyaf				Mostly Pushtun	Purist Islamist
Harakat-i Inqilab-i Islami	Muhammad Nabi				Pushtun	Sufi, traditional
Jabha-i Nejat-i Milli Afghanistan	Sibghatullah Mujaddedi				Pushtun	Sufi, royalist
Mahaz-i Milli Islami	Pir Sayyed Ahmad Gailani				Pushtun	Qadiri Sufi, royalist
Hizb-i Wahdat	Abdul Ali Mazari then Karim Khalili	A unity party formed of all Shia parties in 1988	Iran	Began as an alliance in 1988 but developed into a centralized party	Hazara and some other Shia, notably Quizilbash	Moderate Islamism and Hazara nationalism
Ahl-al-Kitab-wal-Sunna	Jamil al-Rahman (until 1991)	Regionally based, centralized	Saudi Wahhabi groups and Saudi Arabia	Splintered from Hekmatyar's Hizb and later destroyed by it	Kunar and Nuristan Pushtun and Nuris	Salafi/Wahhabi, purist Islamist
"Dawlat" (Islamic State of Afghanistan)	Mawlawi Afzal	Regionally and tribally based Salafi emirate in Nuristan	Saudi Wahhabi groups and Saudi Arabia	Formed in 1978	Mostly the Kati tribe	Salafi/Wahhabi, purist Islamist
Argo emirate	Mawlawi Shariqi	Regionally and tribally based Salafi emirate in Badakhshan	Saudi Wahhabi groups and Saudi Arabia	Split from Jamiat to become an independent organization then joined Hizb after Shariqi was assassinated. Defeated by Massoud in 1991	Tajiks and Uzbek muhajireen	Salafi/Wahhabi, purist Islamist

(*continued*)

Table 7.1. (continued)

ORGANIZATION	LEADER	STRUCTURE	EXTERNAL SUPPORT	ORGANIZATIONAL LIFE	ETHNIC COMPOSITION	IDEOLOGICAL ORIENTATION
Ismaili militia	Sayyid Mansur Nadiri	Militia and clients were said to have peaked at 13,000–18,000 troops, mostly Ismailis.	Supported by Dostum and gradually integrated within his Jumbish	Previous DRA militia, defected with Dostum. Later destroyed by Taliban	Ismailis from northern Afghanistan	Group preservation
Major regional commander shuras						
Herat shura	Ismail Khan	Shura had centralized force called Amir Hamza Division. Vestigial committees	Member of Jamiat	Established in 1987. Overran by Taliban and Dostum in 1996	Mixed	Local concerns
Jallalabad shura	—	Formed mostly by Mahaz (Gailani) and Khalis commanders	—	Largely dysfunctional by end of 1993	Eastern Pushtun	Local concerns
Balkh shura	Mawlawi Alam	Shura had specialized committees and ran a school system	Member of Jamiat	Established in 1988	Tajik	Local concerns
Kandahar shura	Led by executive committee	Loosely organized in committees, weak shura	—	—	Durrani Pushtun	Local concerns
Gardez (Paktia) shura	Jallaludin Haqqani	—	—	—	Eastern Pushtun	Local concerns

Before the Collapse of the Najib Regime

The Najib regime grew increasingly dependent on costly and volatile ties of clientage. One example of such reliance is that thirty thousand of the fifty-five thousand regime troops in Herat province were militiamen in 1988.[29] In 1990, the two main DRA infantry divisions in Herat and Shindand consisted of some five thousand regular troops and twenty-eight thousand militiamen. Overall, militiamen were estimated to number some sixty thousand to seventy thousand, twice the size of the regular army, in 1990.[30]

Soviet advisers realized the dangers of heavy reliance on militias whose leaders they knew to maintain contacts with mujahideen parties and advised Najib to try to increase the number of regular troops instead.[31] The militias were not only costly but also largely disappointing as fighting forces: they knew they could command a high premium from an increasingly desperate regime and had little incentive to create bad blood with neighboring mujahideen that they knew they had to deal with soon. For example:

> Commander Anwar Sayed Ahmed . . . has 8–10,000 men [probably an inflated figure], 10 tanks, 40 other military vehicles and the run of the city [Herat]. Sayed Ahmed recently fell out with mujahideen commander Ismael Khan, and the government snapped him up. The future of Afghanistan is already evident in Herat where local militias have bridged the ideological divide between the Islamic mujahideen and the communist regime. By day they work for the government; by night they maintain contact with their mujahideen friends.[32]

The militias often allowed the mujahideen to move through their roadblocks for a fee, thus increasing their revenues as well as keeping their options open. Regime militias also rarely coordinated with the army, which, in turn, did not intervene when their villages were attacked by mujahideen.[33] The government's desperation was evident from its increasing concessions to its militias and from the price it was willing to pay to maintain their loyalty.[34] After 1987 it offered self-rule to those who joined it as militias, a remarkable change. They were also guaranteed land ownership, free practice of trade, the

29. Giustozzi 2000, 213.

30. Rubin 1995a, 161.

31. Giustozzi 2000, 219.

32. "Herat's Patchwork Peace," *Far Eastern Economic Review* 146, no. 43 (October 26, 1989): 20.

33. Giustozzi 2000, 220–22.

34. Ibid., 156–75.

cancellation of past taxes, allowances to the disabled and families of the deceased, and the right to keep their weapons. Most militias received weapons in larger quantities and of better quality (including tanks and rockets) the more desperate the regime became.[35] They were also given practical assistance, including clinics, fertilizer, seeds, and salaries for village heads, imams, and militia members. In 1990 the government abolished the limitation on ceremonial expenses (*mahr* or the sum given by a man seeking marriage) and drastically reduced its literacy (and indoctrination) program as a further concession, albeit a cheap and largely symbolic one.

Najib's options were limited. The stronger the militias became, the more he needed them and had to give them in return for continuing loyalty. A threat of defection generally provided militiamen with an improved deal. Militias therefore became some of the stronger organizational components of the regime in the post-Soviet withdrawal period.[36] The most powerful militias were Dostum's Jawzajanis, Sayyid Mansur Nadiri's Ismailis, and, perhaps, Jabar Khan's Helmand-based force. The first two increased in importance for the regime, which gave them some of its better weapons in hopes of transforming them into loyal mobile forces that would help project its power in areas beyond their immediate control. The Dostum force was successfully transformed into a mobile force of some forty thousand troops, but the Ismaili militia (said to number thirteen thousand in 1989 and eighteen thousand in 1992) were only occasionally posted outside their strategic location.[37] When Dostum showed signs of defection in early 1992, the Najib regime tried to make Jabar's militia, a full division by then, the main mobile force to project its power, but the regime collapsed soon afterward. The three militias survived the Najib regime and became major players in the post-PDPA/Watan era, in a clear indication of the shift in power from patron to client. The first two survived until the Taliban sweep through northern Afghanistan, and the Jabar force lasted for two years after the collapse of Najib's regime as a cohesive fighting force.[38]

Najib did make one improvement to his centralized command structure: he developed the loyal Special Guard to the sizable twenty to forty

35. Ibid., 247.

36. The militias were given official designations as army divisions, corps, or brigades, but I refer to them as militias because they were outside of the command structure of the ministries of defense and of the interior. They also enjoyed a distinctive patron-client relationship with the regime that differed from the more rigid chain of command that characterized its relationship with its regular troops.

37. Giustozzi 2000, 224.

38. Khan 1993, 59.

thousand–strong mostly Tajik force that saved him from the Tanai coup.[39] The Special Guard increasingly became Najib's necessary last line of defense because the withdrawal of the Soviets allowed the resurgence of intense factionalism within regime institutions. Factionalism was so virulent that Najib could only prop up factions he hoped would remain faithful to him instead of integrating his institutions. His only means of control was the threat of withholding the resources sent to him from Moscow. But even this control mechanism was circumscribed because much of those resources had to cross the territories that some of his supposedly loyal clients controlled, allowing them in the last couple of years to directly expropriate what they believed to be their fair share. Najib's, however, wasn't the only slowly disintegrating patronage-based organization.

Mujahideen commanders became increasingly independent from their parties during the 1989–95 period because of the abundance of available weapons, the less threatening posture of the regime, the increase in direct military aid from foreign sponsors, the increase in direct humanitarian aid from NGOs, the revival of agriculture and particularly opium cultivation, and the emergence of smuggling and the imposition of tolls on road traffic as sources of alternative income.

Weapons became so abundant in Afghanistan after the Soviet withdrawal that they lost value as a currency to buy loyalty. The PDPA/Watan government was estimated to have been the fifth largest importer of weapons in the world between 1986 and 1990.[40] Add military aid channeled through the Iranian and Pakistani borders and Afghanistan might have ranked even higher.

Not only were weapons less valuable, but field commanders were increasingly able to procure them through direct channels. Massoud leveraged his international reputation by sending emissaries to Washington in March 1990 to successfully request that U.S. organized aid be supplied directly to important commanders by circumventing ISI.[41] A new ISI leadership, perhaps taking more seriously threats of U.S. reduction of aid now that the Soviets had withdrawn, accommodated the American desire to directly supply the commanders.[42] Direct aid to commanders was facilitated by new supply lines that were unusable during the days of Soviet air superiority. NGOs and USAID also contributed to weakening patronage ties

39. Rubin 1995a, 156.

40. *SIPRI Yearbook 1991: World Armament and Disarmament* (Oxford: Oxford University Press, 1991), 199, 208.

41. Rubin 1995b, 20–21 and 120.

42. Yousaf 1992, 218.

within Afghan mujahideen parties by directly channeling aid to field commanders.[43]

Aid was not the only source of revenue for the field commanders anymore. The weakening of the regime enabled commanders along major roads to set up roadblocks to levy tolls on road transport, smugglers, and traders supplying the Najib regime's cities. Some became traders themselves and supplied the regime-controlled cities at great profit, leading some to find in this trade an explanation of the endurance of the Najib regime. The retrenchment of regime troops to the cities and the near disappearance of the air threat also allowed the farming of a premium cash crop that transformed several previous commanders and militiamen into drug producers: the opium poppy.

All those factors made loyalty to the Peshawar parties unnecessary. They led to the progressive unraveling of the patronage-based parties, which suffered the ultimate blow when they eventually ceased to be conduits for any more military aid from foreign sponsors—a fate similar to that of the Najib regime. The representative events in Badakhshan Province illustrate how irrelevant patronage-based parties had become by 1992. Basir Khalid, a Jamiat commander from around the provincial capital of Faizabad, teamed up with a Hizb commander to attack and occupy the town in a bloody battle to keep out two other Jamiat commanders, Najmuddin and Aryanpoor.[44] The increased autonomy of field commanders and their diminished need for a party also made it even harder for the Hizb to woo them to join its centralized structure. The increased independence of commanders also manifested itself in resistance to ISI directives.[45]

The decreased relevance of Peshawar leaders allowed important commanders who attracted direct aid (from NGOs, the ISI, USAID, or from Arab organizations, individuals, and states) to become regional patrons or heads of hierarchical shuras. But there were centrifugal forces working even on this level, not the least of which were local means of raising revenue. Even lesser commanders who were getting aid from relief organizations through the dominant commander of a shura sometimes approached them for direct aid, like commander Afzali of Herat did to reduce Ismail Khan's leverage as a regional patron. Several regional shuras, such as the Kandahari and Nangarhari ones, ultimately unraveled by themselves. Attempts by powerful commanders such as Massoud and Ismail Khan to create independent nationwide commanders'

43. Rubin 1995b, 67.

44. Ian MacWilliams and Charles Hoot, "Outside Kabul Is Another Country," *Middle East*, September 1992, 22–23.

45. Rubin 1995b, 118.

organizations were also short lived for similar reasons as well as ethnic and tribal tensions and sabotage by the ISI and the Peshawar parties.[46] The two commanders did manage, however, to create powerful regional shuras held together by their regionally hegemonic centralized organizations and their ability to function as beacons for direct international military and relief aid.

Many mujahideen around Herat were organized from 1987 in a shura under the influence of Jamiat's Ismail Khan, a former Afghan Army officer who built a centralized fighting force of some three thousand to five thousand troops dubbed the Amir Hamza Division.[47] Ironically, the Soviet withdrawal weakened Ismail Khan by depriving him of his $500,000 allocation from ISI and reducing the ideological hurdle traditional commanders resentful of his centralizing effort had to overcome to become government clients.[48] Successful government co-optation was facilitated by an infusion of resources and a generous government program to buy wheat. The collapse of the Najib regime allowed Ismail Khan to expand his control around Herat and to disarm regime militias that had temporarily joined Hekmatyar and taken the Shindand air base.[49] He also disarmed Shiite organizations with little objection from the Shiite population. Ismail Khan remained loyal to the Rabbani regime and skirmished with Dostum in Faryab in early 1994 when tension rose between the Uzbek warlord and the Rabbani government.[50] He used other groups' preoccupation with events in Kabul to consolidate his administration in the city and six adjacent provinces with their 2.5 million ethnically mixed inhabitants. Herat experienced a relative economic revival compared to the rest of Afghanistan during the 1992–96 period. Ismail Khan received some financial and military support from Pakistan and Central Asian states keen on minimizing Iranian influence in his area of control.

Lesser and more loosely structured regional shuras emerged in Kandahar, Jalalabad, Nangarhar, Gardez, and Balkh. They were generally ineffectual and did not lead to the development of local government or integrated military forces.

In addition to regional shuras, at least three Salafi—nonsupporters accusingly say Wahhabi—emirates emerged as regional players with Arab Gulf

---

46. See Rubin (1995b, 119–20) for more on Ismail Khan's attempt to form an independent commanders' organization.

47. For more on Ismail Khan's organization, see Roy (1990, 180–81) and Rubin (1995a, 238–40).

48. Rubin 1995a, 260–1.

49. Ahmed Rashid, "Work in Progress: Self-styled Emir Imposes Order in Turbulent Herat," *Far Eastern Economic Review* 156, no. 41 (October 14, 1993), 24–26.

50. Rubin 1995a, 276–77.

support. In an indication of things to come, they traced their roots and inspiration to the Salafi madrassa of Panjpir. The most significant was Jamil al-Rahman's Jama'at Ahl-al-Kitab wal-Sunna, which he created in Kunar after defecting from Hekmatyar's Hizb in 1985. He was later assassinated, and his organization was defeated in a brutal 1991 Hizb assault. Another Salafi emirate, dubbed Dawlat, was created in Nuristan by Mawlawi Afzal. A third was created by Mawlawi Shariqi's followers in Badakhshan but was defeated by Massoud after Shariqi was assassinated.

After the Collapse of the Najib Regime

There were four significant organizations with national aspirations competing for power after the collapse of the Najib regime: Dostum's Jawzjani militia-turned-army-division, Massoud's organization, Hekmatyar's Hizb, and the Hazara Hizb-i Wahdat. Mujahideen parties besides the Hizb and Jamiat began to dissolve as party leaders gradually lost status and influence. Larger commanders expanded their spheres of influence through patronage. Lesser commanders continued to thrive when they found sources of income to maintain their groups. Remnants of the defunct PDPA/Watan organizations joined the four main organizations: some Parshami leaders including Babrak Karmal joined Dostum; Tajik and other non-Pushtun Parshamis in Kabul and the north joined Massoud; and Khalqis and some previous militias joined Hekmatyar's Lashkar Ithar.

Dostum generally desired a federal system for Afghanistan in which his large organization would control Uzbek and adjacent areas. He had little desire to give up control over his powerful military organization to an ethnically based union with Uzbekistan, and such a union did not interest the newly independent and impoverished Central Asian republic anyway.[51] He enjoyed increased international legitimacy when several states opened consulates in Mazar, and he was received as a statesman in visits to Saudi Arabia, Turkey, Pakistan, and Uzbekistan. The relative peace in his area allowed him to develop the trappings of a state administration that provided essential services, minted currency in competition with the Rabbani government, and collected taxes and customs revenues on the healthy trade then taking place with Uzbekistan.[52]

51. Rubin 1993, 84.

52. Ahmed Rashid, "Master of War: General Dostam Acts as Beacon to Uzbeks," *Far Eastern Economic Review* 156, no. 7 (February 18, 1993), 26. On the currency issue, see "A Thousand Afghanistans," *Swiss Review of World Affairs*, November 1, 1995.

Dostum attracted Nadiri's Ismaili force (80th Division) and previous regime military officers and units (such as the Tajik Abdul Mumin's 70th Division) around Mazar Sharif as semiclients as an expedient alternative to expanding his centralized and mobile force.[53] He also developed patronage ties with previous mujahideen commanders and lesser warlords in adjacent areas by using the immense resources he had accumulated during his years as Kabul's client and that he continued to receive from Central Asia. He partially integrated many previous mujahideen into the hierarchical structure he led along with his two most prominent commanders, Rasul and Ghaffar Pahlawan. His forces may have peaked at anywhere between forty thousand and sixty thousand troops with hundreds of tanks and dozens of serviceable aircrafts. While the centralized portion of Dostum's organization grew considerably after the collapse of the Najib regime, patronage ties—particularly with non-Uzbek groups—grew to form a larger portion of his organization than ever before.

Massoud expanded his control over the Tajik areas after the Soviet withdrawal and integrated the Najib regime's military units in Kabul, Bagram, and Charikar into his centralized force after the regime collapsed. Growth, however, was slowed by Massoud's insistence on carefully integrating former regime officers and new volunteers into his organization in a way that would preserve its integrity and preempt factionalism.[54]

Massoud also developed civilian institutions in the northeast. They functioned well enough without his presence to allow him to focus on national affairs and the battle for Kabul. Massoud received less foreign aid than Dostum but seized many of the collapsed regime's weapons depots and may have received 20 percent of the supplies sent to the Kabul regime through his section of the Salang highway between the Soviet withdrawal and the regime's collapse. He also benefited from the supply of freshly minted banknotes from Moscow and the export of some $2 billion worth of gemstones (emeralds and lesser stones) from Tajik areas.[55] Massoud's fighting force was the well-trained and well-integrated centralized Islamic Army that grew to some twelve thousand troops by the time the Kabul regime collapsed. Massoud played a very limited patronage role through his leadership of Shura Nazar and by leveraging his international notoriety to attract considerable direct aid.

---

53. Davis 1993, 135–38; 1994a, 323.

54. See also Davis (1994a) for more on the inability of Massoud to develop his force the way he hoped because of limited resources and continuing military crises.

55. "A Thousand Afghanistans."

Hizb-i Wahdat had its origin in an 1987 alliance dominated by two pro-Iranian parties (Nasr and Sepah-i Pasdaran) that co-opted all other Hazara and some non-Hazara Shiite organizations. The establishment of Wahdat as a cohesive party under the leadership of Abdul Ali Mazari took place in Tehran on June 16, 1990. By then, it has become a centralized organization with influence over the entire Hazarajat. It had a supervisory council of twenty-four members and a central committee of seventy-five members that served to give status to co-opted traditional leaders. More important, it had a specialized structure it inherited from its two dominant founding organizations, including a well-developed intelligence service.[56] This efficient centralized structure later allowed Wahdat to take advantage of the opening in Kabul provided by the collapse of the Najib regime.

The only centralized organization that mainly recruited among Pushtuns and with any potential to compete with Dostum, Massoud, or Mazari's organizations was Hekmatyar's Hizb. The Hizb tried to leverage this fact and considerable Pakistani aid to increase its support in the Pushtun ethnic space, but it was limited by its image among Durranis as an Eastern Pushtun party and its reputation among the tribes as antitribal. In addition, increasingly independent and self-financed commanders found little reason to sacrifice their autonomy to join its centralized structure. Even the intense desire to reverse the occupation of Kabul by Tajik and, even more unusually, Uzbek and Shiite forces did not motivate Pushtuns to rally around Hekmatyar.[57] The Hizb's violent retaliation against dissenters, such as the attack on Jamil ul-Rahman's group, also raised awareness of the high exit cost for those who decided to join its ranks.

The Hizb's centralized force was composed of its long-standing core fighting organization as well as Sarandoy and other Khalqi troops that defected to it, and a supply of new recruits from the refugee camps. Recruitment in the camps was facilitated by Pakistani support, the Hizb's developed educational system, and the lack of alternative sources of income for the refugees.

Sayyaf's Ittihad was the only other Peshawar party that developed a centralized force. It was fairly small compared to those of the other contenders but benefited from a central training facility that Sayyaf ran in conjunction with Arab volunteers. His organization was generously funded by Gulf Arabs.

---

56. Harpviken 1995, 102.

57. Fänge 1995, 19.

Organizational Performance during the 1989–1992 Period

The significant organizational players between the February 1989 Soviet withdrawal and the April 1992 collapse of the Najib regime were the factionalism-ridden PDPA/Watan and its major clients, increasingly disintegrating patronage-based mujahideen parties, Hekmatyar and Massoud's centralized organizations, and the recently formed Hizb-i Wahdat. The following discussion is best understood with close reference to the previous chapter.

Strategy

The Najib regime simply needed to survive as long as possible, and its best assets were the abundant resources put at its disposal by Moscow. It was structurally incapable of going on the offensive because of the intense factionalism that riddled its structure and the readiness of its troops to defect when outside of their garrisons. It had little to gain anyway from engaging in military offensives because it enjoyed the benefits of the well-constructed defensive structures it inherited from the Soviets. What it tried to do with its relatively abundant resources was to continue to implement divide-and-rule and co-optive strategies initiated under Soviet occupation. Its task was made easier by the Soviet withdrawal and its efforts to distance itself from communism and atheism.

Hizb-i Wahdat adopted an accommodationist strategy toward Kabul because it already dominated its ethnic space in Hazarajat; because the Shia of Kabul were well treated by a regime keen on shoring up minority support; and because Iran and the Najib regime were on good terms. All other organizations avoided the Hazarajat because they had more urgent tasks at hand, and Wahdat therefore did not have to counter any strategies aimed at reducing its territorial space.

Dostum and other Kabul clients tried to extract as much resources as they could from their patron to develop and expand their own organizations and, in the case of the Jawzjanis and Ismailis, to dominate their ethnic spaces. They had little incentive, unless posted out of their base areas, to fight neighboring mujahideen, and they often made deals with them. The militias had no reason to consider exit strategies until the regime failed to supply them with resources.

The patronage-based mujahideen parties' slow degeneration enabled each field commander to have a personal strategy that was mostly motivated by local considerations. The gradual decrease in the amount and value of the resources the parties were able to distribute to their client commanders and the withdrawal of Soviet troops slowly started to loosen the confrontational strategy deadlock that previously exhausted the Soviets. This, however, was not the case for Hekmatyar's Hizb and Massoud's group. Both had a lot to gain from the collapse of the regime but feared that the other would obtain much of the spoils, which included the prime prize of controlling Kabul. They feared each other because they controlled the two largest centralized organizations among the mujahideen. Only they among the mujahideen could take the strategic initiative once Kabul became ripe for the taking. Hekmatyar's and Massoud's troops frequently clashed or tried to sabotage each others' activities on many fronts where they coexisted. For example:

> Massoud's guerrillas captured the town of Khwaja i Ghar last year from General Abdul Rashid Dostum's militia (when Dostum was still loyal to Najibullah), while the local Hizb i Islami commander stood idly by, allegedly even allowing Dostum's men to enter the town unhindered in their effort to defend it. . . . The provincial capital, Taloqan, was also captured by the resistance. The city was divided up between guerrillas loyal to Hekmatyar and Massoud, who soon fell out with each other. The outnumbered Hizb troops were forced to evacuate their half of the city.[58]

While the two centralized organizations clashed continuously, groups affiliated with looser Peshawar parties were generally neutral.[59] Interestingly, Bashir, the Hizb commander in Kunduz, was quoted as saying in an interview more than two years earlier that "Massoud is my enemy" while giving scant attention to the Communists.[60] The enmity around Kunduz went a long way back: Hekmatyar's forces once assassinated a group of top Massoud commanders just before a major, but non-ISI sanctioned, assault planned by Massoud to capture the town, and Massoud retaliated by hanging some Hizb commanders he accused of committing the offense.

Besides direct confrontation, and because of their relatively small sizes that prevented them from overrunning the regime's major towns on their own, the centralized Hizb and Massoud organizations' best strategy was to manipulate factional divisions within the regime. Both succeeded in also eliminating smaller centralized challengers within their vicinity. In 1991,

58. MacWilliams and Hoot, "Outside Kabul Is Another Country."

59. Ibid., 24.

60. *Newsweek*, January 22, 1990, 41.

and in preparation for the coming endgame, Massoud destroyed Mawlawi Shariqi's Argo emirate and Hekmatyar eliminated Jamil ul-Rahman's emirate in Kunar.

Coordination

The PDPA was incapable of efficient coordination among its branches because of intense factionalism within its centralized structure and the increasingly blatant autonomy and assertiveness of its clients. Yet, it achieved good results in coordinating defensive action by relocating troops and using its air force to attack mujahideen concentrations. The bar for necessary coordination is lower in defense than in offense and when the goal is mere survival instead of expansion. The Soviet withdrawal definitely moved the burden of good coordination to the mujahideen.

All of the main centralized organizations (the Hizb, Massoud's force, Wahdat, and the larger militias) took measures to improve coordination among their troops. Power within the resistance was so diffuse, however, that neither Massoud nor Hekmatyar could implement a major attack on his own, and coordination between the two rivals was impossible with their sights set on the endgame. Any attack demanded a herculean effort by either a dominant regional commander or, more often, the ISI to impose coordination among many commanders by offering hefty financial incentives or making credible threats. The ISI's only accomplishment in this respect was the Khost operation, too insignificant a success to make up for the failure to coordinate commanders' actions during the Jalalabad debacle.

One example of how the resistance's divisions hindered its ability to coordinate was Massoud's reluctance to close a stretch of the strategic Salang highway that supplied Kabul. The highway was protected by the regime's Uzbek and Ismaili militias, except for stretches just south of the Ismaili militia's area of control that Massoud occupied in the immediate aftermath of the Soviet withdrawal. The Tajik commander was reported (but this could be baseless propaganda by his rivals) to have rebuffed requests to shut down Kabul's lifeline because he received a fifth of all the supplies that went through his area.[61] Either way, the full amount or the remaining four-fifths that did go through extended the life of the Najib regime and made the job of the mujahideen surrounding Kabul much harder.

61. Rubin 1995a, 259.

Mobilization of Resources

The ability of the Najib regime's military to mobilize resources was closely connected to the general perception of its longevity. The Soviet withdrawal caused desertions to increase, but the regime's ability to defend Jalalabad increased confidence in its ability to endure, thus improving its ability to recruit into its armed forces and to gain new clients. But everyone was on the lookout for signs of the end of the vital Soviet supply effort in order to time their exit.

The regime's clients did much better. The increased resources of the Dostum and Ismaili militias allowed them to mobilize more groups in their periphery through co-option, clientage, or by integrating followers on an individual basis. In a historically surprising development, Nadiri's Ismaili militia was even reported to have recruited non-Ismailis from the surrounding areas by meting out positive sanctions and building a powerful military force.[62]

Massoud and Hekmatyar did the same. They both used their resources to expand their centralized organizations. Their mobilization performances during the 1989–92 phase were similar to the pre-Soviet withdrawal phase, but the Hizb was hindered by the general perception that it was antitribal, anti-Durrani, and bent on reducing independent commanders who joined it to mere salaried officers—a fate no proud Afghan would accept absent dire circumstances.

The ability of the patronage-based organizations to mobilize support became proportional to the value of the resources they could still channel to their supporters. The ideological motivation to belong to a mujahideen party was reduced by the Soviet withdrawal, the government's effort to shed its ideological colors, and its inability to subvert local autonomy. The relatively opulent lifestyle of the traditional party leaders also contributed to the dilution of their influence over commanders leading the rugged life of the jihad. These organizations did not have the means to mete out positive and negative sanctions to drive mobilization like the centralized organizations.

Hizb-i Wahdat strongly dominated the Hazara ethnic space and even mobilized non-Hazara Shia for some time. Only some Shia on the periphery of Hazarajat and in the larger cities were not within its area of control. It also had privileged access to the Hazara refugee population in Iran. It made efficient use of its control of resources to mete out positive and negative sanctions

62. *Far Eastern Economic Review*, July 13, 1989, 16.

and integrate the organizations it co-opted into a single, cohesive, and centralized organization. Wahdat also benefited from the perception that it made little sense for Hazaras to form smaller parties when the only way to have an impact on the national level as members of this historically disadvantaged group was to unite. The endgame in sight improved the largest minority organizations' ability to mobilize within their respective ethnic spaces.

Control and Discipline

The Najib regime and the patronage-based parties increasingly suffered from loosening control over their clients because of the lessening value of the goods they could provide. The clients formulated their own independent local policies, and the best the increasingly weak patrons could do was to keep them from defecting. Dilution of control mechanisms also caused deterioration in discipline that reflected badly on the patrons and created negative incentives to join their institutions. One glaring example of such behavior was the abusive behavior of the Uzbek militias when posted in Pushtun areas and the capital. The regime increasingly posted minority militiamen in Pushtun areas where some used this unexpected reversal of historical power relations to commit abuses that the regime was unable to stop:

> While it is true that even regular army units indulged in various sorts of abuse, particularly in the first years of the conflict, the militias went beyond that: they robbed refugees returning from Iran and Pakistan and on one occasion they sacked a hospital in Kandahar. They also laid mines without any warning and apparently without even noting them on maps. In the town of Balkh militias were reported to "smoke hashish, demand goods at half price and prey on people traveling after dusk." Regular officers acknowledged that militias were "beyond control" and visitors were warned to leave the town by 4 p.m. Unsurprisingly, the population did not seem to like them much.[63]

The unruliness of militiamen in Kabul was such that they were ordered to leave the city in September 1990.[64]

The regime did make use of temporary fixes to improve control and discipline. In the non-Pushtun north, Najib created a fiercely loyal command

63. Giustozzi 2000, 226–27.

64. Rubin 1995a, 160–61.

structure staffed with Pushtun nationalists to coordinate action among the different militias and army units. This mechanism proved to be grossly inadequate when Dostum opened direct talks with Massoud and Nadiri. It also had no effect on Nadiri's long-standing arrangements with neighboring mujahideen. Another mechanism of control consisted of creating redundant structures that kept each other in check. KhAD/WAD was balanced by Sarandoy, the Ministry of Interior by the Ministry of Defense, the army by the militias, Khalqis by Parshamis, and Pushtuns by minorities. The system worked well so long as intense factionalism was kept from tearing down the regime by Najib's monopoly over the distribution of Moscow-supplied resources. Another control mechanism during the 1989–92 period was to confine regime troops and institutions to defensive activities within an easily controllable space to reduce their ability to defect. This effectively ended the regime's ability to take the strategic initiative.

Hekmatyar, Massoud, and Mazari all developed their centralized organizations in a way that did not sacrifice control, but perhaps the thorough Massoud did a better job than the other two in this respect. The use of the term "militia" notwithstanding, Dostum and Nadiri basically developed the command and control structures one normally associates with militaries in developing countries. Only later was Dostum to partially revert to a patronage structure.

Resilience

The PDPA/Watan became more vulnerable to decapitation and organizational dismemberment while the other centralized organizations became less vulnerable as they gained safe havens. Except for the Hizb's assassination of some of Massoud's top commanders, however, none of the centralized organizations scored a coup by decapitating another major organization, perhaps out of fear of retaliation or the efficiency of the cautious leaders' security outfits. Hekmatyar and Massoud did make full use of this approach to weaken smaller centralized rivals when they respectively assassinated the heads of the Kunari and Badakhshani emirates. The Najib regime continued to attempt to assassinate mujahideen field commanders when it could, while neglecting their increasingly irrelevant Peshawar leaders. It did not hesitate, however, to decapitate smaller centralized rivals like the Maoist-style youth group Sofi Shana.[65] The regime's powerful militia leaders were

---

65. *Far Eastern Economic Review*, July 13, 1989, 14.

increasingly looking toward the endgame and therefore wanted to build bridges to mujahideen leaders instead of creating enduring enemies through what could become botched assassination attempts. Different factions within the Najib regime might have avoided the assassination of powerful mujahideen leaders for the same reason. As the endgame neared, Hekmatyar became more brazen and the failed Tanai coup he supported did come close to killing Najib.

Foreign Aid

Things did not change much from the previous period with respect to foreign aid. Moscow financed its client regime and gave it the necessary resources to maintain its increasingly onerous patronage system. The Najib regime could not hope to survive without this aid. Soviet then Russian aid ceased to involve control from Moscow, however, because both Moscow and Najib had convergent goals: the latter's survival. India actively assisted the Najib regime, and Iran provided it with economic assistance in return for a freer hand in Hazarajat, but both aid efforts were miniscule when compared with the assistance provided by Moscow.

The mujahideen continued to receive substantial aid, albeit irregularly and in considerably smaller amounts than Najib, from several sources. Multiplicity of sources allowed overall continuity: when U.S. aid was temporarily halted, for example, Arab Gulf aid was increased. Foreign aid continued to be mostly channeled through the ISI, but the United States increased its ability to influence distribution, and party leaders were increasingly sidelined. ISI control over the Hizb increased, but it waned over the increasingly independent non-Hizb commanders who demanded enormous resources to temporarily contribute to the campaigns it organized. The Saudis and Pakistani Salafi groups did have strong influence over Sayyaf's Ittihad and the centralized Salafi emirates. Hizb-i Wahdat was dependent on the Iranian clergy during this period. The militia leaders were only allowed to receive foreign aid through the Soviet-Watan pipeline.

Intraorganizational Cohesion and Competition

The Massoud organization was so well integrated that it was not vulnerable to organizational manipulation. This was generally also the case for the Dostum and Nadiri organizations as stand-alone units. Hekmatyar's centralized core organization was also well integrated, but the patronage component of his organization was vulnerable to the same centrifugal forces that afflicted the patronage-based parties. The Najib regime's intense factionalism made it particularly vulnerable to the manipulation of its organizational segments. The only rivals capable of taking advantage of its vulnerability were Hekmatyar's and Massoud's organizations because their centralized structures allowed them to credibly commit their organizations to whatever agreements they made with PDPA/Watan faction leaders.

Massoud himself provides a good account of his attempts to manipulate segments of the Najib regime:

> We made very good use of the internal conflicts within the Watan Party, especially after the Tanai coup. . . . We played a major role in creating those problems, exploiting them and using them to our advantage . . . until the regime was on the verge of defeat. Besides that, we had penetrated the regime very deeply, and we had worked hard to have good contacts with regime people. . . . Those regular forces [regime units] belonged to us completely [i.e., were loyal to us] before we came to Kabul. They had a very important role, the main role in defeating Najib's forces in Kabul.[66]

Hizb-i Wahdat was well integrated but suffered from one fault line that no one cared to exploit during this stage of the conflict: the divide between the mostly rural Hazara and the urban Quizilbash faction loyal to Mohsini. Massoud would later ruthlessly exploit this divide.

Generation and Preservation of Knowledge

The PDPA slightly improved its ability to process information by scaling back its activities. Its exclusive focus on defensive operations from a limited territorial base reduced the information-processing burden to more manageable levels. Although it once took the regime's front positions an entire day to see its air force ineffectually strafe the mujahideen positions they located, the military shortened the response time to the point where its air force effectively decimated the mujahideen trying to cross the plains surrounding Jalalabad in 1989. On the other hand, Najib's increased reliance on very independent clients did aggravate the already existing information asymmetry that added to their leverage.

The failure of the mujahideen to centralize after gaining a safe haven hindered their ability to effectively process information. Yousaf (1992, 119)

66. "Massood Reviews History of Victory," 6–8.

provides an example of how the multiplicity of mujahideen parties impeded the efficient flow of information. The ISI received a limited number of long-range secure radio transceivers and more short-range devices that could have functioned optimally if commanders from parties with the long-range devices cooperated with other commanders, from all parties, in their region who had the short-range devices. Party leaders, however, protested the operationally sound but intrusive arrangement and insisted on developing independent radio networks for their parties. This led to inefficiencies in training and the delayed deployment of the helpful communication devices.

Centralized mujahideen organizations, as well as the Dostum, Nadiri, and Wahdat organizations, improved their ability to effectively process essential information. Except for the Hizb, the regional concentration of those organizations facilitated their ability to do so.

How the different organizations performed critical operations, their structure, availability of safe haven, fit of structure with haven, and survival are summarized in table 7.2. I consider all centralized organizations, except for the emirates, to have had safe havens. The emirates were vulnerable to the interruption of their operations by their relatively powerful rivals, the Hizb and Massoud. All patronage-based organizations (PDPA and mujahideen) collapsed while all centralized ones with a safe haven did survive, as the organizational theory would predict.

So why did the PDPA/Watan survive longer than anyone predicted during the post-Soviet withdrawal euphoria, and why did it suddenly collapse in April 1992? The fragmented mujahideen failed to take the strategic initiative by failing to centralize, thus giving the regime a new lease on life and the opportunity to regain its balance. Their failure to centralize also dealt them serious setbacks in Jalalabad and Kabul where the failure to coordinate, an advantage of centralization, was recognized to be their major shortfall.

The regime suddenly collapsed in April 1992 because both its patronage-based and its faction-ridden centralized structures required extensive resources to maintain cohesion and loyalty.[67] The September 1991 cessation of Soviet aid deprived Najib of the necessary stream of resources. He was left with little more than the ability to print more inflation-inducing banknotes to keep the integrity of his organization.[68] The PDPA/Watan fired functionaries and

---

67. Rubin (1995a, chap. 12) and Giustozzi (2000, chap. 19) make this argument.

68. Giustozzi (2000, 23) reports that the PDPA/Watan could fund only 55% of its needs, with the rest coming from Moscow and India.

Table 7.2. How Afghan organizations executed organizational processes between the Soviet withdrawal and the collapse of the Najib regime

PROCESS	PDPA/WATAN	HEKMATYAR'S HIZB	MASSOUD	PATRONAGE-BASED PARTIES	WAHDAT	EMIRATES
Strategy	Can switch to conciliatory strategy. Limited D&C/co-option potential	Very limited ability to adopt conciliatory strategy	Limited ability to compromise	Still stuck in confrontational strategy but client commanders less driven to action	Capable of confrontational and conciliatory strategies	Capable of confrontational and conciliatory strategies
Coordination	Coordination only adequate for defense, not offense	Good coordination	Excellent coordination	No ability to coordinate without ISI intervention	Good coordination	Good coordination within each
Mobilization	Only effective in detribalized cities and adjacent areas	Mostly effective in detribalized refugee camps	Only effective in detribalized Tajik areas	Effective in *qawm*-dominated countryside	Dominated Shia ethnic space	Regional scope and madrassa network
Control and discipline	Fair control mechanisms	Successful control mechanisms	Successful control mechanisms	Alignment of goals but poor control	Good control mechanisms	Probably good
Resilience	Vulnerable to decapitation, internal divisions, geographic isolation	Vulnerable to decapitation and weapons depot seizures	Vulnerable to decapitation	Not vulnerable to decapitation or other counterinsurgency shortcuts	Vulnerable to geographic isolation	Vulnerable to decapitation

Foreign aid	Depended on USSR, some Indian support	Multiple redundant suppliers and logistic lines. Convergence of goals but no control by sponsors except in case of Pakistan and Hizb		Depended on Iran	Arab and Pakistan Salafi support	
Intra-organizational cohesion	Suffered from intense factionalism and loosening of clientage ties	Cohesive but expelled dissenters. Inclusion of Khalqis increased factionalism	Cohesive	Simple structures and effective independence of clients prevented factionalism	Fairly cohesive but Hazara/ Quizilbash fault line	Cohesive
Knowledge and information	Poor but improved implementation	Local information generally reached local decision makers. Commander councils and centralized training facilities diffused knowledge that couldn't be locally generated. Centralization and regional focus helped Massoud, and Hekmatyar to a lesser extent.				Satisfactory for regional focus
Structure	Hybrid centralized and patronage	Centralized	Centralized	Patronage	Centralized	Centralized
Safe haven?	Yes	Yes	Yes	Yes	Yes	No
Good fit?	No	Yes	Yes	No	Yes	No
Survived?	No	Yes	Yes	No	Yes	No

scaled back its propaganda operations. Regime institutions suffered from increased pilferage, corruption, and competition over ever-scarcer resources.[69] The Afghani (the currency) lost all purchasing power, Najib's weapons depots were depleted, and foodstuffs and fuel disappeared from the capital. The air force was also grounded in early 1992 because of the unavailability of aviation fuel.[70] Signs of the nearing end of the regime were everywhere, and regime clients and factions simply executed the exit strategies that would maximize their odds of survival.

What could the PDPA/Watan have done to remain a relevant player in Afghan politics? The PDPA's major post-Soviet withdrawal mistake was to use the resources donated by Moscow as a currency to buy the immediate but unreliable support of the militias. Once given, those resources generated no more return on investment. Even worse, they cheapened all further resources given in following rounds of exchange for continued loyalty. Additional truckloads of freshly minted Afghanis only aggravated hyperinflation, and the abundance of weapons made incremental additions of commoditized light weapons less appealing than before and increased the pressure to transfer larger and more expensive weapons to the militias.[71] Najib would have been better served by using his resources to stamp out factionalism, improve operational performance, and create a better-coordinated and leaner centralized organization, instead of doubling as a patron of militias.

Why did the mujahideen fail to militarily take Jalalabad or Kabul before the implosion of the regime? Observers generally agree that the Jalalabad attack failed because of the mujahideen's inability to coordinate activities locally and nationally. But there is more to the matter than poor coordination. The same processes that explain the unexpected longevity of the Najib regime on the national level also explain its ability to defend its Jalalabad and Kabul strongholds until it imploded.

ISI planners and mujahideen party leaders needed to control a major Afghan city to set up an alternative government, and they therefore poured in resources in a hurry to capture the only such city within easy access of the Pakistani border. Kabul was too well defended, Mazar was too inaccessible, and Kandahar was surrounded by noncooperative Durrani tribesmen who resented the intrusion of out-of-area troops from

---

69. See ibid., chap. 19, for a more detailed account of the internal collapse of the regime.

70. Rubin 1995a, 171.

71. It is reported that, by then, the money the Najib regime gave its clients in return for their loyalty was measured by "container."

non-Durrani parties.[72] Hurried preparations contributed to the debacle by not allowing for the necessary centralization of command, for setting the ground for nationwide cooperation and coordination, and for suitable training. The parties and the Pakistanis threw noncohesive and noncoordinated groups into a protracted battle. On a brighter note, the Pakistanis supplied battle plans and intelligence they acquired through U.S. satellite reconnaissance and may have provided battlefield guidance and some ad hoc training to supplement the structural shortcomings of the mujahideen.

The first assault by some seven thousand mujahideen on March 5, 1989, achieved some initial success because of sheer fervor, motivation, and high morale. The numerically inferior attackers from different parties lacked a unified command, however, and ultimately failed because of poor battlefield and poor national coordination, weak control and discipline, and insufficient training in the new type of warfare.[73] The regime's own performance was enhanced by the easing of the coordination and control burdens of its new defensive position.

The mujahideen failed to tie down the regime's reserve forces by attacking its other strongholds and the airports, from which it launched sorties that decimated many of the Jalalabad attackers.[74] One reason for the lack of nationwide coordination was tension between Hekmatyar and Massoud after Hekmatyar's men assassinated some of the latter's best commanders. Many commanders also stayed put because they resented manipulation by the ISI and disagreed with the "Jalalabad first" strategy.

On the operational level, the eight senior commanders and their mujahideen did not have a unified command. They failed to coordinate their actions, or even their presence, on the battlefield:

> They attacked when the mood took them, and without thought to concentrating or coordinating their efforts. As one exasperated commander was quoted as saying in the *Sunday Times*, "there is no coordination. If the mujahideen attack on one side and keep the government

72. See *Far Eastern Economic Review*, July 13, 1989, 18: "When Hekmatyar [a Ghilzai Pushtun] attempted to spend 10 days with the Kandahar resistance in mid-June [1989], he was expelled at gunpoint after 18 hours."

73. Also argued in Ahmed Rashid, "Siege Mentality: Glaring Weaknesses Exposed in Mujahideen Ranks," *Far Eastern Economic Review* 144, no. 16 (April 20, 1989): 19. Rashid tends to blame discipline problems on the Salafi groups and Arab volunteers in particular, an impression that other sources do not necessarily share.

74. Yousaf 1992, 231.

> busy, the mujahideen on the other side are sleeping." This lack of an overall plan led to many setbacks. The vital highway to Kabul, which, after the airport was closed, was virtually the only way of reinforcing or supplying Jalalabad, was seized by the guerrillas. But instead of closing the road permanently, the mujahideen kept rotating the groups responsible, which enabled the enemy to keep slipping convoys through.[75]

The relatively late appointment of Yahya Nowroz as overall commander of the entire Jalalabad front did little to rectify this shortcoming, because lack of coordination was caused by intragroup rivalry as well as organizational ineptitude. In one attack, for example, one group attacked prematurely to prevent another one from sharing in the eventual victory.[76]

Poor control and discipline also severely impeded the mujahideen attack in more than one way. Some mujahideen massacred regime troops who surrendered during the early successful advances, which deterred other regime troops from surrendering:

> The rebels' lack of discipline also led to the kind of atrocities their leaders had hoped to avoid. At Samarkhel, one Westerner watched as victorious mujahidin massacred two dozen government troops even as they surrendered. Elsewhere, according to several rebel sources, one group of mujahidin sprayed automatic rifle fire into a score of Army soldiers who had been captured by a rival guerrilla band.[77]

The mass surrender of regime troops would have been the rosiest scenario for the numerically inferior attackers. Another way poor control mechanisms impeded the attack was the long-standing and now very damaging practice of the mujahideen leaving their posts to celebrate religious holidays with their families in the nearby refugee camps across the border.[78] This practice wasn't too damaging when they left remote outposts where the Soviets did not leave permanent troops, but it thinned mujahideen lines at a critical juncture around Jalalabad and allowed regime troops to regain strategic terrain.

---

75. Ibid., 228.

76. "An End Game in Afghanistan," *Newsweek*, March 27, 1989, 38.

77. Ibid.

78. Rashid Ahmad, "Out from Under," *Far Eastern Economic Review*, May 25, 1989, 34.

Lack of adequate training in conventional tactics also impeded the attackers' performance:

> Tactically, it was a textbook example of how not to fight a battle. There was no surprise; [numerically] inferior forces attempted to assault prepared positions frontally in daylight. The attacks were poorly coordinated and the mujahideen were subjected to a continuous barrage of shells and bombs from which there was no respite. Logistically it was grossly mismanaged. Due to the U.S. cutback and the loss of all the strategic reserve stocks of arms at Ojhri, there was insufficient ammunition for a large-scale offensive lasting more than a week at most.[79]

Some reported that the Pakistanis hurriedly trained the mujahideen in tank warfare and refurbished some of the armored vehicles they captured, but it is not reasonable to expect them to make good offensive use of such weapons because of the short training period and their poor organization.[80]

Lack of surprise allowed the Kabul regime to send reinforcements (the 11th Division) and to shore up its defensive positions with Soviet advice in anticipation of the attack on Jalalabad. The numerically inferior mujahideen attacked across an open plain by day for reasons grounded in Afghan culture that contradict the most basic principles of modern warfare: bravery can't be demonstrated by night. There was an urge to demonstrate bravery because commanders from different areas and parties were fighting next to each other but not together. Doing so made them vulnerable to the most potent assets in the regime's arsenal: heavy artillery and aerial bombing with devastating cluster bombs. The regime also launched some four hundred of its nerve-rattling and morale-sapping SCUD missiles at mujahideen locations. New technologies and tactics to avoid Stinger missiles allowed the regime's pilots to conduct bolder bombing runs with better accuracy and more devastating results.[81] In addition, the regime's defensive position kept its own troops positioned in an easily controllable space that reduced their ability to defect. It also relieved it of the burden of developing the advanced coordination skills so necessary for offense but less decisive in defense. The imminent danger of being overrun by vengeful

---

79. Yousaf 1992, 231.

80. Ahmad, "Out from Under," 34.

81. "Losing Their Sting," *Far Eastern Economic Review*, July 13, 1989, 20.

mujahideen also increased cohesion among the different regime factions in Jalalabad.

In brief, retired ISI officer Yousaf summed up the situation in Jalalabad well when he wrote in terms inspired by the writings of Mao and Giap:

> One of the most difficult decisions that a guerrilla commander has to make once his forces begin to get the upper hand is the precise moment in the campaign when he should go on the offensive, when he should progress from guerrilla to conventional strategy and tactics. It is a matter of shrewd judgment. He has to assess the enemy's position with care. . . . But before doing so the commander must examine his own forces. Are his men sufficiently trained to adopt coordinated conventional attacks, and if so on what scale? Are they well equipped with heavy support weapons? Can they cope with the enemy's likely control of the air? Can the scattered groups be supplied, concentrated, and then cooperate in joint offensives? . . . if the answers are affirmative, then, probably, it is time to launch the offensive that will end the war.[82]

Things were not too different around Kabul, except that the mujahideen did not push their luck by attempting to mount a decisive assault they simply could not execute given their organization, numbers, and training. The mujahideen faced defensive regime posts that they frequently overran one at a time in small group operations.[83] Their inability to coordinate larger attacks because of their fragmentation prevented them from causing more than pinprick and easily reparable damage to Kabul's defensive belts. According to one observer on the field, lack of coordination was

> one of the main impediments to mujahideen progress around Kabul where a shura council that coordinates among the different fronts is needed. Such coordination would make blows to the regime more painful and damaging. Coordination in some sectors is so poor that military operations often impede each other and operations in one sector negatively affect operations in another. . . . The qawm/tribal system played a negative role when some mujahideen sometimes prevent others from a different area from shelling Kabul from their more advantageous location for tribal or affiliation reasons, or because of the

82. Yousaf 1992, 224.

83. See Mansur (1991, 89) on how the mujahideen performed such operations.

> fear of government retaliation. And sometimes mujahideen in one area do not assist others under attack by regime forces as long as they are spared for similar reasons.[84]

The Kabul regime, on the other hand, was able to concentrate its considerable firepower at will to recuperate breached sections of its security belts. The mujahideen soon realized the futility of conducting uncoordinated attacks. The number of military operations around the capital dwindled from a peak of 100 operations in April 1989 and 113 operations in May to a paltry 30–40 operations per month within a year.[85]

The mujahideen were also numerically weak around Kabul, mostly because of their inability to enforce presence at the front when troops were needed and to concentrate troops where they mattered on the national level. Mansur (1991) estimates that the mujahideen numbered some fifty to sixty thousand around Kabul, a figure that dwindled by two-thirds during winter months. He also estimates the number of regime troops at some three hundred thousand. Just like at Jalalabad, commanders of smaller units often walked away without informing others, leaving fronts understaffed and vulnerable.[86] The regime's effective targeting of field commanders also continued to damage fronts. Mansur (1991, 140–41) lists eleven assassinated field commanders in the Kabul region and quotes a mujahideen leader on how the death of one commander led to the collapse of his front.

The battle for Kabul was also hampered by the rivalry between Hekmatyar and Massoud and the aversion of the almost independent field commanders to supporting the centralized Hizb. Both Massoud and a shura led by the powerful Kabuli leader Abdul Haq (nominally of Mawlawi Muhammad Yunus Khalis's Hizb) opposed Hekmatyar's late 1990 attempt to organize a coordinated assault on Kabul.[87] Massoud refused to obstruct the Salang highway to weaken Kabul, and non-Hizb commanders simply refused to attack when requested to do so. Hekmatyar was just not capable of imposing his will on Kabuli commanders the way Massoud was able to influence northern commanders. He had the only centralized force able to

84. Ibid., 94. Translated from Arabic.

85. Ibid., 93.

86. Ibid.; 43–81 and 94. Regime troops include fifty thousand from the army, twenty thousand from the Special Guard, fifty thousand from the local militias, fifty thousand from the ethnic militias, one hundred thousand KhaD troops, and thirty thousand Sarandoy troops.

87. Ahmed Rashid, "Friendless Foe: Hekmatyar's Kabul Offensive Attracts Little Support," *Far Eastern Economic Review* 150, no. 43 (October 25, 1990), 18.

conduct an effective attack on Kabul but lacked the manpower that the commanders could provide.

The mujahideen also failed to improve their learning processes to transition to the new phase, as many witnesses, including Mansur (1991, 95), tell us. It was mostly Hekmatyar's forces that enjoyed the benefit of training in offensive weaponry and tactics. Most Kabuli commanders continued to use their traditional means of processing information and knowledge, means that served them well when on the defensive but inhibited them when they achieved the potential to take the strategic initiative.

Why did the Iranians succeed in centralizing the Shiite groups but the Pakistanis, Americans, and Saudis failed to unify the Sunni mujahideen? The Hazarajat was exclusively under Iranian influence after 1981, when the Soviets withdrew from the area. The mountainous and completely encircled region was a low priority for the Soviets and PDPA, and they did not recruit significant militias from it. This lack of interest meant that the Hazarajat was less awash with weapons than the rest of Afghanistan and did not experience weapon "inflation." The resources Iran gave its Hazara clients therefore strengthened them vis-à-vis their rivals and helped them mobilize support more than Pakistani-donated aid allowed the Hizb to do in the context of intra-Sunni rivalries. Most of the traditional Hazara elites had already been replaced by Iranian-supported ones by the mid-1980s.[88] There were also fewer alternative sources of income in the impoverished Hazarajat than elsewhere. It is not practical to grow opium poppies in the mountainous area, it is skirted by all significant routes on which traffic could be lucratively taxed, its impoverished population provides a poor tax base, Arab and Western NGOs had little interest in the remote area for lack of jihad activities, and no income could be derived from smuggling because the Hazarajat is not adjacent to international borders. In addition, the many miniscule Hazara parties' fear of Pushtun resurgence and possible persecution grew with the increased likelihood of a Soviet withdrawal. Iranian positive and negative sanctions finally brought about a cohesive alliance of eight Hazara parties under the leadership of their clients in June 1987. The Iranians encouraged the integration of the alliance and its evolution into a single organization, Hizb-i Wahdat, by 1990 by channeling all aid to the Hazara region through its leadership.[89] Iran's influence increased further in Hazarajat when it agreed to supply the Najib regime's troops with oil in western Afghanistan

88. Much of the information on Hazarajat is from Harpviken 1995.

89. Rubin 1995b, 116–17. See Emadi (1997) for a more complete account of the formation of Wahdat.

in return for permission to supply Wahdat through direct flights to Bamyan.[90] Iran was particularly interested in unifying the Hazara in one centralized organization to use them as a counterweight to U.S., Saudi, and Pakistani-supported parties, particularly the Hizb.

The Hazarajat revolt against PDPA encroachment started with patron (*mir*)-client units rising simultaneously but independently to expel the Communists with the sanction of the traditional religious figures (sayyids). The local mirs and sayyids formed a coordinating body in a September 1979 meeting in Waras that they dubbed Shura-i Ittefaq-i Inqilab-i Islami (Council for the Islamic Revolutionary Alliance). The Shura soon evolved from an alliance into a full-fledged party with a burdensome bureaucracy. It grew in power and influence but was soon challenged by two Iranian-backed organizations as well as Mohsini's Harakat-i Islami that adhered to a moderate Islamism that did not agree with Khomeini's creed. The first pro-Iranian Hazara organization was Nasr, but an Iranian delegation that visited the Hazarajat in the summer of 1982 to evaluate its performance was thoroughly disappointed, and the Iranians established another organization, Sepah-i Pasdaran. The new highly centralized party was under the direct authority of its Iranian namesake in Qom and received Iranian weapons and training. Unlike the Pakistanis, the Iranians were not trying to equip their clients for a jihad but to consolidate their own influence in the Hazarajat, and their weapons supply was therefore limited to the parties they controlled.[91] The pro-Iranian Islamist organizations used their newly acquired resources and popular discontent with the increasingly burdensome Shura to expand their influence. In the context of scarce resources, the highly centralized pro-Iranian parties enjoyed a substantial advantage over the traditional patronage-based structures of the Shura:

> Both *mir* and *sayyid* operated in patron/client relations, and the change to Islamist rule also implies a change of organizational mode. Islamists operate in hierarchic, modern organizations, where individual achievement replaces ascribed status. As such, the change can be seen as a transition from a non-representative to a representative system. . . . The *sheikh* [pro-Iranian clerical leaders] might had [*sic*] a comparative advantage through their mode of organization.[92]

---

90. Rubin 1995a, 264.

91. Harpviken 1995, 80.

92. Ibid., 85–86.

The centralized Nasr and Pasdaran made efficient use of the advantages bestowed by their structures: they manipulated segments within the Shura by wooing its most radical members; they created specialized bodies to provide services and efficiently mobilize the population; and they used their comparative advantage of controlling resources to create highly integrated and relatively efficient fighting forces.[93] The very large proportion of Hazara men staying in Iran as laborers or refugees also provided the two centralized organizations with a pool of recruits they were particularly well equipped to mobilize and to whom they had exclusive access.

By 1984, pro-Iranian parties dominated Hazarajat and a rump Shura allied itself with Mohsini's Harakat. Iranian rapprochement with the USSR in 1985 led to an agreement of nonaggression among their Afghan clients and an even freer hand for Iran in Hazarajat. The 1987 all-inclusive Hazara alliance that was to evolve into an integrated centralized organization in 1989–90 was therefore not a coming together of equals who could defect at will in the way that the superficial Sunni alliance members were able to:

> The Hazara parties joined together and formed a single party, Hizb-e Wahdat. Groups that were in conflict merged and the Islamist parties, mainly *sheikh*, dominated. The new party reintegrated people who had been forced out of Hazara politics due to internal struggles. Both negative and positive incentives were important in motivating leaders to join: positively the potential for future political careers, negatively the possibility of being subjected to violence. The integration of the parties was a response to the foreseen disintegration of the Kabul government and the exclusion from the interim government that followed.[94]

In sum, Nasr and the Pasdaran dominated Wahdat and co-opted the other organizations. Traditional elites were given just enough (their lands were returned to them) to join but never assumed positions of leadership again.

The first reason the Pakistanis could not replicate the Iranian feat among Sunni Afghans is that they couldn't give all the resources to the one party they favored because of U.S. pressure and because this approach would have left field commanders who would not join the Hizb either defenseless or with no choice but to defect to the regime. Joining the regime was of course

93. Ibid., 87.

94. Ibid., 94.

not an option in the Hazarajat where neither the Soviets nor the PDPA intervened. Second, the multiplicity of weapons sources and the availability of additional means of generating income allowed traditional elites in Pushtun areas to resist more effectively than the Hazara mirs the rise of Islamist elites. Third, the Pushtun were also divided along rival tribal lineages in a way that inhibited the non-Durrani Hekmatyar's potential to expand his influence in the important Durrani areas.

Unification of mujahideen organizations after the Soviet withdrawal could have accelerated the breakup of the regime by better manipulating its segments. Better control mechanisms would have prevented the vengeful killings of captured regime troops that deterred other troops from defecting at critical junctures, such as during the battle of Jalalabad. The ability to coordinate the actions of mujahideen groups would have forced the regime to spread its resources more thinly and allowed the concentration of mujahideen forces where they would have had a greater impact. The number of Afghan lives spared and amount of destruction avoided could have been considerable.

Because centralized organizations gradually dominated the Hazara, Tajik, and Uzbek ethnic spaces while no such organization was well equipped to mobilize the historically dominant Pushtuns, Afghanistan experienced a rare multipolar moment in its history. Unfortunately, it also proved to be one of its most debilitating ones.

Organizational Performance during the 1992–1995 Period

The four major organizations that survived the previous phase of the conflict to pursue nationwide ambitions were structurally fairly similar. The age of patronage was temporarily over and the centralized organizations—Massoud's Islamic Army, Dostum's Jumbish, Hekmatyar's Hizb, and Mazari's Wahdat—fought over the ruined capital that each associated with international recognition, the power to mint currency, and the potential to become the conduit for international aid. Ismail Khan's emirate in Herat was the fifth substantial and centralized survivor, but it supported the Rabbani government and Massoud instead of pursuing independent national aspirations. The stalemate that characterized this period in spite of shifting alliances can be explained by the failure of the Hizb to effectively mobilize the Pushtun, in spite of its best efforts, and to therefore fail to grow into the only organization capable of effectively projecting power beyond its ethnic space, the way the Taliban later did.[95] Additionally, none of the four organizations was strong enough to overcome the multitude of independent or semi-independent groups that shared their or their rivals' ethnic spaces. Such groups were numerous in Pushtun areas and still persisted in other regions. A failed attempt by Dostum to occupy the northern town of Kunduz, where Tajik Islamists trained, to please his Uzbek backers illustrates the difficulty of expansion because of the presence of many effectively independent armed groups that coalesced under threat.[96]

The difficulty of advancing in rural areas also explains in part why all ambitious organizations focused on Kabul—the only challengers in the capital were the other centralized organizations.

Strategy

Strategies were straightforward during this phase of the conflict: Massoud and Hekmatyar hoped to completely control the capital while Jumbish, Wahdat, and lesser players such as Sayyaf's Ittihad and Mohsini's group tried to maintain a presence there to secure a position in government and the share of resources such a position could bestow. This was a purely conflictual environment that involved short-lived balance-of-power alliances among contending organizations. The centralization of the five surviving major organizations and their ability to force compliance by the rank and file permitted their dramatic shifts of alliances.

Coordination

The way major rivals managed the extensive organizational growth they all experienced affected their ability to coordinate actions among their organizational members. The battles for Kabul and some operations in the north showed that Massoud had the most coordinated forces by far. The Hizb might have been hindered in this respect by the poor integration of previous Khalqi forces into its Lashkar Ithar. Dostum's organization also seemed to have suffered from the rapid incorporation of ethnically diverse and once rival groups. Dostum had to cajole or force the hand of some of the division leaders who joined him after the collapse of the Najib regime (particularly the Tajik Abdul Mu'min of the 70th Division and the Nadiri heads of the Is-

95. For more on the Hizb repositioning itself as a Pushtun party more than ever before, see, inter alia, Ahmad Rashid, "In Pashtun Country," *Far Eastern Economic Review*, May 14, 1992, 12.

96. Davis 1994a, 323; 1994b, 111.

maili 80th Division) to get them to coordinate expansionist moves.[97] Dostum later assassinated Abdul Mu'min when he disagreed with his patron's decision to ally with Hekmatyar against his fellow Tajik Massoud.

Mobilization of Resources

The inability of the Hizb to effectively mobilize resources within the Pushtun ethnic space is the one factor that best explains the stalemate that characterized the 1992–94 period. Effectively mobilizing the traditionally dominant and numerically superior Pushtun would probably have allowed the elimination of rival minority organizations, as the Taliban later demonstrated. The independent Pushtun groups that the Hizb could not mobilize both limited its own organizational space and set the limits for the expansion of minority organizations as well.

Massoud and Dostum had to contend, and sometimes woo as clients, small groups on the peripheries of their organizational space. Dostum in particular used the abundant resources he controlled to reverse his historical role and become a patron in his own right, a mistake whose cost he was soon to pay. The extreme internal cohesion of the groups that joined his Jumbish implies that they were mere clients, not the regular troops he often claimed to lead.

Wahdat remained the only organization in Hazarajat. The collapse of the regime gave it the opportunity to mobilize the substantial Shiite population in southern and western Kabul. Its efficient centralized structure allowed it to promptly take control of almost half of the capital by early May 1992. It dispatched representatives to coordinate the local mobilization efforts that were emerging based on social networks and emphasized the ethnic component of its ideology, instead of its religious dimensions, to appeal to those now frightened Hazara who were once loyal to the Najib regime.[98] It also integrated two Shiite tribal regiments, namely the 95th in Kabul and part of the 96th in Maydan, southwest of the city.[99] Wahdat also extended its efficient and entangling civilian administration and sent fighting units from the secure Hazarajat to the capital. It also used negative sanctions, such as hanging two individuals who surrendered their posts to its Salafi nemesis Ittihad and widely publicized the event. Wahdat's emphasis on its ethnic character drove

97. Ibid.

98. Harpviken 1995, 115.

99. Davis 1993, 135.

non-Hazara Shia, mostly Quizilbash, into joining Mohsini's Harakat, which became an instrumental ally for Massoud during his attacks on Wahdat.

Control and Discipline

Massoud and Hekmatyar continued to exert strong control over their troops. Wahdat was fairly well disciplined, mostly because it was constantly on the defensive after its original expansion into Kabul's Shiite areas. Dostum's organization was less disciplined and had weaker control mechanisms because his ties to several of the "divisions" he hurriedly integrated after the collapse of the Najib regime were de facto ties of clientage. Jumbish's lack of discipline and poor control mechanisms are demonstrated by the brutish behavior of its troops during some of their northern conquests and in Kabul.[100]

Resilience

All five organizations were vulnerable to decapitation, but none of their leaders was assassinated.

Foreign Aid

Foreign sponsors changed as alliances among rivals shifted. Uzbekistan, other Turkic Central Asian states, and Moscow supported Dostum. India, Russia, and Iran intermittently supported the Rabbani regime to counter Saudi and Pakistani influence, but it also earned Saudi sponsorship when it allied with Sayyaf to evict Wahdat from Kabul. Iran supported Wahdat but was ready to withdraw its support to gain Massoud as a client. Hekmatyar depended heavily on Pakistani support but also received some aid from independent Islamist organizations. Ismail Khan received aid through the Rabbani regime.

By virtue of their increased centralization, Afghan rival organizations became more than ever tools for the projection of their sponsors' power. Jumbish, for example, attacked areas where Tajik Islamists trained in order to please its sponsors. This operation resulted in the first defeat of Dostum's troops, some of its best trained ones in fact, since the collapse of the Najib regime. Despite Dostum's best efforts, his forces failed to function as an anti-Islamist buffer on the Tajik border the way they did on the Uzbek one.[101]

---

100. Davis, 1994a.

101. For more information on Dostum's misadventure, see Davis 1994a, 323; 1994b, 111.

Wahdat was so dependent on Iran that it engaged in all alliances arranged or favored by its sponsor, and the Hizb continued to do the ISI's bidding. The Saudi-supported Sayyaf never relented in his attacks on the Shiite Wahdat, and Massoud did the same once he gained Saudi support through his alliance with Sayyaf.

Intraorganizational Cohesion and Competition

Wahdat was vulnerable to organizational dismantling because of the Quizilbash/Hazara divide but each of those two groups was cohesive. Dostum's Jumbish became increasingly vulnerable to being torn apart as it increased the number and size of its clients after the collapse of the Najib regime. The Hizb and Massoud's organization did not suffer from glaring factionalism.

Generation and Preservation of Knowledge

Dostum's, Hekmatyar's, and Massoud's organizations benefited from training by their sponsors in the use of more advanced weapons systems, which they inherited from the defunct regime. They also benefited from recruiting trained personnel from the defunct regime. The Hizb also benefited from Pakistani intelligence and tactical guidance. All organizations developed training camps for their infantrymen, but Massoud was said to have developed the best training programs.[102]

All five organizations started with the advantages of centralization, but Dostum made an organizational blunder by using his abundant resources to woo clients he couldn't effectively transform into more pliant agents. He was able to claim larger numbers of troops, but his clients' units were less useful than the well-coordinated and integrated forces of Massoud and Hekmatyar. He still managed to survive this phase of the conflict, but this hybrid structure would prove to be inadequate when facing the Taliban challenge later. Ironically, Dostum repeated his defunct patron's mistake. How the different organizations performed critical operations, their structure, availability of a safe haven, fit of structure with haven, and survival during this phase of the conflict is summarized in table 7.3.

This short phase of the conflict was characterized by stalemate because none of the ambitious centralized organizations was strong enough to defeat the others. The Hizb was the only organization among the surviving ones

102. Sandy Gall, "Massoud Builds Afghan Power Base with National Army," *Jane's Defence Weekly* 20, no. 14, 17.

Table 7.3. How large Afghan organizations executed processes between the collapse of the Najib regime and the emergence of the Taliban

PROCESS	DOSTUM'S JUMBISH-I MILLI	HEKMATYAR'S HIZB	MASSOUD	PATRONAGE-BASED PARTIES	WAHDAT	ISMAIL KHAN'S EMIRATE
Strategy	Capable of confrontational and conciliatory strategies	Capable of confrontational and conciliatory strategies	Capable of confrontational and conciliatory strategies	Fragmented, no coherent strategies	Flexible but under Iranian influence	Capable of confrontational and conciliatory strategies
Coordination	Fair coordination	Good coordination	Excellent coordination	No ability to coordination	Good coordination	Good coordination
Mobilization	Effective among Uzbeks but increased use of clientage	Mostly effective in detribalized refugee camps, limited in tribal areas	Only effective in detribalized Tajik areas and with previous Jamiat commanders	N.A. Disintegrated into small independent groups	Dominated Shia ethnic space except for Quizilbash	Successful in six multiethnic provinces
Control and discipline	Poor discipline, moderate control	Successful control mechanisms	Successful control mechanisms	No control and discipline	Good control mechanisms	Probably good
Resilience	Vulnerable to decapitation and losing clients	Vulnerable to decapitation and weapons depot seizures	Vulnerable to decapitation	N.A.	Vulnerable to geographic isolation	Vulnerable to decapitation
Foreign aid	Uzbekistan,Russia	Pakistan, independent Islamists	India, Iran, Saudi Arabia, Russia	Dried up	Depended on Iran	Pakistan, Uzbekistan, Rabbani
Intraorganizational cohesion	Clients have leeway to defect but centralized core is otherwise cohesive	Cohesive but expelled dissenters. Inclusion of Khalqis might have increased factionalism	Cohesive	None	Fairly cohesive but Hazara/Quizilbash fault line	Cohesive
Knowledge and information	Good	Good	Good	Commanders' shuras	Fair	Fair
Structure	Centralized but added clients	Centralized	Centralized	Fragmented	Centralized	Centralized
Safe haven?	Yes	Yes	Yes	Yes	Yes	Yes
Good fit?	Mixed	Yes	Yes	No	Yes	Yes
Survived?	Yes	Yes	Yes	No	Yes	Yes

with the potential to mobilize the Pushtun, a necessary condition for monopolizing power in Afghanistan. It failed to do so because of tribal divisions, widespread perception of the Hizb as antitribal and anti—Durrani, and the availability of alternative sources of revenue for commanders not keen on giving up status, autonomy, and local power by joining the centralized organization. Perhaps, if given more time, Hekmatyar or Massoud could have grown their organizations to the point where they would have tipped the balance in their favor, but this was not to be.

CHAPTER 8

The Rise of the Taliban, 1994–2001

The relative winners of the 1989–94 phase of the Afghan conflict did not savor their survival for long. Just when it seemed that they had achieved some sort of balance of power and that lines of conflict had become more clearly drawn, a new organization emerged to dramatically reshape the dynamics of the conflict. The Taliban grew from a small group of idealistic religious students with some military training into a sprawling organization that dominated more than nine-tenths of Afghanistan in less than five years.[1] They swept away all the warlords—petty and mighty alike, with the single exception of Massoud's organization—that had partitioned and terrorized the country to impose a nearly unified political order for the first time since 1979. The rise of the Taliban is one of those events that social scientists have accepted more than they have understood or been able to explain. Most available explanations provide causes (why did the Taliban grow?) but fail to explain the processes that led to its emergence and successful near-unification of Afghanistan (how did they do it?) when all

1. Taliban joins the Arabic noun *talib* (seeker, as in seeker of truth or knowledge) with the plural Dari and Pashto suffix "*an*." I refer to the Taliban in both the singular and plural to reflect current practice. It is more accurate to use the singular tense, however, because the Taliban is an organization with a structure and not an amorphous group of students like the name would indicate and the organization's mythology would imply.

others had failed. Compelling explanations are scarce because of a shortage of reliable information about what really happened during the first critical months of the Taliban's quest. Afghanistan was ignored because of its reduced relevance to the West and because feuding warlords made it one of the least hospitable places in the world for academics and journalists alike. Yet, the rise of the Taliban is a bona fide social scientific puzzle that deserves to be solved.

In this chapter, I discuss existing explanations of the rise of the Taliban. I show that the most popular explanations for the Taliban's success are either inadequate or insufficient. I then explain the rise of the Taliban in its two overlapping stages. The first phase consisted of the Taliban's expansion within the highly fragmented Pushtun ethnic space and shows the weakness of fragmented opposition to a highly coordinated and skilled organization. The second phase of Taliban expansion was in the minority areas and pitted the more streamlined and centralized Taliban against large rivals who came to depend on ties of patronage at their own risk. I explain how the Taliban was able to undermine these organizations by manipulating their ties with their own clients. The only organization that simultaneously did not depend on clientage and did not have a large Pushtun following was Massoud's. Predictably, it was the last holdout against the Taliban. A summary description of the different rival organizations during the 1994–2001 Afghan conflicts is provided in table 8.1.

The Events (1994–2001)

Dostum's Jumbish, Hekmatyar's Hizb, Massoud's Shura-i Nazar, Ismail Khan's Herati organization, and Mazari's Wahdat were not alone in the fragmented Afghanistan of 1994. Although they generally recruited among members of specific ethnic groups, they had to contend with many smaller organizations, often only clans but sometimes loosely structured commander shuras, with whom they shared their ethnic spaces. Among the centralized groups, Hekmatyar's Hizb was the least capable of dominating its ethnic space. The mujahideen parties that were glued together by patronage ties unraveled when foreign aid ceased to reach their leadership in Peshawar. The more centralized Hizb and Jamiat managed to keep the loyalty of some clients alongside their centralized forces by maintaining access to foreign aid, which they disbursed in return for loyalty. Previous clients of largely defunct Peshawar parties substituted local sources of income (e.g., taxation, road tolls, poppy production, banditry) for the resources they used to get from party leaders.

Table 8.1. Significant organizational contenders during the 1994–2001 conflicts

ORGANIZATION	LEADER	STRUCTURE	EXTERNAL SUPPORT	ORGANIZATIONAL LIFE	ETHNIC COMPOSITION	IDEOLOGICAL ORIENTATION
Taliban	Mullah Muhammad Omar	Gradually more centralized and specialized with discipline-enforcing units	Pakistan and Pakistani parties and groups. Saudi Arabia, UAE, traditionalist Muslim groups from the Arabian Peninsula	Started as a band in 1994, grew gradually to take over 90% of Afghanistan, defeated by U.S. in 2001 but continues to exist as decentralized guerrilla movement	Pushtuns majority leadership but all other tribal and ethnic groups are represented	Traditionalist
Jumbish-i Milli	Rashid Dostum	Centralized force with patronage ties to lesser warlords on periphery	Uzbekistan, Turkey, India, Russia, Iran	Defected from Najib regime in 1992 and defeated by Taliban in 1997	Mostly Uzbeks but also some Pushtun and Ismailis	Secular, desired a loose federal state with weak center
Hizb-i Islami	Gulbudin Hekmatyar	Highly centralized, Marxist-like structure. Called its integrated mobile force Lashkar Ithar (Army of Sacrifice)	Pakistani factions until all aligned behind Taliban, independent Islamists.	Oldest Mujahideen party, expelled from the Pushtun belt by Taliban by 1996. Became active again after U.S. occupation.	Probably the most ethnically diverse party, but with a Pushtun Ghilzai majority.	Pragmatic Islamist
Shura-i Nazar-i Shamali	Ahmad Shah Massoud	Highly centralized organization that used old Jamiat superstructure and Rabbani's presence to maintain ties with other commanders	Russia, India, USA, France, Iran	As of mid-2001, Massoud's rump centralized organization was the last organized force still resisting the Taliban	The core organization is mostly Tajik but the umbrella group included a multiethnic coalition	Islamist, pragmatic
Hizb-i Wahdat	Abdul Ali Mazari, then Karim Khalili	A unity party formed of all Shia parties in 1988	Iran, except for period when Iran supported Massoud while he was pouncing on Wahdat	Began as a centralized party under Mazari. Splintered after defeats with Mohsini's faction joining Massoud in	Hazara. Most Quizilbash defected to join Massoud under the leadership of Mohammad Asif	Moderate Islamism and Hazara nationalism

				1995 and others under Ustaz Akbari joining Taliban in November 1998. Others in Hazarajat degenerated into uncoordinated groups with strongest under Khalili	Mohsini	
Herat shura	Ismail Khan	Shura had centralized force called Amir Hamza Division, but gradually maintained more clients on periphery	Member of Jamiat, Iranian and Central Asian support	Established in 1987; overran by Taliban and Dostum in 1995	Mixed	Conservative, local concerns
Ismaili militia	Sayyid Mansur Nadiri	Militia and clients were said to have peaked at 18,000 troops, mostly Ismailis	Supported by Dostum and Massoud, partly integrated into Jumbish	Previous DRA militia, defected with Dostum in 1992; later disarmed by Hizb forces and destroyed by Taliban in 1998	Ismailis from northern Afghanistan	Group preservation
Major regional commander shuras						
Jalalabad shura	Abdul Qadir	Shura functioned as coordinating body among commanders	—	Created after collapse of Najib regime in 1992 and dismantled by Taliban, 1995	Ghilzai Pushtun from area	Local concerns
Balkh shura	Mawlawi Alam	Shura had specialized committees and ran a school system	Member of Jamiat	Established in 1988	Tajiks	Local concerns
Kandahar shura	Led by executive committee; Naqib was most powerful	Loosely organized in committees	—		Durrani Pushtuns from area	Local concerns

The Taliban made their first significant appearance on the Afghan scene when the larger organizations were busy undermining each other around Kabul.[2] In a well-organized assault in September 1993, they took control of Spin Baldak, a rundown town that contained an enormous weapons and ammunition depot under Hizb control.[3] A shocked Hekmatyar attributed the success of the Taliban assault on Spin Baldak to support from Pakistani artillery, which is how he had taken control of the town himself six years earlier. But where did the Taliban come from?

Talibs are students who study in religious schools (madrassas) in Afghanistan or across the border in Pakistan. They frequently participated in the anti-Soviet and anti-Najib jihads as members of mujahideen parties. Once the jihad ended and the surviving organizations turned their guns against one another, many disgruntled former mujahideen crossed the border to take advantage of the free religious education and room and board provided by the madrassas. Most madrassas belonged to sprawling networks set up and managed by two religious Pakistani parties, the Jamiat-i Ulema-i Islam led by Mawlana Fazlur Rahman and the Islamist Jamaʿat-i Islami. Many talibs belonged to the now defunct patronage-based parties and did not share the Hizb's modernist antitribal Islamism, and they therefore did not have an organization to represent them in Afghanistan. The original members of the Taliban came from the pool of talibs who studied in the Jamʿiat-i Ulema schools.

One of the Taliban's key supporters was Nasirullah Khan Babar, Benazir Bhutto's interior minister after October 1993 and her adviser on Afghan affairs. He is said to have been the chief advocate of shifting support from Hekmatyar's Hizb to the Taliban after the Hizb failed to break the stalemate around Kabul and the Taliban proved their mettle by freeing a Pakistani convoy held captive by former PDPA militiamen in Kandahar. The convoy's liberation was a particularly significant feat because Bhutto and Babar were personally involved in making the preparations for the symbolic trip that they hoped would herald a historic resumption of trade with the formerly Soviet Central Asia.

2. Dorronsoro (2000, 269) traces the origins of the Taliban to a client group of Muhammad Nabi's Harakat-i Inqilab created around 1990 called Jamʿiat-i Taliban. Although the name and constituency of the 1990 and 1994 groups are similar, I believe there is little reason to think that this was the same organization.

3. Those who argue that the Taliban were supported by Pakistan from the start point to some evidence to make the case that the Spin Baldak depot was depleted before its seizure by the Taliban. The Pakistanis and Taliban, they say, only pretended it contained enough weapons to equip the organization for years to explain its access to an obviously large supply of weapons.

The Taliban not only freed the Pakistani convoy in November 1994 but they also almost effortlessly swept through Kandahar and dismantled its most vicious criminal bands, which were mostly made up of former government militiamen.[4] They earned much popular approval by disarming all other groups and imposing strict discipline in what had become a lawless and extremely hazardous area. They also tore down the numerous checkpoints that extorted money from traders and travelers, imposed a traditional tribal code of social behavior that provided reassurance to a society traumatized by nearly fifteen years of violence, and burned poppy fields. This last act endeared them to the United States and Pakistan, both of which suffered from the effects of the otherwise pretty flower's narcotic by-products. The Western press was generally positive in its coverage of the emerging movement, comparing the Taliban favorably to the discredited parties that had led the jihad and downplaying their religious zeal.[5]

After taking Kandahar, the Taliban promptly moved to occupy the adjacent provinces of Zabul and Uruzgan in December and then invaded Helmand (a breadbasket province and poppy-growing center) in January. They then expanded through other Pushtun areas where some commanders joined them and others were disarmed. In the process, they eliminated the ubiquitous roadblocks, imposed sharia-based civic order, closed girls' schools, and provided a rare unifying moment in the region's history. Soon thereafter, they reached Hekmatyar's strongholds south and southwest of Kabul and handily routed his forces in January and February 1995. Hekmatyar, the ambitious mujahideen leader who influenced Afghan politics and organized one of the country's most potent organizations, had to flee his base in Charasyab, leaving immense resources behind for the victorious Taliban. He would later become the token Pushtun in Rabbani's government on his way to disappearing for a few years from Afghan political life in exile in Tehran. The Taliban also swept through the two Ghilzai provinces of Paktia and Paktika, which had previously been hotbeds of mujahideen resistance to the Soviets and their puppet regime.

Massoud was at first delighted by the rout of his habitual enemy and contributed to it by increasing pressure on the Hizb's troops when they were attacked by the Taliban. He also took advantage of Hekmatyar's predicament by attacking his Shiite allies in March 1995, finally ending

---

4. The same structural factors that led to the disintegration of Afghan political parties were so extreme in and around Kandahar that even the shura that was formed there after the collapse of the Kabul regime eventually disintegrated.

5. E.g., *Economist*, October 28, 1995, p. 38.

Wahdat's attempt to maintain a presence in Kabul while simultaneously co-opting some Shiite commanders, particularly Mohammad Asif Mohsini.[6] The collapse of the Hizb and the Massoud attack left the weakened Wahdat with no choice but to accept a Taliban mediation effort that involved the surrender of Wahdat posts and heavy weapons to the Taliban in return for their insertion of a buffer force between its troops and Massoud's. Whether it was because of ignorance, confusion, or design, both Massoud's troops and Wahdat troops that preferred to defect to a Shiite faction already co-opted by Massoud attacked the Taliban buffer force instead of giving up their weapons. The Taliban killed Wahdat leader Mazari, who was in their custody at the time, either in revenge or, as they claim, in trying to prevent him from escaping. Massoud took advantage of the confusion by lunching an all-out attack on both the Taliban and the remaining Wahdat forces. He outmaneuvered both and pushed the Taliban out of Charasyab, Hekmatyar's old base, thus putting Kabul out of the range of the rockets they had inherited from the Hizb. Massoud finally controlled all of Kabul. Mazari was succeeded by Abdul Karim Khalili, who reenergized Wahdat, consolidated its control over much of Hazarajat, and slowly reestablished relations with Iran.

The setback at the gates of Kabul shifted the Taliban's attention to Ismail Khan's Herat-based fiefdom in the west of the country. They aggressively moved from Kandahar toward Herat and the strategic airbase at Shindand in March 1995, prompting Massoud to airlift hundreds of fighters to assist his fellow Jamiat commander. Massoud also contributed his air force to defend Shindand, subjecting the attackers to some ten to fifteen sorties a day. Dostum joined the fray by wresting a part of Badghis Province from a distracted Ismail Khan. The Taliban eventually halted their attacks after suffering hundreds of casualties.

Ismail Khan, perhaps heartened by his troops' performance a few months earlier, attacked the Taliban in August. He captured Girishk in what appeared to be a momentous thrust toward Kandahar, but the Taliban counterattacked his overstretched forces with astounding mobility, forcing them into a disorganized retreat that culminated in the fall of Herat on September 5 and the flight of Ismail Khan to Iran. The mobility of the Taliban troops and their tactical aptitude took the seasoned Ismail Khan by surprise and marked a new phase in the conflict. Not only was the Taliban now in control of more than half of the country, including some non-Pushtun areas,

6. See Emadi (1997, 383–85) for more on these events.

they also acquired expertise in the tactics necessary to challenge their large established rivals to the north.

Hekmatyar continued to squabble with Rabbani and Massoud from his remaining base in Sarobi, thirty miles east of Kabul, but finally joined the government as prime minister in June 1996. His situation was desperate: Pakistani support was evaporating and his troops were ready to defect to the Taliban upon contact. Taliban troops advanced with ease in Ghilzai areas, taking Jalalabad and Hekmatyar's remaining stronghold in Sarobi. They then attacked Kabul in September 1996, entering the city on September 27 and dispatching their rivals back to their northern strongholds. The frontline moved to the Shomali Plains north of the capital, an area that would suffer immensely from fighting in the following two years. The loss of Kabul, however, was not fatal for Massoud. The master strategist managed an organized retreat under attack that allowed him to save much of his troops and weapons to fight another day. He also improved his odds of survival by retreating to more favorable terrain and destroying the southern entrance to the Salang tunnel to impede any Taliban push toward the north. The Taliban occupied the area just south of the Salang and Panjshir in February 1997, including the provincial capital of Charikar, but veered toward the Hazarajat to pressure Wahdat instead of pushing north. A few days later, on October 4, member countries of the Commonwealth of Independent States (CIS) met in Almaty, Kazakhstan, to coordinate their response to the rise of the Taliban. The Russians requested a meeting of the UN Security Council on October 22, and Iran convened a conference of anti-Taliban factions that Russian and Indian representatives attended on October 29. The Clinton administration cautiously welcomed Taliban expansion at first but changed its policy a month later because of the approach of U.S. presidential elections, increasing U.S. popular disapproval of Taliban misogyny, and signs of a Taliban alliance with transnational Islamist militants.

The Taliban controlled four of Afghanistan's major cities after the capture of Kabul. They made their first attempt to seize the fifth, Mazar Sharif, in May 1997. Abdul Malik Pahlawan, the largely autonomous Dostum lieutenant whose area of control west of Mazar lay on the frontline with the Taliban, blamed his patron for the death of his brother Rasul and defected to the Taliban on May 19. In the process, he handed them Ismail Khan, who took refuge in the north via Iran after his rout from Herat. Dostum fled Mazar for Turkey on May 24 after fighting broke out in the city. Pakistan recognized the Taliban as the legitimate government of Afghanistan on May 25, 1997, and Saudi Arabia and the United Arab Emirates followed suit within two days. Some Taliban forces were flown to Mazar while others were allowed free passage through the Hindu Kush mountain range by Bashir Salangi, a Massoud commander who claimed to have shifted loyalty to them. Some jubilant Taliban soon attempted to disarm Abdul Malik's troops and those of the Shiite militias in Mazar, but they faced stiff resistance and were soon overwhelmed and isolated. Bashir Salangi, obviously not a sincere convert to the cause, blocked their retreat and prevented reinforcements from reaching the Taliban in Mazar. Hundreds of Talibs perished in battle, and thousands, including key leaders, were imprisoned and then massacred. Some three thousand surviving Taliban in the north withdrew to Kunduz where they occupied the airport and received reinforcements. The Mazar debacle embarrassed states that had extended diplomatic recognition to the Taliban in anticipation of an ultimate victory and provided an opening for Massoud to make a push for Kabul.

Taliban leader Mullah Omar, a largely unknown mujahid before the rise of the Taliban, adopted the title of "prince of the believers" (a title that claims influence beyond state borders) and changed the name of the country to the Islamic Emirate of Afghanistan, but the Taliban seemed unsteady for the remainder of 1997. Massoud advanced to within artillery range of Kabul. An effort by the reinforced Taliban in Kunduz to push toward Mazar was thwarted by fierce resistance. Dostum returned from exile in September to replace his erstwhile betrayer Abdul Malik and send him to exile in Iran. Khalili's Wahdat pushed the Taliban to the western edge of Kabul. The Taliban's rivals proved to be odd bedfellows, however. The forces of Abdul Malik, Wahdat, Massoud, and Dostum wreaked havoc in Mazar after the latter's return. They battled wildly, looted private property and the offices of charities, murdered many civilians, drove UN agencies and NGOs out of the city, depleted the city of necessary staples, and made the once irrelevant trade-off the Taliban offered (security in exchange for the acceptance of a strict social code) particularly appealing for the city's residents. In another indication of the fragmentation of the Northern Alliance, Hekmatyar's rump forces in the north of the country disarmed the Ismaili force of Mansur Nadiri, who was allied with Dostum.[7]

Several meetings by high-level representatives of the Group of Concerned Countries, which was dubbed the Six plus Two (Afghanistan's six neighbors, plus the United States and Russia), did little to assuage the situation, and the Taliban regained the initiative in 1998. They embargoed the impoverished Hazarajat, aggravating the effects of an already debilitating

7. Magnus 1998a.

drought, and initiated a final assault to conclusively occupy Mazar Sharif with some eight thousand troops in August, vanquishing Dostum, and then moved on to occupy Bamyan in September. The Taliban exacted revenge for the massacre of their comrades in Mazar by murdering large numbers of Hazaras in the two towns and killing Iranian diplomats in their Mazar consulate, prompting Iranian mobilization of some two hundred thousand troops and skirmishes on the border. Massoud, under pressure and now without substantial allies in Afghanistan, retreated on several fronts toward the Panjshir and adjacent valleys. Ismail Khan escaped—or was released in a deal with Iran—from Taliban custody in 2000 to join an Iranian-sponsored Northern Alliance whose only significant military force was Massoud's. The concerned leaders of Uzbekistan, Kazakhstan, Kyrgyzstan, Uzbekistan, and Turkmenistan signed an agreement to counter Islamist and other transnational movements in April 2000.[8] President Pervez Musharraf's Pakistan openly declared its support for the Taliban and their summer 2000 campaign, which wrested Taloqan from Massoud and severed his main supply line from Tajikistan. The Taliban occupied more than 90 percent of the country at this point and only faced scattered resistance in Hazarajat and Uzbek regions. The Lion of Panjshir resisted in his stronghold and executed some brilliant, but ultimately inconsequential, operations to expand his zone before he was assassinated by two pro-Taliban Arabs posing as journalists on September 9, 2001. The Taliban was poised to attack Massoud's bastion following his assassination, but the dramatic terrorist attacks that shook the United States soon afterward ushered in a new phase of the conflict that directly involved the world's only remaining superpower.

Explanations of the Rise of the Taliban

Any explanation of the rise of the Taliban must explain how they mobilized the Pushtun. Such an explanation must therefore meet a crucial test: Does it also account for the failure of others (Hekmatyar, the PDPA/Watan and, so far, Afghan president Hamid Karzai) to do the same? The most popular explanations (some are overlapping and complementary) of the rise of the Taliban are that it was merely an extension of Pakistani power; that it bought the loyalty of rivals with Saudi and Pakistani money; that Afghanistan was a political "vacuum" waiting to be filled; that it resulted from popular

8. Ahrari 2000, 658.

discontent with the mujahideen; and that it received an advantage from its religious credentials.

One explanation of the rise of Taliban that is quite popular among its and Pakistan's detractors is that it owes its success to being Pakistan's creature (created, equipped, trained, and directed by Pakistan's intelligence services) and the beneficiary of Arab Gulf financing. Indian writers (e.g., Stobdan 1998, 9–18) are particularly fond of such explanations because of the Indo-Pakistani rivalry, but some of the more savvy observers of Afghan affairs make similar arguments. Anthony Davis (1998, 69) provides a more potent version of this argument:

> The Taliban were pre-eminently a military organisation rather than a political movement. In the short space of two years, their numbers multiplied rapidly from a force of less than 100 men, to one of several thousand and finally to one estimated in late 1996 to number at least 30,000–35,000 troops with a functioning brigade and divisional structure. It was equipped with armour, a notably effective artillery arm, a small air force, an impressive communications network and an intelligence system. The organizational skills and logistical wherewithal required to assemble from scratch, expand, and maintain such an integrated fighting machine during a period of continuous hostilities are simply not to be found in Pakistani madrassas or Afghan villages. . . . Covert Pakistani support for the Taliban can thus be inferred to have been fundamental if not to the movement's political inception then at least to its expansion as a regional and then national force.

Barnett Rubin (2000, 1794) adds a political economy framework to the above explanation of the rise of Taliban:

> Overcoming predation poses a collective action problem: each predatory actor benefits, while a larger but diffuse constituency would benefit from suppressing predation. Both social capital that strengthen networks of solidarity and investments or side-payments from groups benefiting from the suppression of predation can help overcome the obstacles to collective action. The Taliban both mobilized social capital created in madrasas to create a homogeneous leadership group linked to political networks in Pakistan and used assistance from Pakistan and Saudi governments and traders to build up a military force and buy off opponents.

There is little doubt that the Taliban benefited from substantial Pakistani support and Arab Gulf largesse. Yet it is too expedient to explain away their expansion so conveniently, if only because the ISI and Arab donors fully backed another Pushtun organization, the Hizb, for the three years that preceded the rise of Taliban, with paltry results.[9] Pakistani support for the Taliban might have been substantial, but it couldn't possibly compare in scale with Soviet support for the PDPA/Watan or even the resources later poured by Western and other donors in support of the Karzai regime. And, while Pakistan supported the Taliban, its rivals were actively backed by Iran, Russia, and India—the situation was hardly lopsided.[10] Gulf Arabs also simultaneously backed a number of highly conservative Salafi figures with non-negligible support among the Pushtun, including Abd Rab al-Rasul Sayyaf, head of the Ittihad and later a member of the Northern Alliance, and the Kunari Jamil al-Rahman, who headed his own Salafi "emirate" until he was defeated by Hekmatyar. None of them enjoyed the Taliban's success.

Saudi financial support for the Taliban became substantial only after July 1996, after they had swept through most Pushtun areas.[11] Saudi aid dried up by September 1998 over the Taliban's refusal to surrender Osama bin Laden. The Saudis also gave Massoud and Rabbani $150 million in 1993–94 after they distanced themselves from Iran, money that could have been used for purchasing the loyalty of many commanders, if this was indeed the way to extend power in Pushtun areas, as the Taliban's rivals and some scholars alleged.[12] The scale of donations given to the Taliban was also far from enough to dwarf aid given to their combined rivals. The well-connected Ahmad Rashid (2000, chaps. 3 and 14) estimates Pakistani support to the Taliban in 1997–98 at a fairly modest $30 million. It is hard to argue that the Taliban bought their way to power on $30 million a year when the Najib regime only managed to defend itself with ten times this amount every month. All else being equal, both sides would have been able to buy the loyalty of regional leaders, but such leaders do not solely make decisions based on money. At least early on in the conflict, "Saudi money" seems more likely to have been a rhetorical tool used by the Taliban's rivals to discredit them (accusations of association with "Wahhabis" has long been a tactic used to discredit rivals in Afghanistan) and to explain away their own failures.

---

9. Giustozzi (2000, 245) believes that different Pakistani agencies supported both the Hizb and the Taliban during a transition period.

10. For a detailed study of outside aid to the Taliban and its rivals, consult "Afghanistan: The Role of Pakistan, Russia, and Iran in Fueling the Civil War," *Human Rights Watch Report* 13, no. 3 (July 2001).

11. Rashid 1998, 76; 2000, 139 and 201.

12. Ahady 1998, 125.

The political economy explanation put forward by Rubin does not explain why Hekmatyar, who also had exclusive access to young Afghan men in refugee camps and some madrassas, strong connections, and comparable financing, was not able to provide the public good that the diffuse constituency coveted in order to achieve his substantial ambitions. Of course, Afghans suffered for years before the rise of the Taliban from the rapacious behavior of many local leaders. It is also not clear how their "diffuse constituency" (which I understand to mean the general Afghan population), which Rubin implies is critical for explaining the rise of the Taliban, plays a role in the Taliban's interaction with its sponsors and rivals.

Pakistani and Arab support at a crucial juncture of Taliban organizational development probably assisted their rise. Yet, it is impossible to prove that the Taliban would not have achieved similar results absent outside intervention in Afghan affairs at this juncture. After all, Pushtun and other Afghan areas have experienced a large number of tribal upheavals and movements that were not encouraged or financed by outsiders, such as the different anti-British uprisings and the early mujahideen uprising against the PDPA and Soviets. It is too facile to explain the rise of the Taliban by ascribing it to outside assistance—at least part of the explanation of Taliban success must be found in what the Taliban *did*. Even accepting Ahmed Rashid's (1998) powerful thesis that almost reverses the agency relationship between the Taliban and Pakistan—the Taliban had a lock on Pakistani support because of their strong ties to many powerful Pakistani constituencies—does not spare us from having to look at intra-Pushtun dynamics to explain the rise of the Taliban.

Davis (1995, 315) earlier argued that "the speed with which the Taliban burst onto the Afghan scene stemmed from several factors, none of them military. Primarily, the Taliban expanded—faster than they themselves believed possible—to fill what was, in effect, a political vacuum in southern Afghanistan." His use of the "vacuum" metaphor implies that Afghanistan was bereft of political organizations ready to immediately fill the void or willing to grow fast enough to do so. This is an inaccurate description of Afghanistan and the Pushtun areas. Hekmatyar would have been perfectly happy to fill any void in the Pushtun areas long before the Taliban emerged. The reason he couldn't expand his area of influence is that there was no void to be filled. Every area where poppies could be grown, every road where traffic could be taxed, every stretch of border through which goods could be smuggled, and every village that could be exploited or mobilized was already controlled by local, self-financed leaders who sometimes were even part of loose regional shuras. And lest those many local leaders and their armed followers do not seem significant enough, they were in many ways similar to those who bedeviled the Soviets and are now providing an intractable challenge for the United States. The "vacuum" explanation also fails to clarify why Hekmatyar's forces crumbled on the Taliban's approach, when he had a highly centralized and articulated organization with almost all the trappings of a government.

Larry Goodson (2001, 109–11) lists five factors he believes explain the rise of the Taliban:

> First and most telling has been the shared Pushtun ethnicity of the Taliban and the majority of the noncombatant population in most of the area they have come to control. . . . The next two factors in explaining the rise of the Taliban are interrelated. These are their emphasis on religious piety and the war-weariness of the Afghan civilian population. . . . A fourth factor that explains the rise of the Taliban is money. Numerous knowledgeable observers of modern Afghanistan report that the Taliban used money to induce opposing commanders to switch sides or surrender. . . . Finally, the fifth factor that explains the success of the Taliban is Pakistani support. Support for the Taliban within Pakistan's government, army, and society is deep and multifaceted. Indeed, it is not incorrect to say that the Taliban are Pakistan's proxy army in Afghanistan, even though the Taliban leadership has not always followed Pakistan's preferences.

Even if sufficient, necessary, and true, Goodson's factors do not explain *how* the Taliban rose to power. They simply represent empowering and facilitating factors that assisted the organization's execution of the processes essential for its success. Facilitating factors do not an explanation make, but they provide the backdrop for the description of unfolding processes.

Goodson's five factors are not sufficient to explain the rise of the Taliban. Again, Hekmatyar's Hizb failed to overcome the same opponents the Taliban trounced while enjoying the same exact advantages. The Hizb touted itself as a Pushtun party after 1992 while still emphasizing its Islamist pedigree, forcing women to be veiled and limiting "un-Islamic" entertainment. The Hizb also enjoyed access to more resources than it could reasonably use, as its many overstocked weapons depots clearly demonstrated. The Hizb also enjoyed generous Pakistani support through thick and thin for more than fifteen years. Although both the Hizb and the Taliban had the potential to take advantage of the same facilitating factors, the Taliban was much more successful. It is hard to argue that the Taliban expanded by buying off commanders with Arab and Pakistani money when, a few years earlier, Kandahari commanders expelled Hekmatyar from their area in spite of a very generous ISI offer to buy their support for a campaign to liberate the city under his leadership.[13] In this story, money is overrated.

Others also ascribe the rise of the Taliban in Pushtun areas to the appeal of their aura of religious purity and law-and-order agenda in a land ravaged by bandits, smugglers, and other miscreants:

> The Taliban have won support from a people sick of war. The three [*sic*] years since the Soviet army left have been three years of fighting between rival Islamic groups. Traditionally, religious students are held in high esteem. Other Islamic militias find it hard to bring themselves to shoot at them; the people find it easy to follow them. And the Taliban's advertised aim of establishing a government of national consensus, true to Islamic teachings, seems unchallengeable.[14]

There is no doubt that the Taliban's aura of piety and their law-and-order agenda were very appealing to the "people" in Pushtun areas, but how did this popularity translate into the ability to either defeat or co-opt the entrenched local leaders who were benefiting from insecurity and exploitation? Afghanistan was not a liberal democracy in which the will of the people would automatically translate into the emergence of a new regime. The process through which the appeal of the Taliban's agenda was translated into victories on the ground must be understood for this argument to become compelling.

Although there should be room for the factors discussed above in an explanation of the Taliban's feat of mobilizing the Pushtun on their way to controlling much of Afghanistan, their roles must be integrated into a dynamic process-based analytic narrative. Pakistani and Arab Gulf support, for example, was helpful to the Taliban but not to others because of their ability to use it effectively to achieve their goals. It therefore makes sense to explain the rise of the Taliban by focusing on their and their rivals' organizations, perceptions, preferences, and strategies.

Organization, Strategy, and Momentum

The Taliban was able to co-opt or sideline many entrenched and hardened Pushtun local leaders by (1) undermining the leaders' support through a vision that appealed to their followers, (2) making effective use of their specialized

13. Rubin 1995a, 262.

14. "Revenge of the Pathans," *Economist*, February 25, 1995, p. 26. See also Edwards 2002, 293 and 295.

knowledge of the Pushtun power tapestry and sophisticated strategies to sideline opposition at little cost, and (3) benefiting from their own momentum to increase their appeal to local leaders and their followers. These processes sometimes worked simultaneously and at other times independently. They were also *facilitated* by some of the factors identified above: exclusive access to a pool of madrassa students, a widespread yearning for law and order, a desire for a Pushtun political comeback, support from different Pakistani agencies and constituencies, and financing from the Arabian Peninsula.

Several ephemeral Salafi-based movements emerged in Afghanistan—Jamil al-Rahman's emirate in Kunar, Mawlawi Afzal's *dawlat* in Nuristan, Mawlawi Shariqi's followers' tiny emirate in Badakhshan—but they were all defeated by stronger rivals, including Hekmatyar's Hizb. The Taliban's beginnings were therefore not unusual in Afghanistan. Their initial success in Kandahar may have been made possible by the processes I describe below, or by bribery of the dominant Kandahari militia leader, Naqibullah, or foolish orders from his leaders in Kabul to submit to them. Regardless of the exact reasons, the Taliban's management of Afghanistan's second largest city provided them with the credibility to launch their dramatic expansion.

The Taliban's hundreds of small rivals in the Pushtun belt were not all organized along the same lines. Some consisted of independent self-financing bands that thrived on a combination of banditry, taxing traffic, smuggling, and small-scale production of opium poppies. Some commanders managed to develop networks of patronage and economies of scale in the same sectors. Such commanders maintained the loyalty of lesser commanders by providing them with resources they were well positioned to tap, including revenues from smuggling or support from the faraway Rabbani regime or the closer Hekmatyar. Some commanders developed loose coordination and consultation councils where they conferred as equals (e.g., the Jalalabad shura). The only large centralized organization in the Pushtun belt was Hekmatyar's Hizb with its twelve-thousand-strong Army of Sacrifice. Some local leaders tended to dominate their region while others maintained a precarious rivalry with their neighbors. Some leaders maintained their following through their ability to organize resource-generating activities while others also mustered support through a combination of kinship ties, religious authority, and a reputation for valor during the jihad. Some were particularly predatory and hated while others were not. This was a very complex fragmented landscape that provided the Taliban with various types of rivals in different configurations of power in each region they approached.

The Taliban calibrated their image and their message to successive Pushtun neighbors in a way that undermined the loyalty of a commander's following, thus simultaneously increasing his motivation to join the Taliban venture and reducing his ability to resist it.[15] As Taliban forces approached the domain of a field commander or an area shared by rival field commanders, their presence automatically reordered the preferences of field commanders and their followers.

The commanders' followers suddenly had an alternative to being part of a local group engaged in a precarious and brutish rivalry with others and that might have kept itself afloat through predatory behavior. The Taliban's proposition to their Pushtun rivals' followers after they proved their mettle in Kandahar was particularly compelling. It consisted of a mix of the following: they provided moral clarity, a promise of a just and safe society stemming from a potent reconstructed vision of Pushtun authenticity, and the satisfaction of being part of a momentous movement that could accomplish what became the stated goal of the jihad started in 1979 (a just Islamic state) and that could terminate non-Pushtun control of the capital. This vision made the followers of commanders in their vicinity question the wisdom of resisting the Taliban when they seemed to be the credible providers of a better order.

The limited options available to Pushtun commanders when the Taliban approached their region varied depending on their place in the local configuration of power, their size, their own Islamic credentials, and the cohesion of their own rudimentary organizations. Although not all field commanders and local leaders could realistically hope for the entire range of possible outcomes to their interaction with the Taliban, it is reasonable to assume that they would have ranked all theoretically possible outcomes in the following order of preferences (higher first) because they valued their influence, social status, and honor:

1. Maintaining local autonomy and control over local resources by successfully resisting the Taliban (keep influence, status, and honor)
2. Joining the Taliban as a client with a degree of autonomy while maintaining his organization's integrity (keep influence and honor but lose some status)
3. Being rewarded with money or a Taliban post for surrendering local autonomy (exchange influence for increased status or resources)
4. Disbanding or disappearing from public view (lose influence, status, and honor)

---

15. See Giustozzi (2000, 242) for a similar argument.

5. Being defeated in battle (lose influence, status, and maybe life)
6. Being defeated by losing the support of his own troops and clients (lose influence, status, honor, and maybe life)

Those who led tiny bands could not reasonably hope to resist the post-Kandahar Taliban and generally disappeared from view. Established and independently financed commanders who controlled networks of patronage had the option of resisting the Taliban but had to assess whether their client commanders (if any) and their troops would support them. Those who led patronage-based organizations that were kept together by more than money flows could opt to resist, while those who maintained loyalty solely through economic means probably could not rely on their clients to support them. Commanders who generated their revenues by lending their support to the Hizb, Jamiat, or Ismail Khan as opposed to the exploitation of local resources might have perceived the Taliban as an alternative source of patronage. Leaders with Islamic and jihad credentials (e.g., Jalalludin Haqqani) were able to join the Taliban without loss of face or might even have had a dominant strategy of joining them because of their ideological affinity. Weaker commanders in a regional power configuration or ambitious clients of stronger regional leaders could have found in the advance of the Taliban an opportunity to improve their local standing or to survive a precarious situation.

The mere proximity of the advancing Taliban was often enough to strain the elementary organizations and patronage networks of the local leaders they approached, forcing them to evaluate their options and attempt to preempt some of the worse outcomes by making gestures of goodwill (e.g., Abdul Wahid in Helmand). The Taliban astutely used their sophisticated knowledge of the Pushtun tapestry of power to approach different local leaders in ways that convinced them that successful resistance (outcome 1) was impossible and to prompt them to either disband (outcome 4) or to join them while sacrificing autonomy (outcome 3). The Taliban shaped the preferences of local leaders by (1) approaching the most vulnerable ones in a regional power configuration first, (2) approaching key clients before their regional patrons, (3) carefully deciding which commanders to co-opt or discard, and/or (4) calibrating their message to appeal to the local leaders' rank and file.

It made sense for the Taliban to approach the weaker and more vulnerable commander in the context of a regional competition first in order to preempt the creation of a coalition of erstwhile rivals against their advance. A vulnerable commander at risk of elimination by his stronger local rivals was more likely to join the Taliban. In return, he offered them a foothold in his area and specialized local knowledge. The previously dominant commander then found himself as the weaker of two parties locally and had to face the difficult choices discussed above, knowing that he was alone against the Taliban. The pressures in such a dynamic are such that the weaker side often pleaded with the Taliban to support him, presumably in return for his loyalty.

As the largest and most aggressive organization in Pushtun areas, Hekmatyar's Hizb threw more commanders in the Taliban's lap than any other organization. Ghazni fell to the Taliban at the end of January 1995 after an attack by the Hizb meant to preempt Taliban advances drove Governor Qari Baba to ally himself with the Taliban.[16] Davis (1995, 316) reports that this is also how Maidanshahr fell to the Taliban on February 10, 1995. The Taliban also defeated Ghaffar Akhunzadeh's established group, which some estimated at five thousand fighters, in Helmand by leveraging his local rivals in early 1995.[17]

Approaching key clients before their patrons was another strategy that served the Taliban well in Pushtun-majority areas as well as with Pushtun clients of non-Pushtun patrons. An ambitious client could be tempted to switch allegiance in the hope of negotiating a better relationship of clientage, to replace his previous patron, or because of ideological affinity with the newcomers. Clients were also not immune to the Taliban's pull on their followers. Not only were such defections damaging because they reduced morale but also because commanders on the periphery of the patron's domain were generally entrusted with securing strategic areas that blocked the highly mobile Taliban from outmaneuvering their opponents. Indeed, many of those commanders were both valued as clients and targeted for recruitment by the Taliban because of their strategic locations. One or more such defecting commanders allowed the Taliban to control strategic heights, facilitating their first assault on Kabul.[18] And the decisive Taliban push toward Herat was greatly facilitated by the defection of Ismail Khan's Pushtun clients to the south of his domain.[19] Several Pushtun commanders from the Pushtun communities embedded among Uzbek and Tajik regional majorities (particularly around Kunduz) also made the switch at decisive junctures.[20]

16. Dorronsoro 2000, 271.

17. Rashid 2000, 33; Davis 1998, 51; Gélinas 1997, 81.

18. *Asiaweek*, September 22, 1995, p. 35. Also Matinuddin 1999, 88.

19. Davis 1995, 321; Matinuddin 1999, 77; Moshref 1997, 5 and n. 21.

20. Marsden 1998, 55; Matinuddin 1999, 264.

For example, the Taliban's second push toward Mazar Sharif was facilitated by the support of previous Hizb commanders from the area.[21]

The most famous defection by an ambitious client was that of Dostum's client Abdul Malik, who feared for his life after suspecting that Dostum killed his brother Rasul. But Abdul Malik's defection was also induced by Taliban promises of a government post and perhaps money. Abdul Malik's May 1997 defection allowed Taliban forces to enter Mazar Sharif and rout Dostum's forces. Soon afterward, Malik turned against his Taliban allies as they tried to disarm his forces and contributed to their own rout in their first attempt to seize Mazar Sharif. Malik's defection provides us with critical evidence that the Taliban's ability to sideline or co-opt Pushtun leaders hinged on their ability to influence their followers. While the Taliban were able to draw even the best-organized Pushtun troops away from their leaders, Malik was able to switch allegiances at will because he was secure in the loyalty of his non-Pushtun supporters. The Taliban forces in Mazar Sharif must have forgotten why their strategies worked in the past as they became used to easy acquiescence to their monopoly on the use of violence in Pushtun areas.

The Taliban also astutely used their knowledge of the Pushtun landscape to decide whether to co-opt, discard, or assassinate different commanders. The Taliban co-opted local leaders who wouldn't tarnish their finely calibrated image as heralds of a better order and who could enhance their military potential. Jalaludin Haqqani, the master guerrilla leader and uncompromising learned scholar without independent ambitions, was the epitome of the co-optable commander. Commanders tarnished by a history of predation or loyalty to the Hizb or Jamiat were better discarded, and their followers recruited on an independent basis or disbanded. Capable commanders with solid and large followings who could have put up strong resistance were sometimes targeted for assassination.[22] The Taliban assassinated the prominent Durrani leader Abdul Ahad Khan Karzai, father of Hamid, in July 1999, and made several attempts on Abdul Haq's life before they ultimately succeeded after the United States entered the fray in Afghanistan. The assassination of Massoud, with the help of al-Qaida, was the ultimate coup and could very well have led to the collapse of the Panjshiri resistance absent U.S. intervention. Of course, Taliban choices were not always flawless in this regard. They recruited well-trained members of the defunct Communist Khalqi faction (sixteen hundred of them, according to Hekmatyar's

21. Matinuddin 1999, 103–4.

22. Dorronsoro 2000, 280.

claims) to enhance their military capabilities, but discarded them by 1998 after realizing the damage they caused to their image and found alternative sources of expertise.[23]

The carefully calibrated image and message of the Taliban were essential components of their successful expansion across Pushtun areas, and were later tweaked, with somewhat lesser success, to win over other constituencies. The image and message of the Taliban both reduced the ability of rival commanders to rely on their followers' support in case they wanted to resist the Taliban advance and prevented different local leaders from coalescing against them the way they would have were they Soviets, British, Americans, the forces of a regime under the tutelage of a foreign power, or antitribal Islamists such as Hekmatyar.

The identity of the Taliban leaders and the rank and file influenced the way they were perceived and the credibility accorded to their message, but probably not the way most observers believe it did. Some (e.g., Goodson 2001) argue that it is the Pushtun identity of the Taliban that mattered. Others suggest that the identity in question is Durrani as opposed to Ghilzai, but even this should probably be nuanced further because several Taliban leaders (including Mullah Omar) were of Ghilzai extraction.[24] Edwards (2002, 294), who spent considerable time among the Pushtun, probably best isolates the specific flavor of agenda-linked identity that spared the Taliban from being unacceptable to most rural Pushtun:

> Another factor in explaining the Taliban's success is that they consistently downplayed tribal or regional identities in favor of what might be called "village identity." . . . In identifying purist culture and tradition with the Islam of the village, the Taliban were indirectly condemning the Islam of the parties since most of the party leaders were products of Kabul University or had worked for state-sponsored institutions. They were also putting themselves on a par with the people whose support they had to enlist if their movement was going to be successful.

Identity mattered not because of who the Taliban were but because of who they were *not*. The Taliban were not hindered in their expansion within the Pushtun areas by having urban backgrounds, being modernist Islamists with antitribal dispositions, having a long record of ambitious expansion, or

23. Goodson 2001, 125.

24. A list compiled by Rashid (2000, appendix 2) reveals that there were more Ghilzai than Durranis among top-tier Taliban leaders.

being non-Pushtun. Kabuli urbanites (e.g., PDPA leaders) were perceived as wanting to expand the power of a central government and of being culturally alien to rural Pushtun. Modernist Islamists (e.g., Hekmatyar) were perceived as planning to sacrifice local political and cultural autonomy in their effort to create a centralized and modernizing Islamic state. Established organizations that had attempted past expansion (e.g., Hizb, Ismail Khan, Sayyaf) had clashed with many commanders and therefore had lost their ability to claim neutrality. Non-Pushtuns would have been seen as alien and unacceptable by the historically dominant Pushtuns, but Pushtuns were not necessarily unacceptable to minority groups if they did not impose a domineering and discriminatory regime. If the Taliban's identity mattered because of who they were as opposed to who they were not, then Mullah Omar, a Ghilzai of unremarkable lineage, would not have mustered support among Durranis. In spite of his lineage, Mullah Omar was able to woo support across Pushtun areas because of the vision he and his organization articulated and their projected image as credible purveyors of this vision. The credibility of the Taliban's message and image could not be undermined because of who they were, but what really mattered were the message and the image, not the Taliban members' ethnic, tribal, or qawm identities.

A critical component of the Taliban's image is that they were perceived as neutral in the context of ongoing Afghan conflicts. They also suggested at an earlier stage that they were not interested in wresting power for themselves. The Taliban's perceived neutrality made them acceptable neighbors and intermediaries for many commanders. The way the Taliban approached commanders also leveraged the neutral role of religious figures in Pushtun tradition:

> Taliban sent religious envoys ahead to demand that local commanders disarm and dismantle roadblocks. Most duly did. Some even offered money, vehicles and weapons to help Taliban eliminate their rivals. But then Taliban pushed aside these collaborators too.[25]

These religious leaders also paved the way for the Taliban's expansion by communicating their message in at least some areas not yet under their control. Many were trained in the same madrassas as Taliban members and their network represented the only remaining form of organization next to those of local leaders and the Hizb in Pushtun areas.

The Taliban also leveraged cultural knowledge and norms to project an aura of invincibility. This reduced the commanders' perception of their own

25. Emily MacFarquhar, "A New Force of Muslim Fighters Is Determined to Rule Afghanistan," *US News and World Report*, March 6, 1995, 64–66. See also Ghufran 2001, 468.

ability to resist them and the willingness of their fighters to follow them into battle; it also provided assurances for those who would accept surrender or co-option. There is no stronger evidence of the importance the Taliban gave to the preservation of Pushtunwali norms (see glossary) than their willingness to shelter Osama bin Laden until the bitter (possible) end, the way a good Pushtun is expected to do for his guest. As one Taliban leader candidly acknowledged, Taliban leaders would have lost the respect of their followers and consequently endangered the organization's cohesion if they had given up bin Laden. With Pushtunwali came cultural assets that reduced the cost of Taliban expansion. As they expanded, the Taliban brought back collective memories of Pushtun uprisings and symbols that were enshrined in oral culture. Reputation became a valuable asset to risk, thus committing those who declared their loyalty to maintaining it. And even a certain degree of susceptibility to rumors and superstition might have contributed to Taliban victories. Rumors circulated that those who fired on the advancing religious students were miraculously stricken with fear, incapacitated by unexplained bleeding, or fell into a coma. Although there is no evidence that such rumors were decisive, no other force in Afghanistan could have inspired religious and superstitious fear in those who were inclined to believe in it more than the Taliban.[26]

The momentum of the Taliban amplified their message and increased both the perceived and real costs of resisting them. The further and faster they expanded, the more their promises of ushering a better order became credible. Their expansion also brought with it new recruits in the guise of co-opted commanders and volunteers, which made them an ever more formidable force. And the commander who saw dozens of others fall or surrender to the Taliban before him had a robust proxy for what would become of him if he tried to resist. By the time the Taliban reached Hekmatyar's base in Charasyab, their momentum had increased their ability to undermine the capacity of rivals to maintain the loyalty of Pushtun followers to the point that even the Hizb's fairly well-organized and structured force surrendered without a fight. The same scenario was repeated in Sarobi. Even the tenacious Hekmatyar, who had patiently built up his organization over some twenty years of struggle, saw his followers abandon him without even the pretense of a fight.

The Taliban consolidated their monopoly on the use of violence in Pushtun areas by carefully disarming the forces of commanders they did not

26. Mansur 1995, 54.

co-opt. They then maintained some control through a polycentric system of ruling shuras, a network of informants and dedicated followers, their morality police, and by monopolizing the taxation of revenue from poppy production and smuggling.[27] The cost for those Pushtun who wished to organize resistance from scratch to challenge the Taliban became too high. Monopolizing the use of organized violence and reducing the possibility of effective challenge in Pushtun areas allowed the Taliban to expand beyond the Pushtun belt.

The Rise of the Taliban in non-Pushtun Areas

The Taliban had to tweak their message and to adopt different strategies to expand beyond the Pushtun belt. They could not rely on their ability to pull the rug out from under their rivals' feet by appealing to their followers in minority areas the way they did in Pushtun areas. They therefore adopted another mix of strategies: military attacks, assassination of leaders, manipulation of ties of clientage, use of co-optees to mobilize supporters from other ethnic groups, and co-opting minorities (not only Pushtuns) embedded within regional majorities. The Taliban also made efforts to not appear threatening to minority populations including, initially, the Hazara. They added minority members to their governing shura, albeit with inconsequential portfolios, and recruited minority fighters in the north. Their record in wooing minority support was mixed, however, particularly after they assassinated Mazari and violently retaliated against the massacres in Mazar Sharif (both in Mazar itself and in Hazarajat). Yet their ability to use the above combination of sophisticated strategies allowed them to defeat Ismail Khan's organization, Jumbish, and Wahdat, while Massoud's organization held on until the U.S. intervention in October 2001. The evolution of the structures of rival organizations since 1992 explains the ability of the Taliban to successfully implement the above mix of strategies to defeat most of their large rivals.

With the exception of the weakened Wahdat, the Taliban did not have an edge over most of its large rivals because of foreign aid, numbers, experience, training, or mobilization. The Taliban and its rivals all received large amounts of aid from different sponsors who couldn't manipulate them for various reasons. The Taliban's Pakistani sponsors could not control them because of the

27. See Rubin (2000) for a detailed account of the political economy of Afghanistan under the Taliban.

Taliban's influence over several Pakistani agencies and constituencies.[28] The many backers of the Taliban's rivals were more concerned with keeping the Taliban away from Afghanistan's borders with Iran and Central Asia than in projecting their own power within the country. Only Wahdat heavily depended on one sponsor (Iran) and was hurt by the temporary withdrawal of its support. While the Taliban generated income from taxing opium and smuggling, Ismail Khan collected large sums from taxing trade with Iran, and both Dostum and Massoud benefited from a good taxation base, the exploitation of natural gas and gemstones, the printing of money, and the production of opium.[29] The Taliban's troops probably did not exceed those of Ismail Khan's when they trounced him and probably never exceeded the some fifty thousand fighters whose loyalty Dostum claimed to command. The Taliban had only a fraction of the fighters available to its combined enemies by 1996, maybe as little as a third. Taliban fighters were of varying levels of experience, with many fresh recruits experiencing combat for the first time, while all their rivals had combat-hardened troops that had proved themselves, at least in the case of Massoud and Ismail Khan, against formidable opponents. Arabs and Pakistanis trained Taliban forces, but Iran also trained thousands of Ismail Khan's, Wahdat's, and Massoud's troops. While the Taliban was able to draw on thousands of recruits from Pakistani madrassas, Wahdat had access to the Hazara refugee pool in Iran, and all the other rivals controlled large populations from which they could recruit fighters. But even with the supply of madrassa students, the Taliban never gained a numerical advantage. When at one point the Pakistani madrassas shut their doors to provide the Taliban with all the recruits they could send them, they only managed to mobilize eight thousand poorly trained fighters—hardly overwhelming numbers. The secret of the Taliban's success lies elsewhere: their ability to exploit the structural weaknesses of their rivals.

The Taliban was able to successfully execute the complex strategies that facilitated its progress in non-Pushtun areas because it developed into a centralized and specialized organization with strong control mechanisms. This organization was capable of carefully calibrating and coordinating offers and actions on the national level. In contrast, two of the Taliban's key rivals (Dostum and Ismail Khan) left themselves vulnerable to Taliban manipulation

---

28. Rashid (2000, chap. 14) details the Taliban's influence on different Pakistani constituencies.

29. Rashid estimates that the Taliban made some $20 million from taxing opium production in 1997, while Rubin (2000, 1796) estimates their revenue at $45 million in 1999. Rubin (2000, 1795) estimates income from smuggling at $75 million the same year. Massoud was said to make $40–$60 million from gem trading alone.

because of their newly developed reliance on fickle clients in key areas, something that organizations with safe havens should never do. The Taliban's victory over a weakened and divided Wahdat is easily explained. Massoud did develop a centralized and specialized organization in his territory, and it lasted long enough in the face of the Taliban advance to rebound and achieve strong gains with the U.S. intervention.

The Taliban's organizational transformation began some time before its September 1995 conquest of Herat and continued until the U.S. intervention in the country. The Taliban began as an amorphous group and were still grouped in *lashkars*, a term normally used to describe tribal war parties, in 1995.[30] Mullah Omar was a first among equals, but he gained greater influence over time. He made decisions in consultation with a Kandahari shura of top leaders, or even a subset of this shura. The Kandahari shura's size fluctuated to include representatives of groups that gradually came under Taliban control.[31] A separate shura in Kabul had the trappings of a government but was subordinate to the Kandahari shura and shared some of its members. By October 2001, Mullah Omar had centralized power in his hands to the point where Taliban field commanders would fear taking the initiative without his permission.[32]

The Taliban began to address issues of control and discipline immediately after it occupied Kandahar. It developed a specialized policing organization, the ʾAmr bil-Maʿrouf wal Nahi ʿan al-Munkar (Promotion of Virtue and Discouragement of Vice) to impose and enforce a moral order on a city that suffered from the unhindered rule of drug lords, bandits, and other scoundrels. This later became the dreaded department whose enforcement of extreme edicts made news in the Western press. While the zeal of ʿAmr bil-maʿrouf led to excesses that damaged the Taliban's reputation at home and abroad, it helped to keep the rest of the Taliban in check and prevented others from committing crimes in its name.[33] The ʿAmr bil-maʿrouf became the most influential, autonomous, and powerful ministry and received independent funding from the Arab Gulf. The Taliban also enforced discipline by creating a three-tiered judicial system to enforce sharia.[34] Non-Afghan

30. Davis 1995, 316.

31. For greater details, see Rashid 2000, chap. 7.

32. Mozhdeh 2003. See also Rashid (2000, 60) on how even Haqqani couldn't take the initiative on the front. See also "Frozen in Time," *Time International* (May 29, 2000), 36.

33. Gohari 2000, 55–56. For an example of the use of the morality police to enforce frontline discipline, see William Vollman, "Across the Divide," *New Yorker*, May 15, 2000. See also Rashid 2000, 106–7.

34. Dorronsoro 2000, 307–8.

troops that were valued for their advanced tactical training and tenacity, including some followers of Osama bin Laden, were organized as the 055 Brigade to win decisive battles and enforce discipline at the front.

The Taliban leadership prevented the development of cliques, centers of ministerial power, and regional factions by rotating cadres between fronts and civilian appointments and moving provincial governors around.[35] Rotations generally succeeded in maintaining organizational cohesion but resulted in poor administration. The Taliban also carried out aggressive investigations and purges at the first sign of dissent.[36] The training and brotherhood of the madrassas also reduced the cost of keeping the Taliban cohesive.[37] The madrassa education ensured that new organizational members had very similar worldviews, were ready to obey the leadership fanatically, and provided a thorough background check on the pupils. The Dar al-ʿUlum Haqqania madrassa near Peshawar provided the elite training ground and produced much of the cohesive Taliban leadership.

Ismail Khan's and Dostum's organizations had core fighting units that reported directly to their leader but became heavily reliant on client militias on the periphery of their domains. This reliance on strategically located clients contributed to their demise the same way it contributed to the end of the Najib regime. In addition, Ismail Khan disarmed much of the population in his core area of control, which eased Taliban control of the area after his rout. Dostum added a wide assortment of clients to his core organization: Karmalists, Herati militiamen who were defeated by Ismail Khan, some Hizb mujahideen who found little reason to remain loyal to a bankrupt party when squeezed between Dostum and Massoud, and small Uzbek nationalist groups such as Azad Beg's.[38] Even Dostum's generals, including the powerful Pahlawan brothers from Maymana, behaved more like powerful clients than professional officers. Ismail Khan and Dostum wooed clients on the periphery of their domains with their extensive resources because they could claim greater national prestige and larger militaries with the easy additions. There might also have been cultural reasons for extending a network of patronage (this is what the powerful and wealthy have always done in Afghanistan), and both leaders might not have fully considered

35. Rashid 2000, 99.

36. See, for example, Jason Burke, "Brutal Purge by Divided Taliban," *Observer*, November 1, 1998.

37. Dorronsoro 2000, 302.

38. Ibid., 286–87.

the possible downside of their choices at this stage of the conflict.[39] If Ahmed Rashid's (2000, 58) observation of financial strain in Dostum's organization just before it faced the Taliban's advance on Mazar is accurate, then maintaining clients would have been wasteful over time as well as strategically damaging. Dostum and Ismail Khan would have been better served by investing their resources in building larger, centralized, and well-integrated organizations in their safe havens.

Wahdat was much weakened and a mere shadow of its former self by the time the Taliban attacked the Hazarajat. Wahdat had already lost Iranian support, was defeated by Massoud in Kabul, and experienced its first postunification schism when Massoud co-opted one of its leaders and his followers. In addition, the Taliban effectively embargoed the impoverished Hazarajat, thus draining local resources that could have financed the maintenance of Wahdat as a cohesive organization.[40] It wasn't hard for the Taliban to defeat the fragmented Shiite forces in Hazarajat, but it had a difficult time asserting control because of the frequent revolts of local autonomous Hazara groups.

Massoud's organization was the most cohesive and centralized organization facing the Taliban. He continued to develop and integrate his organization the way he did during previous phases of the conflict. He received extensive aid from multiple sources, including help from India and Iran to refit his small air force. He also refitted a considerable number of armored vehicles and used them to equip his elite Guards Division. Massoud indirectly maintained some clients through the Jamiat framework, but they tended to be located away from the front line (e.g., Haji Naqib in Kandahar). Unlike the Hizb, which melted on contact with the Taliban, Massoud's followers consisted of Tajiks who were less susceptible to the Taliban's propositions. Massoud's organization was not vulnerable to organizational manipulation by the Taliban the way Dostum's and Ismail Khan's were. It was therefore not surprising that the Taliban would resort to the assassination of Massoud (September 9, 2001) to reduce the cost of overrunning this last bastion of resistance. Unlike Dostum and Ismail Khan, the astute Massoud structured his organization to maximize its odds of survival (centralization) after he controlled a safe haven. His foresight served his organization well—even without its leader, it survived long enough to fight another day.

39. Dorronsoro (2000, 289) notes in this vein that Dostum had recruited so many of the defunct regime's officers and functionaries that it wasn't surprising that he ran his fiefdom the same way Najib, his previous boss, ran his domain.

40. Rashid 2000, chap. 5.

How the different organizations performed critical operations, their structure, availability of safe haven, fit of structure with haven, and survival in the 1995–2001 period is summarized in table 8.2. The parsimonious version of the organizational theory predicts the survival or elimination of all organizations, except for Wahdat and the Hizb, but this is not a flaw in the theory—when several suitably structured organizations clash in a territorial conflict, some have to ultimately disappear. The theory's framework, as this chapter shows, still allows the researcher to understand why and how the elimination process works in such cases.

Once they had occupied non-Pushtun areas, the Taliban maintained control by using some of the methods they applied in Pushtun areas. In addition, they used violence and revenge massacres as a deterrent against future revolt among the Hazara. Another strategy used by the Taliban, and to a lesser extent by Massoud, to mobilize support among groups under their control other than their core constituency consisted of co-opting minority leaders who could attract support that was unlikely to be accorded directly to the Taliban themselves. Some Uzbeks flocked to Abdul Malik after he briefly joined the Taliban in 1997 and some Hazara joined Muhammad Akbari after he gave them his allegiance in 1997.[41] The Taliban also used Ghilzai figures such as Haqqani to recruit Ghilzai fighters. Massoud did the same with the Shiite Mohsini.

This explanation of the rise of the Taliban in Pushtun areas illustrates the processes that make fragmented opposition highly vulnerable to a coordinated and savvy centralized organization. It also illustrates the sort of dynamics involved in the production of societal outbursts in some acephalous or tribal societies. The dramatic rise of the Taliban provides us with a rare opportunity (perhaps never to be observed again because of the gradual disappearance of acephalous societies) to observe the kind of processes that might have animated much greater ventures from the past. If my understanding of the processes underlying the rise of Taliban is correct, then the power of great ideas should be coupled with an understanding of strategies and organizational features to explain historical events such as the Mongol expansion and past tribal mobilizations in Afghanistan, Algeria, the Arabian Peninsula, and elsewhere. Some of those historical events produced or defeated empires, and it does not suffice to explain their early stages away, the

41. Matinuddin 1999, 98.

Table 8.2. How large Afghan organizations executed processes during the rise of the Taliban

PROCESS	TALIBAN	HEKMATYAR'S HIZB	MASSOUD	DOSTUM'S JUMBISH-I MILLI	WAHDAT	ISMAIL KHAN'S EMIRATE
Strategy	Capable of sophisticated strategies	Capable of confrontational and conciliatory strategies, except versus Taliban	Capable of confrontational and conciliatory strategies	Capable of confrontational and conciliatory strategies, vulnerable to sophisticated ones	Too fragmented and weak to take strategic initiative	Capable of confrontational and conciliatory strategies, vulnerable to sophisticated ones
Coordination	Excellent coordination	Good coordination	Excellent coordination	Fair coordination	Good coordination	Good coordination
Mobilization	Highly effective among Durranis, but also among other Pushtun and Sunni minorities. Exclusive access to large pool of madrassa students	Mostly effective in detribalized refugee camps, limited in tribal areas	Only effective in detribalized Tajik areas and with previous Jamiat commanders	Effective among Uzbeks but increasing use of clientage	Dominated Shia ethnic space except for Quizilbash; Access to refugees in Iran	Successful in six multiethnic provinces but increasing use of clientage
Control and Discipline	Generally good but some breakdown in controlling morality police and some co-opted local leaders	Good control mechanisms, but not when confronting Taliban	Successful control mechanisms	Poor discipline, moderate control of forces. Poor control of clients	Weakened control mechanisms with fragmentation	Probably good except with clients
Resilience	Not particularly vulnerable to decapitation	Vulnerable to decapitation and weapons depot seizures	Vulnerable to decapitation	Vulnerable to decapitation and losing clients	Vulnerable to geographic isolation	Vulnerable to decapitation and losing clients

(*continued*)

Table 8.2. (continued)

PROCESS	TALIBAN	HEKMATYAR'S HIZB	MASSOUD	DOSTUM'S JUMBISH-I MILLI	WAHDAT	ISMAIL KHAN'S EMIRATE
Foreign aid	Pakistan, Saudi Arabia and other Gulf states, private donors, Al-Qaida	Pakistan, independent Islamists	India, Iran, Saudi Arabia, Russia, others	Uzbekistan, Russia, Turkey, others	Depended on Iran	Iran mostly, but also Pakistan, Uzbekistan, Rabbani
Intraorganizational cohesion	Cohesive	Cohesive, except versus Taliban	Cohesive	Clients have leeway to defect but centralized core is otherwise cohesive	Splintered along Hazara/Quizilbash fault line in 1995, more later	Cohesive
Knowledge and information	Excellent	Good	Excellent	Good	Fair	Fair
Structure	Centralized	Centralized	Centralized	Centralized with clients	Centralized	Centralized with clients
Safe haven?	Yes	Yes	Yes	Yes	Yes	Yes
Good fit?	Yes	Yes	Yes	No	Yes	No
Survived?	Yes	No	Yes	No	No	No

way many scholars have done, by referring to facilitating and empowering factors.

The analysis of the Taliban's expansion in non-Pushtun areas confirms the findings from chapter 7 that organizations that have a safe haven should refrain from adopting an organizational structure based on patronage. It also highlights the rapidity with which organizational structures can shift (e.g., Dostum's and Ismail Khan's fatal adoption of patronage just before the rise of Taliban), thus dramatically affecting the dynamics of conflict.

CHAPTER 9

Afghan Conflicts under U.S. Occupation, 2001–

> As the result of two successful campaigns, of the employment of an enormous force, and of the expenditure of large sums of money, all that has yet been accomplished has been the disintegration of the state which it was desired to see strong, friendly and independent.
>
> —Lord Hartington, secretary of state for India, reflecting on the two failed British invasions of Afghanistan, 1880

The September 2001 suicide attacks on the United States ushered in the direct involvement of the United States in Afghan conflicts. Osama bin Laden did not claim responsibility for the 9/11 attacks until well after the U.S. invasion of Afghanistan, probably in an attempt to protect his hosts and to diffuse U.S. energy in the pursuit of unknown attackers. There was little doubt, however, that al-Qaida was behind the attacks, and the United States invaded Afghanistan in October and November 2001 to defeat the organization and its Taliban hosts. The invasion was executed along an innovative model (later dubbed the "Afghan" model in military circles) that consisted of embedding special operations forces with Afghan allies on the ground to help direct massive air strikes to destroy Taliban defenses. The Afghan allies (followers of Dostum, the northern commander Mohammad Atta, Ismail Khan, the deceased Massoud, and minor Pushtun leaders) were expected to overrun the weakened Taliban defenses. This model economized U.S. military losses but provided very limited control over operations. This disadvantage became obvious in Tora Bora and Shah-i Kot where less-motivated Afghan allies of the United States allowed Osama bin Laden and many al-Qaida members to escape from the battlefield.[1] Still, the Taliban collapsed as a

1. For a detailed study of those operations, see Stephen Biddle, "Afghanistan and the Future of Warfare," Strategic Studies Institute, U.S. Army War College, November 2002.

centralized government and military within two months of the beginning of the U.S. attack. Its commanders fanned out across Pushtun areas of Afghanistan and neighboring Pakistan to partly reorganize as an insurgent organization.

The U.S. venture in Afghanistan has been grossly mismanaged and urgently requires stark policy decisions that include difficult trade-offs. Security in Afghanistan has degenerated to the dismal levels that once facilitated the rise of the Taliban; economic growth is driven largely by drug production and the nonsustainable spending of Westerners in Kabul; the state is extremely weak, while many regional leaders (including some particularly brutal and predatory ones) conserve the potential to reemerge; and militiamen still outnumber members of an Afghan army that is completely funded and directly controlled by the United States. At the time of this writing in early 2007, relative stability is based on a precarious equilibrium that is likely to unravel soon because of ongoing trends and inherent contradictions in U.S. policy toward Afghanistan. The resistance could very well spiral into a full-fledged revolt on the scale of the Iraqi insurgency and the anti-Soviet jihad.

In this chapter I present developments in Afghanistan since September 11, 2001, then introduce the current political economy and organization of Afghanistan. I then solve the puzzle of relative early stability in a country famous for its determined resistance to conquering superpowers, including the British and Soviets. Finally, I argue that the ongoing insurgency is likely to become more intense and the U.S. occupation more difficult to maintain.

Political, Organizational, and Institutional Developments since the U.S. Invasion

The collapse of the Taliban allowed the resurgence of many local leaders that the Taliban had suppressed and some new ones as well—this is what some have called, with some justification, the return of "warlordism." Ismail Khan reconstructed his administration in Herat and neighboring provinces; Abdul Rashid Dostum reestablished himself in Uzbek-majority areas; the Panjshiris (the deceased Massoud's followers from the Panjshir Valley) and Mohammad Atta expanded their domains; and Wahdat regained autonomy in Hazarajat. In the Pushtun areas, hundreds of local leaders reemerged to resume many of the predatory practices that had made life unbearable and had facilitated the rise of the Taliban. The fragmented configuration of local organizations facing the Hamid Karzai regime and the United States today is fairly similar to the one that the Taliban defeated during their conquest of Afghanistan.

The United States committed itself to providing better governance to Afghanistan at the time of the invasion. It therefore organized and managed several high-profile events, mobilized some international support, and engaged in limited institution building. The United States convened a November 2001 conference in Bonn, Germany, to appoint an interim administration under Hamid Karzai, a refined Pushtun local leader with longstanding ties to the CIA. It later (2002) convened two large, but not necessarily representative, gatherings of regional representatives (dubbed loya jirga or grand councils) to appoint Hamid Karzai as president of a transitional administration and to develop a constitution for the country.[2] The de facto fragmentation of Afghanistan stands in stark contrast to the highly centralized Afghanistan described in a constitution that reflects the wishes of Karzai.[3] The United States and the United Nations also helped organize an October 2004 presidential election that Hamid Karzai won with 55 percent of the vote. Many of the more influential administrators and ministers who assisted Karzai were expatriates living in the West or militarized local leaders who supported the U.S. overthrow of the Taliban. The technocrats, including expatriates who now have to relinquish their second citizenship to serve, increased their ministerial representation at the expenses of local leaders after the presidential elections.

U.S. attempts to develop the Afghan National Army (ANA) have been fraught with problems. The ANA barely exceeds thirty-three thousand troops five years after the U.S. invasion of Afghanistan, a number that compares unfavorably with the number of armed men under the control of local leaders (tens of thousands, perhaps more than a hundred thousand) or, for purposes of comparison, with the armed forces trained by the Soviets to bolster their own client regime in the 1980s (some 150,000–300,000). U.S. officials, however, have declared that they have accelerated the training program to bring ANA's strength to seventy thousand. Still, it is not obvious how this rapid growth program will be implemented in the face of daunting problems such as high (even if stabilizing) desertion rates, mediocre training, nepotism, and ethnic tensions within the force. Even the inflated salaries paid to ANA recruits (ten times the salaries of police officers) have failed to stem defections. ANA does not have the capability to function without U.S. forces because it lacks an adequate air force (twenty-eight aging helicopters

---

2. For an account of the rubber-stamp quality of the loya jirga, see "The Afghan Transitional Administration: Prospects and Perils," International Crisis Group Afghanistan Briefing, July 30, 2002. For a historically grounded scathing critique, see Hanifi (2004).

3. For more details on the constitution, see "Afghanistan: The Constitutional Loya Jirga," Afghan Briefing, International Crisis Group, December 12, 2003.

and few transports) and advanced officer training. It does not even have an Afghan chain of command—ANA soldiers receive their pay and orders directly from the U.S. military, even though Karzai is theoretically the commander in chief. It is also not clear how the Karzai regime will be able to finance a force of seventy thousand at a cost of $1 billion/year (20–25% of Afghanistan's GDP) after the cessation of foreign aid.[4]

Another force, the sixty-thousand-strong Afghan Military Forces (AMF), which existed until July 2005, was only nominally under the control of the United States or the Karzai regime. It consisted of autonomous militiamen who were willing to provide military support in return for subsidies, just like others did during the days of the Soviet occupation and the Najib regime. Such ties of patronage are notoriously fickle and they led to the rapid unraveling of the Najib regime once its resources dried up in 1992. They also tend to be unreliable in combat because the client militiamen are more likely to want to save their weapons and followers (often by pursuing arrangements with their nominal enemies) than to aggressively pursue their patron's goals. There is little reason to believe that such forces will serve the Karzai government and the United States any better in the long term than they served the Soviets and Najib before them. Members of the AMF were officially disarmed and decommissioned with much fanfare by July 2005, but many continue to be part of mostly autonomous organized units under new designations, such as the highway police.

Although the Karzai regime has touted astronomic growth rates for the devastated economy in the last few years (29% in 2002, 16% in 2003, and 8% in 2004), even a very supportive World Bank acknowledges that this growth is not sustainable and is mostly due to the infusion of spending by foreign NGO personnel in Kabul and to the end of a devastating drought.[5] Economic growth may also have been driven by the trickle-down effects of Afghanistan's successive bumper crops of opium, even if government statistics try to isolate the effect of drugs. Both foreign aid and drug production are very problematic drivers of economic growth: NGO spending is not sustainable and inflates property costs beyond the reach of virtually all Kabulis, and the opium economy, which accounts for almost 40 percent of the entire GDP, is a major source of political instability. The showcase reconstruction

4. Cost estimates from Rubin et. al. 2005, p. 2.

5. "Afghanistan: State Building, Sustaining Growth, and Reducing Poverty," Country Economic Report, World Bank, September 9, 2004. The IMF projects growth of 8–10% for 2004–05 and 2005–06, in "Islamic State of Afghanistan, Third Review under the Staff Monitoring Program," February 3, 2005.

project was supposed to be the two-thousand-kilometer circular highway that joins Afghanistan's larger cities, but only 440 kilometers of the highway has been "rehabilitated" three and a half years into the invasion at the astronomical cost of $300 million, almost ten times more than originally planned. The quality of the work done on the completed Kabul-Kandahar section was so poor that the one layer of asphalt that was laid was degraded by one rough winter.[6] By early 2007, the highway project had cost $1.05 billion, 40 percent of the work was still unfinished, and NATO forces were still fighting to keep Taliban forces from attacking long stretches of the highway.[7]

Afghans are living in misery, with few improvements since the U.S. invasion. Health services have hardly improved but education has expanded noticeably, with the proportion of school-age children receiving schooling increasing from 32 percent to 56 percent between 2000 and 2003.[8] Seventeen to 26 percent of children still die before the age of five.[9] About half of the refugees and internally displaced persons have returned to their home areas or to urban areas, often to face miserable conditions and predatory behavior. Kabul is congested beyond saturation and its infrastructure is in shambles. Drug consumption has become a serious problem in Kabul and elsewhere after the return of addicts from refugee camps and the collapse of the Taliban's strict monitoring system.[10] Such mediocre improvement is not surprising: while $9 billion worth of aid has been committed to Afghanistan since the U.S. invasion, only $3.3 billion had been disbursed to projects that had begun operating as of March 2005, and less than $1 billion worth of projects had been completed, with much of this money wasted on overhead, redundant and ineffective projects, corruption, and huge insurance rates. As Rubin et al. (2005, 61) remind us, $3.3 billion is "half the estimated income from the drug economy ($6.8 bln) during the same period." By comparison, this sum is also less than half of the inflation-adjusted amount the Soviets gave their client regime each year to help it maintain a purely defensive position between 1989 and 1992.[11]

6. Rubin et al. 2005, 18.

7. Paul Watson, "1,373 miles into the Heart of Afghanistan," *Los Angeles Times*, December 31, 2006.

8. "The Road Ahead: Issues for Consideration at the Berlin Donor Conference for Afghanistan," a Center for Strategic and International Studies report by Amy Frumin, Morgan Courtney, and Rebecca Linder, 2004.

9. "Afghanistan: State Building, Sustaining Growth, and Reducing Poverty," x–xi. The higher figure is from UNICEF and the UNDP Human Development Index.

10. "Afghanistan: An Assessment of Problem Drug Use in Kabul City," UN Office on Drugs and Crime, Community Drug Profile, July 2003.

11. Four billion a year in 1992 dollars adjusted for inflation (3%) would equal $7.9 billion in 2005 dollars. Estimates go up to $4.8 billion/year.

The situation of women has improved in a few ways and regressed in many others. Urban Afghan women now have broader access to health care, education, and employment. Some women can now run in elections and voice concerns. The proportion of girls' enrollment in primary schools increased from 3 percent under the Taliban to 40 percent in 2003.[12] They are also freer from the strict dress code of the Taliban, although many Kabuli women still wear the all-encompassing burqa anyway. But most women, even in Kabul, now live in fear for their own safety.[13] Rural women still do not have improved access to health care, education, and employment, but they are now more vulnerable to predatory practices, including rape and kidnapping.[14] The improvement of the legal status of Afghan women does not translate into an improvement of their actual situation. The resumption of conflict and microwars has also made the situation for everyone, including women, more precarious in the countryside. In a chilling reminder of the sort of outrages that threw Afghans into the arms of the Taliban, Human Rights Watch has documented incidents of rape of young boys and girls, as well as women, by soldiers affiliated with the Karzai regime and the United States.[15]

The Karzai government suffers from a narrow base of support. Karzai is generally seen as a figurehead for American and, for the first three years, Panjshiri influence among the Pushtun and, among minorities, as a centralizing ruler trying to limit regional autonomy. Karzai himself could probably rely on no more than the loyalty of some Kandahari tribes such as his own Popolzai. He is not particularly charismatic to Afghans (even if he seems very attractive to Westerners), and he doesn't have particularly relevant military expertise (he claims to never have fired a weapon). He depends heavily on the U.S. and NATO presence for his safety and the consolidation of his government and on an international force (International Security Assistance Force, or ISAF, with eighty-five hundred troops) to maintain security in Kabul. An American shadow cabinet is reported to make most of the important decisions, U.S. advisers write Karzai's major speeches, and the previous

---

12. "The Road Ahead," 6.

13. "Afghanistan: Women Still under Attack—A Systematic Failure to Protect," Amnesty International, May 30, 2005. Accessed online at http://web.amnesty.org/library/pdf/ASA110072005 ENGLISH/$File/ASA1100705.pdf.

14. A number of such instances are documented in, inter alia, " 'We Want to Live as Humans': Repression of Women and Girls in Western Afghanistan," *Human Rights Watch* 14, no. 11 (December 2002).

15. " 'Killing You Is a Very Easy Thing for Us': Human Rights Abuses in Southeast Afghanistan," *Human Rights Watch* 15, no. 5 (July 2003).

U.S. ambassador, Zalmay Khalilzad, was often called "the second president."[16] Karzai's best assets are U.S. support and the broad perception that his government is capable of attracting international financial aid to the country. Karzai's narrow social base and his precarious position made it urgent to hold the October 2004 presidential elections to give him a broader aura of legitimacy and popular appeal.

The presidential election of October 9, 2004, was an encouraging first in Afghan history.[17] The turnout was high at some 70 percent of registered voters, which conveyed the impression that it appealed to the Afghan population. A UN-appointed panel certified the election's results in spite of a number of irregularities, because its members believed that they could not have affected the overall results. Some observers, however, have argued that the international organizations that poured in $200 million (5% of the Afghan GDP) to make this election possible had a vested interest in their success and that their consent was too facile.[18] There is no doubt that Afghans of all backgrounds want to have a voice in the political process, but the implementation of the elections was problematic in at least five ways: (1) it increased and solidified ethnic tensions; (2) it provided no serious alternatives among ethnic candidates from each ethnic background; (3) it was plagued by registration fraud, voter intimidation by local leaders, and abuse of the power of the incumbency by Karzai; (4) it virtually guaranteed the victory of Karzai as the most significant candidate among the plurality Pushtuns; and (5) parliamentary elections were postponed from October to April and then again to September 2005 to prevent the emergence of parliamentary opposition to Karzai.[19] Results of the parliamentary elections of September 2005 confirmed fears that the parliamentary electoral system (a

---

16. Amy Waldman, "In Afghanistan, U.S. Envoy Sits in Seat of Power," *New York Times*, April 17, 2004, p. A1.

17. Parliamentary elections were held in the past, but no Afghan executive had been elected before.

18. "Karzai Wins Afghan Presidential Election," *Guardian*, November 3, 2004.

19. "Afghanistan: From Presidential to Parliamentary Elections," International Crisis Group, Asia Report, No. 88 (November 23, 2004), 2. There were documented cases of warlords collecting voting cards from villagers and promising to vote for them. For example, see Françoise Chipaux, "Guns Still Call the Shots in Afghanistan," *Le Monde*; in English in the *Guardian Weekly*, October 1–7, 2004, p. 21. The media mostly covered Karzai's activities, and he benefited from U.S. transport and protection while campaigning. For a fuller critique, see M. Nazif Shahrani, "Afghanistan's Presidential Elections: Spreading Democracy or a Sham?" *MERIP*, October 8, 2004; "Human Rights Abuses and Political Repression in the Run-up to Afghanistan's Presidential Election," *Human Rights Watch Briefing Paper*, September 2004; and "Free, Fair or Flawed: Challenges for Legitimate Elections in Afghanistan," *Afghanistan Research and Evaluation Unit*, September 2004.

single nontransferable vote) was chosen to produce a weak and fragmented parliament that cannot check Karzai's already overwhelming constitutional powers.[20] Many of those elected to the 249–seat parliament are local leaders with unchecked influence in their home regions; they perceive official positions as yet another dimension of their relation of clientage with the state and international donors.

The Taliban and al-Qaida did not quite disappear after the U.S. invasion of Afghanistan and the standoff in Tora Bora. They reorganized as guerrilla movements and have been harassing U.S. and NATO forces and Karzai supporters. A third group, the rump Hizb-i Islami, also initiated insurgent activities after the return of Hekmatyar from Iran. The insurgency's intensity increased in the spring of 2005, after the winter snow melted, with some fifteen hundred people estimated to die from fighting between March and November. The number of casualties from conflict increased to an estimated four thousand in 2006. The insurgents have been using a broad array of tactics, some of which have been borrowed from Iraqi insurgents. They have been ambushing U.S. and Afghan patrols, using remotely detonated explosives, attacking Afghan police posts, lobbing mortar shells at U.S. bases, attacking NGOs and Karzai administrators to reduce state penetration, assassinating state-appointed clergy, carrying out suicide attacks on ISAF and NATO troops, and reasserting control over some remote areas as bases for future operations. They have also been spreading their message of jihad against what they perceive to be an infidel occupier and its puppet regime by distributing leaflets (night letters) and through broadcasts of Radio Sharia. In return, the United States military has been engaging in a counterinsurgency effort that has caused many civilian deaths, mistreatment and murder of prisoners, arbitrary arrests, and the abuse of civilians by U.S. troops and their Afghan allies.[21] News of the desecration of the Koran and of the abuse of Afghan prisoners by U.S. troops in Afghanistan, Diego Garcia, and Guantanamo caused riots in protest in different parts of Afghanistan. The burning of the bodies of two Taliban fighters by U.S. troops in October 2006 has also produced widespread resentment.

Nineteen U.S., NATO, and New Zealand Provincial Reconstruction Teams of 50–150 soldiers that were meant to win the "hearts and minds" of Afghans have had a very mixed performance and have endangered the staff

---

20. "Political Parties in Afghanistan," *International Crisis Group Asia Briefing*, no. 39, June 2, 2005.

21. " 'Enduring Freedom': Abuses by U.S. Forces in Afghanistan," *Human Rights Watch* 16, no. 3, March 2004.

of international NGOs who did effective relief work.[22] The assassination of dozens of NGO personnel has led to the withdrawal of key organizations and the cessation of most humanitarian work in the south and east of the country. Efforts to destroy poppy fields often produce the intensification of insurgent attacks in the area. The Pushtun belt is simmering.

The Political and Economic Organization of Afghanistan after the U.S. Invasion

The Karzai government directly controls a very small portion of Afghanistan, mostly Kabul and some areas in the west and south of the country. An international force of some eighty-five hundred soldiers under NATO command helps it maintain security in Kabul and some areas of the north. Some forty thousand U.S. and NATO troops are mostly engaged in counterinsurgency and the effort to seize al-Qaida and Taliban leaders in the Pushtun belt, without trying to reduce the influence of local leaders. Much of the country is under the influence of armed local leaders whose forces range in size from a few ragtag soldiers to hundreds, and perhaps thousands. Leaders with larger organizations are based in minority areas, while Pushtun areas are much more fragmented. Dedicated insurgents such as the rump Taliban, Hizb-i Islami (the former mujahideen party), and al-Qaida forces can function fairly freely across the border in Pakistan and in some of the more remote regions of Helmand, Uruzjan, Zabul, Paktia, and Kunar.

Local leaders, in true Afghan tradition, are generally concerned with maintaining maximum local autonomy. The Karzai regime must weaken militarized local leaders to improve its long-term odds of remaining in power. The U.S. presence officially aims to consolidate a strong Afghan state but often works at cross-purposes to that goal. Dedicated insurgents want to remove the United States from Afghanistan and establish a different regime.

Two resources will greatly affect the ability of the United States, the Karzai regime, local leaders, and dedicated insurgents to achieve their goals: money and weapons. Different streams of income into the impoverished Afghan economy (which had a $4 billion GDP, or $200 per capita, in 2005) strengthen the state, militarized local leaders, or both.

22. "Provincial Reconstruction Teams and Humanitarian-Military Relations in Afghanistan," Save the Children, September 2004, accessed online on August 1, 2005 at http://www.savethechildren.org.uk/scuk_cache/scuk/cache/cmsattach/2029_PRTs%20in%20Afghanistan_Sep04.pdf.

The largest source of economic activity in Afghan is the production and export of opium and its derivatives. It strengthens autonomous local leaders who tax poppy cultivation and participate in its processing and transport. In 2004, this industry generated up to 40 percent of Afghanistan's GDP, spread to all Afghan provinces, and provided much of the income for 2.3 million Afghans, one-tenth of the population.[23] Afghanistan had three consecutive bumper crops of opium in 2002, 2003, and 2004 in spite of promises by the United States, Britain, and Karzai to eradicate poppy fields or facilitate the transition to other crops. Production remained relatively stable in 2005 but soared by 59 percent, to sixty-one hundred tons of opium, in 2006—providing 92 percent of the world's supply.[24] In addition, much more processing of opium into heroin and morphine is taking place within Afghanistan's borders. This increases the profit margins of the drug refinement and export operations, which benefits militarized leaders in particular.[25] The U.S. military has been resisting the extension of its mission to include eradication out of fear of stoking resistance and distraction from its main mission of capturing al-Qaida leaders. Highly publicized destruction of opium fields and even the use of aerial spraying of harsh chemicals (a so-called Agent Green, according to sources familiar with the program) have had little impact except to aggravate some desperately impoverished farmers. The inability of the Karzai regime, NGOs, and others to deliver on promises to compensate and train farmers who have forfeited poppy production has lessened their readiness to take such offers seriously. A forceful destruction of Afghan poppy fields, even if possible, would eliminate a third of the Afghan economy and push famished and disgruntled farmers into joining the insurgents.[26] On the other hand, income from this industry can finance a full-fledged insurgency on the scale of the anti-Soviet jihad: the estimated $1 billion a year that the smugglers, local leaders, and refiners make today dwarfs the foreign aid given to the mujahideen during most years of the jihad, even when the sums are adjusted for inflation.

---

23. "Afghanistan Opium Survey 2004," UN Office on Drugs and Crime and government of Afghanistan's Counter Narcotics Directorate, November 2004. Accessed online on August 1, 2005, at http://www.unodc.org/unodc/en/crop_monitoring.html. See also previous years' reports.

24. "Afghan Opium Cultivation Soars 59 percent in 2006, UNODC Survey Shows," UN Office on Drugs and Crime and government of Afghanistan's Counter Narcotics Directorate. Accessed online January 22, 2007, at http://www.unodc.org/unodc/press_release_2006_09_01.html.

25. Barnett Rubin, "Road to Ruin: Afghanistan's Booming Opium Industry," Center on International Cooperation Report, October 7, 2004, online at http://www.cic.nyu.edu/pdf/RoadtoRuin .pdf, accessed August 1, 2005.

26. Barnett R. Rubin and Omar Zakhilwal, "A War on Drugs or a War on Farmers," *Wall Street Journal*, January 11, 2005, p. A20.

International aid, at perhaps a quarter of GDP, is the second largest stream of income into the Afghan economy. Western aid is channeled through the Karzai regime, disbursed by NGOs, or meted out by the U.S. military. The portion given to the Karzai government contributes to its consolidation, or at least to its ability to act as a patron. The effect of the portion disbursed directly by NGOs in Kabul and other areas is not obvious: it might show the merits of having a centralized state, but it might also create a skewed economy that alienates many of those who do not benefit from it. Aid disbursed by the U.S. military is the most problematic. It consists of direct subsidies to militarized local leaders in return for operational help (safeguarding the perimeter of bases, help in operations) and developmental projects. Some reports even claim that the United States has been unwittingly supporting Taliban units by giving money to their tribal kith and kin.[27] Subsidies for militarized local leaders obviously go against the grain of the policy of creating a strong centralized state. Development projects, on the other hand, might create goodwill for the regime that the U.S. military is supporting.

Taxes on imports are another major stream of income. Most of those taxes are levied on the borders with Iran, Pakistan, Turkmenistan, and Uzbekistan. Until recently, only the stronger local leaders benefited from such taxes, but a successful operation by the United States, Karzai regime figures, and some militarized local leaders dislodged Ismail Khan, the generally successful and well-liked emir of Herat, from his fiefdom and put income from trade with Iran (estimated at up to $300 million per year) under the control of the government.[28] Ismail Khan is the only major local leader who has been removed by the Karzai government and the United States so far.[29]

Smuggling to Pakistan, taxing agriculture and even people, and road tolls provide an additional stream of income to militarized local leaders. Smuggling

---

27. Syed Saleem Shahzad, "Taliban Profit from U.S. Largesse," *Asia Times*, May 5, 2005. Also, Syed Saleem Shahzad, "The Face of Afghanistan's Resistance," *Asia Times*, August 26, 2003.

28. A Human Rights Watch report ("Our Hopes Are Crushed" 14, no. 7, November 2002) presents Ismail Khan in a much more negative light. Still, and in spite of his many transgressions, he was one of the best local leaders in Afghanistan. Accounts of his administration were generally favorable and he is not known to have engaged in large-scale atrocities like other local leaders. See, for example, Radek Sikorski, "Meanwhile in Afghanistan," *National Review*, October 11, 2004, and Barry Bearak, "Unreconstructed," *New York Times Magazine*, June 1, 2003.

29. It is debatable whether the unsavory Pushtun warlord Padshah Khan Zadran with his three-hundred-men militia was significant enough to be included in this statement. At any rate, he was attacked by the U.S. military because he threatened a U.S. Special Forces unit, not because he was trying to scuttle Karzai's administrative appointments in Paktia (International Crisis Group Asia Report no. 65, pp. 14–18).

is fueled by high Pakistani tariffs on imports and has been practiced by Afghan tribes for decades. Some roadblocks are reported to have been torn down by the U.S. military and ANA, but many persist.

One possible future stream of income would help consolidate the state, but it is unlikely to become significant soon: revenue from an oil pipeline that transports Central Asian oil to Pakistani ports through Afghanistan. Building such a pipeline would require a degree of security that only a strong state could provide, and it is therefore not likely that the income it would generate will arrive in time to assist the state to defeat its entrenched rivals. Another potential future stream of income would weaken the state—aid from U.S. rivals or potential rivals, such as Iran, Pakistan, China, or Russia, to challengers of the Karzai regime.

Weapons are the other significant resource in current Afghan conflicts. The country is awash with weapons of all calibers because of the largesse of the motivated sponsors of Afghan factions since 1979. There are millions of small arms and tens of thousands of heavy weapons in Afghanistan. Between 65,000 and 120,000 men are under arms on a permanent basis, and many more could mobilize for local defense or feuds.[30] A disarmament, demobilization, and reintegration (DDR) scheme targeted militias that affiliated themselves, even if nominally, with the Karzai government. The DDR project, dubbed Afghanistan's New Beginnings Programme, claimed to have collected 36,431 weapons, including 10,888 heavy weapons, by the time its mandate ended in July 2005.[31] Not only is this number miniscule when compared to estimates of weapons in Afghanistan but a good portion of those weapons are older and unusable ones. It is very likely that many soldiers who surrendered small arms in return for the promised incentive package (money, food, and vocational training) gave up older, largely useless weapons and kept newer ones. This DDR program did not target armed groups (estimated to number 850 to a thousand groups with at least sixty-five thousand fighters) that were not affiliated with the regime. The program was also diluted by the transfer of many "decommissioned" militias to the highway police, an appointment that allows them to easily engage in smuggling opium while pocketing inflated salaries from USAID.

30. Numbers and other information in this paragraph are from "Afghanistan: Getting Disarmament Back on Track," International Crisis Group Asia Briefing, no. 35, February, 23, 2005; Robin-Edward Poulton, "Afghanistan: New Approaches for Weapons Management," *Small Arms and Human Security Program* 4, October 2004; and Françoise Chipaux, "Guns Still Call the Shots in Afghanistan," *Guardian Weekly*, October 1–7, 2004, p. 21.

31. From official website at http://www.anbpafg.org/, accessed August 1, 2005.

The tiny ANA is not capable of controlling a country still saturated with weapons and fighters and those wealthy enough from the drug trade to organize them. The corrupt police forces are mostly extensions of the militias and cannot be relied on to subdue them. The Karzai regime is considerably outmatched, both militarily and financially.

Solving the Puzzle of Early (Relative) Stability

Limited (albeit rising) resistance to the foreign presence might seem surprising in a country whose people (particularly the Pushtun) have little tolerance for foreign occupation and externally imposed rulers. The British, the hyperpower of the time, twice failed miserably to occupy Afghanistan, losing in one instance almost every member of their nineteen-thousand-strong Army of the Indus. The Soviet Red Army lost some thirty thousand of its soldiers in Afghanistan in the 1980s. Not a single Afghan ruler that was imposed by an outside power survived the withdrawal or defeat of the invading army, whether it was the Communist Najib, Shah Shuja, or Yaqub Khan—who followed the withdrawing British and was reported to have sheepishly said, "I would rather be a grass cutter in a British camp than to be the ruler of Afghanistan."[32]

Karzai and his backers in the Bush administration found in early limited military resistance hope that their state-building venture would succeed. But a lack of large-scale military resistance to the Western presence did not necessarily reflect consent or support among Afghans. It was simply the result of four internal and five facilitating regional factors that have already begun to wither away.

The first internal factor is the debt of gratitude the reemerging leaders felt toward the United States. Most of them would not have reemerged as players on the Afghan scene if it weren't for the U.S. intervention. Gratitude, however, will erode quickly if the United States decides to comprehensively disarm local militias, undermine local autonomy by extending the writ of Kabul across the country, or actively reduce local leaders' sources of income, such as the production of opium poppies, smuggling, and direct subsidies. Local leaders would then become much more dangerous to U.S. troops than the dedicated Taliban, al-Qaida, and Hizb. But, most likely, they will use the Taliban and Hizb as a convenient umbrella for their activities if they decide

32. Ewans 2001, 89.

to resist. Keeping a foot in each camp to hedge for contingencies is a very old and wise Afghan practice.

The second internal factor is fear of the impressive military might of the United States, particularly its air force. There are already signs, however, that dedicated insurgents have adapted to U.S. military tactics and found effective ways to ambush U.S., NATO and ANA troops. The Afghans' learning curve did catch up with the British Army of the Indus and with the Soviet Red Army in the past, and fear of mighty enemies dips with small successes. Guerrilla attacks on NATO and government troops have lately become more frequent, bold, and effective. Of even greater concern to the U.S. military, Afghans seem to be copying successful tactics used by Iraqi insurgents, probably with the help of seasoned Arab mujahideen.

The third domestic factor that helps keep local leaders in check is the distribution of resources and even direct subsidies by the U.S. and Western organizations. Many, including former members of the Taliban who now support local leaders, are benefiting from the price the Americans are willing to pay because of their desire to catch Taliban and al-Qaida leaders. One U.S. officer described some of the ways local leaders benefit from U.S. subsidies:

> At least some of these incidents (mortar attacks), especially those around Bagram [the U.S. base north of Kabul], are crude attempts at extortion. In some places, the U.S. pays local warlords to use their armed paramilitary groups to provide some security around bases and along roads. Many of these warlords are no more than boorish gangsters, and their paramilitary armies are gangs of bandits with nothing else productive to do in a destroyed economy. The local warlord controls, by force and fear, which local nationals get to work at the air base, and we employ hundreds here. The workers don't make much, but the warlord extorts a hefty percentage of their pay in exchange for allowing them to continue to work at the base. The warlord also extorts money from the vendors who sell goods at the weekly bazaars we have sponsored on base in the past. The extortion theory argues that the warlord is behind the rocket incidents, and that he thinks the rockets will scare the U.S. into paying him more to provide even more security.[33]

The disbanded Afghan Military Forces and the possible creation and maintenance of a national guard—a project under consideration by the

33. Unpublished Afghanistan journal, February 13, 2003, Col. Bruce Wood, Georgia National Guard, chief of information warfare for the U.S. contingent, Bagram Airbase.

Bush administration—aim at subsidizing local militias in return for military support. The United States and other donors will ultimately have to stop direct subsidies and the disbursement of aid. A good indication that donor fatigue is increasing is that international donors are made to repledge their multiyear commitments every year by the United States. No subsidies, no loyalty.

The fourth domestic factor is the weakness of the state and the tepid nature of the efforts to undermine local autonomy. This situation is nearly ideal for local leaders: the state serves as a conduit for subsidies but doesn't undermine their autonomy, and efforts to disarm them and cut their sources of income have been timid. Local leaders have little reason to revolt until they become even stronger, the United States leaves, or they feel threatened.

The first facilitating regional factor that explains limited early resistance to U.S. occupation is the general quiescence of the Pushtun tribes across the border in Pakistan. Although they welcomed Taliban and Arab Islamists and voiced hostility toward U.S. actions and increased Pakistani penetration of their tribal domain, they haven't actively pushed for a jihad in Afghanistan yet. Pakistan is a very unstable country, however, and there are many possible scenarios that would result in increased cross-border Pushtun guerrilla activities. A successful coup or assassination attempt against Pakistani president Pervez Musharraf could very well let loose the massive resentment that has been building up in Pakistan against U.S. policies.[34] The electoral victories of Pakistani Islamist parties in the North-West Frontier and Baluchistan provinces (the same parties that sponsor the religious schools that gave birth to the Taliban movement) make this an even more likely scenario. As of January 2007, the Pakistani government seemed to have all but given up on deterring Pakistani Pushtun tribesmen from supporting the Taliban and, some suspect, might even be assisting them in their cross-border activities.

The second facilitating factor is the support of the Uzbek, Kyrgyz, and Pakistani governments. The three governments have allowed the United States to operate bases in support of military operations in landlocked Afghanistan. Pakistan also allowed some U.S. troops to discretely operate on its soil to help locate Taliban members and their non-Afghan supporters within

34. According to the Pew Global Attitudes Project (*A Year after Iraq War*, March 16, 2004, online at http://people-press.org/reports/pdf/206.pdf), only 21% of Pakistanis had a favorable opinion of the United States in 2004 (10% in 2002) while 50% held a very unfavorable opinion. Sixty percent of Pakistanis also oppose and 16% favor the "US War on Terrorism," and 51% have confidence in Osama bin Laden as a world leader.

its own borders. The three countries are very unstable, however, and U.S. ability to base troops and air force assets within their borders has always been precarious. Uzbekistan's Islam Karimov felt slighted by U.S. protests over his brutal crackdown on protesters in the Ferghana Valley, and did request in July 2005, with Russian and Chinese encouragement, that the United States vacate the base within 180 days.[35] The Americans left in October, and Karimov also notified other NATO members with operations in Afghanistan that they could not use Uzbek soil anymore.[36] Kyrgyz president Kurmanbek Bakiyev might have been appealing to the Kyrgyz Russian vote during the July 2005 elections when he threatened to close the Manas base in Bishkek.[37] There are already signs that Pakistan, even under Musharraf, is adopting an independent policy in Afghanistan, including support for some Taliban, which is not compatible with U.S. goals. The loss of bases and support in Kyrgyzstan and Pakistan would make it much more difficult and costly to support U.S. military operations in Afghanistan.

The third regional factor is Russia's and China's acquiescence to the U.S. presence in Afghanistan in return for the United States conveniently overlooking their oppression of their own Muslim minorities. This is already changing, however, and it is not far-fetched that one day Russia might support Afghan groups to avenge the U.S. support for the mujahideen in the 1980s, or that China might find in Afghanistan a convenient way to distract the United States from intervening on the Korean Peninsula or in Taiwan. U.S. hesitation to support Russia in its intrusive attempt to displace Chechen rebels from their refuge in Georgia, lack of economic rewards, and the U.S. invasion of Iraq have already freed Russian leaders from any misconceptions they might have had of the advantages to be gained from supporting the U.S. presence in Afghanistan. More important, Russia and China have coordinated their efforts to induce and pressure Uzbekistan and Kyrgyzstan to close U.S. bases within their borders.[38] The regular presidential-level meetings of the Shanghai Cooperation Organization (which includes Russia, China, Kazakhstan, Kyrgyzstan,

35. Jim Garamone, "Uzbeks Ask U.S. to Leave Karshi-Khanabad," American Forces Press Service, August 1, 2005; "Uzbekistan Mulls Future of U.S Air Base," Associated Press, July 7, 2005; "US Military Shifts Afghan Support from Uzbek Base," Reuters, June 15, 2005.

36. "Uzbekistan: No More Help on Afghanistan," Associated Press, November 23, 2005.

37. Aida Baltabaeva, "Kyrgyzstan President-Elect Raised Issue of U.S. Base Withdrawal," *Caucasus Analyst*, July 13, 2005.

38. C. J. Chivers, "Central Asians Call on U.S. to Set a Timetable for Closing Bases," *New York Times*, July 6, 2005.

Uzbekistan, and Tajikistan) provide the recurrent mechanism through which this pressure is applied.

The fourth regional factor is Iran's fear of provoking U.S. wrath by supporting dissenters in Afghanistan and in Iraq. But despite discreet contacts between Washington and Tehran since the invasion of Afghanistan, the Bush administration hasn't been mincing words when it comes to Iran, and there is little doubt that the Iranians feel threatened by the U.S. focus on their nuclear program and their continuing demonization (a reciprocal behavior) by members of the Bush administration. While attempting to avoid being next in the administration's crosshairs, there is no doubt that Iran has the kind of relationships it could leverage to weaken the U.S. presence on both its Afghan and Iraqi borders if it is attacked. The Iranians already have strong ties to the Tajik, Hazaras, Ismail Khan, and Hekmatyar in Afghanistan, and they have strong ties to sectors of the Iraqi Shiite and Kurdish populations. Iranian support for current and potential Afghan challengers would fundamentally alter the security situation for the United States and Karzai.

A fifth regional factor is the draw of the Iraq conflict on transnational Islamist militants. Iraq is more attractive to Arab militants than Afghanistan because of its greater proximity, ethnic and linguistic ties, and because the Iraqi resistance has been much more vibrant than the Afghan one. Ironically, however, the success of the Iraqi insurgency in tying down the U.S. military and undermining America's image and foreign policy is helping revitalize the Afghan insurgency. Iraqi insurgents have shown that U.S. technology cannot prevent committed and innovative insurgents from operating effectively. Some Iraqi methods and tactics have been copied by Afghan insurgents. Some reports indicate that al-Qaida has opted to open a second, more active, front in Afghanistan to stretch American capabilities to the limit after ensuring that the insurgency in Iraq has gained sufficient momentum. This is a sensible strategy because the U.S. military has few troops to spare given its current deployment configuration, its huge commitment in Iraq (some 150,000 troops on the ground in early 2007, with twice as many at different stages of rotation), and its inability to meet recruitment targets since the eruption of the Iraqi insurgency.

The United States could continue to have a favorable environment in Afghanistan if these factors do not change. Many are already unraveling, however. Time is not on the side of the U.S. occupation in Afghanistan: the longer it stays, the more likely it is that domestic or regional changes will encourage a cascade of anti-American and anti-Karzai activities.

Why Is This Stability Illusory?

The underpinnings of stability in Afghanistan are crumbling. Three inherent contradictions in the Bush administration's Afghan policy will have to be decisively resolved as part of a comprehensive strategy before any serious progress can be made.[39]

The first contradiction is between the perhaps inadvertent but very real ethnic divide-and-rule strategy that has permeated the administration's policies and the need to create a unified Afghan polity. The U.S. invasion and many postinvasion practices have leveraged and aggravated ethnic tensions. The U.S. invasion was done in alliance with organizations that have adopted overtly ethnic agendas (Dostum's and Wahdat) and that later abused Pushtun minorities in the north and massacred Pushtun prisoners in the presence of U.S. troops.[40] Later, the United States invited Panjshiri (Tajik) troops to support military operations in the Pushtun belt, something that hasn't happened since the collapse of the Najib regime, and helped impose unpopular Pushtun commanders.[41] The U.S.-orchestrated loya jirgas emphasized ethnic representation and encouraged ethnic politics. The presidential elections also emphasized ethnic loyalty and amounted to ethnic polling—each ethnic group voted almost en masse for the one candidate from its ranks with the best chance to win. Ministerial appointments and even the composition of ANA units followed an ethnic logic. Karzai deftly manipulated ethnic divisions to win the presidential election and to keep himself relevant in a new Afghanistan where different ethnic groups fear one another much more than they fear him. The United States also stoked ethnic rivalries in its effort to fight the Taliban, sideline Ismail Khan, and subdue parts of the country. Ethnic politics and the practices of counterinsurgency, however, are in opposition to practices of nation building. Nation building consists of creating a sense of common destiny among members of the population, not fear and destructive rivalry. The United States and Karzai must transition away from divisive ethnic politics if they are to create a stable Afghan state, but this may not be possible anymore.

---

39. For other discussions of contradictions in the management of development aid and other areas, see Maley (2006) and a working paper by Astri Suhrke, "The Dangers of a Tight Embrace: Externally Assisted Statebuilding in Afghanistan," accessed online January 15, 2007, at http://state-building.org/resources/Suhkre_RPPS_October2006.pdf.

40. "Paying for the Taliban's Crimes: Abuses against Ethnic Pashtuns in Northern Afghanistan," *Human Rights Watch* 14, no. 2 (April 2002).

41. For more details, see "Afghanistan: The Problem of Pashtun Alienation," International Crisis Group Asia Report, no. 62, August 5, 2003.

The second inconsistency in the Bush administration's policy is between calling Afghans to abide by the rule of law when the U.S. military is consistently flouting their own rights and their own government cannot provide even a modicum of security. There is no such thing as the rule of law in Afghanistan. The law of the land applies to few regions, mainly Kabul, while the balance is under the yoke of local leaders whose often arbitrary behavior is unchecked. More important, Afghanistan is a country occupied by a foreign power whose behavior is above both local and international laws. In 2005 Karzai signed an agreement that affirmed the U.S. military's right to operate without any restrictions or accountability to the Afghan state.[42] The military of the United States has engaged in extremely abusive behavior against Afghan civilians, even drawing repeated protests from a largely impotent Karzai. Afghan prisoners have been tortured to death in U.S. custody, and many have been held incommunicado for years or shipped to prisons outside of Afghanistan without due process.[43] The U.S. military has also killed a substantial number of Afghan civilians in military operations, such as during the revenge bombing of an Afghan compound after the July 2005 downing of a U.S. military helicopter. U.S. military units engage in search-and-seizure operations that often humiliate and sometimes kill those whose property is targeted. Western mercenaries and contractors have followed the U.S. military into Afghanistan to commit abuses of their own, including kidnapping and torturing Afghan civilians. Spread of the news of the defilement of the Koran, the Muslim holy book, by American officers in Afghanistan and in Guantanamo has dispelled among Afghans any illusions that this occupation is meant to bring the rule of law. Afghans in ten provinces risked their lives protesting the U.S. occupation in response to news of the desecrations. Seventeen were killed and scores were wounded when the police fired into the crowds in May 2005.[44] Again, U.S. counterinsurgency involves abusive behavior that goes against the grain of democracy and the rule of law. The Bush administration will have to decide at some point which of the two it wishes to pursue.

---

42. The "Joint Declaration of the United States-Afghanistan Strategic Partnership," May 23, 2005, states (p. 864) that "U.S. and Coalition forces are to continue to have the freedom of action required to conduct appropriate military operations."

43. Those events have been widely covered in international and Afghan media. See the *Report of the Independent Expert on the Situation of Human Rights in Afghanistan*, M. Cherif Bassiouni, UN E/CN.4/2005/122, March 11, 2005. Accessed online January 22, 2007 at http://www.law.depaul.edu/institutes_centers/ihrli/pdf/Bassiouni_Afghanistan_Final_05.pdf.

44. Jon Lee Anderson, "The Man in the Palace: Hamid Karzai and the Dilemma of Being Afghanistan's President," *New Yorker* 81, no. 16 (June 6, 2005), 60–73. Also, "Protests against U.S. Spread across Afghanistan," *New York Times*, May 13, 2005, p. A1.

The third and most problematic contradiction in the administration's Afghanistan policy is that it simultaneously nurtures unifying (the state) and centrifugal (militarized local leaders) forces. The United States allowed the return of warlordism because it wanted to conduct the invasion of Afghanistan on the cheap and without risking the lives of many American soldiers. The invasion was conducted brilliantly from a military perspective, but the cost of this frugality was loss of control over the kind of organizations and institutions that filled the vacuum left by the collapse of the Taliban. Instead of weakening the militarized local leaders when they were still vulnerable in 2001–02, the Bush administration decided to leverage them to achieve further objectives at a manageable cost. The United States tolerated militarized local leaders consolidating their power by engaging in narcotics trafficking and other predatory practices; it has even helped strengthen some of them with direct subsidies. The Afghan state cannot have a reasonable chance to survive beyond a U.S. occupation if it is left to face on its own a large number of well-financed and well-armed rival organizations. The Bush administration, or its successor, will have to decide: Will it maintain or tolerate local client militias and postpone comprehensively disarming local leaders to avert a large-scale insurgency or will it actively try to establish a state with a reasonable chance of survival beyond a U.S. occupation at the risk of facing a broad insurgency?

If the history of patronage in Afghanistan is any indication, the current delicate equilibrium (the state and a large number of militarized local leaders coexisting under U.S. patronage) will not last for long. The many local leaders are independent and rational political actors who make strategic decisions to support or resist the outsider's venture based on their desire to increase their local autonomy, influence, and income. Centralization of the polity obviously goes against their interests, but they might accept becoming loyal clients of the regime so long as they are the beneficiaries of its generosity. The currency to buy the short-term loyalty of Afghan local leaders, weapons and money, has always been the means to strengthen their long-term independence, which goes a long way to explain the fragility of such arrangements.

The ability of an Afghan regime to woo clients increases if there are fewer of those resources circulating, if local competition is more intense, and if it is perceived to be more Islamic. If the country is saturated with weapons, as was the case during the later years of the Najib regime, then the regime will have to offer more and better weapons to keep the loyalty of its clients. Local competition inevitably produces losers who would be ready to provide an opening for the government in return for improving their odds for survival. Loyalty to an un-Islamic regime or foreign occupier could alienate a commander's followers or potential followers, which in turn would require him to both disburse and request more resources. The availability of alternative sources of income or weapons (poppy production, road tolls, outside sponsors) also reduces the ability of the regime to attract clients, while the ability to effectively mete out punishment to those who are not ready to join increases it.

The United States currently plays the role of overarching patron in Afghanistan, in an environment that has been conducive to the maintenance of ties of clientage. The regional leaders and chieftains running the lives of Afghans entered a period of intense competition as they struggled to reestablish themselves after the elimination of the Taliban as a centralized government. They were ready to ingratiate themselves with the Americans to buy time and receive the critical resources they needed to reestablish control, keep rivals at bay, and buy the loyalty of lesser commanders in some cases. The earlier allocations of money and weapons were the most valuable for the insecure local leaders, particularly because the Taliban and the rump Northern Alliance (the Panjshiris and their then defeated allies) monopolized the use of most large weapon systems right before the U.S. intervention. Resources dispensed later are less critical to the local leaders' survival (particularly if they manage to eliminate some of their immediate rivals) and are therefore less valuable. To attempt to deprive militarized local leaders of the critical (not superfluous or unusable) weapons in their possession (a stated U.S. and Karzai goal) in return for official positions would immediately alienate them. Political appointments under the leadership of a weak regime with an uncertain future are a poor substitute for governing autonomous fiefdoms. They would only accept such a deal on the verge of defeat, as Ismail Khan's experience has shown. Contrary to U.S. hopes, and if the Soviet experience in Afghanistan is any indication, local leaders will soon begin asking for more resources, including larger weapons, in return for maintaining loyalty or participating in military operations in the south and east of the country. And their loyalty will become ever more symbolic as they become stronger.

Although the alien identity of the occupiers is currently tolerated because of the need for the resources disbursed by the United States and the debt of gratitude the local leaders owe the Americans for their comeback, it will become a hindrance to maintaining clients as popular discontent begins to affect the decisions of local leaders. And the Karzai regime (widely perceived as a dependent puppet government) will continue to be tolerated only so long as its technocrats are capable of wooing foreign aid.

Even absent the correct inducements, overt rebellion against the U.S. occupation is not an appealing option for any militarized local leader because of U.S. military might and the unattractiveness of having to sustain its impact when an ambiguous position is costless. Some leaders, such as Dostum and Massoud's successor Mohammad Qasim Fahim, seem to think that avoiding direct confrontation is even worth giving up a portion of their arsenals, particularly when future income would easily allow them to purchase better weapons. Dissatisfied leaders could, however, resist the U.S. occupation in more discrete ways (e.g., sheltering Taliban fighters, sabotage, anonymous military operations) that signal to others that there are like-minded resistors. Once enough commanders who are secure in their turfs signal their restiveness, resistance could break out in an acephalous jihad that would dwarf in scale the current Taliban, Hizb, and al-Qaida resistance. The dedicated insurgents are, of course, trying to trigger such a jihad cascade themselves by increasing the intensity of resistance.

The current U.S. policy in Afghanistan is simply not sustainable. It will soon crumble under the weight of its own contradictions and as the underpinnings of stability continue to fray.

On the Outcome of a Full-fledged Insurgency

Both the U.S.-led occupation and its challengers are likely to experience changes in organizational structure and to adopt different strategies in the future, but the current patterns favor the insurgents.

The U.S.-Led Occupation

The coalition that aims to consolidate the Karzai regime is highly fragmented and suffers from the divergent goals of its members. Troops under NATO command are in charge of counterinsurgency and security while eight thousand or so U.S. troops are in charge of pursuing al-Qaida leaders. Troops from some NATO member countries avoid fighting, leaving the burden mostly to Canadian and British troops in the restive south. Provincial Reconstruction Teams, military-led groups that provide services to help counterinsurgency efforts, are led by militaries from different countries with different levels of commitment to counterinsurgency. The work of PRTs has also angered civilian NGOs who do not want their work to be associated with military activities. The United Nations Assistance Mission in Afghanistan (UNAMA) has a nonintrusive approach (a light footprint) that contrasts sharply with NATO's strategy of expanding its presence and the U.S. military's intrusiveness. UN agencies and NGOs often work at cross-purpose for bureaucratic reasons. Westerners control a parallel administrative and financial system that dwarfs those of Karzai's government: ANA is controlled by the U.S. military rather than the Afghan Ministry of Defense, donor countries control three-quarters of expenditures with no input from the Afghan Ministry of Finance, and U.S. officers, rather than Afghan judges, decide the fate of detainees and suspects accused of resistance.

This jumble of discordant organizations is incapable of meeting the challenges of a sophisticated insurgency. It is not capable of formulating coherent and sophisticated strategies or of adequately performing all other necessary processes to defeat a rising insurgency. The goodwill this coalition has lost in Pushtun areas now prevents it from implementing sophisticated strategies such as hearts and minds—the real strategy developed in Malaya and Kenya, not what NATO believes it is doing with the PRTs. This coalition needs to centralize quickly, expand, and develop a coherent set of strategies that actually helps the Afghan population while fending off challengers if it is sincere in its intention of consolidating the Karzai regime. Even then, it will face an uphill battle with poor odds of success because of the legacy of its inefficiencies and mistakes.

The Challengers

The Taliban and Hizb appear, albeit based on limited information, to have adopted centralized structures. No rival leaders to Mullah Omar or Hekmatyar seem to have emerged within either organization. They both benefit from safe havens across the border in Pakistan. And while cross-border havens are normally inferior to ones within the contested territory because neighboring countries may prevent their use at will, the North-West Frontier and Baluchistan provinces of Pakistan are inhabited by tribesmen who effectively keep the Pakistani government at bay and are committed to sheltering their ethnic kin from Afghanistan. This centralization, in combination with a safe heaven for planning and training, has allowed both organizations to adopt sophisticated guerrilla strategies to exhaust and overstretch occupation forces, weaken the penetration of the state, expel Western NGOs, and impede the progress of occupation-led development projects that would have facilitated a hearts-and-minds strategy. By attacking government representatives and supporters, the Taliban convince local leaders not to commit their support to the government or at least to keep a foot in each camp. By disturbing NGO and reconstruction efforts, they show the population that little good can come from occupiers. By attacking NATO troops, they attract brutal retaliation and a more visible military presence, shifting Pushtun public opinion to their side and increasing the costs of occupation. All those activities are probably accompanied with ongoing negotiations with local leaders and the recruitment of new fighters. When these activities reach a tipping point, change in Pushtun areas will come abruptly for the Karzai regime and its supporters. And once Pushtun resistance organizations gain momentum, other organizations from ethnic minorities will have to become active again to avoid being overwhelmed by a Taliban comeback. NATO's mission will then have to encompass both counterinsurgency and the policing of ethnic conflict, at a much higher cost than most contributors would be willing to sustain.

The cost of this insurgency is very small (probably no more than $30 million a year) and can be sustained from income from the opium trade and support from within Pakistan. In contrast, the U.S. military presence alone costs more than $1 billion a month and another billion or so a year is needed to maintain the ANA and other Karzai institutions.[45] And while the unruly U.S.-backed coalition could unravel under pressure for any number of reasons, the Taliban are not under the pressure of deadlines or domestic politics. This is why one of the Taliban leaders' most popular sayings is "The Americans have the watches, but we have the time."

The Soviets poured $4 billion per year and committed 120,000 soldiers and 10,000 advisers in their attempt to consolidate their client regime, and yet they failed to accomplish their goal. The United States today is committing a quarter as much money, a sixth as many boots on the ground, and only a tiny group of advisers, in the hope of achieving the same Sisyphean goal in a process plagued by inefficiency and with a strategy based on contradictions. The United States is also repeating the fatal Soviet mistake of acting as a patron of militias and has formed a discordant coalition to consolidate the highly vulnerable Karzai regime. It is facing sophisticated opponents with time on their side and a landscape of skeptical local leaders who can suddenly shift their support to them. If Washington fails to quickly restructure operations in Afghanistan to really help improve the lives of Afghans while engaging in effective counterinsurgency, then it might soon have to choose between fighting a full-fledged counterinsurgency and leaving Afghanistan as yet another defeated superpower.

Sadly, the suffering of the Afghans will likely continue for many more years.

---

45. Kenneth Katzman, "Afghanistan: Post-war Governance, Security, and U.S. Policy," *Congressional Research Report for Congress* (RL 30588), updated April 21, 2005.

PART THREE

And Beyond . . .

CHAPTER 10

The Organizational Theory beyond Afghanistan

Will the organizational theory's predictions hold beyond Afghanistan? My findings are not unique to Afghanistan, nor even to the Muslim world.

I test the ability of the organizational theory of group conflict and others to postdict the survival of organizations involved in conflicts and the outcomes of the conflicts in which they participated on an original ad hoc data set. The conflicts in the data set consist of all revolutionary, resistance, separatist, civil, and ethnic confrontations that I believe satisfy the following criteria:

1. All such conflicts from two broad regions: North Africa, the Middle East, the northern tier of the Indian subcontinent (MENA for short), and the Americas.
2. Cases are limited to the period from the end of World War II to the end of 2001.
3. All conflicts lasted longer than three years and killed at least 250 persons in each of those years.

This last criterion excludes from the sample "palace" revolutions, military coups, or confrontations in which the occupier did not care to remain. The passage of three years attests to the determination of all sides to the conflict to achieve their goals. Some might argue that the three-year threshold would leave out the successes of highly effective centralized regime factions that captured power precisely because of their centralization (e.g., the Egyptian Free Officers in 1952, Muʿammar Gadhafi in 1969, and Afghan Communists in 1978). Although the criticism is valid concerning what this criterion leaves out, this is a book about conflicts among distinct rival organizations, not among different regime factions or institutions. The sample is also not biased by ignoring societies where revolt or resistance never occurred (the equivalent of failure) because, even if the population is aggrieved and wishes to overthrow the powers that be, the lack of effective organized resistance only proves the point that atomization (extreme fragmentation) is very disadvantageous.

The data set includes only substantial organizations or classes of similar organizations. I used my judgment and consulted with area specialists to decide whether an organization is substantial enough to be included or not. The size and impact of a militant organization is difficult to gauge, and the judgment of the area specialist is often the best estimate. Conflicts are delineated by the entry or exit of a significant organization, its restructuring, or its acquisition of a safe haven. Conflicts begin when the activities of the involved organizations result in more than 250 deaths per year and conclude when they result in fewer than 100 deaths per year for at least three consecutive years. Deciding whether a settlement is a true compromise settlement (Sudan 1972), a tactical move by an organization waiting for a more opportune time to eliminate rivals (e.g., temporary concessions made by successive Iraqi regimes to the Kurds), or a mere ceremony to consolidate defeat (Yemen 1970) is a more subjective matter. I distinguish genuine negotiated settlements from tactical concessions by requiring that the arrangement last for at least ten years. I distinguish between genuine agreements and those designed to consolidate an outcome decided on the battlefield by assessing whether they contain provisions for the preservation of the involved organizations and whether they allow them to exit the arrangement fairly intact if the powers that be renege on their commitments. The 1972 negotiated settlement between the Sudanese regime of Jaafar Nimeiry and Anya Nya, the southern Sudanese insurgents, is the only genuine negotiated settlement among MENA conflicts that satisfies both requirements. Anya Nya troops were integrated into the Sudanese army as cohesive separate units and were not rotated out of their home areas. When Nimeiry violated the provisions of the Addis Ababa accords eleven years later by imposing sharia (the religious law southerners opposed) on the south and dividing it into three administrative units, the old Anya Nya units mutinied and regrouped to resume resistance. The 1970 agreement between North Yemeni republicans and royalists fails to meet the second requirement. The royalists did achieve immediate gains from the negotiations (up to five ministries, a seat on the Republican Council, and a number of governorships), but their organization, which was based on patronage and depended on Saudi aid, collapsed and could not challenge the gradual erosion of the gains they achieved. Only four years later, the 1974 military coup of Ibrahim al-Hamdi ended all these arrangements, and the designation "Royalist" even ceased to have any political meaning.[1]

Descriptive Statistics

I found that 133 organizations or groups of organizations that participated in forty-one conflicts met my selection criteria. Ninety-four organizations participated in twenty-seven conflicts from the MENA region and its periphery, and thirty-nine participated in fourteen conflicts from the Americas. Of the forty-one conflicts, four were ongoing as of 2001 (Sudan, Colombia, occupied West Bank and Gaza, and Kashmir) and two culminated in a durable negotiated settlement (El Salvador 1991 and Sudan 1972). Of the 133 organizations, forty are incumbents (governments or occupiers) and ninety-three are not. In one case, Afghanistan under the Taliban, there was no incumbent. Thirty-eight of the incumbents had a generally centralized structure, but two relied heavily on patronage. Nonincumbents were more diverse in their structures: fifty-five were centralized, nineteen were decentralized, six were based on patronage, and thirteen consisted of more than four uncoordinated groups (fragmented). Seventy-nine organizations had a good structural fit with the availability of safe haven (thirty-eight incumbents and forty-one nonincumbents), and fifty-four did not (two incumbents and fifty-two nonincumbents.) Incumbents won half the conflicts, lost 22.5 percent of them, and settled or are still fighting the balance.

On the Fate of Organizations

Again, the organizational theory's testable hypothesis is:

> H_1: Organizations that have the right fit of structure with the availability of safe haven are more likely to survive by the end of the conflict. Organizations with a safe haven should adopt a centralized structure, and those without such a haven should adopt a noncentralized one.

1. Gregory Gause kindly provided this information, but we disagree in our assessments of the quality of the agreement.

I code for *Fit* of structure with the availability of a safe haven by giving a score of 1 for good fit (centralization with safe haven or noncentralization without one) and a score of 0 for poor fit (centralization without safe haven or noncentralization with one, and fragmentation.)

A serious concern is that the organizational theory, a complex theory, overshoots by considering the fit of structure with the availability of safe haven—perhaps one of the two variables suffices to explain the fate of an organization. To check for this possibility, I include the two variables in some models. I code each organization dichotomously for *Haven* (1 = organization has such a safe haven). I code *Structure* on a scale that very roughly reflects the organization's degree of centralization—1, centralized; 2, decentralized, decentralized with board or precentralized Mao-like structure; 3, patronage-based; 4, fragmented.[2]

Because very little rigorous research has been done on the outcome of conflicts, I suggest other hypotheses drawn from studies on the onset and duration of conflict. Many military specialists and observers associate the length of civil wars with the availability of outside aid to belligerents. It is therefore reasonable to consider:

> H_2: The more aid an organization receives, the more likely it is to survive.

Unfortunately, it is difficult to know the exact amount of aid given to organizations in conflict because much of it is clandestine. I therefore code for *Aid* by using the following scale: 3 = Two or more state backers, considerable support; 2 = Support by a single state actor; 1 = Support by nonstate actors such as diasporas, transnational militants, or other militant organizations; 0 = No outside support. The number of sponsors is an accessible proxy for the quality of outside aid and perhaps even its quantity. Having more than one sponsor shields the beneficiary organization from the abrupt cessation of aid if one sponsor decides to withhold support.

Some (e.g., Ross 2004) have argued that the availability of extractable resources increases the likelihood of civil war, hence it seems reasonable to suggest:

> H_3: Organizations that control extractable resources are more likely to survive.

---

2. Two research assistants and I independently collected this data from secondary sources. I consulted with country experts when I did not find strong evidence on the distribution of power within organizations in conflict. The data on Afghanistan and Lebanon are at least partly informed by my own field research.

I code for the availability of exploitable natural *Resources* (such as gems, drugs, or oil) dichotomously.

Fearon and Laitin (2003) found evidence that rough terrain encourages the use of guerrilla tactics by aggrieved groups, so perhaps it also helps them to overthrow the powers that be:

H_4: Organizations that dwell in rough terrain are more likely to survive.

For the variable *Topography*, I give a score of 1 to an organization that performs its operations in a terrain that is difficult for opponents to penetrate (mountains, swamps, or jungles) and a score of 0 if it dwells in rural, desert, or urban areas that provide poor shelter. As a check on this variable, I also borrow from Fearon and Laitin another variable that I rename *Percent Topography*—the percentage of the country's area that is mountainous.

Perhaps experience advantages organizations in conflict as they learn to better perform their craft. The length of time (*Age*, in years) the organization spent engaging in conflict would then affect its ability to survive by the end of the conflict:

H_5: The longer an organization engages in conflict, the more likely it is to survive by the end of the conflict.

Other factors are generally considered to advantage insurgents, including larger populations, larger geographic areas, cross-border bases, ethnic and religious fragmentation, and perhaps the political aims of the organization. Therefore:

H_{6a}: The larger the population, the more likely an insurgent organization is to survive.

H_{6b}: The larger the country or contested area, the more likely an insurgent organization is to survive.

H_{6c}: The more ethnically or religiously divided the country, the more likely an insurgent organization is to survive.

H_{6d}: Insurgent organizations with bases across the border are more likely to survive.

H_{6e}: Separatist insurgent organizations are more likely to survive than those that want to control the entire country.[3]

---

3. This is suggested in Walter 1997, 343.

Population Size is in millions during the last year of the conflict. I code for *Size* in two different ways: the overall size of the country and the size of the contested territory. The two measures of area differ in the case of secessionist movements and wars of liberation. I use two indices from the State Failure Project to code for *Ethnic Diversity* and *Religious Diversity*. The indices estimate the degree of ethnic and religious fragmentation for the country based on the sizes of its largest seven ethnic and religious groups between 1960 and 1990. I include the values of the indices at the date closest to the end of the conflict and impute for missing values for the years 1950 and 2000 by assuming linear tendencies when necessary. I code a dummy variable *Aim* for whether the organization aims to control the entire territory or a portion of a contiguous territory not separated by an international border. Another dummy variable, *Cross-border*, reflects the availability of bases across international borders to the organization at any point during the conflict. Occupying powers that share an international border with territories they are trying to control are considered to have cross-border bases.

Some practitioners and researchers argue that economic performance, high population density, urbanization, and rentier economies advantage incumbents. A larger economic pie can defuse grievances or equip a larger military, and a rentier economy puts enormous resources in the hands of the powers that be, allowing them to strategically influence societal groups. Dense population patterns and high urbanization would facilitate counterinsurgency operations through more easily available intelligence.[4] Urbanized areas are also less likely to feature pervasive social structures that would shelter insurgents.

> H_{7a}: The higher the per capita income, the more likely an incumbent organization is to survive.

> H_{7b}: The denser and more urbanized the population, the more likely an incumbent is to survive.

> H_{7c}: Rentier economies increase the odds of the incumbent's survival.

I borrow and rename the variable *Wealth* (real GDP per capita, base 1985 dollars) from the State Failure Project and supplement it with estimates from other sources. *Density* (people per square kilometer) and *Urbanization* (the fraction of the population that lives in towns and cities) are

---

4. Mark Lichbach (1995, 158–65) and Matthew Kocher (2002) link population density to the onset of civil war.

also from the State Failure data set with missing values imputed by assuming geometric growth from existing estimates. *Rentier* (adapted from the Fearon and Laitin data set) is a binary variable that measures whether oil exports account for more than one-third of GDP at any point during the conflict.

I also include a number of control variables to verify that the results are not influenced by whether the winner is the incumbent (*Incumbent*) or insurgent (*Insurgent*), the conflict ended during the cold war (*Cold War*, 1 for conflicts that end between 1953 and 1989), the conflict is from the MENA region (*Mena*, dichotomous), the length of the conflict in years (*Length*), and the number of deaths resulting from the conflict (*Death*).

Empirical Findings and Interpretation

I present the results of several multivariate logistic regression models in table 10.1. I code the dependent variable *Survival* as 1 for all organizations that survived by the end of a conflict in which they engaged and 0 for those that lost by the end of the conflict. Survival does not include ongoing conflicts and negotiated settlements, which reduces the cases to 111 out of 133.[5] Model 1 is inspired from the organizational theory and uses variables (including all of *Fit*, *Haven*, and *Structure*) that are organization-centric as opposed to those that are country- and conflict-centric. Model 2 is nested in model 1 and omits the theory's key *Fit* variable to allow for likelihood ratio (LR) tests and for Bayesian Information Criterion (BIC) and other measures of goodness of fit. Model 3 uses conflict-centric variables thought to advantage either insurgent or incumbent organizations. Model 4 is a "political economy" model that emphasizes variables that suggest that resources influence the evolution of conflicts. Model 5 is a hybrid parsimonious model that includes all variables that are statistically significant in models 1 to 4. All models use the same selection of control variables: incumbency, whether the conflict ends during the cold war, and region. The following paragraphs interpret and discuss the coefficients, particularly from models 1 and 5.

Goodness of fit tests provide very strong support for the organizational theory's model (model 1) and the hybrid model (model 5) over the incumbent/

5. I estimate the same models in table 10.1 with an alternative dependent variable that does not omit organizations engaged in ongoing conflicts or party to settlements (all coded as 1) with similar results, except that length of the conflict and population density become significant in model 3.

Table 10.1. Logit analysis of organizational survival by the end of a conflict

	Model 1 OTGC	Model 2 OTGC minus Fit	Model 3 Incumb/insurg.	Model 4 Political economy	Model 5 Parsimonious
Fit	2.344 (0.653) **				2.729 (0.811) **
Haven	-0.829 (0.923)	0.286 (0.701)			-2.404 (1.327)
Structure	-0.631 (0.337) [a]	0.474 (0.246) [a]			-0.409 (0.349)
Aid	0.446 (0.235) [a]	0.484 (0.219) *		0.328 (0.231)	0.276 (0.275)
Age	0.035 (0.039)	0.041 (0.037)			
Resources	-0.333 (0.747)	-0.558 (0.69)		-1.084 (0.763)	
Cross-border bases	-0.16 (0.589)	-0.049 (0.542)			
Topography	0.495 (0.597)	0.547 (0.537)			
Aim	0.23 (0.644)	0.125 (0.589)			
Insurgent*Aim			0.214 (0.154)		
log(Size)			-1.324 (2.530)		
log(Size)*Insurgent			3.415 (2.102)		
log(Population size)			2.634 (2.486)		-0.305 (0.331)
log(Population size)*Ins			-6.724 (2.970) **		0.101 (0.325)
Ethnic diversity			3.143 (4.272)		
Ethnic diversity*Ins			-6.202 (6.648)		
Religious diversity			2.46 (5.583)		
Religious diversity*Ins			-8.86 (7.468)		
log(% Topography)			-0.737 (0.924)		
log(% Topography)*Ins			2.037 (1.197)		
log(Wealth)			-1.666 (1.301)	-0.816 (0.347)**	-1.380 (0.479) **
log(Wealth)*Inc			2.958 (2.104)	2.150 (.706)**	2.699 (0.798) **
log(Density)			2.665 (2.365)		1.186 (0.453) **
log(Density)*Inc			-3.489 (1.649) **		-1.219 (0.681)
Urbanization			-0.022 (0.038)		
Urbanization*Inc			0.012 (0.057)		
Rentier			3.253 (2.164)	-0.764 (0.831)	
Rentier*Incumbent			-4.686 (3.209)	1.649 (1.630)	
log(Death)			-0.207 (0.405)		
Length			0.146 (0.104)		
MENA	0.421 (0.629)	0.454 (0.576)	-0.481 (1.703)	0.442 (0.627)	0.316 (0.708)
Cold War	0.706 (0.621)	0.765 (0.557)	1.826 (1.471)	0.731 (0.564)	0.99 (0.744)
Incumbent	0.488 (0.89)	1.05 (0.787)	-7.467(14.789)	-14.587(5.117) **	-13.778(5.706) *
Constant	-2.261 (1.248)	-1.895 (0.916)	1.003(17.256)	4.461 (2.609)	5.576 (3.125)
N	111	111	111	111	111
% predicted	75%	66%	83%	76%	77%
Pseudo R^2	0.256	0.145	0.476	0.239	0.408
AIC	1.266	1.401	1.176	1.234	1.073
BIC'	17.21	29.482	39.789	5.616	-1.488

Note: The dependent variable is coded "1" if the organization survives at the end of the conflict, "0" otherwise. Negotiated settlements and ongoing conflicts not included.
Standard errors in parentheses. Estimations performed using Stata 8.2. $^{*}p<.05$; $^{**}p<.01$
[a] p=0.06

insurgent model (model 3).[6] An LR test performed on nested models 1 and 2 suggests that fit of structure with safe haven (*Fit*) matters much more than structure and haven independently or together.[7] The *Fit* of structure with the availability of a safe haven is highly significant with an intuitively positive coefficient. *Structure* or *Haven*, jointly or alone, fail to reach significance

6. I use Scott Long's SPost package to conduct goodness of fit tests. A difference of twelve points in the Bayesian Information Criterion (BIC) provides very strong support by Raftery's (1995) generally accepted guidelines for the fully specified organization-centric model when compared with the nested model that excludes fit. The alternative Akaike Information Criterion (AIC) also suggests stronger support for the unrestricted model. Model 1 also predicts correctly 9% more cases that model 2. The same information measures also provide very strong support for the organizational theory's model (model 1) and the parsimonious hybrid model (model 5) over the incumbent/insurgent model (model 3).

7. A z-test also confirms that *Fit* is significant beyond the .01 level, which suggests that the fit of structure with safe haven matters much more than each of them independently or together. *Fit* and

at the .05 level although *Structure* comes close when *Fit* is absent. The level of outside *Aid* to the organization is the only other significant or marginally significant variable in models 1 and 2, with the expected positive coefficient.

Most variables normally included in studies on the onset of conflict (model 3) do not seem to influence the odds of organizational survival. That rough terrain encourages the onset of armed political challenge (Fearon and Laitin 2003) but does not necessarily improve the insurgents' odds of success might suggest that insurgents believe that mountains would provide them with protection while in fact they fail to do so in the modern era. I carry the two statistically significant variables (the interaction of population size and density with incumbency) to the parsimonious model (model 5) to interpret their effect.

Other political economy variables dilute the effect of outside aid to organizations in model 4. The only variables that are statistically significant in this model are wealth, incumbency and their interaction, and I therefore also include them in the parsimonious model.

Resources available to the organization have no noticeable effect over its odds of survival by the end of a conflict. Findings are also consistent for both MENA and Latin America, two very different regions, which makes it likely that they can be generalized. The end of the cold war also does not seem to influence the odds of organizational survival.

The combined effects of fitted structure and aid, the two statistically significant variables in model 1, on the probability of an organization to survive by the end of the conflict are illustrated in figure 10.1. I vary *Fit* and *Aid* while holding all other variables constant at the (sometimes artificial) mean. Dashed lines represent the 95 percent confidence intervals.

Outside aid has a substantial effect on the probability of the organization's survival by the end of the conflict. Organizations are approximately four times more likely to survive if they have access to two or more state sponsors than if they don't receive any foreign aid. The effect of fit, however, is more dramatic. An organization is almost eleven times more likely to survive if it is adequately structured than if it is not. Well-structured organizations with no outside support are three times more likely to survive by the end of the conflict than badly structured organizations with abundant support (54% versus 30%). Aid does matter, but fit is paramount.

Haven together or *Fit* and *Structure* together are also jointly significant at the .01 level. I found it prudent to conduct such tests even though *Fit* is not really an interaction term.

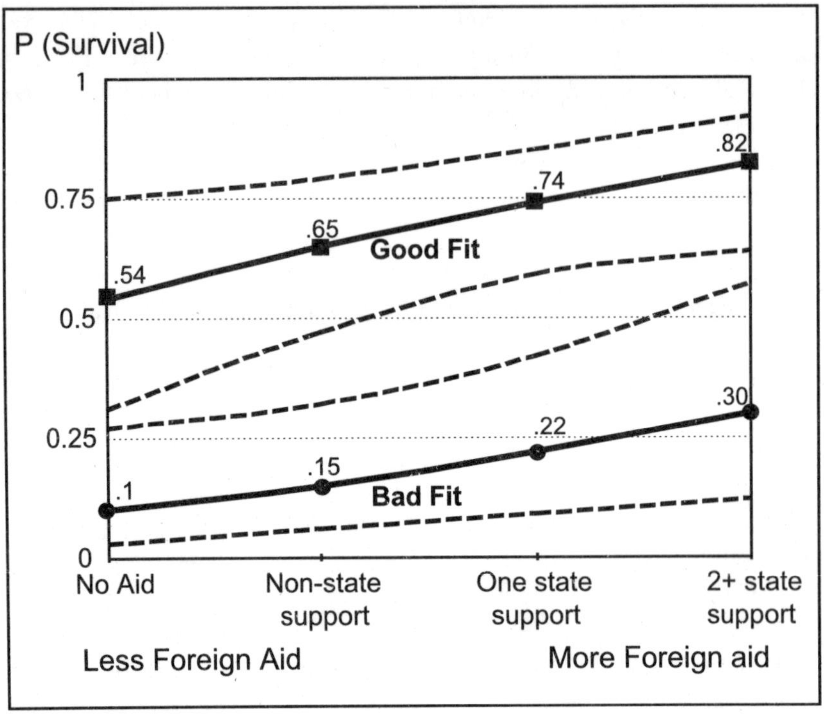

FIGURE 10.1. The effect of fit and aid on the probability of organizational survival, with 95 percent confidence intervals

Figure 10.2 presents the combined effects of foreign aid, structure, and the availability of safe haven on an organization's probability of survival by the end of the conflict—it unravels the combined *Fit* variable in figure 10.1. All other variables are held at the mean while *Fit* is varied to match the combination of structure and safe haven.[8] All structures that are well fitted according to the organizational theory have a higher probability of survival by the end of the conflict than all badly fitted structures. An adequately centralized state with abundant foreign support facing an insurgency has an 80 percent probability of overcoming the challenge and would see its odds of success fall to one-half if it loses its foreign support. Adequately structured insurgents have similar odds. A centralized insurgent organization without a safe haven (a state by definition has a safe haven) has almost a 50% probability of win-

8. Results are not much different if *Fit* is held at a substantively meaningless mean as opposed to 1 (structures that make a good fit with haven) or 0 (those that don't). Most probabilities vary within ±0.1 range from the values in figure 10.2. The only major difference is that patronage-based organizations seem to do less well.

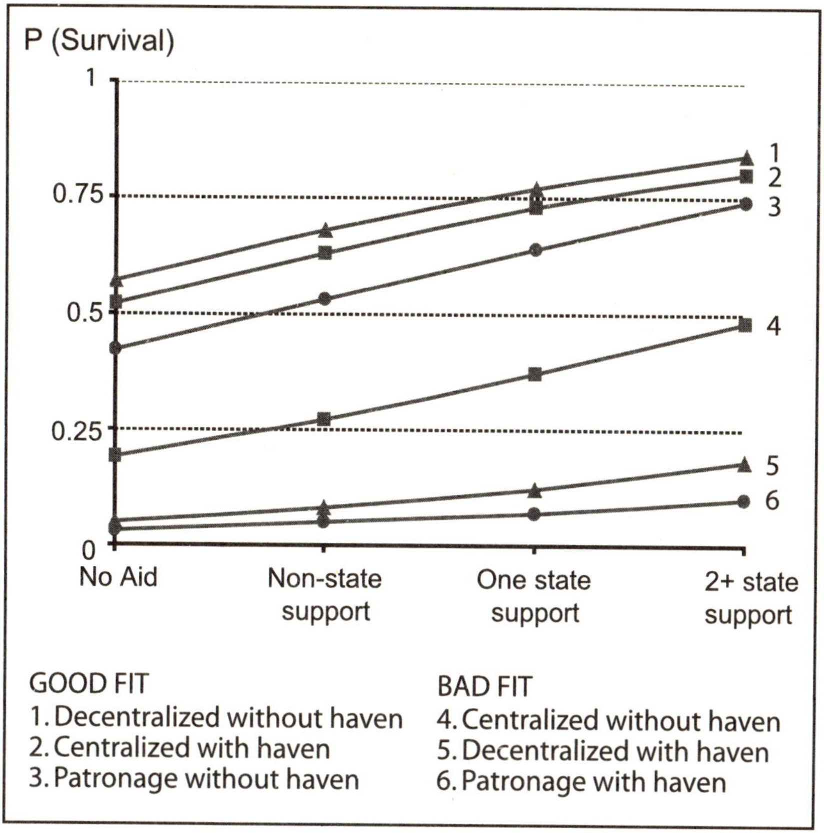

FIGURE 10.2. The effect of fit and foreign aid on the probability of organizational survival by the end of the conflict for different organizational structures

ning if it receives abundant foreign aid but would find its odds brought down to 1 in 5 if this aid is completely withdrawn. Well-structured insurgents are not as vulnerable: they have a good probability of survival even without any outside aid (from 42% to 57% depending on the specific structure).

The effect of outside aid is significant for all types of structures, but, again, fit matters most. All well-fitted structures have comparable success odds but centralized organizations with bad fit do better than other badly fitted ones. Any poorly fitted organization will dramatically increase its odds of survival merely by restructuring. Decentralized organizations with a safe haven would improve their odds by roughly twenty times by centralizing. Centralized organizations without a safe haven would increase their odds sixfold by decentralizing.

The statistically significant coefficients from model 5, which includes all variables that are statistically significant in the other models, are interpreted

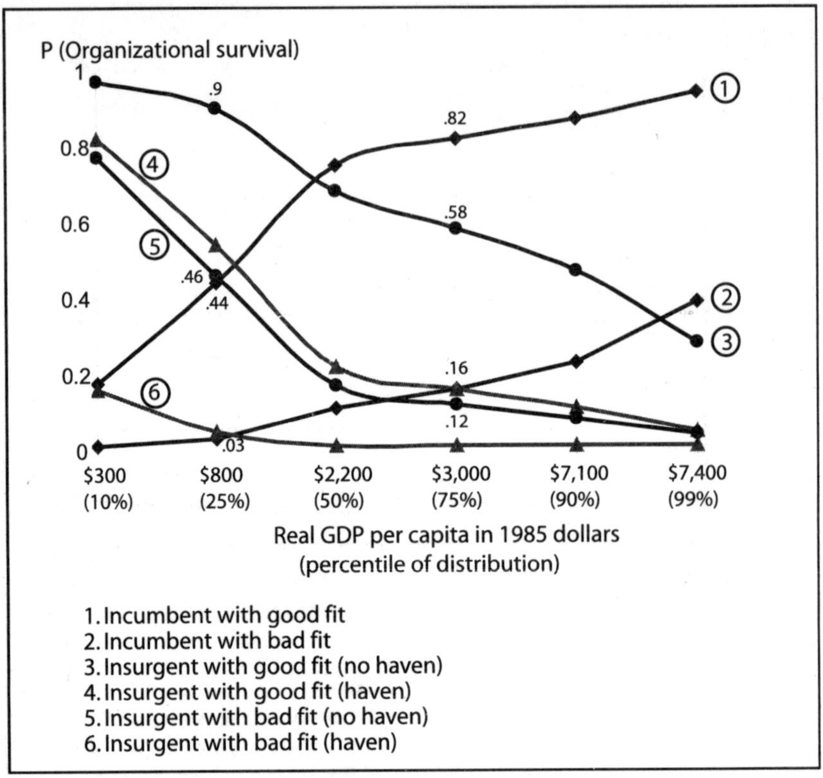

FIGURE 10.3. The effect of wealth on the probability of the survival of incumbent and insurgent organizations by the end of the conflict (model 5)

in figure 10.3. Both *Aid* and *Population Size* are not significant in this model, in spite of being highly or marginally significant in other models. I do not interpret the effect of *Density* because it influences the odds of the incumbent's survival by the end of the conflict in a way contrary to the prediction of H_{7b}. Figure 10.3 therefore represents the combined effects of *Wealth*, *Fit*, *Incumbency*, and *Haven* on the probability of the organization's survival by the end of the conflict.[9]

There is a strong agreement in the literature that higher economic development reduces the probability of the onset of civil war (State Failure Project 2000; Henderson and Singer 2000; Fearon and Laitin 2003). Model 5 implies

9. This graph only represents the effect of centralized and decentralized organizations for purposes of simplification. The expected probabilities for patronage-based organizations fall within .1 from those of decentralized organizations. All interaction terms and fit, structure, and haven are fixed in a consistent manner and other variables are held at the mean.

that wealth also favors the incumbent if a conflict develops in spite of the odds. An incumbent with a good fit (centralized with haven) is almost six times more likely to survive if real GDP per capita (1985 dollars) is $3,000 (75% percentile) instead of $800 (25%). Conversely, an insurgent organization's odds diminish six times as the GDP increases from $800 to $3,000 per capita.

Just as in model 1, fit matters most. Along the same GDP per capita interval discussed above, an incumbent with a bad fit would increase its odds twenty-five times by restructuring, and an insurgent organization (no haven) would increase its odds more than ten times by doing the same.

The findings from models 1 and 5 are different, but both deserve to be examined. There are good theoretical reasons to include the variables in model 1 together (focus on organization-specific variables), and there is no good reason for not considering a parsimonious hybrid model, because outcomes might very well depend on the combined effect of factors that scholars categorize under different theoretical perspectives. Most importantly and interestingly for the general thrust of this book, both models suggest that fit of structure with the availability of a safe haven matters the most in affecting the odds of organizations to survive by the end of the conflicts in which they participate. But how do such odds relate to the outcomes of conflicts?

On the Outcomes of Conflicts

An organization that survives beyond the ability of all its rivals to challenge it practically wins the conflict. If the last organization (or group of organizations with converging interests) standing is one of the challengers to the powers that be, then one can say that the country has been liberated, a territory has seceded, or that the revolution has happened. By postdicting the survival of organizations by the end of the conflicts in which they were engaged, the organizational theory also explains the outcome of conflicts. Figure 10.4 distinguishes among the structures of challengers from the MENA region and correlates them to the outcome of the conflict.[10] The underlying assumption is that incumbents are generally adequately centralized.

10. I did not include the 1994–2001 phase of the Afghan conflict because it did not feature an incumbent. I did not include the 1967–70 phase of the North Yemeni conflict in figure 10.4 because it features a patronage-based organization with a safe haven—I discuss it further below. I do not include Afghanistan (1989–92) in figure 10.4 because it would be too much of a stretch to approximate the patronage-based incumbent (the regime of Najib) with a centralized model. The Lebanese and Eritrean conflicts, which involved effective restructuring by successful insurgents, are reduced to one entry each. Conflicts in bold represents cases where challengers successfully restructured into

	Structure of challengers without safe haven				
Outcome of conflict	Fragmentation	Patronage-based organizations	2-3 major organizations	One major decentralized organization	One major centralized organization
Incumbent defeated or withdraws		Afghanistan (1979-89) Yemen (1962-67) **Iran (1963-79-81)**	Israel (1945-48) S. Yemen (1962-68) **Eritrea (1961-85-91)** **Lebanon (1982-85-2000)**	Algeria (1954-62)	
Ongoing or inconclusive conflict	Kashmir (1989-)	Iraqi Kurds (1961-91)	Algeria (1992-) Iraqi Kurds (1991-) Intifada (1987-) **Sudan (1983-)**		
Negotiated settlement					Sudan (1962-72)
Challengers defeated	Turkey (1971-80)			Syria (1964-82)	Egypt (1952-90) Iranian Kurds (1979-86) W. Sahara (75-91) Dhofar (1965-75) Turkish Kurds (1980-2001)

FIGURE 10.4. Relationship between the structure of challengers without a safe haven and the outcome of conflicts

A disheartening observation from figure 10.4 is that only one conflict from the MENA region and its periphery concluded with a durable settlement (one that lasted for longer than ten years), but even this one resumed afterward. Perhaps negotiated settlements are so rare because their success is contingent on both negotiating partners being centralized enough to enable the leaders to bring along the rank and file while negotiating and implementing the agreement. Unfortunately, the same centralization that makes the challengers capable of adhering to agreements also makes them vulnerable to the stronger incumbent's efforts to destroy them, thus reducing the incumbent's desire for a genuine compromise. Except for the first Sudanese conflict, all conflicts that mainly featured centralized challengers resulted in their defeat. The Sudanese exception itself is easy to explain from a structural perspective: the Sudanese government and military were so poorly integrated and inept and the country was so vast that they couldn't effectively take advantage of Anya Nya's cen-

a centralized organization after achieving control of territory. The structure they featured before restructuring is what allowed them to last long enough to be able to control a safe haven, and they are therefore listed under this earlier structural form.

tralization. While President Nimeiry was able to impose an agreement on his army by withdrawing its units from the south, he couldn't hope to defeat Anya Nya because of his own state organization's shortcomings. Joseph Lagu, the head of Anya Nya, managed to centralize the organization only two years before the agreement was reached, thus making it vulnerable for only a very short time and eight years into the conflict. The Sudanese government probably never understood the advantage it gained when Lagu centralized Anya Nya.

The evidence seems to be mixed in the case of decentralized organizations but much stronger in the cases of multiplicity and patronage. All cases featuring multiple (two to four) major organizations or patronage-based ones (there is an overlap between the two categories) either concluded with the defeat of the incumbent (seven of twenty-two conflicts) or are ongoing (five of twenty-two). Four of the conflicts from those two categories feature organizations that restructured successfully on gaining control of a safe haven (in bold): Lebanon's Hizballah, the Eritrean People's Liberation Front (EPLF), the Sudan People's Liberation Army (SPLA), and Iran's postrevolution Islamic Republican Party (IRP). At least three of the four benefited greatly from restructuring at the right juncture, as the theory predicts, and the fourth (SPLA/M) achieved great strides subsequently.

The theory suggests that organizations should centralize after achieving firm control of a portion of the contested territory. The conflict outcome for insurgents who restructured or failed to do so following the theory's prescription is considered in table 10.2. I do not include conflicts from the data set that mainly feature a single centralized challenger—I have already established that almost all such organizations were defeated and never survived long enough to gain control of a safe haven. I also only include conflicts that concluded—the only ones that could help us glean useful conclusions. For purposes of illustration, I added to table 10.2 some of the most notorious conflicts from the past century. Although the additions still do not make the sample large enough to be tested statistically and are not randomly chosen, it is encouraging that none of the cases contradicts expectations. I also add a few subconflicts that nicely illustrate my point—the Battle of Algiers, early Chinese Communist efforts, and the Tet offensive. The additions (in italics) are consistent with the results from the unbiased sample.

The first interesting insight from table 10.2 is that weak organizations do not need to be able to keep rivals out of a slice of territory to win, particularly in colonial and secessionist conflicts where it suffices to be resilient enough to take advantage of international or domestic changes that reduce the occupier's ability or desire to sustain the cost of occupation. This was the

Table 10.2. Fate of noncentralized and multiple challengers, based on whether they restructured or not

CONTROLLED	CENTRALIZED AFTER CONTROLLING A SAFE HAVEN	FAILED TO CENTRALIZE AFTER CONTROLLING A SAFE HAVEN	CENTRALIZED BEFORE CONTROLLING A SAFE HAVEN	NEVER A SAFE HAVEN
Defeated		Afghanistan (1989–94) Yemen (1962–70)	Battle of Algiers *Malaya* *Huk rebellion* *Viet Cong—Tet* *Greece* *China 1927–34* *China 1940* Shining Path 1992	Syria (1964–82) Turkey (1971–80)
Not defeated	Eritrea (1961–91) Iran (1963–81) Lebanon (1982–2000) *Russia post-1917* *Indochina* *North Vietnam* *China post-WWII*			Algeria (1954–62) Afghanistan (1979–89) Israel (1945–8) South Yemen (1962–8) *Yugoslavia* *Russia pre-1917*

case in Algeria, Afghanistan, Palestine (international and British desires to accommodate the decimated European Jewry), and South Yemen (Britain's fiscal problems). But for challengers to centralize absent a safe haven, we must not forget, would be a fatal mistake.

All out-of-sample centralized organizations without a safe haven in conflicts only featuring such challengers were defeated, just as in the sample. The Battle of Algiers provides a crucial test for the theory because Algiers was the only area where the F/ALN adopted a centralized structure. While the ALN survived throughout Algeria, it was eradicated in Algiers. The Tet offensive, another case of premature centralization, led to the near-demise of the South Vietnamese Viet Cong—the adequately highly centralized North Vietnam ultimately won the war. Years earlier, Giap's restructuring of his forces on gaining a territorial base during his conflict with the French in Indochina allowed him to take the strategic initiative that led to his victories in the field. The Chinese Communists tried twice to centralize without a safe haven, twice suffering terribly from the mistake and only miraculously surviving to fight another day. The third try, following the Japanese defeat and the liberation of a vast territory, was the charm. The Huk rebellion was going quite well for the rebels until the Communist Party decided to centralize the rebels under one structure, leading to the ultimate demise of their venture through a well-calibrated government hearts-and-minds strategy that isolated them from their most likely constituency. The highly centralized Malay Communists succumbed to the same finely tuned British strategy as well as to their leader's treachery. The activities of the Peruvian Shining Path were considerably reduced after the 1992 capture of its charismatic leader, Abimael Guzmán, whose decision to renounce violence (just like the Kurdish Ocalan) was heeded by the rank and file even though he was in prison.

On achieving the ability to protect its space, a noncentralized challenger must centralize. The performance of both Afghan and Yemeni patronage-based organizations suffered on failing to restructure after reaching this stage. Conversely, the Iranian clergy was able to eliminate all rivals and to exclusively dominate state institutions after it centralized its institutions under the IRP following the collapse of the imperial regime in 1979. Centralization on controlling a safe haven also enabled Hizballah and the Eritrean EPLF to take the strategic initiative and drive their powerful adversaries from the territories they contested. In Russia, resistance to the tsar was resilient because of the multiplicity of challengers. When the regime collapsed in the aftermath of its capitulation to Germany, however, only Lenin's centralized Bolsheviks were able to take the strategic initiative to seize power and eliminate rivals that were structurally impeded from doing the same.

On Mechanisms

So how did the losers lose and the winners win? The processes behind the demise of organizations with and without safe havens are, as the theory predicts, different. In seven of the eight conflicts where the incumbent lost, the occupier or central government gave in after dramatic changes in its domestic or international situation. The Egyptians withdrew from North Yemen in the wake of their 1967 defeat by Israel; the British left South Yemen after reeling from fiscal problems and from Palestine for similar reasons as well as international pressure to accommodate a decimated Jewry; the Israelis withdrew from Lebanon after a change in political leadership; and the Ethiopians gave up on Eritrea after a military coup and the demise of their Soviet backers. A weaker party is more likely to be successful by organizing in a way that allows it to be resilient enough to take advantage of opportunities that weaken the resolve or ability of its stronger opponent than by taking the strategic initiative.[11] The weak must persevere to see the occupier withdraw

11. This agrees with an argument made in Merom 2003.

or to someday have the opportunity to control a safe haven that would allow them to take the strategic initiative after restructuring. Iran is both the only nonseparatist conflict and the one exception to this rule—the United States maintained its support for the shah until the end, but the resilience of the Iranian opposition was critical for its success as well.

There are many ways to overcome centralized challengers without a safe haven. The PKK gave up a year after the capture of its leader, Abdullah Ocalan, something less-centralized organizations such as Hamas—whose leader was incarcerated for many years and then assassinated—would not do.[12] The Turkish military realized the advantages of capturing or killing Ocalan long before it succeeded in doing so, as shown by its previous attempts.[13] The Dhofaris were trounced by a well-implemented hearts-and-minds strategy designed by the sultan's seasoned British mercenaries to deprive them of popular support, a strategy that is only effective against centralized organizations without a safe haven. The Sahrawi Polisario lost its ability to put up a challenge after its two main backers (Libya in 1984, Algeria in the early 1990s) withdrew assistance because of their desire to improve relations with Morocco. The many tiny centralized Turkish challengers were destroyed piecemeal by the country's effective military. There are many ways to destroy centralized organizations without a safe haven, which goes a long way to explain their near universal demise.

The introduction or existence of a second challenger increases radicalization and resilience. This happened among the Iranian Kurds, Iraqi Kurds, Jewish organizations in Palestine, South Yemeni organizations, Afghan mujahideen, Eritreans, and with the creation of Hizballah (Kramer 1991). The only exceptions are the Sudan, where Anya Nya II members defected to the government when the SPLA gained in power, and Algeria, where the GIA's brutality drove the FIS to compromise with the regime. The existence or introduction of an additional challenger increases radicalization because the new challenger finds it convenient to demonstrate its dedication to a purist cause through militant activities in the hope of swelling its ranks and widening its appeal. When, for example, the Kurdish Democratic Party of Iran (KDPI) wanted to negotiate with Tehran, the much smaller Komaleh intensified its operations. Komaleh gained in popularity, and the KDPI immediately backtracked from attempts to negotiate. In another example, the Iranians withdrew their support from the Iraqi Democratic Party of Kurdis-

12. Reuters, "Kurdish Rebels Say They'll Pull Out of Turkey," August 6, 1999.

13. Imset 1992, 83–84.

tan (DPK) in 1975 as part of the Shatt-al-Arab agreement with Iraq. The demoralized leadership of the DPK, which received all of its aid through Iran, declared the struggle over. Syria later encouraged the formation of a splinter organization that soon began military operations (Jalal Talibani's PUK, which had merged with the DPK years earlier) in the hope of undermining the Iraqi regime. Prompted by its loss of popular support to the PUK, the DPK resumed militant activities in 1977, two years after it gave up.

Details from some of the cases also support my argument that states and other organizations with safe havens should not act as patrons. Both Turkey and Iraq, in addition to using their formidable centralized militaries, became patrons of Kurdish tribes, clans, and organizations, with very mediocre results. They did not suffer like Afghanistan's Najib regime, which relied on its clients more than on its own forces, but one could see the same damaging processes at work on a smaller scale:

> The majority of *jash* [the Iraqi government's client militias or clans] were half-hearted. Some had considered the choice of fighting for the Kurdish forces, but were discouraged from joining. Both the KDP and PUK were unable to meet the potential supply of recruits, for the simple reason that they would increase the administrative burden and undermine the effectiveness of Kurdish forces. As a result some jash acted as informants for their favorite party and others sheltered wounded *peshmergas* [Kurdish guerrillas]. Some went further. In May 1986, for example, the KDP had captured Manjish because the local Duski chief switched allegiance from Baghdad to the KDP.[14]

Statistical evidence supports the theory's ability to consistently postdict organizational survival and the outcomes of complex conflicts over half a century in two large geographic areas. One would hope that the theory could also predict the outcomes of current and future conflicts. So what is the domain of applicability of the theory, and what does it tell us about the development of current and future conflicts?

Domain of Applicability and Significance

The organizational theory is not a universal theory in the sense that it is useful in the analysis of all social and revolutionary conflicts—it is a contingency

14. McDowall 1997, 356.

theory that applies to a subset of those conflicts and is universal within this subset. The subset is that of zero-sum territorial conflicts. The theory does not apply to conflicts where rivals aim for recognition, compromise, or co-optation as outcomes for their struggles. The framework needs to be modified to be useful for the study of such interactions.

By way of illustration, consider Gamson's (1975) analysis of the performance of fifty-three randomly selected movement organizations active in the United States between 1800 and 1945. Gamson measures success by using two criteria: the provision of tangible benefits that meet goals established by the social movement organizations, and their formal acceptance by their antagonists as rightful representatives of a legitimate set of interests. Movement outcomes fall into four categories: full success, co-optation (acceptance but no benefits), preemption (benefits but no acceptance), and failure. In general, Gamson found, successful movement organizations were "bureaucratic" while decentralized ones generally failed. His results could simplistically be viewed to be in disagreement with the organizational theory, but they are not. The discrepancy is easy to account for: noncentralized structures are more advantageous than centralized ones for a vulnerable underdog in a zero-sum conflict, while centralized organizations are better equipped than noncentralized ones to co-opt institutional resources and mobilize "grassroots" participation to accomplish policy change in the U.S. context (Starr 1979). Different types of conflicts advantage different types of organizations, but an organizational approach is always relevant.

The organizational approach suggests that durable compromise settlements can only be achieved between (not among) centralized organizational rivals that strongly control their members and are capable of preempting the rise of alternative organizations to represent the interests of those who do not favor an agreement. This was the case for the only negotiated settlement from North Africa and the Middle East in the sample—Joseph Lagu had to centralize Anya Nya and consolidate his control over its rank and file before negotiating with Khartoum.[15] Centralization, and the ability it generally confers to control the rank and file, is an important prerequisite for effective negotiation because of the frequent need to rein in spoilers, to use Stephen Stedman's (1997) terminology, who disagree with the leadership's conciliatory goals. Spoilers can sabotage negotiations by committing confrontational acts that undermine the perceived sincerity of organizational leaders, who will be blamed for them. The ability to effectively preempt the

15. Rothchild and Hartzell 1993, 69–70.

emergence of new rival organizations is necessary because such rivals are likely to adopt, as their strategy for rapid growth at the expense of the conciliatory organization, an uncompromising line that appeals to those conditioned during years of conflict to believe that negotiation is tantamount to betrayal.[16] A thorough study of the effect of organizational structure on conflict resolution, a generally still uncharted territory with room for innovation and substantial policy relevance, might produce many more insights.

Globalization and today's unipolar configuration of power also make the organizational theory curiously relevant to the ongoing conflict of the United States with transnational militants. Some argue that new technologies (weapons, communications, the Internet, media, transportation) both require and encourage new organizational structures and strategies. Breakthroughs in information technologies and the pervasiveness of the Internet facilitated the work of transnational militants and activists who adopted a "networked" structure. Arquilla and Ronfeldt (1996; 2001) even argue in studies meant to guide U.S. policymakers and strategists that states that are trying to reduce the influence of networked militants should adopt similarly networked structures. I couldn't disagree more.

I generally accept that dramatic changes in the environment or organizational goals (settlement as opposed to exclusionary goals) could advantage organizations that are structured differently from the way the organizational theory suggests. Interestingly, however, the effects of globalization, technological developments, and the end of the cold war have expanded the domain of applicability of the theory to the global confrontation between the United States and its transnational challengers. The shift of the global configuration of power to a strictly unipolar one, and the ability of both the hegemon and transnational challengers to work across state borders, make the dynamic of their confrontation similar to the one between a government and its domestic challengers. The same noncentralized structures that assist vulnerable challengers in domestic confrontations now favor transnational militants. The proper response for the United States government (a behemoth organization with a safe haven) is not to decentralize but to further centralize those institutions that are engaged in countering transnational challengers. The same technologies that allow decentralized networks to work would allow the effective centralization of large institutions and complex organizations. Indications are that the Bush administration and

16. For an illustration from Kosovo of how compromise could be impeded by a lack of centralization, see Chris Hedges, "Serbs Ready for Large-Scale Attacks on Kosovo Rebels," *New York Times*, June 27, 1998.

most members of Congress understood the necessity and urgency of centralizing operations after 9/11 but were too sensitive to the difficulties involved in restructuring large agencies with entrenched interests.[17]

So which revolutionaries whose perspectives on organizational matters we explored at the beginning of this book were right? This study confirms the wisdom of Mao and Giap's approach and suggests that the recommendations of the Islamists Qutb and Yakan (his recommendation for local organization) are misleading. Those who are concerned with the challenge from the Islamist al-Qaida to the United States should not get solace from the ideological background of those thinkers, however, because revolutionaries adopt organizational strategies across ideological divides. Al-Qaida has adopted the structures that benefited it best in the past: the organization was centralized in Afghanistan when its forces provided support for the Taliban under the designation Brigade 055, but restructured after the last stand in Tora Bora. Globally, it always had a suitably decentralized structure (Deibert and Gross Stein 2002).

What would it mean if people accept that it is organizations—not ethnic groups, classes, civilizations, ideologies, or religions—that engage in war? It may make it easier for people to forgive and forget after the conflict is over. I remember, growing up in the Lebanese civil war, how consciously very careful my Sunni Muslim family was about choosing terms to describe the traumatic events the country went through. We used to say, for example, that "al-Quwat" (the so-called Lebanese Forces militia that claimed to represent Maronite Christians) massacred the refugees, not the "Christians" or "Maronites." The use of precise language allowed us to maintain good relations with our many Christian friends and neighbors, kept us from sinking into the cycle of hatred, and allowed us to remain objective in our discussions. The war has ended, most militias have disbanded, and the friendships and social ties still endure.

Another advantage is that it may demystify conflict. Imagined epic ideological, religious, and civilizational battles tend to grab the imagination of those who are too excitable and those with little awareness of the horrors of war. This is why the Bush administration has tried to frame its confrontation with militant Islamist organizations as a war against "Islamo-fascism," a term that fallaciously joins a great world religion with a loathed European totalitarianism. This, however, is a war, like any other, of self-serving organizations. Acceptance of the Bush administration's ideological frame, or the

17. James Risen, "Little Change in a System That Failed," *New York Times*, September 8, 2002.

civilizational and religious frames, will only extend and deepen the conflict. If members of the Bush administration actually believe in their own conceptual frame, they may well be undermining their ability to successfully engage in conflict.

For al-Qaida, the ongoing conflict is an asymmetric one meant to undermine U.S. influence in the Muslim world, both direct and through co-opted authoritarian governments. This is a grand global insurgency, and al-Qaida's attacks on U.S. soil can best be understood in this context. Al-Qaida's goal, a tried-and-tested insurgent strategy, was to provoke the U.S. government to overreact to the 9/11 attacks in a way that would make it easier to mobilize support among the world's 1.3 billion Muslims. Americans asked the wrong question after 9/11. Instead of "Why do they [Muslims] hate us?" they should have asked "What are they [al-Qaida] trying to get us to do?" The United States, of course, played into the hand of al-Qaida when it invaded Iraq. Support for the United States in the Muslim world has sunk to dismal levels because of the destruction of Iraq and the apparent U.S. disregard for Muslim lives, dignity, and welfare.[18] Al-Qaida–like groups sprouted across the Muslim world in a clear indication that the organization's strategy is working. The Bush administration has already lost the more important battle, the one for the hearts and minds of the world's Muslims, by thinking that it was fighting a threat from within a world religion (Islamo-fascism) instead of one emanating from a miniscule organization.

Al-Qaida, according to bin Laden himself, also intended to bleed, exhaust, and bankrupt the United States by overstretching its global military activities. He envisioned that the United States would get bogged down in conflict in Afghanistan the way the Soviets did before them. This is happening in Afghanistan a bit later than bin Laden anticipated, but the bigger quagmire, of course, has been in Iraq. The war in Iraq is costing more than $200 billion a year in direct and indirect costs by most estimates, has overstretched and exhausted the U.S. military, and weakened U.S. ability to attend to challenges elsewhere.[19]

Perhaps the findings of this book will give pause to those who are tempted to use powerful militaries to impose new regimes beyond their

---

18. See in particular the surveys conducted by the Pew Global Attitudes Project in Muslim countries and elsewhere. Online at http://www.pewglobal.org.

19. For a discussion of different cost estimates by economists (totals varying between $700 billion and $2 trillion as of January 2007), see David Leonhardt, "What $1.2 Trillion Can Buy," *New York Times*, January 17, 2007.

borders when they realize that victory in intrastate conflicts has little to do with boots on the ground, the latest matériel, or large economies. Good organizational and strategic choices can be great equalizers in asymmetric warfare. They also make the illusion of wielding power highly dangerous for the reckless and those who follow them.

Glossary of Terms

Afghani. The Afghan unit of currency.

Alim. Sunni religious scholar.

Allah. The one and only God in Arabic.

Badal. Revenge or feud.

Baluch. A mostly tribal and nomadic people, the small Afghan Baluch community was mainly concerned with continuing its smuggling operations and played little role in Afghan conflicts.

Basmachi. Soviet derogatory term meaning "bandit" used to describe anti-Soviet freedom fighters in Central Asia.

Burqa. Afghan-style veil that covers a woman from head to ankle.

Daʿwa. The call to join Islam or the act of preaching Islam.

Durrani Pushtun. Members of the historically dominant Durrani tribal coalition that produced Afghan kings since the inception of Afghanistan.

Fatwa. Religious edict given by a prominent *alim.*

Ghilzai Pushtun. Members of an important Pushtun tribal coalition.

Ghund. Military base.

Hazara. Shiite people of central Afghanistan, a mountainous area called Hazarajat. They speak a distinctive language, Hazaraji, and have pronounced Asiatic features. They were historically marginalized and mistreated by the Afghan central government and Pushtun tribes. They were largely autonomous during the Soviet occupation, but their Wahdat Party was defeated by the Taliban. The Hazara make up some 15 percent of the Afghan population.

Imam. Leader of Muslim prayers. Also head of an Islamic community or group.

Ismaili. Follower of a sect that holds that the Muslim imamate passed from the Prophet to his daughter Fatima's descendents and through the seventh imam, Ismail. Ismailis number some 150,000 to 200,000 in Afghanistan.

Jabha. Front or just a group of politicized people in an area.

Jihad. Striving in the way of Allah. Fighting to defend one's Muslim community is considered a jihad. The term also describes spiritual self-improvement.

Jirga. Council or assembly held for the settlement of a dispute in a locality.

Khan. Head of a tribe or community who has the allegiance of subordinate community leaders. Originally a Mongol term, it is often used as an honorary title nowadays.

Lashkar. A tribal army.

Loya Jirga. Ad hoc grand assembly or council that brings together prominent leaders to address urgent national issues.

Madrassa. School of Islamic studies.

Malik. A state-appointed head of a clan or tribe.

Markaz. Mujahideen base.

Mawlawi. Traditional religious scholar.

Mir. Hazara chief or ruler.

Muhajirin. Those who leave their homes under duress. The term *hijrah* (migration, Arabic) was originally used to describe the Prophet Mohammad's move from Mecca to the more hospitable Medina. Muslim refugees in the Indian subcontinent and Central Asia have used the term to describe their own act of taking refuge in more hospitable lands when persecuted in their homes.

Mujahid. He who engages in Jihad.

Mujahideen. Plural of *mujahid*. Those who engage in jihad. Islamically oriented opponents of the Kabul regime were called mujahideen.

Mullah. Prayer leader or village-level scholar.

Namus. Honor with a social dimension. It specifically refers to the womenfolk (*zan*) of one's own and of one's father's household. But also refers to gold (*zar*) and land (*zamin*), the two other elements to defend to preserve one's honor.

Nang. Honor.

Naqshbandiyya. A Sufi (Islamic mystic) order.

Nuristani. Nuris, previously Kafiris, converted to Islam in the nineteenth century and have been staunch Muslims ever since. Their areas were generally resistance hotbeds to the Soviet occupation.

Pathan. The name the British gave to the Pushtun.

Pir. Head of a mystic order or a religious person with great influence and strong following.

Pushtun or Pukhtun. The dominant ethnic group in Afghanistan. The Pushtun are divided into the Durrani, Ghilzai, and Eastern tribal coalitions. Afghan kings were traditionally Durranis from Kandahar while most resistance leaders were from the two other segments. Pushtun make up some 40–45 percent of the population.

Pushtunwali. Social and legal code of the Pushtun. Includes the duty to grant asylum for those who seek it (*ninawatay* is the act of seeking it) and *nirkh*, its disciplinary and punitive aspects.

Qadiriyya. A Sufi (Islamic mystic) order.

Qawm. A group united by solidarity and rivalry with other groups. The term could refer to a tribe, clan, regional, ethnic, or professional group.

Quizilbash. Urban Shia, they are the descendents of the Persian administration that once ruled Afghanistan.

Saur revolution. The April 1978 coup in which Khalqi officers overthrew the Daoud regime.

Sayyid. A real or assumed descendent of the Prophet Mohammad through Fatima, his daughter.

Sharia. Islamic law comprising the interpretations of the Hanafis, Shafi'i, Maliki, and Hanbali schools. Afghans are generally Hanafis.

Shia. Group of Muslims who believe that the imamate passed through Ali, the prophet's cousin, to his descendents and stopped with the twelfth, the Mahdi. The majority sect in Iran, Iraq, Azerbaijan, Bahrain, and the central area of Hazarajat in Afghanistan.

Shura. Council. A principle or institution in Islamic leadership or government.

Tajik. The second largest ethnic group in Afghanistan (some 30% of the population), the Tajik are mostly Hanafi Sunni Muslims like the majority Pushtun. Their most prominent leaders after the Soviet invasion were Ahmad Shah Massoud and Burhanuddin Rabbani.

Talib. Seeker of knowledge or student.

Taliban. Plural of *talib*.

Tanzim. Organization or political party. Used to describe each of the Peshawar parties.

Ulama. Plural of *alim*. Religious scholars among Sunni Muslims.

Ummah. The Muslim community, Islamdom. Given a political dimension in the writings of Sayyid Qutb and Sayyid Abu Ala Maududi.

Uzbek. Uzbeks make up some 6 percent of the Afghan population and were historically mistreated by Pushtuns and Afghan central governments. They managed, however, to provide the Najib regime with its strongest militia. Its defection contributed to the regime's collapse in 1992. Uzbek areas fell to the Taliban in the late 1990s.

Wahhabi. Follower of Mohammad bin Abdel-Wahhab, who was a proponent of a puritanical Islam that is pure of all perceived innovation. The term was frequently used by Kabul regime propagandists to drive a wedge between Afghan mujahideen whose Islamic practices contained a substantial cultural component and their Arab supporters.

Watan. Homeland.

Participants in Post-1978 Afghan Conflicts

Abdul Haq (1958–2001). Pushtun from Ningarhar, Hizb-Khalis. One of the most prominent field commanders around Kabul during the Soviet occupation. He was known for his network of agents inside the city, but his organization was undermined by KhAD. Later killed by the Taliban.

Abdullah ʿAzzam. A Palestinian from Tulkarm, he promoted the Afghan jihad among non-Afghan Islamists and organized their financial and physical participation in it. He was assassinated in a sophisticated operation in 1989.

Abdul-Malik, General. Uzbek. Dostum client who switched allegiance to the Taliban in May 1997 after Dostum killed his brother and one of his commanders. His defection led to Dostum's defeat a few days later. He was named deputy foreign minister by the Taliban but turned against them and forced them out of Mazar Sharif with the help of Hizb-i Wahdat in what became one of their worse temporary setbacks. He fled to Iran when Dostum returned.

Abdul Rahman, Akhtar. Pakistani general and director general of ISI, 1977–85. Chairman of the Chiefs of Staff committee, 1985–88. He was one of the main architects of Pakistan's strategy in Afghanistan. Died with Zia ul-Haq in airplane explosion. His role in the Afghan conflict is described by his subordinate, Brigadier Mohammed Yousaf in *Silent Soldier.*

Afzal, Muhammad. Mawlawi of Kam tribe in Nuristan. Founder and amir of the Salafi, some say Wahhabi, Islamic State of Nuristan.

Ahmad, Qazi Husayn. Amir of Jamaʿat-i Islami of Pakistan.

Al-Azhar University. A major center of Islamic learning in Cairo, where some of the leaders of the mujahideen earned their higher degrees in theology and were exposed to the ideas of the Muslim Brotherhood and the writings of Sayyid Qutb.

Amin, Hafizullah (1929–79). Khalqi Pushtun from Paghman in Kabul Province. He had a master's degree in education from Columbia University where he returned in the 1960s to complete a PhD but soon went back to Afghanistan. He was active in student politics and joined the PDPA. He built a strong support base among Pushtun students and teachers at home and in the United States. He played a key role in initiating the April 1978 coup. His strong personality and strong constituency within the PDPA allowed him to become the strongman during the months that preceded the Soviet invasion. He angered the Soviets by physically eliminating their protégés, particularly Nur Muhammad Taraki, and they killed him during their invasion even though he hoped they would provide him with a reliable personal guard.

Andropov, Yuri. General secretary of the Communist Party of the Soviet Union, 1982–83. There is some evidence that he wanted to withdraw Soviet troops from Afghanistan, but he wasn't able to achieve this goal before the deterioration of his health and subsequent death. Mentor of Gorbachev.

Babar, General Nasirullah Khan. Pakistani. Pushtun general appointed as interior minister by Benazir Bhutto in 1993. He became one of the main proponents of shifting support from Hekmatyar's Hizb to the Taliban.

bin Laden, Osama. The youngest of many children of a Saudi building magnate of Yemeni origin, he went to Afghanistan in the mid-1980s with the goal of assisting the mujahideen. He used his knowledge to dig tunnels and shelters and part of his considerable wealth to assist their families. He later organized the influx of volunteers from the Arabian Peninsula and reinvented his calling in a way that put him in confrontation with the United States after the first U.S.-Iraq War and the positioning of U.S. troops in Saudi Arabia. Assisted the Taliban as head of al-Qaida. Engaged in attacks on the United States that motivated the U.S. invasion of Afghanistan.

Brezhnev, Leonid. General secretary of the Communist Party of the Soviet Union from 1964 until his death in 1982. He was one of a handful of people who made the decision to invade Afghanistan, but he is thought to have been mentally incapacitated at the time.

Chernenko, Konstantin. General secretary of the Communist Party of the Soviet Union, 1983–85. A conservative who believed that the military tide in Afghanistan could turn in Moscow's favor through a more aggressive approach.

Cordovez, Diego. United Nations undersecretary general for special political affairs and personal representative of the Secretary General in Afghanistan between 1982 and 1988. He mediated the Geneva negotiations.

Daoud, Mohammed (1910–78). First cousin of King Zahir Shah, he overthrew him with Parshami help in 1973 to set up a republic. He was overthrown in turn and killed by Khalqi officers in April 1978.

Democratic Republic of Afghanistan (DRA). The official name of the state of Afghanistan under PDPA rule. The "democratic" label was later dropped by Najib, who was trying to make it seem that his regime had shed all connections to Marxist ideology.

Dostum, General Abdul Rashid (1955–). Uzbek from Jawzjan. Leader of the Uzbek militia (later the 53rd Division) that sided with the Soviet forces and the Najib regime. His defection in April 1992 contributed to the downfall of Najib and made him one of the most powerful warlords in the country with a force of perhaps fifty thousand militiamen. Yet, he was swept away by the Taliban advance in May 1997 and fled to Turkey. He then made a brief comeback but could not resist the second Taliban thrust into Mazar Sharif. He made a comeback after the U.S. invasion.

Durrani, Asad. Pakistani general and head of ISI in 1990–91.

Gailani, Pir Sayyid Ahmad (1932–). Leader of the moderate Sunni Mahaz-i Milli party. He was also a leader of the Qadiriyya mystic order and espoused fairly liberal political views.

Ghaus, Mullah Muhammad. Durrani Pushtun from Kandahar. Acting foreign minister of the Taliban government until 2001.

Gorbachev, Mikhail. First secretary of the Communist Party of the Soviet Union, 1985–91, and president of the USSR, 1986–91.

Gul, Hamid. Pakistani general who replaced General Abdul Rahman Akhtar as head of the ISI until June 1989 when he was removed because of his responsibility for the Jalalabad debacle.

Gulabzoy, Sayyed Mohammad (1951–). An illiterate Khalqi Paktia Pushtun, he became minister of interior and head of the Sarandoy where he consolidated Khalqi power after the Soviet invasion.

Haqqani, Jalaluddin. Jadran Pushtun from Paktia. A major commander of Mawlawi Muhammad Yunus Khalis's Hizb. Member of the National Commanders Shura (NCS) who led forces that took Khost in March 1991. Later joined the Taliban and resisted U.S. troops.

Harakat-i Inqilab-i Islami (Revolutionary Islamic Movement). The traditionalist party of Muhammadi. See table 6.1 for more details.

Harakat-i Islami. Small pro-Iranian party led by Mohammad Asif Mohsini that later merged with other Hazara parties to form Hizb-i Wahdat.

Hekmatyar, Gulbuddin (1948–). Ghilzai Pushtun born in a Tajik-majority area in the north of Afghanistan. He could not finish his engineering studies because of political developments. He was a founder of the Muslim Youth branch of the Islamic movement in the late 1960s. He left Kabul after being released from jail in the early 1970s and became active in Islamist politics in Peshawar. He formed the Hezb-i Islami after a 1975 Islamist revolt in Afghanistan failed. He was a shrewd and very ambitious political entrepreneur and a talented orator who strived to create a dynamic and centralized organization that would overwhelm less-structured rival groups. He returned from exile in Iran to organize resistance to the United States after the U.S. invasion.

Hizb-i Islami (Islamic Party) of Gulbuddin Hekmatyar. A centralized Islamist party. It had a relatively efficient bureaucracy and propaganda machine, a two-year military academy, and organized tank units that were later included in its army, Lashkar Ithar. Its main strength was in Pushtun areas, but it commanded support in other regions as well. It relied much more on ideological appeal than on clan and tribal affiliation for recruitment. It had substantial stocks of weaponry and following in the refugee camps. The Hizb tried to bring down the Kabul regime by manipulating its Khalqi segment but failed. It was routed by Taliban in the mid-1990s.

Hizb-i Islami of Mawlawi Yunis Khalis. A splinter party from the Hizb-Hekmatyar, it officially espoused radical Islamist views but enjoyed mostly traditional Pushtun backing. It depended on regional and tribal loyalties and was strong in southern Afghanistan and north of Kabul. It had a weak and unstructured bureaucracy.

Hizb-i Wahdat (Unity Party). Shia party formed under pressure from Iran that brought together almost all the small Hazara parties in 1988. It was headed by Abdul Ali Mazari then by Karim Khalili. The party was virtually destroyed by the advancing Taliban.

Hizbullah (Afghanistan). Small pro-Iranian party led by Shaikh Wusoqi that later merged with other Hazara parties into Hizb-i Wahdat.

Ikhwan al-Muslimeen (Muslim Brotherhood). Loosely structured Islamic movement that was launched in Egypt by Hassan al-Banna and produced the theologian and ideologue Sayyid Qutb who influenced many Afghan mujahideen leaders.

Inter Services Intelligence (ISI). The Pakistani secret service largely in charge of logistics, guidance, and tactical support of Afghan mujahideen parties during the Soviet occupation and of the Taliban after 1995.

Ismail Khan. Of uncertain ethnicity, from Shindand. Military officer who mutinied after the Saur revolution to lead mujahideen around Herat and join Rabbani's Jamiat. Amir of Herat shura after April 1992. He was defeated by the Taliban in 1996 but made a comeback after U.S. invasion, only to later be sidelined by Hamid Karzai and the United States.

Ittihad-i Islami bara yi Azad-yi Afghanistan (Ittihad). The small Sunni party led by Abd Rab al-Rassoul Sayyaf that had its origin in a 1980 mujahideen alliance.

Jabha-i Najat-i Milli Afghanistan (Afghan National Liberation Front). The small traditionalist party led by Sibghatullah Mujaddedi.

Jamaʿat Ahl-al-Kitab wal-Sunna. A Salafi organization that dominated Kunar Province after its leader Jamil al-Rahman defected from Hekmatyar's Hizb in 1985. It enjoyed strong Arab Gulf support but was later defeated by the Hizb after the assassination of Jamil al-Rahman.

Jamaʿat-i Islami (Pakistan). Influential Islamic Pakistani party that supported mujahideen parties, particularly the Hizb, then the Taliban.

Jamiat-i Islami (Afghanistan). The large but militarily loosely organized party led by Burhanuddin Rabbani. Ahmad Shah Massoud was its dominant field commander. It had a very well structured, efficient, and highly ideological bureaucracy in Peshawar.

Jamiat-i Ulema-i Islam (Pakistan). Influential traditionalist Pakistani party led by Mawlana Fazlur Rahman that supported the Taliban through its alliance with Benazir Bhutto and its sprawling network of madrassas.

Jamil al-Rahman, Mawlawi Husayn. Formed the Salafi Jamaʿat Ahl-al-Kitab wal-Sunna that dominated Kunar Province after defecting from Hekmatyar's Hizb in 1985. He was assassinated by an Egyptian gunman in 1991.

Jawzjani militia. The Dostum militia. Most sources and interviewees say that it is the one also designated as the Ghulam Jam (mujahideen eater) militia because of the ferocity and brutality of its Uzbek warriors, but Giustozzi (2000, 203) reports that the Ghulam Jam was another Mazar Sharif-based militia founded by Amanullah, a Communist teacher whose entire family was killed in a mujahideen attack.

Juma Khan Andarabi. Tajik from Andarab, close to Panjshir. Joined Hekmatyar but lost his valley to Massoud in 1983 and then joined the government in 1984. He was assassinated in November 1986.

Jumbish-i Milli-i Islami (National Islamic Movement). The political organization Abdul Rashid Dostum created in Mazar Sharif after defecting from the Najib regime.

Kallu, Shamsu al-Rahman. Pakistani general and head of ISI, 1989–90.

Karmal, Babrak (1929–). Parshami of uncertain ethnicity, perhaps from a Tajikized Kashmiri family. He was installed as Afghan leader with no real power by the Soviets after they assassinated Amin until they replaced him with the more capable Najib in 1986.

Karzai, Hamid. A minor local leader with close relations to the CIA during the jihad. He was put at the head of the Afghan state after the 2001 U.S. invasion and elected president in 2004.

KhAD (Khidamat-i Ittilaat-i Dawlati). The Kabul regime's brutal Parshami-controlled security service with its own military units. It was elevated to ministry status and renamed WAD (Wizarat-i Amaniyyat-i Dawlati) in January 1986.

Khalili, Abdul Karim. Leader of Hizb-i Wahdat after the death of Mazari. He was supported by Iran and controlled Bamyan as part of the anti-Taliban alliance until its fall to the Taliban.

Khalis, Mawlawi Muhammad Yunus (1919–). A respected Pushtun scholar from Ningarhar. A senior member of Hekmatyar's Hizb, he broke away in 1979 and created his own party with the same name. He personally participated in the jihad in spite of his old age.

Khalq (Masses). The PDPA faction led by Nur Muhammad Taraki and Hafizullah Amin that took power after overthrowing Mohammad Daoud. The Soviet invaders reduced Khalqi power to the Ministry of Interior, but the mostly Pushtun-speaking Khalqis continued to be a majority among army officers. Many joined Hekmatyar when the regime's collapse appeared imminent.

Kishtmand, Sultan Ali (1936–). An Ismaili Hazara Parshami and founding member of the PDPA. He became prime minister in June 1981 and was a driving force behind the execution of the Soviet divide-and-conquer policy. He resigned from the Watan Party in 1991 to protest Pushtun domination and was later wounded in an assassination attempt.

Lashkar Ithar. The Army of Sacrifice, created by Hekmatyar to liberate Kabul.

Mahaz-i Milli Islami (National Islamic Front for Afghanistan). The loosely structured traditionalist and pro-monarchy party led by Pir Sayyid Ahmad Gailani.

Massoud, Ahmad Shah (1953–2001). A Tajik from the Panjshir Valley. A brilliant strategist and organizational entrepreneur, Massoud studied the military writings of Giap and Mao and applied his version and interpretation of their experiences very successfully. He became one of the most prominent faces of the resistance in the West, and particularly in France where he was popular because of his French education. He earned his nickname Sheer Panjshir (Lion of Panjshir) as he successfully and skillfully resisted eight major Soviet offensives in his valley. No field commander reached Massoud's prominence and ability to affect national events during the conflict. His organization was the one that lasted the longest in the face of the Taliban sweep. He was assassinated by two al-Qaida agents posing as journalists in September 2001.

Mazari, Abdul Ali. Leader of the Shiite Hazara Hizb-i Wahdat until he died in an altercation with the Taliban.

Militias. The Kabul regime bought the allegiance of several militias, the most important of which were the Jawzjani and Ismaili militias. It also had a more structured but less significant militia system in the cities, particularly Kabul.

Mohammadi, Mawlawi Muhammad Nabi (1920–). Ghilzai Pushtun from Logar. Leader of the centrist Peshawar party Islamic Revolutionary Movement. He received much of his support from traditional mawlawis.

Mohsini, Mohammad Asif. A Hazara leader co-opted by Rabbani and Massoud while they were trying to dislodge Hizb-i Wahdat from Kabul.

Mujaddedi, Sibghatullah (1929–). Scion of a powerful family of pirs of the Naqshbandiyya order. He graduated from al-Azhar and was imprisoned for his anti-Soviet views. He founded and led the small and traditionalist National Front for the Rescue of Afghanistan. He later became interim president of Afghanistan, April–June 1992.

Nadiri, Sayyid Mansur. Pir of Ismaili Hazaras of northern Afghanistan. He led a large pro-Kabul Ismaili militia but later defected with Dostum. He allied himself with Dostum and Massoud against the Taliban.

Najib (ullah), Mohammad (1947–1996). Ghilzai Pushtun from Paktia, a medical doctor. Made head of KhAD by the Soviets after their invasion, his tenure was memorable for its brutality. They later promoted him to the top post in 1986. He was toppled while resigning in April 1992. He took refuge in UN offices until he was hanged by the Taliban when they entered Kabul in 1996.

National Commanders Shura (NCS). A shura formed in 1990 by increasingly independent field commanders to protest ISI tactics and the Khalqi-Hizb connection. Massoud was the dominant figure of this shura.

National Fatherland Front (Jabha-yi Milli-yi Padarwatan). An organization set up by the PDPA in June 1981 to co-opt commanders or khans in a nonideological context. Its success was exaggerated by the regime.

Omar, Mullah Muhammad. Ghilzai Pushtun from Kandahar Province. The Taliban's founder and Amir-ul-mumineen or commander of the faithful. He was given the title by a congregation of some fifteen hundred mullahs in Kandahar in April 1996. He fought the Soviets under different commanders with some distinction; he was injured four times and lost an eye in combat. He has an imposing physique, at six feet six inches tall, and leads a very secluded and modest life. He was never able to finish his religious studies but led a small madrassa where he taught some forty students. He went into hiding after the U.S. invasion of 2001.

Pankin, Boris. USSR minister of foreign affairs, August–December 1991.

Parsham (Banner). The PDPA faction that originally supported Daoud. They were sidelined and purged by the Khalqis after the Saur revolution. Later, the

Dari-speaking and mostly minority Parshamis regained control of much of the state apparatus, except for the Ministry of Interior, with the help of the Soviet invaders. Many among them joined Massoud when the regime's collapse appeared imminent.

People's Democratic Party of Afghanistan (PDPA). The Communist party formed from the union of Khalq and Parsham that toppled Daoud in April 1978 and remained in control of Kabul with Soviet support until early 1992. The party's name was changed to Watan (Homeland) Party in June 1990 to distance it from communism.

Rabbani, Burhanuddin (1940–). A Tajikized ethnic Yaftal from Badakhshan. A graduate of al-Azhar where he translated some of Sayyed Qutb's books. One of the earlier members of the Afghan Islamist movement, he succeeded Ghulam Niazi as the amir of the Islamic Association in 1972. He later fled to Peshawar to avoid arrest. The association became one of the larger mujahideen parties with a mostly Tajik constituency. He later became president of Afghanistan.

Rabbani, Mullah Muhammad. Durrani Pushtun from Kandahar. Number-two man in the Taliban shura and head of its provisional government. He fought in the anti-Soviet jihad. He made the decision to hang Najib after the Taliban entered Kabul without consulting Mullah Omar, who banished him from the leadership for a while because of that act.

Sarandoy. The Khalqi-controlled police force with military units of the Afghan regime's Ministry of Interior.

Sayyaf, Abd-Rab al-Rassul (1947–). Ghilzai Pushtun from Paghman. A graduate of al-Azhar where he joined the Muslim Brotherhood. He was arrested by Daoud in 1975 but was later spared execution by Khalqis because he was a cousin of Hafizullah Amin. After his release in 1980, he went to Peshawar and was chosen to lead the Islamic Union for the Liberation of Afghanistan—a union of the different mujahideen parties—because of his perceived neutrality. After the union failed, he kept the name to create his own party. He was supported by Arab donors who responded well to his imposing oratorical skills in Arabic.

Sazman-i Mujahidin-i Mustazafin (Organization of the Defenders of the Dispossessed). Small pro-Iranian party that later merged with other Hazara parties into Hizb-i Wahdat.

Sazman-i Nasr (Victory Organization). Small pro-Iranian party led by Shaikh Wusoqi that later merged with other Hazara parties into Hizb-i Wahdat.

Sepah-i Pasdaran (Revolutionary Guard, Afghanistan). Small pro-Iranian party led by Muhammad Akbari that later merged with other Hazara parties into Hizb-i Wahdat.

Shevardnadze, Eduard. USSR minister of foreign affairs, 1985–90, and later president of Georgia. He assisted Gorbachev in developing "New Thinking" in foreign affairs.

Shura-i Hal-o-aqd. A handpicked council loyal to Rabbani that elected him president.

Shura-i Hamahangi (Coordination Council). The name given to the alliance that joined Hekmatyar's Hizb, Dostum's Jumbish, and Wahdat against Massoud in early 1994.

Shura-i Ittefaq-i Inqilab-i Islami (Council for the Islamic Revolutionary Alliance). Small Shia party led by Sayyid Ali Behishti that later merged with other Hazara parties into Hizb-i Wahdat. Originally the major party in the Hazarajat.

Shura-i Nazar-i Shamali (Council of the North). Ahmad Shah Massoud's organization.

Taliban. The organization led by Mullah Omar that swept through Afghanistan to dominate the country and disarm almost all remnants of the mujahideen parties and previous government militias. It was overthrown by invading U.S. forces and allied Afghans in 2001. More recently, it has reformed itself into an insurgent organization to resist U.S. and NATO occupation.

Tanai, Shahnawaz. Khalqi Pushtun from Paktia. Soviet-trained general, chief of the army staff (1986–88), and minister of defense (1988–90). He staged a failed coup against Najib in March 1990 and then joined Hekmatyar's Lashkar Ithar after fleeing Kabul.

Taraki, Nur Muhammad (1917–79). Ghilzai Pushtun from Ghazni. Founder of PDPA. He became the first president and prime minister of Afghanistan after the April 1978 coup. He endeared himself to Brezhnev, who felt personally offended when he was assassinated by Hafizullah Amin.

Watan Party. The new name given to the PDPA in June 1990 to distance it from Marxism.

Yousaf, Mohammad. Pakistani army brigadier. Appointed to the Pakistani ISI between 1984 and 1987, he was in charge of the logistics of the jihad and the coordination of operations under General Akhtar. His 1990 book contains a wealth of information and a reliable firsthand account of events during his years at the ISI.

Zabihullah. Tajik from Balkh. Capable Jamiat commander in Balkh whose assassination by KhAD in December 1984 permanently set back the resistance in the area.

Zahir Shah, Mohammad. King of Afghanistan from 1933 till 1973, when he was overthrown by his cousin Mohammad Daoud with Parshami help. He was invited back to Afghanistan after the U.S. invasion.

Zia ul-Haq, Muhammad. Chief martial law administrator and then president of Pakistan between 1979, when he overthrew Zulfiqar Ali Bhutto, and August 17, 1988, when he perished in an explosion on a military aircraft. He was an early and persistent supporter of the Afghan Peshawar parties.

References

Ahadi, Anwar-ul-Haq. 1998. "Saudi Arabia, Iran and the Conflict in Afghanistan." In *Fundamentalism Reborn? Afghanistan and the Taliban*, edited by William Maley, 117–33. Lahore: Vanguard.

Ahmed, Akbar, and David Hart, eds. 1984. *Islam in Tribal Societies: From the Atlas to the Indus*. Boston: Routledge and Kegan Paul.

Ahrari, M. Ehsan. 2000. "China, Pakistan, and the 'Taliban Syndrome.' " *Asian Survey* 40, no. 4: 658–71.

Akcali, Pinar. 1998. "Islam as a 'Common Bond' in Central Asia: Islamic Renaissance Party and the Afghan Mujahidin." *Central Asian Survey* 17, no. 2: 267–84.

Alexiev, Alex. 1985. "Soviet Strategy and the Mujahidin." *Orbis* 29, no. 1: 31–40.

Apter, David. 1967. *The Political Kingdom in Uganda*. Princeton: Princeton University Press.

Arnold, Anthony. 1983. *Afghanistan's Two-Party Communism: Parcham and Khalq*. Stanford: Stanford University Press.

——. 1985a. *Afghanistan: The Soviet Invasion in Perspective*. Stanford: Hoover Institution Press.

——. 1985b. "The Stony Path to Afghan Socialism: Problems of Sovietization in an Alpine Muslim Society." *Orbis* 29, no. 1: 40–57.

——. 1993. *The Fateful Pebble: Afghanistan's Role in the Fall of the Soviet Empire*. Novato, Calif.: Presidio.

Arquilla, John, and David Ronfeldt. 1996. *The Advent of Netwar*. Santa Monica, Calif.: RAND.

——, eds. 2001. *Networks and Netwars*. Santa Monica, Calif.: RAND.

Arrow, Kenneth. 1974. *The Limits of Organization*. New York: Norton.

Axelrod, Robert. 1984. *The Evolution of Cooperation*. New York: Basic Books.

Bacharach, Samuel, and Edward Lawler. 1980. *Power and Politics in Organizations*. San Francisco: Jossey-Bass.

Barrett, Archie. 1983. *Reappraising Defense Organization*. Washington, D.C.: National Defense University Press.

Barry, Brian. 1970. *Sociologists, Economists, and Democracy*. London: Collier-Macmillan.

Beals, Carleton. 1970. *The Nature of Revolution*. New York: Thomas Y. Crowell.

Beckett, Ian, and John Pimlott. 1985. *Armed Forces and Modern Counterinsurgency*. New York: Saint Martin's Press.

Bedeian, Arthur. 1980. *Organizations: Theory and Analysis*. Hinsdale, Ill.: Dryden Press.

Bell, J. Bowyer. 1976. *On Revolt*. Cambridge: Harvard University Press.

Bendor, Jonathan. 1985. *Parallel Systems: Redundancy in Government.* Berkeley: University of California Press.

Berman, Paul. 1974. *Revolutionary Organization.* Lexington, Mass.: Heath.

Binder, Leonard, ed. 1999. *Ethnic Conflict and International Politics in the Middle East.* Gainesville: University of Florida Press.

Blacker, Coit. 1993. *Hostage to Revolution: Gorbachev and Soviet Security Policy.* New York: Council on Foreign Relations Press.

Borer, Douglas Anthony. 1993. "Superpowers Defeated: A Comparison of Vietnam and Afghanistan." PhD diss., Boston University.

Borovik, Artyom. 1990. *The Hidden War.* New York: Atlantic Monthly Press.

Bracken, Paul. 1990. *Strategic Planning for National Security: Lessons from Business Experience.* Santa Monica, Calif.: RAND.

Bradsher, Henry. 1985. *Afghanistan and the Soviet Union.* Durham: Duke University Press.

——. 1999. *Afghan Communism and Soviet Intervention.* New York: Oxford University Press.

Brand, Laurie. 1999. "Al-Muhajirun w-al-Ansar: Hashemite Strategies for Managing Communal Identity in Jordan." In *The International Dimensions of Ethnic Conflict in the Middle East*, edited by Leonard Binder, 279–306. Gainesville: University of Florida Press.

Brigot, André, and Olivier Roy, eds. 1985. *La guerre d'Afghanistan: Intervention Soviétique et résistance.* Paris: La Documentation Française.

Brown, Nathan. 1989. "The Conspiracy of Silence and the Atomistic Political Activity of the Egyptian Peasantry, 1882–1952." In *Everyday Forms of Peasant Resistance*, edited by Forrest Colburn, 93–121. London: Sharpe.

Bunge, Mario. 1996. *Finding Philosophy in Social Science.* New Haven: Yale University Press.

Burton, Richard, and Borge Obel. 1984. *Designing Efficient Organizations.* Amsterdam: Elsevier.

Callwell, Charles. 1976 [1906]. *Small Wars: Their Principles and Practice.* 2nd ed. East Ardsley, England: EP Publishing.

Canfield, Robert. 1989. "Afghanistan: The Trajectory of Internal Alignments." *Middle East Journal* 43: 635–48.

Chaliand, Gerard. 1982. *Guerrilla Strategies.* Berkeley: University of California Press.

Clapham, Christopher, ed. 1982. *Private Patronage and Public Power.* New York: St. Martin's Press.

Colburn, Forrest, ed. 1989. *Everyday Forms of Peasant Resistance.* New York: Sharpe.

Collins, Joseph J. 1986. *The Soviet Invasion of Afghanistan.* Lexington, Mass.: Lexington.

Cooley, Alexander. 2005. *Logics of Hierarchy.* Ithaca: Cornell University Press.

Cordesman, Anthony, and Abraham Wagner. 1990. *The Afghan and Falklands Conflicts.* Boulder, Colo.: Westview Press.

Cordovez, Diego, and Selig Harrison. 1995. *Out of Afghanistan: The Inside Story of the Soviet Withdrawal.* New York: Oxford University Press.

Daley, Tad. 1989. *Afghanistan and Gorbachev's Global Foreign Policy.* Occasional paper. Santa Monica, Calif.: RAND.

———. 1995. "Gorbachev and Afghanistan: The Soviet Debate over the Lessons of Afghanistan, and Consequent Directions in Russian Foreign Policy." PhD diss., RAND Graduate Institute.

Daly, M. W., and Ahmad Alawad Sikainga. 1993. *Civil War in the Sudan*. London: British Academic Press.

Dar, Saeeduddin A. 1986. *Selected Documents on Pakistan's Relations with Afghanistan*. Islamabad: Printways International.

Davis, Anthony. 1993. "The Afghan Army." *Jane's Intelligence Review* 5, no. 3: 134–39.

———. 1994a. "The Battleground of Northern Afghanistan." *Jane's Intelligence Review* 6, no. 7: 323–38.

———. 1994b. "Peace Eludes Afghanistan." *Jane's Intelligence Review* 6, no. 12: 111–14.

———. 1995. "Afghanistan's Taliban." *Jane's Intelligence Review* 7, no. 7: 315–21.

———. 1998. "How the Taliban Became a Military Force." In *Fundamentalism Reborn? Afghanistan and the Taliban*, edited by William Maley, 43–71. Lahore: Vanguard.

DeNardo, James. 1985. *Power in Numbers: The Political Strategy of Protest and Rebellion*. Princeton: Princeton University Press.

Deibert, Ronald, and Janice Gross Stein. 2002. "Hacking Networks of Terror." *Dialogue-IO* (April): 1–14.

Dorronsoro, Gilles. 2000. *La révolution Afghane: Des communistes aux Tâlebân*. Paris: Karthala.

Dorronsoro, Gilles, and Chantal Lobato. 1989. "The Militia in Afghanistan." *Central Asian Survey* 8, no. 4: 95–108.

Drenick, R. F. 1986. *A Mathematical Organization Theory*. New York: North Holland.

Duncan, Raymond, and Carolyn McGiffert Ekedahl. 1990. *Moscow and the Third World under Gorbachev*. Boulder, Colo.: Westview Press.

Dupree, Louis. 1980. *Afghanistan*. Princeton: Princeton University Press.

Duverger, Maurice. 1959. *Political Parties*. New York: Wiley and Sons.

Edwards, David. 2002. *Before the Taliban: Genealogies of the Afghan Jihad*. Berkeley: University of California Press.

Eisenstadt, S. N., and Louis Roniger. 1984. *Patrons, Clients and Friends: Interpersonal Relations and the Structure of Trust in Society*. Cambridge: Cambridge University Press.

Ekedahl, Carolyn, and Melvin Goodman. 1997. *The Wars of Eduard Shevardnadze*. University Park: Pennsylvania State University Press.

Emadi, Hafizullah. 1990. *State, Revolution, and Superpowers in Afghanistan*. New York: Praeger.

———. 1993a. "China's Politics and Developments in Afghanistan." *Journal of Asian and African Studies* 28, nos. 1–2: 107–17.

———. 1993b. "Minority Group Politics: The Role of Ismailis in Afghanistan's Politics." *Central Asian Survey* 12, no. 3: 379–92.

———. 1997. "The Hazaras and Their Role in the Process of Political Transformation in Afghanistan." *Central Asian Survey* 16, no. 3: 363–87.

Etzioni, Amitai. 1975. *A Comparative Analysis of Complex Organizations*. New York: Free Press.

Evans, Sara. 1979. *Personal Politics*. New York: Knopf.

Ewans, Martin, Sir. 2001. *Afghanistan: A New History*. Richmond, U.K.: Curzon.

——. 2005. *Conflict in Afghanistan: Studies in Asymmetric Warfare*. New York: Routledge.

Fänge, Anders. 1995. "Afghanistan after April 1992: A Struggle for State and Ethnicity." *Central Asian Survey* 14, no. 1: 17–24.

Farr, Grant, and John Merriam, eds. 1987. *Afghan Resistance: The Politics of Survival*. Boulder, Colo.: Westview Press.

Fearon, James D., and David D. Laitin. 2003. "Ethnicity, Insurgency, and Civil War." *American Political Science Review* 97: 75–89.

Flamholtz, Eric. 1996. *Effective Management Control: Theory and Practice*. Boston: Kluwer Academic.

Fortes, M., and E. E. Evans-Pritchard, eds. 1940. *African Political Systems*. London: Oxford University Press.

Freeman, Jo. 1972. "The Origins of the Women's Liberation Movement." *American Journal of Sociology* 78: 792–811.

Friedland, William, and Amy Barton. 1982. *Revolutionary Theory*. Totowa, N.J.: Allanheld, Osmun.

Frisch, Hillel. 1993. "The Druze Minority in the Israeli Military: Traditionalizing an Ethnic Policing Role." *Armed Forces and Society* 20: 51–67.

Galeotti, Mark. 1995. *Afghanistan, the Soviet Union's Last War*. London: Frank Cass.

Gamson, W. 1975. *The Strategy of Social Protest*. Homewood, Ill.: Dorsey Press.

Gargiulo, Martin. 1993. "Two-Step Leverage: Managing Constraint in Organizational Politics." *Administrative Science Quarterly* 38: 1–19.

Garthoff, Raymond. 1994. *Détente and Confrontation: American-Soviet Relations from Nixon to Reagan*. Washington, D.C.: Brookings.

Geertz, Clifford. 1973. *The Interpretation of Cultures*. New York: Basic Books.

Gélinas, Sylvie. 1997. *Afghanistan du communisme au fondamentalisme*. Paris: L'Harmattan.

Gellner, Ernest, and John Waterbury, eds. 1977. *Patrons and Clients*. London: Duckworth.

Gerlach, Luther, and Virginia Hine. 1970. *People, Power, Change*. New York: Bobbs-Merrill.

Ghufran, Nasreen. 2001. "The Taliban and the Civil War Entanglement in Afghanistan." *Asian Survey* 41: 462–87.

Giap, Vo Nguyen. 1961. *People's War, People's Army*. Hanoi: Foreign Languages Publishing House.

——. 1970. *The Military Art of People's War: Selected Writings*. New York: Monthly Review Press.

Gibson, James, John Ivancevich, and James Donnelly. 1973. *Organizations*. Dallas: Business Publishing.

Giddens, Anthony. 1979. *Central Problems in Social Theory: Action, Structure, and Contradiction in Social Analysis*. Berkeley: University of California Press.

Girard, René. 1977. *Violence and the Sacred*. Baltimore: Johns Hopkins University Press.

Girardet, Edward. 1985. *Afghanistan, the Soviet War*. New York: St. Martin's.

Giustozzi, Antonio. 2000. *War, Politics and Society in Afghanistan, 1978–1992*. London: Hurst.

Gohari, M. J. 2000. *The Taliban Ascent to Power*. Oxford: Oxford University Press.

Goldstone, Jack, Ted Robert Gurr, Barbara Harff, Marc A. Levy, Monty G. Marshall, Robert H. Bates, David L. Epstein et al. 2000. *State Failure Task Force Report: Phase III Findings*. Online at http://globalpolicy.gmu.edu/pitf/SFTF%20Phase%20III%20Report%20Final.pdf.

Goodson, Larry Preston. 1990. "Refugee-Based Insurgency: The Afghan Case." PhD diss., University of North Carolina.

——. 2001. *Afghanistan's Endless War: State Failure, Regional Politics, and the Rise of the Taliban*. Seattle: University of Washington Press.

Gorbachev, Mikhail. 1986. *Speeches and Writings*. Oxford: Pergamon Press.

——. 1995. *Memoirs*. New York: Doubleday.

Grau, Lester. 1996. *The Bear Went Over the Mountain: Soviet Combat Tactics in Afghanistan*. Washington, D.C.: National Defense University Press.

Greene, Thomas. 1974. *Comparative Revolutionary Movements*. Englewood Cliffs, N.J.: Prentice-Hall.

Griffin, Michael. 2001. *Reaping the Whirlwind: The Taliban Movement in Afghanistan*. Sterling, Va.: Pluto Press.

Guevara, Che. 1961. *Guerrilla Warfare*. New York: Vintage Books.

Gustafson, Thane, and Dawn Mann. 1986. "Gorbachev's First Year: Building Power and Authority." *Problems of Communism* 35: 1–19.

Haddad, Yvonne. 1983. "The Qur'anic Justification for an Islamic Revolution: The View of Sayyid Qutb." *Middle East Journal* 37: 14–29.

Halbach, Uwe. 1990. "The Military Withdrawal from Afghanistan." In *Soviet Union, 1988–89*, edited by the Federal Institute for Soviet and International Studies, 283–91. Boulder: Westview Press.

Hanifi, Jamil M. 2004. "Editing the Past: Colonial Production of Hegemony through the 'Loya Jerga' in Afghanistan." *Iranian Studies* 37, no. 2: 295–322.

Hardin, Russell. 1982. *Collective Action*. Baltimore: Johns Hopkins University Press.

——. 1995. *One for All: The Logic of Group Conflict*. Princeton: Princeton University Press.

Harpviken, Kristian. 1995. "Political Mobilization among the Hazara in Afghanistan: 1978–1992." PhD diss., University of Oslo.

——. 1996. *Political Mobilization among the Hazara of Afghanistan*. Oslo: Department of Sociology, University of Oslo.

——. 1997. "Transcending Traditionalism: The Emergence of Non-State Military Formations in Afghanistan." *Journal of Peace Research* 34, no. 3: 271–88.

Hart, Douglas. 1982. "Low-Intensity Conflict in Afghanistan: The Soviet View." *Survival* 24: 60–70.

Hatch, Mary Jo. 1997. *Organization Theory*. New York: Oxford University Press.

Hatem, Robert. 1999. *From Israel to Damascus*. La Mesa, Calif.: Pride International.

Hauner, Milan. 1991. *The Soviet War in Afghanistan*. Philadelphia: Foreign Policy Research Institute.

Hauner, Milan, and Robert Canfield. 1989. *Afghanistan and the Soviet Union: Collision and Transformation*. Boulder: Westview.

Hayden, Tom. 1966. "The Politics of the 'Movement.' " *Dissent* 13: 75–87.

Hayek, Friedrich. 1945. "The Use of Knowledge in Society." *American Economic Review* 35: 519–30.

Hechter, Michael. 1987. *Principles of Group Solidarity*. Berkeley: University of California Press.

Hedberg, Bo. 1981. "How Organizations Learn and Unlearn." In *Handbook of Organizational Design*, edited by Paul Nystrom and William Starbuck, 3–27. New York: Oxford University Press.

Hemsley, John. 1982. *Soviet Troop Control*. New York: Brassey's.

Henderson, Errol, and J. David Singer. 2000. "Civil War in the Post-Colonial World, 1946–92." *Journal of Peace Research* 37, no. 3: 275–99.

Heraclides, Alexis. 1987. "Janus or Sisyphus? The Southern Problem of the Sudan." *Journal of Modern African Studies* 25, no. 2: 213–31.

Herbst, P. G. 1968. *Autonomous Group Functioning*. London: Associated Book.

Hoffer, Eric. 1951. *The True Believer*. New York: Harper and Row.

Hui, Victoria. 2005. *War and State Formation in Ancient China and Early Modern Europe*. New York: Cambridge University Press.

Hyman, Anthony. 1984. "Afghan Resistance: Danger from Disunity." *Conflict Studies* 161: 1–24.

——. 1992. *Afghanistan under Soviet Domination*. London: Macmillan.

Ianni, Francis. 1972. *A Family Business: Kinship and Social Control in Organized Crime*. New York: Russell Sage Foundation.

Ibn Khaldun. 1989. *The Muqaddimah: An Introduction to History*. Translated by Franz Rosenthal. Princeton: Princeton University Press.

Imset, Ismet. 1992. *The PKK: A Report on Separatist Violence in Turkey, 1973–1992*. Ankara: Turkish Daily News.

Isby, David. 1989. *War in a Distant Country: Afghanistan*. London: Arms and Armour.

Jalali, Ali Ahmad, and Lester Grau. 1999. *The Other Side of the Mountain: Mujahideen Tactics in the Soviet-Afghan War*. Quantico, Va.: U.S. Marine Corps, Studies and Analysis Division.

Janda, Kenneth, ed. 1980. *Political Parties: A Cross-National Survey*. New York: Free Press.

Jenkins, Craig. 1983. "Resource Mobilization Theory and the Study of Social Movements." *Annual Review of Sociology* 9: 527–53.

Jensen, Michael, and William Meckling. 1995. "Specific and General Knowledge and Organizational Structure." *Journal of Applied Corporate Finance* 8, no. 2: 4–18.

Johnson, Chalmers. 1962. *Peasant Nationalism and Communist Power: The Emergence of Revolutionary China*. Stanford: Stanford University Press.

Kakar, Hassan. 1995. *Afghanistan: The Soviet Invasion and the Afghan Response, 1979–1982*. Berkeley: University of California Press.

Kalyvas, Stathis. 2003. "The Ontology of Political Violence: Action and Identity in Civil Wars." *Perspectives on Politics* 1: 475–94.

——. 2006. *The Logic of Violence in Civil War*. New York: Cambridge University Press.

Kaplan, Robert. 1990. *Soldiers of God*. Boston: Houghton Mifflin.

Karnow, Stanley. 1983. *Vietnam: A History*. New York: Viking.

Karp, Aaron. 1987. "Blowpipes and Stingers in Afghanistan: One Year Later." *Armed Forces Journal* (September): 36–40.

Kasza, Gregory. 1993. *The State and the Mass Media in Japan, 1918–1945*. Berkeley: University of California Press.

Katz, Mark. 1989. *Gorbachev's Military Policy in the Third World*. New York: Praeger.

Kerkvliet, Benedict. 1977. *The Huk Rebellion*. Berkeley: University of California Press.

Khalilzad, Zalmay. 1995. "Afghanistan in 1994: Civil War and Disintegration." *Asian Survey* 35, no. 2: 147–53.

Khan, Riaz. 1993. *Untying the Afghan Knot: Negotiating the Soviet Withdrawal*. Lahore: Progressive Publishers.

Klass, Rosanne. 1988. "Afghanistan: The Accords." *Foreign Affairs* 66: 922–45.

——., ed. 1990. *The Great Game Revisited*. New York: Freedom House.

Klibanoff, Peter, and Jonathan Morduch. 1995. "Decentralization, Externalities, and Efficiency." *Review of Economic Studies* 62: 223–47.

Kochen, Manfred, and Karl Deutsch. 1980. *Decentralization*. Cambridge: Oelgeschlager, Gunn and Hain.

Kocher, Matthew. 2002. "Is Immunity from Insurgent Challenges Bought or Found?" Paper presented at the Comparative Politics Workshop, University of Chicago, May 29, 2002.

Kornienko, G. M. 1994. "The Afghan Endeavor." *Journal of South Asian and Middle Eastern Studies* 17: 2–17.

Kowalewski, David, and Dean Hoover. 1995. *Dynamic Models of Conflict and Pacification*. Westport: Praeger.

Kramer, Martin. 1991. "Sacrifice and Fratricide in Shiite Lebanon." *Terrorism and Political Violence* 3: 30–47.

Kuhn, Alfred, and Robert Beam. 1982. *The Logic of Organization*. San Francisco: Jossey-Bass.

Kuran, Timur. 1991. "Now Out of Never: The Element of Surprise in the East European Revolution of 1989." *World Politics* 44: 7–48.

Laitin, David. 1989. "Linguistic Revival: Politics and Culture in Catalonia." *Comparative Studies in Society and History* 31: 297–317.

——. 1993. "National Revivals and Violence." Paper presented at the Center for Advanced Study in the Social Sciences of the Juan March Institute, March 29.

Lammers, Cornelis J., and David Hickson, eds. 1979. *Organizations Alike and Unlike*. London: Routledge.

Landau, Martin. 1969. "Redundancy, Rationality, and the Problem of Duplication and Overlap." *Public Administration Review* 29: 346–58.

Leites, Nathan, and Charles Wolf. 1970. *Rebellion and Authority: An Analytic Essay on Insurgent Conflicts*. Chicago: Markham.

Lenin, V. I. 1967. *Selected Works*. New York: International Publishers.

Le Quang, Gerard. 1973. *Giap ou la guerre du peuple*. Paris: Denoel.

Lichbach, Mark. 1995. *The Rebel's Dilemma*. Ann Arbor: University of Michigan Press.

Lohbeck, Kurt. 1993. *Holy War, Unholy Victory*. Washington, D.C.: Regnery Gateway.

Lohmann, Susanne. 1994. "The Dynamics of Informational Cascades: The Monday Demonstrations in Leipzig, East Germany, 1989--91." *World Politics* 47: 42–101.

Magnus, Ralph. 1998a. "Afghanistan in 1997: The War Moves North." *Asian Survey* 38, no. 2: 109–16.

——. 1998b. *Afghanistan: Mullah, Marx, and Mujahid*. Boulder, Colo.: Westview Press.

Magnus, Ralph, and Eden Naby. 1995. "Afghanistan and Central Asia: Mirrors and Models." *Asian Survey* 35, no. 7: 605–21.

Maley, William. 1998. *Fundamentalism Reborn? Afghanistan and the Taliban*. Lahore: Vanguard.

——. 2002. *The Afghanistan Wars*. New York: Palgrave Macmillan.

——. 2006. *Rescuing Afghanistan*. London: Hurst and Company.

Maley, William, and Fazel Haq Saikal. 1992. *Political Order in Post-Communist Afghanistan*. Boulder, Colo.: Lynne Rienner.

Mamdouh, Farid. 1990. "The Structure of the Corporate Intelligence System." In *Global Corporate Intelligence*, edited by George Roukis, Hugh Conway, and Bruce Charnov, 123–35. New York: Quorum Books.

Mansur, Ahmad. 1991. *Mustaqbal Kabul*. Al-Mansurah, Egypt: Dar al-Wafa'.

——. 1995. *Mustaqbal Afghanistan*. Beirut: Dar Ibn Hazm.

Mao Tse-tung. 1962. *On Guerrilla Warfare*. Translated by Samuel Griffith. New York: Praeger.

——. 1966a. *Basic Tactics*. Translated by Stuart R. Schram. New York: Praeger.

——. 1966b. *Selected Military Writings*. Peking: Foreign Language Press.

March, James, ed. 1965. *Handbook of Organizations*. New York: Rand McNally.

——. 1978. "Bounded Rationality, Ambiguity, and the Engineering of Choice." *Bell Journal of Economics* 9: 587–608.

March, James, and Herbert Simon. 1958. *Organizations*. New York: John Wiley.

Margolis, Howard. 1982. *Selfishness, Altruism and Rationality*. Cambridge: Cambridge University Press.

Marsden, Peter. 1998. *The Taliban: War, Religion and the New Order in Afghanistan*. Karachi: Oxford University Press.

Mason, T. David, Joseph P. Weingarten, and Patrick J. Fett. 1999. "Win, Lose, or Draw: Predicting the Outcome of Civil Wars." *Political Research Quarterly* 52: 239–68.

Matinuddin, Kamal. 1999. *The Taliban Phenomenon*. Karachi: Oxford University Press.

McAdam, Doug, John McCarthy, and Mayer Zald, eds. 1996. *Comparative Perspectives on Social Movements*. New York: Cambridge University Press.

McCarthy, John, and Mayer Zald. 1973. *The Trend of Social Movements in America: Professionalization and Resource Mobilization*. Morristown, N.J.: General Learning Press.

——. 1977. "Resource Mobilization and Social Movements: A Partial Theory." *American Journal of Sociology* 82, no. 6: 1212–41.

McDowall, David. 1997. *A Modern History of the Kurds*. London: I. B. Tauris.

McKenna, Thomas M. 1998. *Muslim Rulers and Rebels*. Berkeley: University of California Press.

McMichael, Scott. 1991. *Stumbling Bear: Soviet Military Performance in Afghanistan*. London: Brassey's.

Mendelson, Sarah Elizabeth. 1993a. "Explaining Change in Foreign Policy: The Soviet Withdrawal from Afghanistan." PhD diss., Columbia University.

——. 1993b. "Internal Battles and External Wars: Politics, Learning, and the Soviet Withdrawal from Afghanistan." *World Politics* 45: 327–60.

——. 1998. *Changing Course: Ideas, Politics, and the Soviet Withdrawal from Afghanistan*. Princeton: Princeton University Press.

Merom, Gil. 2003. *How Democracies Lose Small Wars*. Cambridge: Cambridge University Press.

Michels, Robert. 1949. *Political Parties*. Glencoe, Ill.: Free Press.

Migdal, Joel. 1977. *Peasants, Politics, and Revolution*. Princeton: Princeton University Press.

——. 1988. *Strong Societies and Weak States: State-Society Relations and State Capabilities in the Third World*. Princeton: Princeton University Press.

Mintzberg, Henry. 1979. *The Structuring of Organizations*. Englewood Cliffs, N.J.: Prentice-Hall.

Moe, Terry. 1980. *The Organization of Interests*. Chicago: University of Chicago Press.

——. 1984. "The New Economics of Organization." *American Journal of Political Science* 28, no. 4: 739–77.

Morgan, Gareth. 1997. *Images of Organization*. Thousand Oaks, Calif.: Sage.

Moshref, Rameen. 1997. *The Taliban*. East Hampton, N.Y.: Afghanistan Forum.

Mozhdeh, Waheed. 2003. *Afghanistan va Panj Sal Salteh-yi Taliban*. Tehran: Nashrani.

Mustafa, Masoud Ahmad. 1990. *Aqalim al-Dawla al-Islamiyya Bayn al-la-Markaziyya al-Siyasiyya wal la-Markaziyya al-Idariyya*. Cairo: al-Hay'a al-Masriyya al-ʿama lil-Kitab.

Namlah, Ali ibn Ibrahim. 1994. *Al-Jihad wa-al-Mujahidun fi Afghanistan: Waqafat Taqwim*. Riad: Maktabat ʿUbaykan.

Neuman, Stephanie. 1986. *Military Assistance in Recent Wars*. New York: Praeger.

Niskanen, William. 1971. *Representative Bureaucracy*. New York: Aldine-Atherton.

Nojumi, Neamatollah. 2002. *The Rise of the Taliban in Afghanistan*. New York: Palgrave.

Nonaka, Ikujiro, and Hirotaka Takeuchi. 1995. *The Knowledge-Creating Company*. New York: Oxford University Press.

O'Ballance, Edgar. 1993. *Afghan Wars, 1839–1992: What Britain Gave Up and the Soviet Union Lost*. New York: Brassey's.

O'Donnell, Guillermo, and Philippe Schmitter. 1986. *Transitions from Authoritarian Rule: Tentative Conclusions about Uncertain Democracies*. Baltimore: Johns Hopkins University Press.

Olson, Mancur. 1971. *The Logic of Collective Action*. Cambridge: Harvard University Press.

Ouchi, William. 1980. "Markets, Bureaucracies, and Clans." *Administrative Science Quarterly* 25: 120–41.

Parker, John W. 1991. *Kremlin in Transition: Gorbachev, 1985 to 1989*. Boston: Unwin Hyman.

Peirce, Charles Sanders. 1878. *How to Make Our Ideas Clear*. N.p.

Pellissier, Pierre. 1995. *La bataille d'Alger*. Paris: Perrin.

Petersen, Roger. 1993. "A Community-Based Theory of Rebellion." *European Journal of Sociology* 34, no. 1: 41–78.

——. 2001. *Resistance and Rebellion: Lessons from Eastern Europe*. New York: Cambridge University Press.

Pfeffer, Jeffrey. 1981. *Power in Organizations*. Marshfield, Mass.: Pitman.

Pirouet, Louise M. 1976. "The Achievement of Peace in Sudan." *Journal of Eastern African Research and Development* 6, no. 1: 115–45.

Plato. 1999. *Cratylus*. Hazleton, Penn.: Pennsylvania State University.

Poladi, Hassan. 1989. *The Hazaras*. Stockon, Calif.: Mughal Publishing.

Popkin, Samuel. 1979. *The Rational Peasant*. Berkeley: University of California Press.

Putnam, Robert. 1988. "Diplomacy and Domestic Politics: The Logic of Two-Level Games." *International Organization* 42: 427–60.

Qutb, Sayyid. N.d. *Ma'alim fil-Tariq*. N.p.

Radu, Michael, ed. 1990. *The New Insurgencies: Anticommunist Guerrillas in the Third World*. New Brunswick, N.J.: Transaction Publishers.

Raftery, Adrian. 1995. "Bayesian Model Selection in Social Research." *Sociological Methodology* 25: 111–63.

Rais, Rasul Bakhsh. 1994. *War without Winners*. Karachi: Oxford University Press.

Rashid, Ahmed. 1998. "Pakistan and the Taliban." In *Fundamentalism Reborn? Afghanistan and the Taliban*, edited by William Maley, 72–88. Lahore: Vanguard.

——. 2000. *Taliban: Militant Islam, Oil, and Fundamentalism in Central Asia*. New Haven: Yale University Press.

Rastegar, Farshad. 1991. "Education and Revolutionary Political Mobilization." PhD diss., University of California, Los Angeles.

Reeves, Edward. 1990. *The Hidden Government: Ritual, Clientelism, and Legitimation in Northern Egypt*. Salt Lake City: University of Utah Press.

Rice, Edward. 1972. *Mao's Way*. Berkeley: University of California Press.

——. 1988. *Wars of the Third Kind*. Berkeley: University of California Press.

Ries, John. 1964. *The Management of Defense*. Baltimore: Johns Hopkins University Press.

Rogers, Tom. 1992. *The Soviet Withdrawal from Afghanistan*. Westport: Greenwood Press.

Ross, Michael. 2004. "What Do We Know about Natural Resources and Civil War?" *Journal of Peace Research* 41, no. 3: 337–56.

Rothchild, Donald, and Caroline Hartzell. 1993. "The Peace Process in the Sudan." In *Stopping the Killing: How Civil Wars End*, edited by Roy Licklider, 63–93. New York: New York University Press.

Roukis, George, Hugh Conway, and Bruce Charnov, eds. 1990. *Global Corporate Intelligence*. New York: Quorum Books.

Roy, Olivier. 1989. "War as a Factor of Entry into Politics." *Central Asian Survey* 8, no. 4: 43–62.

——. 1990. *Islam and Resistance in Afghanistan*. Cambridge: Cambridge University Press.

——. 1991. *The Lessons of the Soviet-Afghan War*. Adelphi Paper No. 259. London: International Institute for Strategic Studies.

——. 1995. *Afghanistan: From Holy War to Civil War*. Princeton: Darwin Press.

Rubin, Barnett. 1993–94. "The Fragmentation of Tajikistan." *Survival* 35 (Winter): 71–91.

——. 1994. "Afghanistan in 1993, Abandoned but Surviving." *Asian Survey* 34: 185–91.

——. 1995a. *The Fragmentation of Afghanistan*. New Haven: Yale University Press.

——. 1995b. *The Search for Peace in Afghanistan*. New Haven: Yale University Press.

——. 2000. "The Political Economy of War and Peace in Afghanistan." *World Development* 28, no. 10: 1789–1803.

Rubin, Barnett, Hmayun Hamidzada, and Abby Stoddard. 2005. "Afghanistan 2005 and Beyond: Prospects for Improved Stability Reference Document." Netherlands Institute of International Relations, Conflict Research Unit.

Rubinstein, Alvin. 1988. "The Soviet Withdrawal from Afghanistan." *Current History* 87: 333–40.

Russell, D. E. H. 1974. *Rebellion, Revolution, and Armed Force*. New York: Academic Press.

Russian General Staff. 2002. *The Soviet-Afghan War: How a Superpower Fought and Lost*. Translated and edited by Lester Grau and Michael Gress. Lawrence: University Press of Kansas.

Saikal, Amin, and William Maley. 1989. *The Soviet Withdrawal from Afghanistan*. Cambridge: Cambridge University Press.

Sahlins, Marshall. 1985. *Islands of History*. Chicago: University of Chicago Press.

Saivetz, Carol, ed. 1989. *The Soviet Union in the Third World*. Boulder: Westview Press.

Sakwa, Richard. 1991. *Gorbachev and His Reforms*. New York: Prentice-Hall.

Sartori, Giovanni. 1968. "Political Development and Political Engineering." *Public Policy* 17: 261–98.

Saward, Michael. 1992. *Co-optive Politics and State Legitimacy*. Aldershot, U.K.: Dartmouth.

Schelling, Thomas. 1978. *Micromotives and Macrobehavior*. New York: W. W. Norton.

Schmidt, S. W., J. C. Scott, C. Lande, and L. Guasti, eds. 1977. *Friends, Followers, and Factions: A Reader in Political Clientelism*. Berkeley: University of California Press.

Schwartz, M., and E. A. Thompson. 1986. "Divisionalization and Entry Deterrence." *Quarterly Journal of Economics* 101: 307–21.

Scitovsky, Tibor. 1976. *The Joyless Economy*. New York: Oxford University Press.

Scott, James. 1976. *The Moral Economy of the Peasant*. New Haven: Yale University Press.

———. 1977. "Political Clientelism: A Bibliographical Essay." In *Friends, Followers, and Factions: A Reader in Political Clientelism*, edited by S. W. Schmidt et al., 483–505. Berkeley: University of California Press.

———. 1986. *Weapons of the Weak: Everyday Forms of Peasant Resistance*. New Haven: Yale University Press.

Scott, Richard. 1981. *Organizations*. Englewood Cliffs, N.J.: Prentice-Hall.

Selznick, Philip. 1948. "Foundations of the Theory of Organizations." *American Sociological Review* 13: 25–35.

———. 1949. *TVA and the Grass Roots: A Study in the Sociology of Formal Organization*. New York: Harper and Row.

———. 1952. *The Organizational Weapon: A Study of Bolshevik Strategy and Tactics*. New York: McGraw-Hill.

Shahrani, Nazif M. 2002. "War, Factionalism, and the State in Afghanistan." *American Anthropologist* 104, no. 3: 715–22.

Shahrani, Nazif M., and Robert Canfield. 1984. "Revolutions and Rebellions in Afghanistan." *Institute of International Studies* 57: 371–90.

Shalinsky, Audrey. 1979. *Central Asian Émigrés in Afghanistan: Problems of Religious and Ethnic Identity*. Occasional Paper 19. New York: Asia Society.

Shevardnadze, Eduard. 1989. *Foreign Policy and Perestroika*. Moscow: Novosti Press.

———. 1991. *The Future Belongs to Freedom*. New York: Free Press.

Shultz, George. 1993. *Turmoil and Triumph: My Years as Secretary of State*. New York: Scribner.

Siccama, Jan G., and Theo van den Doel, eds. 1994. *Restructuring Armed Forces in East and West*. Boulder: Westview Press.

Siddiqui, Muhammad Yasin. 1987. *Organization of Government under the Prophet*. Delhi: Muhammad Ahmad.

Simon, Jeffrey. 1989. *Revolutions without Guerrillas*. Santa Monica, Calif.: RAND.

Sivan, Emmanuel. 1985. *Radical Islam: Medieval Theology and Modern Politics*. New Haven: Yale University Press.

Skocpol, Theda. 1979. *States and Social Revolutions*. Cambridge: Cambridge University Press.

Sloan, Alfred. 1964. *My Years with General Motors*. Garden City, N.Y.: Doubleday.

Stam, Allan C. 1996. *Win, Lose, or Draw: Domestic Politics and the Crucible of War*. Ann Arbor: University of Michigan Press.

Starr, Paul. 1979. "The Phantom Community." In *Co-ops, Communes, and Collectives*, edited by John Case, 245–73. New York: Pantheon.

Stedman, Stephen. 1997. "Spoiler Problems in Peace Processes." *International Security* 22, no. 2: 5–53.

Stobdan, P. 1998. *The Afghan Conflict and India*. New Delhi: Institute for Defense Studies and Analyses.

Stubbs, Richard. 1989. *Hearts and Minds in Guerrilla Warfare: The Malayan Emergency, 1948–1960*. Singapore: Oxford University Press.

Summers, Harry. 1982. *On Strategy: A Critical Analysis of the Vietnam War*. Novato, Calif.: Presidio.

Tarzi, Shah. 1991. "Politics of the Afghan Resistance Movement: Cleavages, Disunity, and Fragmentation." *Journal of Contemporary Asia* 21: 479–95.

Taylor, Michael, ed. 1988. *Rationality and Revolution*. Cambridge: Cambridge University Press.

Tilly, Charles. 1978. *From Mobilization to Revolution*. Reading, Mass.: Addison-Wesley.

Tocqueville, Alexis de. 1873. *State of Society in France before the Revolution of 1789*. London: John Murray.

——. 1980. *Selected Writings on Democracy, Revolution and Society*. Edited by John Stone and Stephen Mennel. Chicago: University of Chicago Press.

Tullock, Gordon. 1971. "The Paradox of Revolution." *Public Choice* 11: 89–99.

Urban, Mark. 1988. *War in Afghanistan*. London: Macmillan.

Van Creveld, Martin. 1991. *The Transformation of War*. New York: Free Press.

Walter, Barbara. 1997. "The Critical Barrier to Civil War Settlement." *International Organization* 51: 335–64.

Weber, Max. 1947. *The Theory of Social and Economic Organization*. London: Oxford University Press.

Weinbaum, Marvin. 1994. *Pakistan and Afghanistan: Resistance and Reconstruction*. Boulder: Westview Press.

Weingrod, A. 1968. "Patrons, Patronage and Political Parties." *Comparative Studies in Society and History* 10: 377–400.

Weinstein, Jeremy 2006. *Inside Rebellion: The Politics of Insurgent Violence*. New York: Cambridge University Press.

Welch, Claude. 1980. *Anatomy of Rebellion*. Albany: State University of New York Press.

Weller, Robert, and Scott Guggenheim, eds. 1982. *Power and Protest in the Countryside*. Durham: Duke University Press.

Wilson, James. 1978. *The Investigators: Managing FBI and Narcotics Agents*. New York: Basic Books.

Wolf, Eric. 1974. *Peasant Wars in the Twentieth Century*. New York: Harper and Row.

Yacef, Saadi. 1962. *Souvenirs de la bataille d'Alger*. Paris: René Julliard.

——. 1982. *La bataille D'Alger*. Paris: Éditions du Témoignage Chrétien.

Yakan, Fathi. 1989. *Ihzharu al-Aydz al-Haraki* [Beware of Activism AIDS]. Beirut: al-Mu'assassa al-Islamiyya.

——. 1993. *Nahwa Haraka Islamiyya ʿAlamiyya Wahida* [Toward a United Worldwide Islamic Movement]. Beirut: al-Risalah.

Yapp, M. E. 1980. *Strategies of British India*. New York: Oxford University Press.

Yousaf, Mohammed. 1991. *Silent Soldier: The Man behind the Afghan Jehad: General Akhtar Abdur Rahman Shaheed*. Lahore: Jang.

——. 1992. *The Bear Trap: Afghanistan's Untold Story*. Lahore: Jang Publishers.

Yunas, Fida. 1998. *Afghanistan: Organization of the PDPA/Watan Party, Governments and Biographical Sketches 1982–1998*. Peshawar: Shinwari Press.

Yusufzai, Rahimullah. 1985. "Massoud." Unpublished manuscript.

——.1993. "Dostum." *Afghanistan Forum* 5 (September): 8–68.

Zagorin, Perez. 1982. *Rebels and Rulers, 1500–1660*. Cambridge: Cambridge University Press.

INDEX